CW00520006

THE FAR EAST AND THE ENGLISH IMAGINATION, 1600–1730

In the seventeenth and eighteenth centuries China, Japan, and the Spice Islands dazzled the English imagination as insatiable markets for European goods and as vast, inexhaustible storehouses of spices and luxury wares. Robert Markley explores the significance of attitudes to the wealth and power of East Asia in rethinking conceptions of national and personal identity in seventeenth- and early eighteenth-century English literature. Alongside works by canonical English authors, this study examines the writings of Jesuit missionaries, Dutch merchants, and English and Continental geographers, who directly contended with the challenges that China and Japan posed to visions of Western cultural and technological superiority. Questioning conventional Eurocentric histories, Markley examines the ways in which the writings of Milton, Dryden, Defoe, and Swift deal with the complexities of a world in which England was marginalized and which, until 1800, was dominated – economically at least – by the empires of the Far East.

ROBERT MARKLEY is Professor of English at the University of Illinois and editor of *The Eighteenth Century: Theory and Interpretation.* He has published widely on Restoration and eighteenth-century literature, and his most recent books include *Dying Planet: Mars in Science and the Imagination* (2005).

THE FAR EAST AND THE ENGLISH IMAGINATION, 1600–1730

ROBERT MARKLEY

CAMBRIDGE
UNIVERSITY PRESS

CAMBRIDGE UNIVERSITY PRESS
Cambridge, New York, Melbourne, Madrid, Cape Town, Singapore, São Paulo

CAMBRIDGE UNIVERSITY PRESS
The Edinburgh Building, Cambridge CB2 2RU, UK

Published in the United States of America by Cambridge University Press, New York

www.cambridge.org
Information on this title: www.cambridge.org/9780521819442

First published 2006

Printed in the United Kingdom at the University Press, Cambridge

A catalogue record for this book is available from the British Library

ISBN-13 978-0-521-81944-2 hardback
ISBN-10 0-521-81944-X hardback

Contents

Illustrations

Acknowledgements

This book began to take shape more than a decade ago, and during its long gestation I have had the opportunity to discuss aspects of my argument with a number of people who have contributed, in various ways, to its final form. During the research and writing of this study, I have benefited from grants from the National Endowment for the Humanities, the Beinecke Library of Yale University, the Huntington Library, the University of Washington, and West Virginia University that have allowed me, in the days before the availability of Early English Books Online and the Eighteenth-Century Catalogue Online, to conduct research at the Folger Shakespeare Library, the British Library, and the Huntington. I sincerely appreciate the support. Various parts of chapters have been presented as invited lectures or keynote addresses at the University of Washington, the University of Auckland, the Humanities Research Centre at the Australian National University, Canterbury University (NZ), the University of Otago (NZ), the University of Melbourne, Princeton University, the University of Chicago, the University of Pittsburgh, McMaster University, the University of Exeter, Carnegie Mellon University, the State University of New York at Stony Brook, the New York Eighteenth-Century Seminar at Fordham University, Otterbein College, and the University of Oklahoma.

A work of this sort invariably is a collaborative process, and during the past ten years I have benefited from conversations with a great many people. I would like to thank (in no particular order) Rajani Sudan, Tom DiPiero, Pat Gill, Cynthia Klekar, Rachel Ramsey, Hans Turley, Tita Chico, Aleksondra Hultquist, Jeannie Dalporto, David Porter, Marshall Brown, Paul Remley, Ronald Schleifer, Tom Lockwood, Jean Marsden, Suvir Kaul, Ania Loomba, Richard Wheeler, Bruce Boehrer, Dan Vitkus, Bernadette Andrea, Bruce Clarke, Srinivas Aravamudan, Paula Backscheider, Catherine Ingrassia, Barbara Fuchs, David Baker, Balachandra Rajan, Elizabeth Sauer, Deborah Payne Fisk, Lucinda Cole, Andrew McRae, Sandra McPherson, Neil Chudgar, Tony Brown,

Cynthia Wall, Shef Rogers, Tanya Caldwell, Bridget Orr, Jonathan Lamb, Mona Narain, Gillian Russell, Iain McCalman, David Shumway, Frances Loughrey, Brian McHale, Paul Armstrong, Heidi Hutner, Kristina Straub, Zachary Lesser, Lori Newcomb, Tony Pollock, Michael Keevak, Helen Thompson, Erin Mackie, Martha Koehler, Andrew McGann, Deepika Bahri, Ian Donaldson, Ann Kaplan, Peter Walmsley, Daniel Carey, Susan Naquin, Mark Elvin, Jeng-Guo Chen, Eun Kyung Min, Laura Rosenthal, Elizabeth Johnston, Marilyn Francus, Duane Nellis, Jonathan Burton, Jeanne Hamming, Helen Burgess, Bruce Mazlish, Laurie Finke, Stephen Markley, and Hannah Markley.

Skeletal versions of the arguments and examples in several chapters have appeared elsewhere. In each case, the original articles have been expanded, cut, reworked, and in some cases traduced, yet I acknowledge with thanks Duke University Press for permission to reprint parts of chapters four, six, and seven that originally appeared in *Eighteenth-Century Life* (1993, 1998) and *South Atlantic Quarterly* (2004); Blackwell Publishers for permission to rework a version of two sections of chapter one that appeared in *Renaissance Studies* (2003); Associated University Presses for permission to revise (at times almost beyond recognition) a previously published version of chapter three that originally appeared in *Passionate Encounters in a Time of Sensibility*, edited by Anne Mellor and Maximilian Novak in 2000; and Duquesne University Press for permission to reprint shreds and patches of chapter two that appeared in *Milton and Imperialism*, edited by Balachandra Rajan and Elizabeth Sauer in 1999. I would also like to thank the British Library for permission to reproduce the illustrations in chapters one, three, and seven.

Dedications of works are always inadequate. They are gestures as much as tributes. Nonetheless, this one is for my father, Henry E. Markley, and my stepmother, Nicki Markley.

Introduction: British literature of the late Ming and early Qing dynasties

When those creatures of my imagination, the Galactic Museum-Keepers, look back on our past, with the objectivity of a vantage point near the edge of the universe, ten thousand years in the future, they will center their display on China, and cram Western civilization into a corner of some small vitrine.   Felipe Fernandez-Armesto[1]

EUROCENTRISM AND ITS DISCONTENTS

For many scholars, England's interactions with and understanding of the Far East in the seventeenth and eighteenth centuries remain an area of vague assumptions and misconceptions. Although there are obvious political differences between traditionalists, who celebrate the spreading of "civilization" to the non-European world, and their revisionist critics, who decry the violence and socioeconomic devastation of European imperialism, both camps share a fundamentally Eurocentric perception of early modern history. Both rely on historical narratives and analytical models – colonialist or postcolonialist – that retell an old story: the technological inferiority, economic backwardness, and political conservatism of oriental cultures spelled their inevitable defeat by European colonizers. In this respect, many scholars read the presuppositions of nineteenth-century colonialism back into the 1600s, taking for granted that the English and other Europeans assumed a national and racial superiority to all non-European peoples with whom they came in contact; that the same political dynamic, predicated on overwhelming European techno-military power, which operated in the Americas, functioned in Asia as well; and that intellectual, religious, cultural, and financial contacts between western Europe and Japan, China, and the sultanates of Southeast Asia were comparatively unimportant in the early modern period. All of these assumptions are false; to dislodge them is to contest traditional histories that posit European "mercantilism" in the sixteenth, seventeenth, and eighteenth centuries as the engine of worldwide economic change.[2] In subsuming the shifting and unstable relations between western merchants, diplomatic emissaries, and mariners (on the one hand) and local rulers, tax officials, suppliers, and translators (on the other) within a one-size-fits-all model of postcolonialism, many critics may invert the moral valence of Eurocentric history but ironically reproduce many of its assumptions, values, and interpretations.

The Far East and the English Imagination offers a historical and theoretical critique of some of the fundamental assumptions, values, and inter-pretations of a Eurocentric modernity. My readings of the fictional and non-fictional literature of the period between 1600 and 1730 build on the profound challenges to Eurocentrism offered in recent years by K. N. Chaudhuri, Jack Goldstone, J. M. Blaut, Frank Perlin, Paul Bairoch, R. Bin Wong, Andre Gunder Frank, Kenneth Pomeranz, and Geoffrey Gunn, among others.[3] In different ways, these historians argue that until 1800 an integrated world economy was dominated by China and to a lesser extent Japan and Moghul India, and that our recognition of this domin-ation requires a fundamental reassessment of both neoclassical and Marxian accounts of the economic "rise" of the West. In Japan and China during the early modern era, something close to the inverse of common-sense propositions seems to have been the case. As Claudia Schnurmann puts it, "compared to the Far East's progressive medicine, industry, and *savoir vivre*, even the Dutch, although highly sophisticated from a European perspective, at best measured up to what today would be considered 'third world' inhabitants in Asian eyes."[4] Behind this statement lies a complex history of the early modern world.

To write the history of English literature in an Asian-dominated world is not to minimize the near-genocidal horrors of the conquest of the Americas beginning in the sixteenth century or the costs and consequences of later European colonization in Africa, Asia, and Australasia. The valuable contributions of many postcolonial critics (some of them discussed below) to challenging traditional literary, economic, social, and cultural histories of the early modern world have tended to concentrate on European encounters with the Ottoman, Persian, and Moghul Empires. In devoting this study to the countries east of the Indian subcontinent, I want to emphasize the crucial differences between western reactions in the seventeenth and eighteenth centuries to Islamic cultures – long known and feared – and responses to China and Japan.[5] This vast but diffuse body of literature is crucial to an understanding of the early modern world and western Europe's place within it.

Literary texts by John Milton, John Dryden, Daniel Defoe, and Jonathan Swift and the geographies, travel narratives, and histories of Peter Heylyn, Thomas Mun, Matteo Ricci, Martino Martini, Jan Nieuhoff, Evret Ysbrants Ides, and many others reveal a variety of compensatory strategies to deal with Europe's marginalization in a global economy dominated by the empires of the Far East. Asia could be ignored or depicted as a vast region of pagans ripe for conversion; and European technological, military, and political power in the Americas could be invoked to counter the limitations of the Dutch, Portuguese, Spanish, and English in East Asia. If narratives of New World colonization reinforced Eurocentric beliefs in national greatness, universal monarchy, and Christian triumphalism, the experience of Europeans in China, Japan, and (before 1716) Moghul India radically challenged all of these ideological constructions.

No literate man or woman in western Europe could plead ignorance of the relative size, wealth, and natural resources of, say, England and China. By the middle of the seventeenth century, China had become a crucial site of contention and speculation in a variety of fields: Chinese chronicles called into question the dating of the Flood in the Masoretic text of the Old Testament, provoking seemingly endless controversies about the dating of the Bible; the fall of the Ming dynasty in 1644 and the "sinification" of the conquering Manchus led to encomiums for the resiliency of Chinese culture; the size and wealth of the empire provoked (as we shall see) an almost ritualistic praise of the country's natural wealth and the industry of its people; and, most significantly, the wealth of the nation whetted a seemingly insatiable desire for Chinese goods and what seemed, for many merchants, an infinitely profitable trade.[6] As David Porter demonstrates, the continuity of China's culture, language, and Confucian precepts through millennia became emblematic strategies of patrilineal legitimation: for many sinophiles in the seventeenth century, the Middle Kingdom symbolized the very principles of sociopolitical stability and transcultural moral value on which European elites depended.[7]

The two hundred or so primary sources that I cite in this study represent a small fraction of the texts on the Far East available to eighteenth-century readers. Donald Lach and Edwin van Kley count 1,500 works published in Europe between 1500 and 1800 dealing with Asia, and they admit to erring on the side of conservatism; widely reprinted and cannibalized reports (such as those compiled by Samuel Purchas) were recycled in atlases, travelogues, economic treatises, and natural histories.[8] In discussing this material, I concentrate on works that went through multiple editions (often in several languages and often in lavish folio volumes) and that were ransacked for information about the peoples and cultures of the Far East by editors who converted firsthand accounts into seemingly authoritative commentaries. This body of work, until 1750, dwarfs the amount of material published on the colonization of the Americas.

Europe's fascination with the Far East reflects the complex ways in which China, Japan, and the Spice Islands functioned in economic theorizing in the early modern world. Writers in England and elsewhere recognized that "the Far East" could be described holistically; it existed as a complex network of ports, agricultural regions, and trading opportunities. The prospect of tapping into the markets of Aceh, Canton, Nagasaki, and Agra between 1600 and 1740 became a crucial element in European economic thought because it allowed writers to displace domestic problems – ranging from high tax rates, to environmental degradation, to lagging productivity in some sectors and unmarketable surpluses in others – onto the vision of a theologically sanctioned and enormously profitable commerce. For England, largely excluded from trade east of India, China, Japan, and the Spice Islands fulfilled two crucial and imaginary roles, promising both an insatiable market for European exports and a vast, inexhaustible, storehouse of spices, luxury goods (from tea to textiles), and raw materials. If China, Japan, and India represented the apex of civilization – idealized embodiments of the sociopolitical order and cultural sophistication necessary to carry on an ever-expanding trade – the islands of the Indonesian archipelago and the imaginary continent, Terra Australis Incognita, offered visions of exotic realms where the East India Company could either gather commodities with little effort or strike good deals with cooperative natives. The Far East thus serves as a fantasy space for mercantile capitalism because it allows for the rigorous externalization of costs: profits can be tallied (or future profits imagined) without calculating (to take only two examples) either the value of lost lives, ships, and cargoes, or the value, in devastated local ecologies, of the deforestation necessary to build ships for the British navy and East India Company (EIC) fleets.[9]

The Far East and the English Imagination examines critically this widespread faith in the benefits of trade. As Josiah Child, a sometime governor and long time director of the EIC, put it in 1681, "Foreign Trade produceth Riches, Riches Power, Power preserves our Trade and Religion; they mutually work one upon and for the preservation of each other."[10] The crucial term in this logic is "produceth"; like many of his contemporaries, Child assumes that trade itself can generate wealth in excess of the expenditures of labor and capital required to man and provision ships for multi-year voyages, that it can be both mutually beneficial for all (civilized) parties concerned and yet always work to the economic advantage of England. This rhetoric of mutual enrichment dominates European defenses of trade in the seventeenth century and underlies the promise that the lands of the East Asia hold as both producers of desirable commodities and insatiable consumers of English goods, especially textiles. At the same time, however, Asian markets were also perceived as the sites of rags-or-riches competition with rival European and indigenous powers, and English writers from Queen Elizabeth on qualify Child's assertions by enlisting various nations as allies against England's commercial rivals, particularly the Dutch. In different ways, as I argue in each of the chapters below, these writers employ exclusionary, triangular models of politics, communication, and commerce to isolate (if only imaginatively) these antagonists and to protect their ideological investment in the self-perpetuating logic of infinite riches, unchallenged power, expanding trade, and true religion.

The fantasy of infinite productivity and profit requires a concomitant and profoundly anti-ecological faith in the existence of inexhaustible resources that can be endlessly exploited. In an important sense, the ideology of trade between 1500 and 1800 is a response to ecological and demographic crises in northwestern Europe. The widespread perception in the first half of the seventeenth century that England's resources were inadequate to support its population, or that nature itself had been corrupted by humankind's sins, placed the burden on international trade to solve complex ecological, demographic, and economic crises.[11] This "general crisis" of the seventeenth century requires, in effect, an eco-cultural approach of the kind outlined, in very different ways, by Goldstone, Pomeranz, and Perlin, among others – an approach that calls into question the economic premises of Eurocentric conceptions of modernity. In the rest of this Introduction, I lay out both the premises of Eurocentrism and its critique by postcolonial critics, then describe briefly the fundamentals of an eco-materialist approach to the early modern world.

ECONOMICS, MATHEMATICS, AND POSTCOLONIALISM

Eurocentrism rests on the belief that beginning in the seventeenth and eighteenth centuries, northwestern Europe, led by England, rapidly progressed toward the industrialized, coal-based economy of the nineteenth century. Debates still rage about what factors made England unique, and a good deal of economic history is devoted to assessing which characteristics of the English economy contributed decisively to its emergence as a world power. In general, historians emphasize various combinations of factors in their efforts to describe the causal narrative of English exceptionalism.[12] England developed and benefited from institutions such as the Bank of England to improve the climate for commercial enterprises and capital investment; this financial revolution led to both increased investment in the country's infrastructure and new technologies to improve trade, transportation, and communication. At the same time, England's civil service grew significantly in order to collect taxes and appropriate monies levied to support wars on the Continent and in the Americas. The development of a complex fiscal-administrative state fostered the professionalization of economic bureaus, agencies, and experts. The growth in the nation's military and naval finances, in turn, stimulated developments in a range of technologies useful for mining, textile manufacturing, and energy production. At roughly the same time, the agricultural revolution increased the efficiency of crop production to feed England's rapidly growing (after 1720) population. After 1688, liberal or "Enlightenment" values both strengthened and were strengthened by the codification of property rights and, for a small but increasing number of male property-owners, political rights. For many economic historians, then, the combinations of these factors, both ideational and material, made England the first country to industrialize, and the industrial revolution marks the advent of the modern world.[13]

Other countries or regions in southern and eastern Europe, Asia, South America, and Africa typically are evaluated according to this Anglocentric model of early nineteenth-century industrialization. If England is both the harbinger and exemplar of worldwide socioeconomic progress, then other nations must exist at more primitive stages of economic development. Invariably, China loses in such Eurocentric histories because it is treated as a wealthy nation that "failed" to modernize and consequently suffered the indignities of defeat, de facto colonization, and eventually communism. Not only is the senescence of the late Qing dynasty used to justify these views of China's failure but the very analytical vocabularies of a progressivist historiography reinforce an overall narrative of western Europe's economic dominance in the early modern period.

Yet as Greg Dening suggests, "historians always see the past from a perspective the past could never have had," and traditional accounts of the rise of England and northwestern Europe often assume that progress in technology, science, agriculture, industrial production, and finance is inscribed more or less self-consciously in the seventeenth and eighteenth centuries.[14] Crucial to this narrative of the rise and progress of modernity are the principles and assumptions – often decontextualized and reified as transhistorical "truths" – of neoclassical economics. In neoclassical economics, all economic activity can be described in terms of a rational calculus; the process of reducing complex behaviors to the key variables of choice and utility has two important consequences: it treats real-world exchanges and negotiations as expressions of underlying mathematical laws; and it distinguishes modern principles that foster technological innovation, capital formation, and overall growth from retrograde or primitive practices that lead to stagnation and lack of competition.[15] Because choice and utility can be modeled and generalized, neoclassical economic theory creates a virtual space of calculation where the costs and consequences of, say, resource extraction and environmental degradation can and must be rendered as functions of objective laws of the market.[16] While individual experiences and fortunes may vary considerably, the mathematics of neoclassical economics offers a universal standard of measurement: the *form* of the equation remains constant even as the value of variables and consequently solutions vary.

While several historians have noted the ways in which mathematics became a crucial instrumental technology for economists in sixteenth and seventeenth-century Europe, the values and assumptions of neoclassical economics have been challenged on both historical and theoretical grounds by Philip Mirowski, and the implications of his argument are far reaching.[17] Mirowski demonstrates that the neoclassical fascination with mathematics derives from a nineteenth and early twentieth-century misreading of the second law of thermodynamics. At the time, both economics and energy physics confronted profound discrepancies between theories (expressed in mathematics) and empirical observations; for complex reasons, both disciplines came to detach "progress" in mathematical theory (defined by internal consistency) from actual observations and experiments. In searching for ways to legitimate these radical moves, researchers in each field took the other discipline's constitutive metaphors as objectively true, then used these supposedly acknowledged truths to legitimate their own programs. Put simply, mathematical consistency – paradoxically because it does *not* conform to perceived physical reality – became an end in itself. Economics was thus cut free from the kinds of social and ecological considerations that had marked the discourses of economics prior to the mathematicizing of nature.[18] Consequently, the virtual spaces of economic thought and representation could be extended indefinitely, both across the globe and through time: profits yet to be realized could be projected onto the blank spaces of the map – in Asia, Africa, and the Americas – and extrapolated into the future. In both cases, a faith in the new sciences of economics could displace the environmental and social

consequences of resource depletion into the mathematics of unending profits and infinite exploitability. Whatever resisted short-time quantification –
deforestation, soil exhaustion, and water pollution – could be disregarded.

One of the problems in the historiography of the early modern world, as
Frank argues, is that Marxist historians tend to share Eurocentric perceptions of both progressivist narratives of technological and socioeconomic
development and theories of value that treat the natural world as though it
were primarily a storehouse of resources for labor to exploit. While
Marxism defines progress in terms of the equitable distribution of the
goods and services according to a labor theory of value, making workers,
not capital, the engine of technological, industrial, and social development
does not in itself safeguard humankind from the consequences of resource
depletion and pollution.[19] To promote this version of socioeconomic progress, Marx paradoxically must follow John Locke in treating use value as
(in theory) infinitely elastic: a collectivist future depends on resources
remaining abundant.

Eurocentric, that is, modern, economic theory, whether neoclassical or
Marxist, describes both a history and a historiography of the "rise" of
capitalism. In this sense, the quest for the "origins" of western "imperialism"
in Asia paradoxically remains bound to progressivist and self-reflexive
narratives: searching for the origins of western-style economic "progress"
produces a narrative that reifies discrete practices, data, and texts as
evidence of such progress, even if the specific instantiations of bourgeois
capitalism are perceived, in Marxian terms, as ultimately subject to the
same inexorable laws of socioeconomic progress. Postcolonial critiques of
empire in the early modern period thus run the risk of getting caught
between condemning European military, political, and economic imperialism and a paradoxical reliance on either liberal or Marxist narratives of
colonialist domination. In this respect, the narratives of Eurocentrism – as
the intellectual DNA of our economic, social, political, scientific, and
technological history – tend to be accepted and reproduced as accurate,
if deplorable, descriptions of the genealogy of empire.

Ironically, many postcolonial studies rely on neoclassical or narrowly
Marxian economic histories that reinforce myths of European technological,
military, and economic superiority. In otherwise valuable works, for
example, Shankar Raman in 2001 and Balachandra Rajan in 1999, follow
G. V. Scammell's Eurocentric histories in their descriptions of European
trade in India, but do not discuss (or footnote) the work of Frank, Perlin,
Goldstone, or Bairoch – all of whom had published their major critiques of
Eurocentrism before 1997.[20] "Traditional" postcolonialism has no way to

account for a Sinocentric world, and therefore tends either to ignore Japan and China or read European–Asian encounters in the seventeenth and early eighteenth centuries through the lens of the nineteenth-century European domination of India.[21] In concentrating on European contacts with the Ottoman, Persian, and Moghul Empires, many critics and historians assume that the Far East lies outside of the circuits of trade, linguistic contact, and religious confrontation in the Mediterranean and Near East. John Michael Archer, for example, asserts that "China, Japan, and the Moluccas . . . effectively fall outside the overlap of early modern trade with the geo-historical itinerary of Mediterranean antiquity."[22] This seems, at best, a debatable point: Heylyn, John Webb, and Sir William Temple, among many other writers (as I argue in later chapters), explicitly compared the empires of the ancient world to China, and found that Greece and Rome suffered by comparison to the Ming and Qing dynasties. It is significant, in this regard, that there is no discussion of China or Japan in either David Armitage's *The Ideological Origins of the British Empire* or Anthony Pagden's *Lords of All the World: Ideologies of Empire in Spain, Britain and France c. 1500–1800*. China and Japan are also absent from the essays collected in *Empire and Others: British Encounters with Indigenous Peoples, 1600–1850*.[23] At the very least, this neglect gives a skewed perspective of what authors, editors, and apparently readers found appealing in collections such as those of Purchas and Heylyn. In emphasizing European encounters with the Far East, I argue throughout this study that the confrontation of English writers with China and Japan became a catalyst for their recognition that the discourse of European empire was an ideological construct – part self-conscious propaganda, part wish fulfillment, and part econometric extrapolation to sustain fantasies of commercial prosperity, if not imperial conquest.

That said, some first-rate postcolonial studies of eighteenth-century literary culture have revealed the ways in which the contradictions within the ideology of empire worked to suture over fissures within social and political institutions as well as within unstable conceptions of colonialist subjectivity. In her provocative study of science, ecology, race, and colonialism in British India, Kavita Philip demonstrates convincingly that "local knowledges from the periphery of empire were constitutive of both the form and content of science at the metropolitan center," and, consequently, of one of the key forms of modernist self-definition: the self-consistent and internalist progress of universal scientific knowledge, a knowledge that is then used to denigrate "primitive" belief systems and the peoples who practice them.[24] As Rajani Sudan argues, the colonizer's

belief in his or her cultural and political authority is introjected so that the
corollary of colonialist agency becomes xenophobia – the fear of others that
forces the European self into ever more emphatic, even hysterical assertions
of racial purity and sociopolitical authority. The threat posed by the
racial other, she argues, can be contained only by the ongoing process of
repressing the "profound insecurities" on which Eurocentrism and its
"belief in an essential authorial subjectivity" rests.[25] This decentering of
the colonizer's subjectivity is mirrored by the construction of hybrid
identities by and for colonized peoples who participate in, resist, and
reshape imperialist practices. Srinivas Aravamudan calls attention to the
significance of the "tropicopolitans," that is, those "subjected to the politics
of colonial tropology, who correspondingly seize agency through contesting
language, space, and the language of space that typifies justifications of
colonialism."[26] The contested space of the tropics thus implicates English
writers and readers in contestations of language, space, and political
economy in the domestic as well as the public sphere. In this respect,
Betty Joseph reminds us of the crucial importance of the myriad "transformations within everyday cultural spaces of empire." The colonial project,
she argues, in her study of East India Company archives between 1720 and
1840, reinforces the separation of the public and private spheres, thereby
helping to reinforce an ideology of biological and cultural reproduction for
the British colonial powers.[27] In different ways, then, Philip, Sudan,
Aravamudan, Joseph, and Felicity Nussbaum, among others, contest the
history and historiography of Eurocentrism on moral, political, and
evidentiary grounds by providing a collective archaeology of the colonizers'
model of the world. As valuable as these studies are, they leave open
questions about western Europe's relations between 1600 and 1750 with
the non-tropical world – the Asian metropoles of Beijing, Canton, Tokyo,
Nagasaki, and many other centers of international and regional significance. These questions can be addressed only by resituating postcolonial
critiques of European encounters with the Far East within the context of
non-Eurocentric perceptions of global economic culture.

WORLD SYSTEMS THEORY

In the last fifteen years, historians such as Goldstone, Frank, and
Pomeranz, among others, have challenged the seemingly bedrock assumptions of Eurocentrism – the interlocking "rises" of financial and then
industrial capitalism in northwestern Europe – on both factual and conceptual grounds. In different ways, they reject or severely qualify the idea

that Europe occupied the center of an emerging world system between 1500 and 1800, and they call into question the very analytic vocabularies that historians such as Immanuel Wallerstein and Fernand Braudel have employed to describe progressivist histories of a Eurocentric world.[28] In challenging some fundamental assumptions about agricultural and proto-industrial productivity in the global economy of the early modern era, this revisionist project has profound implications for how scholars treat the "postcolonial past." While their arguments have stirred some debate among Marxist economic historians, I want to argue that the postcolonial critique of empire has far more to gain than lose by treating skeptically progressivist narratives of early modern history, and that considering seriously the implications of these historians' arguments offers a crucial means to recontextualize the literature and history of the early modern era.[29] By recognizing, as Felipe Fernández-Armesto suggests in the epigraph to this Introduction, that western dominance is *atypical* of world history, postcolonial critics have surer grounds from which to argue that our contemporary "global economy" is historically and environmentally contingent – and therefore more open to change and resistance than the discourses of Eurocentrism (and twenty-first-century Americocentrism) would have us believe.

The arguments of Pomeranz, Goldstone, and Perlin resist quick synopsis because their works are predicated on dismantling from within the economic principles on which the entwined narratives of Eurocentrism and modernism depend. Very briefly, they muster a wide range of data – from China, Japan, India, Persia, and the Ottoman Empire as well as western Europe – to demonstrate that there is little historical evidence to support the exceptionalist view that England, the Netherlands, and France became world powers in the sixteenth century and consolidated their pre-eminence in the seventeenth and eighteenth centuries. Frank is the most assertive in arguing that before 1800 "the entire world economic order was – literally – Sinocentric," but this view has been seconded by other historians of China.[30] Rather than being hamstrung by its retrograde "Asiatic mode of production" and stunted by its "oriental despotism," China emerges as the economic engine for the early modern world – the most populous, wealthiest, and among the most technologically sophisticated nations before 1800. Its insatiable thirst for silver (its basic currency) drove the long-distance trade of European maritime powers for three hundred years. Europeans manufactured almost nothing that was in demand in the Far East, and consequently the bulk of their exports – almost 80 percent of the English and Dutch East India Companies' before

1800 – were in bullion, which paid for luxury items: cottons from India, silks, porcelain and increasingly tea from China, and spices from Southeast Asia and India.[31] Except on the small islands of the Indonesian archipelago, the European powers were suitors for trading privileges, not colonists, in East Asia; indeed "colonialism" seems a problematic term to apply to factories (trading outposts) that usually contained fewer than one hundred resident Europeans at any one time. To speak of the Far East in the European imagination, as I argue in each of the chapters below, is to recognize the significance of these limitations on European power and influence.

In challenging Eurocentric economic histories, Pomeranz argues that China, not England or the Netherlands, was closer to Adam Smith's conception of a neoclassical economy than any nation in Europe. Drawing on studies of economic data on Qing China (much of which had been inaccessible until the 1980s), he demonstrates that the very criteria that have been used to champion English exceptionalism actually show that in many ways the heavily populated coastal provinces of China equaled or surpassed the "advanced" economies of northwestern Europe. Labor markets in China and Japan were freer than they were in England or France; and the Qing and Tokugawa administrations were committed to fostering increased productivity through technological advances in small industries and innovative agricultural practices. The diet of Chinese peasants and urban laborers was at least as good as the diet of their counterparts in western Europe; in fact, between 1500 and 1800 per capita consumption of meat declined in Europe, and in England, France, and parts of Germany, the laboring classes suffered from stagnant living standards and increased pressures on available resources. In China, life expectancies were higher and infant mortality rates comparable to those in northwestern Europe. Wage differentials between men and women in the crucial weaving industries, the major employer for women working outside the home, were far less in China than in Britain.[32] The Qing administrations also had a sophisticated and effective granary system to deal with floods, droughts, and bad harvests. The heroic efforts of Qing officials during the El Niño droughts in northern China in 1743–44 saved two million peasants from starvation; in Ireland, France, and central Europe between 1740 and 1743, harvest failures led to the deaths by starvation and disease of perhaps as many as three million peasants.[33] In brief, there is no evidence to support traditional views that workers in western Europe lived longer or better than their counterparts in China and Japan. As significantly, Europe enjoyed no decisive technological advantages over Japan or China before 1800 – a fact noted by almost all European merchants and missionaries who visited these countries in the seventeenth and eighteenth centuries and marveled at the variety, quality, and low price of Chinese and Japanese goods.[34]

To answer the crucial question of why the industrial revolution occurred in Great Britain rather than China, Pomeranz argues that ecological factors – broadly understood – were far more important than social liberalization, financial capitalism, or technological innovation. In a detailed investigation of the circumatlantic trade, he suggests that the monoculture of the American colonies, predicated on slave labor and the comparatively low costs of planting sugar and cotton, provided England with a crucial influx of "real resources" at a time when England's agriculture and forests could no longer keep pace with a rapidly increasing population. Sugar provides a crucial instance of his approach, what we might term eco-cultural materialism. In 1800, sugar made up approximately 4 percent of the average worker's diet in England (and 18 percent in 1900), assuming (generously) that an average male worker consumed 2,500 calories daily. While 4 percent seems negligible, consider the costs and ecological implications of this change in diet: one acre of tropical sugar produces as many calories as four acres of potatoes and nine to twelve acres of wheat. If no sugar were imported into England, an additional 1,300,000 to 1,900,000 acres of farm land would have had to have been devoted to food production in 1800 – land that either did not exist or was unavailable or unsuitable for cultivation.[35] These "ghost acres" represent the net gain to England of its American imports, computed not in terms of, say, a percentage of the overall economy, but as a measure of the pressures relieved on England's resources.

After 1800, imports of American cotton and timber also rose rapidly. Citing studies by Joel Mokyr, Samuel Mintz, and others, Pomeranz calculates that raising enough sheep to replace imported cotton with wool would have required an additional 9,000,000 acres of land in 1815 and over 23,000,000 acres in 1830 – a figure that exceeds Britain's total combined crop and pasture land. By 1815, England's annual energy output from coal was the equivalent of 15,000,000 acres of forest, but cotton, sugar, and timber combined saved twice as many "ghost acres" – the land under cultivation that would have been required to feed, clothe, and fuel Britain's growing population.[36] Without these imports from Canada and the fledgling United States and its own substantial coal deposits, England would have faced the same structural demographic and ecological crisis that overtook China. Pomeranz's analysis thus supplements the arguments of Goldstone, Frank, and Wong, who, in different ways, argue that coal production fired Britain's industrial revolution at a time when other countries – notably China – would have required massive, even unprecedented investments of time, labor, capital, and resources in mining and transporting coal to densely populated areas. For England, cheap American imports provided a comparatively inexpensive way to circumvent the crises of intensification that overtook China at the beginning of the nineteenth century when growth in energy-intensive industries was hampered by a lack of resources, a deficiency that trade with East Asian hinterlands could not solve. While these hinterlands boomed in population and productivity, their exports of resources to the cloth-producing Yangzi Delta slowed, and the Chinese were forced to rely on labor-intensive and resource-husbanding paths of agriculture and small-scale manufacturing throughout the eighteenth century.

ECONOMICS AND HISTORICAL ECOLOGY

Pomeranz's work describes accurately the conditions that European travelers described in China from the sixteenth century on. If the rhetoric about the riches of China and the benefits of trade with the Far East often seems repetitive by the eighteenth century, it is because writers share the ideological assumptions and values that foster a belief in the glories of a godly commerce with Aceh, Canton, and Nagasaki. The English fascination with the Far East in the works of Milton, Dryden, and their contemporaries was conditioned by more than a century's experience of increasing demographic and ecological pressures, culminating in the upheavals of the Civil War and Interregnum. Between 1500 and 1650, the population of England more than doubled to over five million; the increase in "marginal" groups who were excluded from owning or inheriting property (younger sons, sisters, and daughters among the upper and middle classes; displaced agricultural laborers who gravitated toward London or retreated to the waste areas of fens and forests among the property-less classes) exceeded the growth of the general population by several fold. Grain prices during this century and a half rose by 600 percent, but wages by only 200 percent. The human misery of this imbalance only can be imagined – or experienced secondhand by reading the radical writers of the 1640s. Fixed rents and a greater population of underemployed laborers and younger sons of the gentry clamoring for government positions created intensifying pressures on the Crown to raise duties and taxes to meet expenditures, particularly paying for military forces. Allowing for inflation and the discrepancy between rising food prices and the much slower increase in land rents and other revenues, Goldstone estimates that the cost of running the government in 1640 was twelve times what it had been for Henry VII. Charles I's revenues were only 10 percent higher than Elizabeth's had been in the 1580s, but the population of England had grown by two-thirds in this half century, and the gentry, "always hungry for patronage," had tripled.[37] Significantly, these structural and demographic changes were not confined to the British Isles: the costs of government in France, the Ottoman Empire, and China as well as in England by the middle of the seventeenth century, Goldstone argues, fragmented elite classes, provoked rebellion among workers whose living standards had been declining rapidly, and led to fiscal crises that traditional state institutions and tax structures could not solve. The breakdown of the old order in these states was halted only after warfare, civil unrest, disease, and declining birth rates halted decades of population growth. To many writers who lived through the Civil War, the Interregnum, the Restoration, and three wars with the Dutch within twenty years, the financing of a would-be commercial empire through trade with the Far East seemed an ideal way to overcome economic, political, and environmental crises at home. Even earlier in the seventeenth century, debates between economic writers such as Gerald Malynes and Thomas Mun focused on the relationships among trade, production, and credit as merchants and government officials tried to foster conditions that would alleviate a seemingly pervasive economic crisis.[38]

Goldstone's "demographic/structural" model of history, like Pomeranz's analysis, brings the seemingly arcane debates of seventeenth-century political economy within the context of recent work in historical ecology. This cross-disciplinary field emphasizes, in Carole Crumley's words, that all landscapes are manifestations of "ongoing dialectical relations between human acts and acts of nature."[39] Nature and culture are not distinct entities but parts of a complex matrix of multiple causal pathways and feedback loops. In this context, to appreciate the efforts of writers such as Milton to think through seemingly intractable economic and ecological problems, we need to jettison the assumption – common to all forms of exploitative economics – that the natural world is susceptible to infinite manipulation and strategies of control. The crises of the seventeenth century that fueled English fascination with international trade can be described in terms of *intensification*. Marvin Harris describes intensification as "the investment of more soil, water, minerals, or energy per unit of time or area," which is humankind's "recurrent response to threats against living standards."[40] But even if it raises living standards temporarily, the practices of intensification – from cutting down more trees to build more houses to draining marsh lands to provide more land for agriculture – invariably prove counter-productive over time because, in Harris's words, "the increased effort sooner or later must be applied to more remote, less reliable, and less bountiful animals, plants, soils, minerals, and sources of energy." As resources become increasingly scarce or disappear entirely, living standards decline and unrest spreads, until cultures collapse into anarchy or "invent new and more efficient means of production which sooner or later again lead to the depletion of the natural environment."[41] Harris's description calls attention to the complex interactions among population pressures, technological developments, rates of resource extraction, environmental degradation, fluctuations in living standards, distribution networks for food and water, communication, labor, political power, tax structures, and the creation of symbolic systems of value that favor those in positions of authority. These interdependent factors, in turn, cannot be divorced from larger ecological considerations. While England benefited from its coal and comparatively cheap American imports, China confronted growing ecological problems without the resources to defer their consequences.[42]

In different ways, Pomeranz, Goldstone, Harris, and Crumley offer fundamental challenges to after-the-fact theorizing that attributes socio-historical change to "ideas," "discourses," "ideologies," "philosophies," or, more generally, human intentions imposed on a feminized natural world. Modern explanations of cultural and conceptual transformations in the seventeenth and eighteenth centuries characteristically downplay the techno-logical developments, demographic pressures, and unintentional conse-quences of intensification. Because, as Greg Dening suggests, "surrenders to conventionality are what disciplines are," cross-disciplinary and cross-cultural studies must resist the temptation to retreat to disciplinary modes of thinking without questioning the principles and narratives that they take for granted.[43] One of the effects of Eurocentric economic theory has been the denigrating of non-western means of assessing and negotiating the exchange values necessary for sophisticated commercial enterprises. In suggesting that "the organizational characteristics of past economic activities were not necessarily poorer in quality or complexity than those of the present day," Perlin argues that we need to recognize the significance of differentiation in a variety of systems of preindustrial exchange: plant species no less than manufactured goods were produced to enhance "micro-differentiation" in response to supply and demand. Rather than accepting Marx's description of the money form of value as the ultimate basis for commercial transactions, he suggests that complex taxonomies of value included wide ranges of goods that enhanced rather than stymied the ability of agricultural societies to convert plant species and seed varieties into other fungibles, even as they maintained "predictable collective identities" as aspects of dynamic and coherent socioeconomic practices.[44] Cultivated varieties of Indonesian pepper, for example, represent sophisticated agro-economic responses to market demands, consumption habits, and ecological variations long before the arrival of European traders – and before the cultures of the archipelago had developed written records. Perlin's work, like Goldstone's and Pomeranz's, demonstrates that "economics" cannot be restricted to a narrative of deterministic causes and effects, nor to a progressivist history of the growth and maturation of a "modern" world system. Between 1600 and 1730, its discourses remain embedded in discussions of trade, theology, warfare, missionary work, technology transfer, ecology, and diplomacy – in short, in *ideology*: the practices, beliefs, and negotiations of value and meaning that dynamically redefine and constrain horizons of expectation and intelligibility.

The eco-cultural materialism that I have described offers a powerful analytic to explain a wider range of phenomena than conventional "intellectual" history, and it brings higher standards of interdisciplinary accountability to bear on the literary culture of the seventeenth and eighteenth centuries. Milton, Dryden, Defoe, Swift, and their contemporaries may have written about the crises of their times in the discourses of religion, classical precedent, and socioeconomic and masculinist privilege, but their texts are nonetheless powerful efforts, using the analytic vocabularies they had available, to make sense of complex relationships among contemporary crises of intensification, the promise of international trade, and challenges posed by the Far East to Eurocentric conceptions of historiography, theology, and national identity.

CHAPTER DESCRIPTIONS

The Far East and the English Imagination follows a rough chronological order even as it studies the recursive qualities of European writing on China, Southeast Asia, and Japan. Sources, accounts of historical incidents, and truisms recur throughout English writing on the Far East in the seventeenth and eighteenth centuries: the torture and execution of a dozen English merchants on the Dutch-held island of Amboyna, for example, is debated by English and Dutch pamphleteers in the 1620s; the incident becomes the subject of John Dryden's 1672 tragedy; it is invoked repeatedly by Defoe in his fiction and non-fiction; and it serves as the name of the ship on which Gulliver returns to England from Japan at the end of the third book of his adventures. This interweaving of history, literature, and economic theory reveals the complex ways in which political revolutions, technological innovations, and socio-economic changes paradoxically seem to make a wide variety of writers cling ever more fiercely to Child's identification of riches, power, trade, and religion.

Chapter one examines the literature of commercial adventurism in early seventeenth-century writing on Southeast Asia. The travel journals of Jan Huighen van Linschoten, the diplomatic correspondence of Queen Elizabeth with the Sultan of Aceh, the account of John Saris of his voyage to the Spice Islands and Japan, and the influential geography by Peter Heylyn register both the complex politics of the region and the limitations of European military and economic power. Rather than imposing orientalist assumptions on the East Indies, these accounts describe shifting alliances among European and regional powers, internal conflicts within Southeast Asia, and changing opportunities for trade. These texts demonstrate an endless fascination with economic, agricultural, climatological, and cultural practices, and the peoples of these regions present European travelers with projections of their own desires and fears. For Thomas Mun, an EIC official, the Far East confirms the principles of mercantile capitalism; trade to the Spice Islands, Japan, and China offers a fantasy space for the endless generation of wealth. In his *Discovrse of Trade* he reshapes the complexities of international commerce into a dynamic ideology that presumes that the spice trade can enrich European trading companies, individual merchants, and the nation as a whole. These assumptions inform Heylyn's *Cosmographie* as it reworks firsthand descriptions into truisms about race, national identity, and civilization in the Orient.

Chapter two examines Milton's fascination with trade to the Far East in the context of Jesuit apologetics and Chinese writings about Europeans. For Milton and his contemporaries, China offers the promise of riches that will help Europeans overcome the curses of sin and scarcity, even as it poses a formidable challenge to Eurocentric visions of history, politics, and theology. Milton's voluntarist theology and republican politics lead him to distance himself from the Jesuit accounts of China, by Matteo Ricci, Martino Martini, and British royalists such as John Webb, that celebrated the country's wealth, socioeconomic stability, and presumed monotheism. The prospect of an empire resistant to his voluntarist critiques of tyranny, sin, and idolatry forces Milton to try to separate the potential benefits of trade to the Far East from the challenges that China poses to his vision of providential history – including the threat represented by the assimilation of the Jews of Kaifeng to Chinese culture. In this regard, Milton's rejection of Jesuit accommodationism – the efforts of missionaries in China to minimize or efface differences between Christianity and Confucian moral philosophy – defines the ways in which responses to China help to constitute political and theological forms of self-identification in seventeenth-century England.

Chapter three concentrates on two trade missions to Beijing: the Dutch East India Company (VOC) embassy in 1655–56, chronicled by Jan Nieuhoff, and the Russian mission conducted by the Czar's emissary, Evret Ysbrants Ides, in 1690. Both accounts were quickly translated into English and other European languages, and both articulate the conviction that favorable trading rights can be secured from the Qing dynasty by appealing to the shared upper-class, transcultural values of civility. Projecting their own desires for trade onto their Manchu and Chinese hosts, Nieuhoff and Ides have trouble negotiating the complex intrigues of the court, notably the efforts of Jesuits in Beijing to undermine their missions. Although they failed to secure the trading privileges they sought, both men reassert their faith in seventeenth-century ideologies of trade; as they leave China, they remain convinced that the United Provinces and Russia can establish a lucrative commerce with China. In turn, the response of the Qing officials to these European missions offers a means to explore Manchu and Chinese perceptions of trade and civility. By deferring and ultimately frustrating the goals of the Dutch and Russian emissaries, the court officials reassert a very different set of values from those that the red-haired barbarians assume all civilized people must possess.

Chapter four discusses the volatile and violent rivalry between the Dutch and English over the riches of Southeast Asia as it figures in two works by John Dryden. In his 1666 poem *Annus Mirabilis*, Dryden maintains that England's future greatness depends on securing trade to the Spice Islands. Glorifying the inconclusive battles of the Second Dutch War, the poet celebrates a vision of London's resurrection after the Plague in alchemical images that link England's prophesied future to a revival of its commerce in the East Indies. Several years later, his tragedy *Amboyna* recasts England's humiliation in 1622 as the martyrdom of national virtue, liberty, and nobility. By simplifying a complex history of international rivalry as a mercantile morality play, Dryden mystifies the sources and nature of Anglo-Dutch conflict. Paradoxically, his tragedy stages the instabilities within the discourses of nationalism, free trade, and gentlemanly civility that the play overtly champions. In this respect, *Amboyna* displaces profound insecurities about the economic strength and political will of England into the theatrics of political martyrdom.

Chapter five concentrates on the second volume of Daniel Defoe's Crusoe trilogy, the *Farther Adventures of Robinson Crusoe*, to challenge the tendencies within eighteenth-century studies to write the histories of modernity, identity, the rise of the novel, and the rise of financial capitalism in mutually reinforcing terms. Crusoe's abandoning of the island midway through *Farther Adventures* represents the novelist's self-conscious *rejection* of the interlocking discourses of "psychological realism," economic self-sufficiency, and European colonialism. While trade in the Far East offers the promise of endless profits, it also confronts Crusoe with the challenges posed by China to western conceptions of identity and theology. The threat posed by non-Christians lead to the hero's (and his creator's) fervent assertions of British and Protestant superiority to the cultures of China and Siberian Tartary. In this regard, Crusoe's career as a merchant becomes a compensatory means to reestablish a religious and national identity that both depicts and seeks to counter nightmare visions of an embattled English identity in a hostile world.

Chapter six investigates Defoe's longstanding advocacy of British trading ventures to the South Seas. Undaunted by the South Sea Bubble, Defoe uses his final novel, *A New Voyage Round the World*, to promote schemes for English colonization in Southeast Asia and the unexplored interior of South America. *A New Voyage* fictionalizes the constitutive assumptions of previous travel writers – that the lands and peoples of the Pacific can produce wealth in excess of the capital expenditures required to exploit them. But in this novel, this faith comes close to self-parody: Defoe sends his nameless narrator and crew to Terra Australis Incognita where they trade trinkets for huge amounts of gold and then to a verdant and unpeopled South America where gold lies on the ground waiting to be picked up. Banishing the hardships and horrific mortality rates suffered by sailors in eighteenth-century voyages to the Pacific, *A New Voyage* projects onto little known continents and imaginary islands the fantasy of unending profits that informs both speculative ventures to the South Seas and the logic of Defoe's economic theorizing.

Chapter seven explores a crucial but often neglected episode in Gulliver's adventures in the western Pacific: his encounters with natives of Japan in book three. His capture by a Japanese pirate captain at the beginning of the book and his audience with the Emperor of Japan at its end provide Swift with opportunities both to revile the Dutch and to demonstrate the limits of his contemporaries' Eurocentric vision of world. Gulliver's voyage to Japan draws on three important bodies of literature: accounts of the short-lived English trading post in Hirado (1613–23); histories of the expulsion of the Jesuits and the suppression of Catholicism in Japan; and narratives of the Dutch willingness to trample on the crucifix in order to maintain their trading privileges. In their combination of fantasy and realism, Gulliver's encounters with the Japanese register profound anxieties about the limitations of English economic power, national identity, and morality. Like China, Japan presented fundamental challenges to the rhetoric of European imperialism: works such as Jean Crasset's *History of the Church of Japan* and Engelbert Kaempfer's *History of Japan* reflect a consensus among European commentators that the Japanese rivaled or surpassed the English, French, and Dutch in their standards of living, technological sophistication, and military prowess. Gulliver's audience with the Emperor demonstrates ironically the *irrelevance* of the assumptions, values, and logic on which Eurocentrism depends.

CODA: AMERICOCENTRISM

"History," as Dening reminds us, "is not the past: it is the consciousness of the past used for present purposes."[45] In an important sense, the consciousness of the early modern past has been used both to justify and to question the values and principles of the world order ushered in during the nineteenth century but it has done little to encourage investigations in comparative imperialisms.[46] In studying the literary and cultural responses to European encounters with the Far East in the seventeenth and eighteenth centuries, I have my own purposes in mind – calling into question the belief that Eurocentric modernity is now, and has been since Columbus, an inevitable and continuing state of affairs, that we live in an open-ended era of western dominance. The five-hundred-year history of the modern world system favored by Wallerstein and Braudel looks almost immutable compared to the two-hundred-year epicycle of Eurocentrism described by Frank and Pomeranz. Five hundred years is too much for most people to imagine: few buildings from 1505 remain standing; books, documents, and maps from the early sixteenth century are exceedingly rare. Two hundred years, in contrast, hovers on the verge of historical re-enactment, if not recovery. On my wall hang maps of Asia from the seventeenth and eighteenth centuries; like many scholars, I own a few books published before 1800. The town in which I was born in Connecticut features a handful of houses that date to the Revolutionary War, still standing and still occupied. In the United States, lawyers debate incessantly the intentions of what eighteenth-century merchants, slaveowners, and printers meant in cobbling together, in secrecy, various articles and phrasings in the Constitution. By locating the origins of Eurocentric modernity in the coalfields of late eighteenth and early nineteenth-century Britain, Pomeranz and other historians bring the prospect of a Sinocentric world into an uncomfortable proximity to the values, assumptions, and ideologies of our own time.

Ultimately, although some readers may disagree, early modern studies may be at the beginning of a paradigm shift away from Eurocentric discourses, narratives, and habits of thought that invest post-1800 conceptions of empire, technology, science, and economics – the ideology of modernity – with a transhistorical status. Eurocentric and Americocentric modernity currently may be subject to endless qualification and questioning, but such discussions tend to reify its underlying values, assumptions, and beliefs. At the end of *Revolution and Rebellion in the Early Modern World*, Goldstone describes what is at stake in his revisionist argument about the general crisis of the seventeenth century and, more broadly, the "cyclic crises that shook, but often failed to fundamentally change, rigid institutions and economies." If, he argues, "most social theory has fundamentally misunderstood the dynamics of the early modern period," then what he calls "selfish elites" perpetuate such misunderstandings in enforcing legislation predicated on the dubious assumptions that economic growth is open-ended, that the aggrandizement of resources by a small minority of wealthy individuals is inevitable, and that unrealistic tax structures are essential for prosperity.[47] His solution for the United States – increased taxes to reflect the real costs of rising expenditures – strikes me, if anything, as optimistic, particularly in the context of the deadly combination of ecological crises and unrestrained capitalism that, according to Mike Davis, ushered in the modern world.[48] As a thought experiment, one might read Chalmers Johnson's *The Sorrows of Empire: Militarism, Secrecy, and the End of the Republic*, a sobering look at the political, military, and economic costs and consequences of an American empire headed toward a seemingly irrevocable decline, in conjunction with Ray Huang's classical study, *1587, A Year of No Significance: The Ming Dynasty in Decline*.[49] The uncanny similarities between these two works suggest the need for new modes of thinking about the relationships between the early modern and the all-too-modern world.

NOTES

1. Felipe Fernández-Armesto, *Civilizations: Culture, Ambition, and the Transformation of Nature* (New York: Free Press, 2001), 22–3.
2. Although he is writing about nineteenth-century culture, Edward Said, *Orientalism* (London: Routledge, 1978), has influenced many accounts of Europe's relationship to Asia in earlier periods. Because Said concentrates on the Middle East, his arguments have less relevance for this study than they do for the critics (cited below) who work on Anglo-Ottoman and Persian relations. On the problems of imposing nineteenth-century conceptions of orientalism on the early modern world, see Janet Abu-Lughod, *Before European Hegemony: The World System A.D. 1250–1350* (New York: Oxford University Press, 1989).
3. K. N. Chaudhuri, *Asia before Europe: Economy and Civilisation of the Indian Ocean from the Rise of Islam to 1750* (Cambridge: Cambridge University Press, 1990); Jack Goldstone, *Revolution and Rebellion in the Early Modern World* (Berkeley and Los Angeles: University of California Press, 1991); J. M. Blaut, *The Colonizer's Model of the World: Geographical Diffusionism and Eurocentric History* (New York: Guilford Press, 1993); Frank Perlin, *"The Invisible City": Monetary, Administrative and Popular Infrastructure in Asia and Europe 1500–1900* (Aldershot: Variorum, 1993); Perlin, *Unbroken Landscape. Commodity, Category, Sign, and Identity: Their Production as Myth and Knowledge from 1500* (Aldershot: Variorum, 1994); Paul Bairoch, *Economics and World History: Myths and Paradoxes* (Hemel Hempstead: Harvester/ Wheatsheaf, 1993); R. Bin Wong, *China Transformed: Historical Change and the Limits of European Experience* (Ithaca: Cornell University Press, 1997); Andre Gunder Frank, *ReOrient: Global Economy in the Asian Age* (Berkeley and Los Angeles: University of California Press, 1997); Kenneth Pomeranz, *The Great Divergence: China, Europe, and the Making of the Modern World Economy* (Princeton: Princeton University Press, 2000); and Geoffrey Gunn, *First Globalization: The Eurasian Exchange, 1500–1800* (Lanham, MD: Rowman & Littlefield, 2003).
4. Claudia Schnurmann, "'Wherever profit leads us, to every sea and shore ...': The VOC, the WIC, and Dutch Methods of Globalization in the Seventeenth Century," *Renaissance Studies* 17 (2003), 483.
5. On England and the Ottoman Empire, see Nabil I. Matar, *Islam in Britain, 1558–1685* (Cambridge: Cambridge University Press, 1998); Matar, *Turks, Moors, and Englishmen in the Age of Discovery* (New York: Columbia University Press, 1999); Daniel Vitkus, *Turning Turk: English Theater and the Multicultural Mediterranean, 1570–1630* (London: Palgrave, 2003); Bernadette Andrea, "Columbus in Istanbul: Ottoman Mapping of the 'New World'," *Genre* 30 (1997), 135–65; Kenneth Parker, "Introduction," in *Early Modern Tales of Orient: A Critical Anthology* (New York: Routledge, 1999), 1–35; Gerald MacLean, *The Rise of Oriental Travel: English Visitors to the Ottoman Empire, 1580–1720* (London: Palgrave, 2004); and Jonathan Burton, *Traffic and Turning: Commerce, Conversion, and Islam in English Drama* (Newark: University of

Delaware Press, 2005). The extraordinarily complex problem of India in the literary imagination and global economy of the eighteenth century lies beyond the scope of this study. But see Balachandra Rajan, *Under Western Eyes: India from Milton to Macaulay* (Durham: Duke University Press, 1999); Shankar Raman, *Framing "India": The Colonial Imaginary in Early Modern Culture* (Stanford: Stanford University Press, 2001); and John Michael Archer, *Old Worlds: Egypt, Southwest Asia, India, and Russia in Early Modern English Writing* (Stanford: Stanford University Press, 2001).

6. On biblical controversies see Edwin J. van Kley, "Europe's 'Discovery' of China and the Writing of World History," *American Historical Review* 76 (1971), 358–85, and van Kley, "News from China: Seventeenth-Century Notices of the Manchu Conquest," *Journal of Modern History* 45 (1973), 361–82; and Paolo Rossi, *The Dark Abyss of Time: The History of the Earth and the History of Nations from Hooke to Vico*, trans. Lydia G. Cochrane (Chicago: University of Chicago Press, 1984), 141–67. On the influence of Chinese thought in seventeenth-century Europe see, Yuen-Ting Lai, "Religious Scepticism and China," in *The Sceptical Mode in Modern Philosophy: Essays in Honor of Richard H. Popkin*, ed. Richard A. Watson and James E. Force (Dordrecht: Martinus Nijhoff, 1988), 11–41.

7. David Porter, *Ideographia: The Chinese Cipher in Early Modern Europe* (Stanford: Stanford University Press, 2001).

8. Donald Lach, with Edwin J. van Kley, *Asia in the Making of Europe*, 3 vols. (Chicago: University of Chicago Press, 1965–93).

9. On deforestation, see Andrew McRae, *God Speed the Plough: The Representation of Agrarian England, 1500–1660* (Cambridge: Cambridge University Press, 1996), and Robert Markley, "'Gulfes, deserts, precipices, stone': Marvell's 'Upon Appleton House' and the Contradictions of 'Nature,'" in *The Cultural Life of the Country and City: Identities and Spaces in Britain, 1550–1860*, ed. Donna Landry, Gerald MacLean, and Joseph Ward (Cambridge: Cambridge University Press, 1999), 89–105.

10. Sir Josiah Child, *A Treatise Wherein is Demonstrated . . . that the East-India Trade is the Most National of All Trades* (London, 1681), 29.

11. See Kenneth Knoespel, "Newton in the School of Time: The *Chronology of Ancient Kingdoms Amended* and the Crisis of Seventeenth-Century Historiography," *The Eighteenth Century: Theory and Interpretation* 30 (1989), 19–41, and Robert Markley, "Newton, Corruption, and the Tradition of Universal History", in *Newton and Religion*, ed. James E. Force and Richard Popkin (Dordrecht: Kluwer Academic Press, 1999), 121–43.

12. On English exceptionalism, see François Crouzet, *A History of the European Economy, 1000–2000* (Charlottesville: University Press of Virginia, 2001), 110–16.

13. For representative histories see Geoffrey Holmes, *The Making of a Great Power: Late Stuart and Early Georgian Britain 1660–1722* (London: Longman, 1993); John Brewer, *The Sinews of Power: War, Money and the English State, 1688–1783* (Cambridge, MA: Harvard University Press, 1990); C. G. A. Clay, *Economic Expansion and Social Change: England 1500–1700*, 2 vols. (Cambridge:

Cambridge University Press, 1984); Larry Neal, *The Rise of Financial Capitalism: International Capital Markets in the Age of Reason* (Cambridge: Cambridge University Press, 1990); Joel Mokyr, *The Lever of Riches: Technological Creativity and Economic Progress* (New York: Oxford University Press, 1990); Robert Brenner, *Merchants and Revolution: Commercial Change, Political Conflicts, and London's Overseas Traders, 1550–1633* (Cambridge: Cambridge University Press, 1993); and David Hackett Fischer, *The Great Wave: Price Revolutions and the Rhythm of History* (New York: Oxford University Press, 1996), 91–106.

14. Greg Dening, *Performances* (Chicago: University of Chicago Press, 1996), 58.
15. See Donald N. McCloskey, "The Economics of Choice: Neoclassical Supply and Demand," in Thomas G. Rawski, Susan B. Carter, Jon S. Cohen, Stephen Cullenberg, Peter H. Lindert, Donald N. McCloskey, Hugh Rockoff, and Richard Sutch, *Economics and the Historian* (Berkeley and Los Angeles: University of California Press, 1996), 122–58.
16. On mathematics and its implications, see Brian Rotman, *Ad Infinitum: The Ghost in Turing's Machine. Taking God Out of Mathematics and Putting the Body Back In* (Stanford: Stanford University Press, 1993). My critique in this section is indebted to Bruno Latour, *We Have Never Been Modern*, trans. Catherine Porter (Cambridge, MA: Harvard University Press, 1993).
17. Philip Mirowski, *More Heat than Light: Economics as Social Physics, Physics as Nature's Economics* (Cambridge: Cambridge University Press, 1989); Richard W. Hadden, *On the Shoulders of Merchants: Exchange and the Mathematical Conception of Nature in Early Modern Europe* (Albany: SUNY Press, 1994), 46–56; Susan Buck-Morss, "Envisioning Capital: Political Economy on Display," *Critical Inquiry* 21 (1995), 434–67; and Alfred W. Crosby, *The Measure of Reality: Quantification and Western Society* (Cambridge: Cambridge University Press, 1997), 199–223.
18. See Joyce Oldham Appleby, *Economic Thought and Ideology in Seventeenth-Century England* (Princeton: Princeton University Press, 1978).
19. I treat seventeenth-century discussions of the labor theory of value and its ecological consequences in Robert Markley, "'Land Enough in the World': Locke's Golden Age and the Infinite Extensions of 'Use'," *South Atlantic Quarterly* 98 (1999), 817–37.
20. Rajan, *Under Western Eyes*; and Raman, *Framing "India"*; G. V. Scammell, *The First Imperial Age: European Overseas Expansion, c. 1400–1715* (London: Unwin Hyman, 1989); and Scammell, *The World Encompassed: The First European Maritime Empires, c. 800–1650* (Berkeley and Los Angeles: University of California Press, 1981).
21. Jyotsna G. Singh, *Colonial Narratives/Cultural Dialogues: "Discoveries" of India in the Language of Colonialism* (London: Routledge, 1996); Singh, "History or Colonial Ethnography: The Ideological Formation of Edward Terry's *A Voyage to East India* (1655 & 1665) and *The Merchants and Mariners Preservation and Thanksgiving* (1649)," in *Travel Knowledge: European "Discoveries" in the Early Modern Period*, ed. Ivo Kamps and Jyotsna G. Singh (London: Palgrave, 2001),

197–210; and, in the same volume, Ivo Kamps, "Colonizing the Colonizer: A Dutchman in *Asia Portuguesa*," 166–84.

22. Archer, *Old Worlds*, 19.

23. David Armitage, *The Ideological Origins of the British Empire* (Cambridge: Cambridge University Press, 2000); Anthony Pagden, *Lords of All the World: Ideologies of Empire in Spain, Britain and France c. 1500–1800* (New Haven: Yale University Press, 1995); and Martin Daunton and Rick Halpern, eds., *Empire and Others: British Encounters with Indigenous Peoples, 1600–1850* (Philadelphia: University of Pennsylvania Press, 1999).

24. Kavita Philip, *Civilizing Natures: Race, Resources, and Modernity in Colonial South India* (Rutgers: Rutgers University Press, 2004), 6.

25. Rajani Sudan, *Fair Exotics: Xenophobic Subjects in English Literature, 1720–1850* (Philadelphia: University of Pennsylvania Press, 2002), 1, 16.

26. Srinivas Aravamudan, *Tropicopolitans: Colonialism and Agency, 1688–1804* (Durham: Duke University Press, 1999), 6. See also Felicity Nussbaum, *Torrid Zones: Maternity, Sexuality and Empire in Eighteenth-Century English Narrative* (Baltimore and London: Johns Hopkins University Press, 1995).

27. Betty Joseph, *Reading the East India Company, 1720–1840: Colonial Currencies of Gender* (Chicago: University of Chicago Press, 2004), 92. Even in India, the situation was vastly different in 1700 from what it would be a century later. Writing of the humiliating conditions imposed by the Moghul Emperor on the EIC in 1690, after the defeat of the British and their allies in the Moghul War, John Keay asserts that "politically, the [Dutch and English East India] companies were an irrelevance [in South Asia] and would long remain so" (*India: A History* [New York: Grove Press, 2000], 323).

28. Immanuel Wallerstein, *The Modern World System*, vol. I: *Capitalist Agriculture and the Origins of the European World-Economy in the Sixteenth Century* (New York: Academic Books, 1974); *The Modern World System*, vol. II, *Mercantilism and the Consolidation of the European World-Economy, 1600–1750* (New York: Academic Books, 1980); *The Modern World System*, vol. III, *The Second Era of Great Expansion of the Capitalist World-Economy 1730–1840* (New York: Academic Books, 1989); Fernand Braudel, *The Wheels of Commerce*, vol. II of *Civilization and Capitalism: 15th–18th Century* (Berkeley and Los Angeles: University of California Press, 1982); and *The Perspective of the World*, vol. III of *Civilization and Capitalism, 15th–18th Century* (Berkeley and Los Angeles: University of California Press, 1992).

29. For a Marxist critique of Frank's *ReOrient*, see Ricardo Duchesne, "Between Sinocentrism and Eurocentrism: Debating Andre Gunder Frank's *ReOrient: Global Economy in the Asian Age*," *Science and Society* 65 (2001–02), 428–63. A measure of Pomeranz's success has been the awards that *The Great Divergence* has won (the 2000 John K. Fairbank Prize of the American Historical Association; the 2001 World History Association Book Prize) and the praise his study has received from both historians of European economics (Joel Mokyr, Deidre McCloskey) and historians of Asian economics (Robert Marks, Jack Goody).

30. Frank, *ReOrient*, 127; on China see Timothy Brook, *The Confusions of Pleasure: A History of Ming China (1368–1644)* (Berkeley and Los Angeles: University of California Press, 1998); Madeleine Zelin, *The Magistrate's Tael: Rationalizing Fiscal Reform in Eighteenth-Century China* (Berkeley: University of California Press, 1984); S.A.M. Adshead, *Material Culture in Europe and China, 1400–1800: The Rise of Consumerism* (London: Palgrave, 1997); Gao Xiang, "On the Trends of Modernization in the Early Qing Period," *Social Sciences in China* 22, 4 (2001), 108–27; and John E. Wills, Jr., *1688: A Global History* (New York: Norton, 2001).

31. Frank, *ReOrient*, 159.

32. Pomeranz, *Great Divergence*, 92–93; 105–06. Japan, too, can be compared favorably to western Europe. See Susan B. Hanley, "Tokugawa Society: Material Culture, Standard of Living, and Life-Styles," in John W. Hall and James L. McCain, eds., *Early Modern Japan*, vol. IV in *The Cambridge History of Japan* (Cambridge: Cambridge University Press, 1997), 660–705; Hanley, *Everyday Things in Premodern Japan: The Hidden Legacy of Material Culture* (Berkeley: University of California Press, 1997); and Hanley and Kozo Yamamura, *Economic and Demographic Change in Preindustrial Japan, 1600–1868* (Princeton: Princeton University Press, 1977).

33. See Mike Davis, *Late Victorian Holocausts: El Niño Famines and the Making of the Third World* (London: Verso, 2001), 281–85.

34. Joseph Needham's multivolume work, *Science and Civilization in China*, remains a crucial resource for understanding the complex interactions among eastern and western technologies, and for appreciating the achievement of the Chinese in science, technology, and engineering. On shipbuilding, to take only one example, see Joseph Needham, with Wang Ling and Lu Gwei-Djen, *Science and Civilization in China*, vol. IV, part three (Cambridge: Cambridge University Press, 1971), 433–695. See also Mark Elvin, *The Pattern of the Chinese Past* (Stanford: Stanford University Press, 1973); Michael Adas, *Machines as the Measure of Men: Science, Technology, and Ideologies of Western Dominance* (Ithaca: Cornell University Press, 1989); Joanna Waley-Cohen, *The Sextants of Beijing: Global Currents in Chinese History* (New York: Norton, 1999); Francesca Bray, "Technics and Civilization in Late Imperial China: An Essay in the Cultural History of Technology," *Osiris* 13 (1998), 11–33; and Mokyr, *Lever of Riches*, 209–38.

35. Pomeranz, *Great Divergence*, 274–76, draws on the work of a number of historians including Sidney Mintz, *Sweetness and Power: The Place of Sugar in Modern History* (New York: Penguin, 1985); Mokyr, *The Lever of Riches*; and Gregory Clark, Michael Huberman, and Peter H. Lindert, "A British Food Puzzle, 1770–1850," *Economic History Review* 48 (1995), 215–37.

36. Pomeranz, *Great Divergence*, 276–77.

37. See Goldstone, *Revolution and Rebellion*, 93–100; quotation on 97.

38. Gerald Malynes, *Consuetudo vel Lex Mercatoria, or the Ancient Law-Merchant* (London, 1629); Thomas Mun, *England's Treasure by Forraign Trade* (London, 1660).

39. Carole Crumley, "Historical Ecology: A Multidimensional Ecological Orientation," in *Historical Ecology: Cultural Knowledge and Changing Landscapes*, ed. Crumley (Santa Fe: School of American Research Press, 1994), 9.

40. Marvin Harris, *Cannibals and Kings: The Origins of Cultures* (New York: Random House, 1977), 5.

41. Ibid., 5.

42. On environmental pressures in late Ming and Qing China see Peter C. Perdue, *Exhausting the Earth: State and Peasant in Hunan, 1500–1850* (Cambridge, MA: Harvard University Press, 1987); Robert B. Marks, *Tigers, Rice, Silk, and Silt: Environment and Economy in Late Imperial South China* (Cambridge: Cambridge University Press, 1997); and the essays collected in *Sediments of Time: Environment and Society in Chinese History*, ed. Mark Elvin and Liu Ts'ui-jung (Cambridge: Cambridge University Press, 1998): Anne Osborne, "Highlands and Lowlands: Economic and Ecological Interactions in the Lower Yangzi Region under the Qing," 203–34; Eduard B. Vermeer, "Population and Ecology along the Frontier in Qing China," 235–79; Robert B. Marks, "'It Never Used to Snow': Climatic Variability and Harvest Yields in Late-Imperial South China, 1650–1850," 411–46; Li Bozhong, "Changes in Climate, Land, and Human Efforts: The Production of Wet-Field Rice in Jiangnan during the Ming and Qing Dynasties," 447–85; and Helen Dunstan, "Official Thinking on Environmental Issues and the State's Environmental Roles in Eighteenth-Century China," 585–615; Pierre-Etienne Will and R. Bin Wong, *Nourish the People: The State Civilian Granary System in China, 1650–1850* (Ann Arbor: University of Michigan Press, 1991); and Pierre-Etienne Will, *Bureaucracy and Famine in Eighteenth-Century China* (Stanford: Stanford University Press, 1990).

43. Dening, *Performances*, 39.

44. Frank Perlin, "The Other 'Species' World: Speciation of Commodities and Moneys, and the Knowledge-Base of Commerce, 1500–1900," in *Merchants, Companies, and Trade: Europe and Asia in the Early Modern Era*, ed. Sushil Chaudhury and Michel Morineau (Cambridge: Cambridge University Press, 1999), 146. On the problem of value, see James Thompson, *Models of Value: Eighteenth-Century Political Economy and the Novel* (Durham: Duke University Press, 1996); and Jean-Joseph Goux, *Symbolic Economies after Marx and Freud*, trans. Jennifer Curtiss Gage (Ithaca: Cornell University Press, 1990).

45. Dening, *Performances*, 72.

46. On comparative imperialism, see, for example, Balachandra Rajan and Elizabeth Sauer, "Imperialisms: Early Modern to Premodernist," in *Imperialisms: Historical and Literary Investigations, 1500–1900*, ed. Rajan and Sauer (London: Palgrave, 2004), 1–12; and, in the same volume, Nabil I. Matar, "The Maliki Imperialism of Ahmad al-Mansur: The Moroccan Invasion of Sudan, 1591," 147–62; Dorothea Heuschert, "Legal Pluralism in the Qing Empire: Manchu Legislation for the Mongols," *International History Review* 20 (1998), 310–24; Laura Hostetler, *Qing Colonial Enterprise: Ethnography and*

Cartography in Early Modern China (Chicago: University of Chicago Press, 2001); and Felicity A. Nussbaum, "Introduction," in *The Global Eighteenth Century*, ed. Nussbaum (Baltimore: Johns Hopkins University Press, 2003), 1–18.

47. Goldstone, *Revolution and Rebellion*, 484, 496.

48. Davis, *Late Victorian Holocausts*; see also Alfred W. Crosby, *Ecological Imperialism: The Biological Expansion of Europe, 900–1900* (New York: Cambridge University Press, 1986).

49. Ray Huang, *1587, A Year of No Significance: The Ming Dynasty in Decline* (New Haven: Yale University Press, 1981); Chalmers Johnson, *The Sorrows of Empire: Militarism, Secrecy, and the End of the Republic* (New York: Metropolitan Books, Henry Holt, 2004).

CHAPTER I

The Far East, the East India Company, and the English imagination

In 1580, the year that Sir Francis Drake returned from his circumnavigation of the globe, the Portuguese crown passed to Philip II of Spain, and this dynastic union dramatically altered politics and commerce in western Europe. The Anglo-Portuguese alliance came to an abrupt end, and prices for pepper and other spices rose significantly; this trade was controlled by an international cartel of bankers and merchants who dealt directly with Lisbon and then added huge mark-ups before reselling the spices to a network of suppliers across Europe. Philip banned ships from England and Holland from anchoring in Lisbon, and consequently merchants in both countries saw their supply of spices cut off almost completely.[1] This embargo led to shortages, higher prices, and involuntary changes in the diets of many well-to-do consumers in northern Europe, and it had complex effects on conceptions of trade, economy, and luxury. For two thousand years, spices had been a prized luxury in Europe, carried laboriously by caravans across Asia; but in the sixteenth century spices became a staple for urban elites, gentry, and middle-class European consumers, useful for flavoring many foods and essential for preserving meat. By sailing around the Cape of Good Hope, the Portuguese had reached Java in 1511 and began shipping cloves and nutmegs from the Moluccas, spices indigenous only to these volcanic islands at the eastern end of the Indonesian archipelago.[2] Spices were an almost ideal cargo: clove, pepper, mace, and nutmeg weighed little and were easy to transport; they could be dried, husked, and bagged, then stored for long sea voyages, and later broken down into small loads for distribution. Ten pounds of nutmeg in the Banda Islands sold for a half pence, and ten pounds of mace for less than five pence. In Europe, these pound weights in the sixteenth century could sell respectively for £1 12s and £16, an increase of some 32,000 percent.[3] The mark-up on these products meant that they acquired a metonymic fascination for those wealthy enough to afford and consume exotic commodities. Spices symbolized an ongoing transformation of the idea of surplus value: rather than a luxury, they increasingly seemed a necessity for maritime nations that made international trade a crucial component of their tax structures, financial planning, labor markets, investment strategies, and ideological self-definition. The challenge for the merchants of England, the United Provinces, and Portugal was to ensure that the extraordinary prices paid for pepper, nutmeg, mace, and cloves would offset the costs and risks of sending men, money, and ships halfway around the world and generate profits large enough to fund ongoing ventures.

In 1579, Drake had stopped at Ternate, the small island sultanate east of Sulawesi, and had procured a cargo of cloves. His success fired the imagination of investors in London's Levant and Muscovy Companies, merchants experienced in the complexities of international trade, and eager to find ways to circumvent the Portuguese domination of the spice trade. A voyage was quickly fitted out to return to Ternate, but the ships could not negotiate the Cape and never made it to the Indian Ocean. With tensions between Spain and England mounting, the English turned to their principal instrument of foreign policy – piracy on the high seas. In 1587, Drake's capture of a Portuguese galleon worth £100,000 precipitated Philip II's mustering of the Invincible Armada that was defeated in the English Channel. In the English fleet of defense in the Channel in 1588 was the captain of a Levant Company vessel, James Lancaster, who had studied navigation in Portugal. Three years later, he was selected by a cartel of London investors to command a fleet of three ships bound for the Spice Islands. The hardships this mission suffered provided a good indication of the costs and consequences of sending ships tens of thousands of miles to procure spices. Wracked by scurvy, one ship turned back to England before reaching the Cape; the flagship was lost with all hands off the coast of Africa; and thirty of Lancaster's men were killed by natives in the Comoro Islands. With little cargo left to trade, Lancaster turned to piracy, plundering Portuguese, Burmese, and Indian vessels off the Malay coast. The ship then limped back across the Indian Ocean before heading to the West Indies; only twenty-five out of the 198 men on the two ships that had rounded the Cape made it back to England.[4] Such disasters became horrifyingly familiar for European vessels well into the eighteenth century; with some exceptions, subsequent voyages to the Far East were beset by storms, shipwreck, scurvy, piracy, violence from indigenous peoples in Africa and Asia, and ships that almost literally rotted from beneath the sailors' feet.[5]

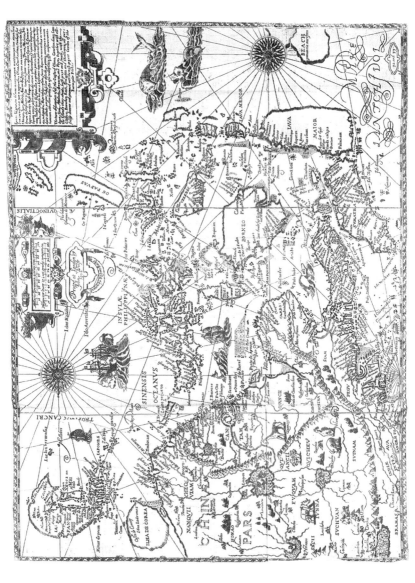

FIGURE 1. Asia, from Jan van Linschoten, *Iohn Huighen van Linschoten his Discours of Voyages into ye Easte and West Indies* (1598). Reproduced by permission of the British Library.

The Levant Company was in no mood to finance another voyage, but a consortium of Amsterdam investors, the Far Lands Company, had better financing and better intelligence than the English, including firsthand information from Jan Huygen van Linschoten, who had sailed through Asia while in the service of the Portuguese archbishop of Goa between 1583 and 1588. In 1595, the first Dutch voyage left for the East Indies, and returned two years later with just enough spices for the investors to break even. This one-shot venture cost the lives of three-quarters of the original crew but demonstrated that the Portuguese, thinly stretched from Goa to the Philippines, could be circumvented and that their vaunted empire had only intermittent control of a few sea lanes between Europe and the Far East. By 1601, eight companies had financed fifteen fleets, totaling sixty-five ships, for the eastern trade, and the fierce competition produced a glut of spices on the market throughout the United Provinces.[6] Alarmed by the prospect of being shut out of the spice trade, English merchants in 1599 petitioned Queen Elizabeth, then in negotiations with Spain, to charter a company that would trade with ports and countries, including China, Bengal, and Japan, not claimed by the Portuguese or Spanish.[7] The Queen stalled for a year until negotiations with Spain faltered, then granted a charter to the 218 petitioners, the original shareholders in the East India Company (EIC). Lancaster was given command of the Company's first voyage that left for Sumatra in 1601. With the chartering of the Dutch East India Company (VOC) the following year, the trade war among England, Portugal, and the Netherlands began in earnest.

On his second voyage, Lancaster had a better idea of the political and economic situation in Southeast Asia than he had a decade earlier. In 1596, a Dutch edition of Linschoten's travels through Asia had been published, and an English translation followed in 1598.[8] Part navigation treatise, part geography, and part commercial espionage manual, this extraordinarily important book described Portuguese vulnerabilities in the Indonesian archipelago. Both English and Dutch editions included detailed maps of East Asia that were emblematic of the importance attached to cartography by Dutch merchants and printers (see figure 1). The exaggerated size of the islands of the archipelago suggests both the importance of this region in the European imagination and a limited understanding of its political and strategic complexities. Linschoten's map is crowded with place names: cities, ports, rivers, and sea passages. Distances are often foreshortened so that Southeast Asia seems a compact and abundantly rich area of the world that invites European merchants to take advantage of seemingly innumerable places to trade. The map, in this respect, plots European desire for the products and commerce of the Far East. With Linschoten's atlas presumably in hand, the petitioners to Queen Elizabeth had a good idea of their best opportunity for finding a willing partner in the region: the sultanate of Aceh on Sumatra. Lancaster carried a letter from Queen Elizabeth to Sultan Ala'ad-din Ri'ayat Syan al-Mukammil (ruled 1588–1603) that discloses the logic motivating England's bid to gain a foothold in the lucrative spice trade by forming a trading alliance with an important regional power.

Linschoten's description of Aceh testified to its strategic significance as both an international trading center and a military bulwark against the Portuguese factory in Malacca. Situated on the northwest coast of Sumatra, Aceh commanded the entrance to the Straits of Malacca and therefore was in a position to enforce its power against lightly armed merchant vessels of all nationalities. Its political and economic control of much of Sumatra kept the Portuguese in check. "The Portingals," wrote Linschoten, "dwell not therein in any place [on Sumatra], but deale and traffique in some pleaces thereof, yet very few, for that the inhabitants themselves doe bring many of their commodities vnto *Malacca*" (32). His descriptions of the precise locations of cities – Aceh "lyeth vpon a point of the lande, vnder 4. degrees and a halfe on the North side" of the island – provide invaluable signposts for merchants and mariners feeling their way along unfamiliar coastlines and sailing through poorly charted waters and dangerous currents. As significantly, his sketches of the political situation on Sumatra neatly lay out the tensions in the region and define the extent and limitations of Portuguese power:

The Island hath many kings, the principallest is the king of *Dachem* ... This *Dachem* is very mightie and a great enemie to the Portugals, he hath besieged *Malacca*, and done it great mischiefe, as it happened in the time of my biding in *India*, by stopping the passage of all victuals and other Marchandise comming to *Malacca*, as also by keeping the passage of the straight betweene *Malacca* and *Sumatra*, so that the shippes of *China*, *Iapen*, and the Islands of *Molucco*, were forced to sayle about, whereby they passed much dayes, to the great discommoditie and hindrance of travelling Marchants[.] (32)

Linschoten's descriptions offer a corrective to the heroicizing of commercial ventures in quasi-commercial epics like the *Lusiads*, a work written with an eye toward patronage and future expansion rather than toward exploring the complexities of commercial rivalry, economic negotiation, and the comparative weakness of European powers.[9] His thumbnail sketch of the conflicts between Aceh and the Portuguese in Malacca testifies to the sultanate's power: a strong enough navy to blockade the Iberians' key port on the Malay peninsula and to disrupt their seaborne commerce. Beginning in the sixteenth century, Aceh had established a vigorous trade in spices directly with Red Sea ports in Africa and Arabia, bypassing Portuguese outposts in India; at least until the middle of the century, Aceh shipped, by volume, as much spice as the Portuguese carried to Lisbon.[10] As the principal competition for the Portuguese in the spice trade, Aceh posed political and economic challenges to the expansion of European trade in Southeast Asia. The antipathy between the Sultan and the Portuguese in Malacca and Goa, as Anthony Reid demonstrates, had religious as well as economic and military dimensions, and these conflicts between the sultanate and Portugal are crucial to understanding the situation that Lancaster encountered.

Islamic conversion had taken root throughout the Indonesian archipelago among merchants and seamen and became a cohesive force for redefining cultural as well as spiritual identity. In contrast to the local allegiances to family, ancestors, village, and the immediate environment that structured animistic beliefs, Islam offered a universal faith with prayers that could be performed and moral codes that could be obeyed throughout the world. For those in Southeast Asia who left or were forced to leave familiar surroundings for a world of heaving seas, endless horizons, strange ports, unfamiliar people, and bizarre tongues, Islam offered a morality and ethics that stressed mercantile virtues such as hard work, asceticism, and deference to religious authority, and provided a means to reorient personal identity in relationship to both metaphysical absolutes and a transcultural community of believers.[11] In the 1560s, with the establishment of commercial and diplomatic relations between Turkey and Aceh, pan-Islamism became an important component of the resistance of Aceh, Ternate, Brunei, and other sultanates to Portuguese authorities who saw their colonial ventures, at least in part, as an extension of their crusade against infidels.

Aceh's naval power made the sultanate an essential destination for the English and Dutch merchant fleets that reached Sumatra in the 1590s and after. Throughout the region, the increasing wealth of royal centers such as Aceh in the sixteenth century was pumped into larger naval fleets rather than into cargo vessels; the militarization of the indigenous fleets of Southeast Asia allowed Portuguese, Japanese, Gujarati, and Chinese merchants to exploit the commercial potential of the "country trade" within the region.[12] Instead of imposing their will on outgunned natives, the Europeans found themselves entangled in long-standing rivalries and intermittent hostilities; like Aceh and other sultanates in the region, the

Portuguese made seizing ships, blockading ports, and setting fire to towns and trading centers instruments of policy. Linschoten relates a tale of one such Portuguese raid intended to disrupt the alliance between the royal families of Aceh and Johor. This brief narrative, interestingly enough, is inserted within a description of Sumatra's mineral wealth:

The Island is very rich of mynes of Gold, Silver, Brasse, (whereof they make greate Ordinance) precious stones, and other mettal: of all kinde of Spices, sweete woode, rootes, and other medicinable Herbes and Drugges . . . it hath likewise great store of Silke. At this last besieging and troubles of *Malacca*, the king of *Acheijn* sent out a piece of Ordinance, the like is hardly to bee founde in all Christendome, which he gave in marriage with his daughter to the king of *Ior*, a town lying by *Malacca*. [The ship and the canon are captured by the Portuguese, then Johor is] besieged, and at the last wonne and by them rased to the ground, and for euer made wast, wherein they found 150. Brasse pieces smal & great . . . very cunningly wrought with flowers and personages, which I have purposely set down to let you know that they have other kindes of Mettals, and know how to handle them. (33)

The attack that Linschoten describes punctuates a series of raids and naval battles between the Portuguese and Aceh. Johor presumably was put to the torch because it had participated in the 1560s and 1570s in "a series of *jihad*" against the Portuguese.[13] But this description also testifies to the socio-political, technological, and symbolic currency of metal working and military ordinance in Southeast Asia during the period. The wedding present, a massive canon, is technologically advanced, as are apparently the 150 pieces; these armaments indicate that the workmen of Aceh have the metallurgical abilities to fashion weapons and create designs that rival the decorated military hardware of Europe. This dissemination of such military technology in Sumatra, Java, and the Malay Peninsula meant that the grand schemes hatched in Lisbon or Goa for colonial conquest had to confront the political realities of power, profit, and dynastic alliances in the region. Linschoten remarks that

It was long since concluded & determined by the King of Portugale and Viceroye [in Goa], that the Isle of *Sumatra* should be conquered, and at this present there are certaine Captaines that to the same end haue the kings pay, with the title of Generals and chiefe Captaines or *Adelantado* of this conquest, but as yet there is nothing done therein, although they still talke thereof but doe not it. (32–33)

While their rhetoric of conquest echoes the religious and military language of the Spanish conquest of the disease-ravaged New World, the King and Viceroy can only plan, bluster, and pour money into a scheme that never comes to fruition. In contrast to the heroic idealization of the *Lusiads*,

Linschoten's account repeatedly voices such skepticism. The plan to conquer Sumatra – and to eliminate Aceh as a commercial rival – remains on the drawing board; the gentlemen-adventurers may have titles but they lack the military means to take and hold territory, to colonize the island in the manner that the Dutch were to do beginning in the late seventeenth and eighteenth centuries.

ELIZABETH AND HER ''LOVING BROTHER'' IN ACEH

Elizabeth's decision to write to the Sultan of Aceh indicates a sophisticated understanding of what it would take to establish an English commercial presence in Southeast Asia: a string of factories, good relations with ruling elites, and a viable network of ports, trading partners, and allies stretching from Arabia, to India, to Southeast Asia, and even on to Japan and China. Aceh was crucial strategically and economically to British efforts: with its energetic Arab and Indian communities, it controlled much of the pepper trade in western Sumatra, and, as Linschoten recognized, provided a check on the expansionist plans of the Portuguese and harassed their shipping in the Straits of Malacca. In this context, Elizabeth's letter to the Sultan of Aceh is a small masterpiece of diplomacy, and it testifies to her sensitivity to the interrelated issues – political, theological, economic, and ecological – that structured European perceptions of East Asia between 1600 and 1800. It begins with a ceremonious, and symbolically significant, greeting to a brother monarch, then offers a theological justification for international trade:

ELIZABETH by the Grace of God, Queene of England, France, and Ireland, defendresse of the Christian Faith and Religion. To his great and mightie King of Achem, &c. in the Iland of Sumatra, our loving Brother, greeting. The Eternall God, of his divine knowledge and providence, hath so disposed his blessings, and good things of his Creation, for the use and nourishment of Mankind, in such sort: that notwithstanding they growe in divers Kingdomes and Regions of the World: yet, by the Industrie of Man (stirred up by the inspiration of the said omnipotent Creator) they are dispersed into the most remote places of the universall World. To the end, that even therein may appeare unto all Nations, his marvellous workes, hee having so ordained, that the one land may have need of the other. And thereby, not only breed intercourse and exchange of their Merchandise and Fruits, which doe superabound in some Countries, and want in others: but also ingender love and friendship betwixt all men, a thing naturally diuine.[14]

Elizabeth invokes a shared monotheistic religion in order to establish a basis for her offer of friendship and alliance with an Islamic monarch thousands of miles away: common cultural, commercial and political interests unite England and Aceh. This opening promotes a mutually profitable trade, "a thing naturally diuine," as both a means to ensure "love and friendship" between England and Aceh and an end for fulfilling God's plan for humankind. By exchanging goods "which doe super-abound" in their own realms for others they lack, both nations can compensate for their limited resources and take advantage of the industry and ingenuity of each other's labor force by exchanging "Merchandise" – ideally, for the English, trading European cloth for silks and spices. Trade, at least in theory, can overcome the entwined evils of sin and scarcity that have plagued humankind since the expulsion from Eden. Materially as well as theologically, this "exchange of . . . Merchandise and Fruits" can redeem a fallen world.

After staking out a common religious ground, Elizabeth proceeds to the business of forging political and economic links between the two nations. To entice the Sultan into allowing the East India Company to trade in Aceh, Elizabeth must construct for herself an authority that mirrors his. She employs the rhetoric of absolute monarchy – of regal brotherhood – to appeal to him by describing the Company's merchants as her "subjects" and implying that she wields the same kind of power over them that he claims over his traders. But Elizabeth knew that this was not the case; the very articles which she was seeking to negotiate were intended to guarantee that English merchants in Aceh would retain control over their property, goods, and persons as guaranteed by English common law rather than being subject to an absolute monarch. In the Indonesian archipelago in the seventeenth century, as Jeyalamar Kathirithamby-Wells has demonstrated, control of trade, tax and custom revenues, and investment capital lay entirely in the hands of monarchs: strict controls existed on the sale and ownership of property, and there was no independent class of merchants or administrators, except for palace favorites. Consequently, foreign merchants – whether Chinese, Dutch, Portuguese, Japanese, or English – were essential to the region's international trade.[15] In effect, then, Elizabeth needed the Sultan of Aceh to decree, with his absolute power, favorable trading conditions for her subjects, while downplaying the independence of the EIC merchants, their de facto freedom at the end of lengthy chains of supply and communication, from her or her government's authority.

Elizabeth's chief rhetorical strategy in her letter, though, is to exploit the networks of communication, commerce, political alliances, and naval rivalries that structure the dynamic relationships among the English,

Dutch, and Portuguese merchants and the sultanates of the Indonesian archipelago. Religious differences between Christian and Moslem are elided to allow the Queen to emphasize the theological, political, and economic enmity between Protestant England and Catholic Iberia and to promote the common interests that she and the Sultan share in frustrating Spanish and Portuguese designs in the East Indies:

your Highnesse shall be very well served, and better contented, then you have heretofore beene with the Portugals and Spaniards, our Enemies: who only, and none else, of these Regions, have frequented those your, and the other Kingdomes of the East. Not suffering that the other Nations should doe it, pretending themselves to be Monarchs, and absolute Lords of all those Kingdomes and Provinces: as their owne Conquest and Inheritance, as appeareth by their loftie Title in their writings. The contrarie whereof, hath very lately appeared unto us, and that your Highnesse, and your royall Familie, Fathers, and Grandfathers, have (by the grace of GOD, and their Valour) knowne, not onely to defend your owne Kingdomes: but also to give Warres unto the Portugals, in the Lands which they possesse: as namely in Malaca, in the yeere of the Humane Redemption 1575 under the conduct of your valiant Captaine, Ragamacota, with their great losse, and the perpetuall honour of your Highnesse Crowne and Kingdome. (II: 154)

Rather than an oppositional model that sets a European "self" against a non-European "other," Elizabeth describes the discourse of trade in terms of triangular relationships – efforts to forge alliances with "others" against a third disruptive or threatening force. Michel Serres argues that because the "other" is a projection of the negative qualities of a solipsistic identity, no communication can take place without the presence of a "third man" or parasite who creates the noise against which – and only against which – meaning can emerge.[16] In this respect, the relations between England and Aceh need to be understood not as the clash of antagonistic cultures, but as efforts to exclude the "third men," the Spanish and Portuguese, who are essential to English–Sumatran relations: they must be excluded as the basis for Elizabeth's overtures of friendship and her vision of a mutually profitable trade between the two countries.

This triangular model of communication and politics was well understood in Aceh. When Lancaster arrived in 1602, the Sultan congratulated him on the defeat of the Spanish fleet. According to Lancaster, he "seemed to be very well pleased" with the Queen's letter, and responded with a likeminded appeal to forge a lasting friendship based on their mutual animosity to the Catholic powers of Iberia. In his reply to Elizabeth (translated from the Arabic by William Bedwell, the foremost English translator of that language at the time), he granted the East India Company merchants free entry and trade into Aceh; absolute control over their own property, including the ownership, sale, and inheriting of land, chattels, and inventories; "stability of bargaines and orders of payment by [his] subjects"; and legal jurisdiction over all English citizens in his country. "Our joy [is] increased and our societie confirmed," in this agreement, the Sultan wrote to Elizabeth, because the English provide a bulwark against Portuguese and Spanish encroachment on Aceh's trade: the Iberians "are our enemies in this world, and in the world to come: so that we shall cause them to die, in what place soever we shall meete them, a publicke death" (II: 160). Like the English monarch, the Sultan employs a transhistorical rhetoric: his nation's conflict with Spain and Portugal over the strategic control of the spice trade through the Straits of Malacca and in the Indian Ocean will continue indefinitely, even into a monotheistic afterlife. Elizabeth's claim "that this beginning shall be a perpetuall confirmation, of love betwixt our Subjects on both parts" (II: 154) also suspends the mutability of historical time by envisioning unending cargoes from the East and an untroubled future of domestic production to supply the presumptive demands of Southeast Asian markets. Because it is constituted by bodily metaphors of integration, circulation, and order, this mutually beneficial commerce can fail only if it is disrupted by the machinations of malicious rivals – the very enemies who provide the basis for the monarchs' professions of friendship.[17]

In yoking theology and economics, Elizabeth assumes a shared perception of the moral and material world in England and Aceh, a shared conceptual vocabulary. Balance sheets, prices, exchange rates, credit, and the honoring of contracts are embedded within a language of political values as well as theological imperatives. Their mutual distrust of the Spanish and Portuguese allows Elizabeth to play shrewdly on the Sultan's fears that her European rivals represent threats to his political position as well as to Aceh's trade; she flatters him with her knowledge of his and his father's victories, and appeals to the primal fear of absolute rulers – usurpation. Elizabeth tars the Spanish and Portuguese with illegitimacy. Her indictment of their false claims to sovereignty in Southeast Asia seems intended to resonate with a monarch who must remain constantly vigilant against foreign incursions and the intrigues of his own court. By emphasizing the Catholic threat, the Queen can turn the ambitions of EIC merchants into a mechanism for offering the Sultan a profitable alternative to Spanish, Portuguese, and Bengali shipping: English bullion and (she hopes) woolens to India; Indian goods to Sumatra and the Moluccas; and, in return, pepper, nutmeg, mace, and cloves that can be resold in

Europe at a substantial profit. In this regard, her letter represents a shrewd effort to insinuate the fledging EIC into the "endless struggle for people, for trade, and for status between rival centers" that defined the Indonesian archipelago in the early modern era.[18] While her protestations of friendship may be sincere, that sincerity can be measured only as an expression of her country's desire for a "perpetuall trade," for mutually amicable relations that never deteriorate into the self-interest, suspicion, and single-minded pursuit of profit that attend England's commercial relations in Europe.

Having delivered his letters, Lancaster embarked on what would become a familiar itinerary for EIC vessels on its first dozen voyages. He captured a Portuguese galleon, loaded with Indian cottons, in the Malaccan Straits; he traded this cargo for spices, which he then sent back on two of the smaller ships in his fleet, then continued on to Bantam on the west coast of Java. Java offered tantalizing opportunities for both the English and the Dutch; despite its population base and large markets, there were no Portuguese factories on the island, and Lancaster left a handful of British merchants at Bantam to establish a factory. In September 1603, he returned to England with 500 tons of peppercorn, but the Company ran into difficulties selling their cargo in a city wracked by plague.[19] Even after the plague subsided, there was not much of a market for pepper in London because the new King, James I, had released a large quantity of pepper, apparently captured from a Portuguese ship, to a handful of wealthy merchants and favorites; they already had swamped London's wholesalers, and Dutch ventures to the East Indies had glutted the markets of Amsterdam. Much of the pepper remained unsold for more than a year – an indication that no matter how valuable spices might appear to be on paper, they could be sold only to a comparatively small segment of the population. The large-scale availability of spices would have to be matched by changes in the diets, recipes, and tastes of Englishmen and women to transform what were still were luxury condiments into essential foodstuffs.[20] The investors in the original EIC voyage were now told that they would have to reinvest £200 of their original £250 in a second venture. Subsequent voyages proved to be more profitable, but financing voyages as one-shot ventures left the Company during its first decades scrambling to raise the necessary capital to compete effectively with the Dutch in the spice trade.

TRADING WITH THE EAST: PRACTICE AND THEORY

The early ventures of the East India Companies of England and the United Provinces took place within the complex circuits of a global seaborne commerce.[21] Trade between Europe and Asia throughout the seventeenth century depended on shipments of New World silver from Amsterdam, Lisbon, and London to India and China in exchange for finished goods and luxury items, often textiles that competed directly with European products. The slave trade between Africa, America, and western Europe, with its genocidal horrors, functioned as one aspect of larger economic networks. African slaves mined precious metals in South America and produced cash crops (tobacco, sugar, and molasses) in the Caribbean and Carolinas that were sent to Europe in exchange for manufactured goods, including luxury items (porcelain, pepper, and clothing) imported from Asia. Gold and silver were shipped from South and Central America to Spain to finance the cost of maintaining a colonial empire, and then from Iberia to northern Europe to purchase cloth, manufactured goods, raw materials, and more African slaves from Dutch, French, and English traders.[22] Silver also went west from Acapulco to the Philippines to allow the Spanish and Portuguese to buy their way into markets that gave them access, often through expatriate Chinese merchants scattered throughout East Asia, to the restricted markets of China and Japan. The networks of trade among these communities were complicated and often difficult for Europeans to negotiate, and VOC and EIC merchants often overpaid for goods to buy their way into small shares of this intra-Asian or country trade. Bullion from the Netherlands and England was shipped east, often through the Ottoman Empire and Persia, to India where it allowed Europeans to enter the long-established and complex South Asian market. Indian cloth and manufactured goods were traded to Southeast Asia for cloves, nutmeg, mace, and pepper; spices were shipped throughout Asia, in response to local and international surges in demand; Chinese commodities (porcelain, tea, and silk) attracted much of the region's silver and copper; and spices were imported to Europe and helped to finance the Dutch commercial empire.[23] The propaganda of EIC officials notwithstanding, England and the Netherlands paid hard cash for what many considered luxury goods.

Seventeenth-century accounts of a world dominated by Chinese demands for silver provide an indispensable context for discussions of European ventures to the Far East, and the most important contemporary account of world trade is also the most unabashed defense of the East India Company during the first half of the seventeenth century, Thomas Mun's *A Discovrse of Trade, from England vnto the East-Indies*, first published in 1621, and then reprinted in Purchas's *Pilgrimmes* in 1625.[24] Having been a merchant for many years in Italy and Turkey Mun (1571–1641) became a director of the EIC in 1615. Although his *Discovrse of Trade* and post-humously published treatise, *England's Treasure by Forraign Trade*, have been treated by economic historians as classic texts in the development of mercantilist theory, his arguments for the significance of international trade are colored both by his practical experience and by his perception of the fortunes of the EIC in 1621.[25] It is significant that Mun wrote his *Discovrse* at a high point in the Company's early history when arguments for the benefits of the Asian trade for national prosperity and security may have seemed particularly strong. In 1620, the Company operated thirty to forty ships, many of which it owned outright and which had been built at its dockyards at Deptford and Blackwall. These dockyards employed 200 craftsmen, and, because several ships were being outfitted each year for ventures to India and beyond, crewing requirements made the EIC one of London's largest employers. In addition, Company officials and agents were in contact with financial markets throughout Europe. One measure of the Company's fortunes was the investment capital it attracted: the first joint-stock offering between 1613 and 1616 raised £418,000, but the joint-stock for voyages between 1617 and 1622 soared to £1,600,000.[26] By 1623, the EIC had been all but driven out of the spice trade in the Indonesian archipelago (see chapter four below), and shipping began to drop dramatically. In the decade between 1611 and 1620, the Company sent fifty-five ships to the East, and returned profits of 155 percent on the initial offering. In the 1620s, however, that total dropped to forty-six ships, and the second joint-stock offering returned only a 12 percent profit for a longer period of investment. During this period, pepper made up the bulk of the Company's shipping volume and import value. Between 1613 and 1616, the price of pepper averaged twenty-six pence a pound in London; by 1627, it had dropped to seventeen pence a pound.[27]

In his posthumously published *England's Treasure*, written in 1630, Mun describes international trade in more general and abstract terms. This language may seem evocative of an emerging "modern" discourse of economics, but, in an important sense, he is forced to generalize beyond the grim circumstances of the Company's finances after a decade of set-backs. His earlier *Discovrse of Trade* responds directly to attacks leveled at the EIC, the most serious being that it exports bullion (it was allowed £30,000 per ship) to the East in exchange for "vnnessary wares." In countering this charge, Mun argues that "Drugges, Spices, Raw-silke, Indico, and Callicoes" from Asia are more valuable than other imports, notably tobacco from the Americas and "cambrick" and other cloths manufactured on the continent, because they yield larger profits and therefore are more valuable for re-export to Europe and the American colonies than other goods (1: 733). He then derides the critics who argue against the novelty and danger of the trade, and his response is cast in both historical and conceptual terms:

It is an error in those men ... who thinke that the trade of the East *Indies* into *Europe* had first entrance, by the discouerie of the Nauigation by the Cape of *Good Hope*. For many yeeres before that time, the trafficke of those parts had his ordinary course by shipping from diuers places in the *Indies*, yeerely resorting with their wares to *Mocha* in the Red-Sea, and *Balsera* in the *Persian* Gulfe: From both which places, the Merchandise (with great charges) were after transported ouer-land by the *Turkes* vpon Cammels, fiftie dayes iourney, vnto *Aleppo* in *Soria*, and to *Alexandria* in *Egypt*, (which are in the Mart Townes, from whence diuers Nations, as well *Turkes* as *Christians* doe continually disperse the said Wares by Sea into the parts of *Europe*:) by which course, the common enemie of Christendome (the *Turke*) was Master of the Trade, which did greatly imploy, and inrich his Subiects, and also the Coffers of his owne Customes, which he exacted at very high rates; But by the prouidence of Almightie God, the discouerie of that Nauigation to the East *Indies* by the Cape of *Good Hope* (now so much frequented by the *English*, *Portugals*, and *Dutch*; and also attempted by other Christian Kingdomes) hath not onely much decayed the great Commerce betweene the *Indians* and the *Turkes* in the Red Sea; and in the *Persian* Gulfe (to their infinite hurt, and to the great increase of Christian Trade,) but it hath also brought a further happinesse vnto Christendome in generall, and to the Realme of *England* in particular, for the venting of more *English* Commodities. (1: 734)

Mun demonstrates a sophisticated knowledge of the history of European trade to the East and an awareness of the costs and difficulties of the caravan trade. The East Indies is neither a vaguely defined or undifferentiated region nor a fantastic space of surmise and myth; rather, it is defined by its vast networks of trading ports, merchants, customs officials, manufacturing centers, and agricultural regions whose connections to European markets antedate the Portuguese ventures of the sixteenth century. Mun describes the two primary routes of international commerce: the markets and ports controlled by "infidels" are set against the sailing routes, that allow "the *English*, *Portugals*, and *Dutch*" to circumvent Turkish control of overland trade and the Red Sea. The question for England is not whether spices and silks will continue to pour into Europe, but whether the EIC will be allowed, as the agent of a larger national interest, to get a share of the enormous profits derived from "the trade of the East *Indies* into *Europe*." Although he casts his appeal in terms of religious solidarity and national identity, that identity is defined oppositionally: the infidel Turks not only are enemies to Christendom, but force European merchants to pay astronomical mark-ups on what otherwise would be reasonably priced goods. These taxes, duties, and marketing costs are passed on to Mun's readers in England. The Turks turn affordable items into luxury goods.

The centerpiece of Mun's argument is a detailed comparison of prices for spices and silk in Aleppo, after the Turks have added their carrying charges and duties, and the price of those same commodities in "Ports of the East *Indies*." In the 1621 edition of *Discovrse of Trade*, these comparisons are presented in tables that allow the reader to take in at a glance the benefits of the Company's trade for consumers and, at the same time, invite him or her to reflect on larger principles of international commerce. These figures for the "quantitie of Spices, Indico, and *Persian* raw Silk (which is yeerely consumed in *Europe*)," "the cost with the charges to lade the same Commodities [in] *Aleppo*; and the like of all the selfe same wares, as they haue beene vsually dispatched from the Ports of the East *Indies*" are calculated to the shilling and pence. In Aleppo, 6,000,000 pounds of pepper cost two shillings a pound ("with charges") for a total of £600,000; in the East Indies the same quantity costs "two pence halfe pennie the pound" (also "with charges") or £62,500. The price for 450,000 pounds of cloves in Aleppo at 4 shillings 9 pence a pound is £106,875 10s; in the East, at 9 pence a pound, the same quantity can be purchased for £16,875. In Aleppo, 150,000 pounds of mace cost £35,626, but only £5,000 in the Spice Islands; 400,000 pounds of nutmeg, £46,650 13s 4d versus £6,656 13s 4d. Similar mark-ups for indigo and "*Persia* raw Silke" drive the price of these goods as well, although for 1,000,000 pounds of the latter, the difference between 12s per pound in Aleppo versus 8s per pound in the Persian Gulf is not of the same magnitude. The total cost for these goods in Aleppo is £1,465,001 10s; purchased at the source, £511,458 5s 8d (1: 734–35). This annual savings of £953,543 4s 4d becomes an almost totemic figure, a quantitative measure, Mun maintains, of the value of the Company to consumers across Europe.

Mun's comparison of the wholesale prices in the East Indies to those charged by merchants in Aleppo presents the Company's business in the abstract and generalized semiotics of mathematics. His averages and calculations define trade in the terms of a nascent science of rationalized economics that both structures and is structured by the self-consistent operation of general laws of "the market"; these laws are distinct from traditional conceptions of a "moral economy" that treats economic factors as part of a complex social matrix.[28] Mun's abstract space of economic calculation offers an illusion of absolute precision and regularity so that imports and wholesale and retail prices take on a certainty that seemingly removes them from the contingencies of lost ships, glutted markets, and falling prices. In this respect, the tables in the 1621 edition and the long lists of figures in Purchas allow Mun to freeze historical time to promote the general laws that underlie his conception of the international market.[29]

Even as he abstracts the relative costs of commodities in the East Indies and at Aleppo, Mun implicitly treats consumption and consumer desire as constants that too are subject to quantification and measurement. In his discussion of the increase of England's wealth by the East India Company's sale of £100,000 worth of imported pepper, cloves, nutmeg, mace, indigo, "China Raw silkes," and calico in England, he renders complex economic transactions as mathematical abstractions. The 2,500,000 pounds of pepper imported into England cost 2 1/2d per pound, £26,041 13s 4d, and can be resold for 20d per pound, £208,333 6s 8d. Because cloves, nutmegs, and mace come into London in smaller quantities, their resale value is significantly higher. The 150,000 pounds of cloves bought at 9d per pound (£5,626) are resold at 6s per pound (£45,000); the same amount of nutmeg, purchased at 4d per pound (£2,500) brings in, at 2s 6d, £18,750; and 50,000 pounds of mace (8d per pound: £1,666 13s 4d) retail at 6s per pound for £15,000. The 107,140 pounds of Chinese raw silk, at 7s per pound, cost £37,499 in the East and have a resale value in England of 20s per pound, grossing £107,140. At 7s each (on average), 50,000 calicoes cost £15,000 in the East Indies and can be resold in England at 20s each, for £50,000. In sum, spices, Indigo, and silks that cost £100,000 in bullion in the East Indies sell in England, by Mun's reckoning, for £494,223 6s 8d (1: 737–38). His elaboration of these prices defines a multiplier effect: the Company's imports increase the "stock" of the nation by generating custom duties, taxes, and wages to the shipbuilders, mariners, "victuallers," and other employees on the payroll. The importation of spices and silks, Mun argues, generates economic growth, stimulates employment, and adds almost £500,000 to the nation's wealth. To calculate this value, he must render the desire for these products as a quantifiable function of the prices he lists: the ratio of costs to prices mathematicizes the wealth and material well-being of the nation.

Because *A Discovrse of Trade* presents its quantitative evidence as an objective representation of economic realities, Mun has little difficulty in responding to the other objections raised by the EIC's critics. He argues that cutting down trees for shipbuilding is good for employment, national wealth, and the defense of the realm: "what more noble or profitable vse" for oaks, he asks rhetorically, "then goodly ships for Trade and Warre? Are not they our Barnes for wealth, and plentie, seruing as wals and bulwarkes for our peace and happinesse?" (739). His solution for timber shortages is more trade and more intensification: importing lumber from Ireland or shipping it from Hampshire, Essex, Kent, and Berkshire.[30] To counter the argument that voyages to the East Indies are too dangerous and the returns too uncertain, Mun provides a list of all seventy-nine ships financed by the EIC through 1620 and enumerates their fates: "thirtie foure are alreadie come home in safetie richly laden"; four have been "worne out by long seruice"; two were "ouer-whelmed in the trimming there"; six lost at sea; "twelue haue beene taken and surprized by the *Dutch*"; and twenty-one ships are still in the Indies. He meticulously calculates costs in exports, losses, and profits: although England has exported almost £550,000 in bullion and another £293,300 in commodities, the returned ships brought back £356,288 in goods that, according to his multiplier effect, means that the EIC has "produced here in *England* towards the generall stocke" £1,914,000, with another £400,000 on its way from the East Indies (741–42). While he is willing to write off almost £85,000 of potential profit aboard these ships to the depredations of the Dutch, his characterization of long-distance trade presumes the ability of his calculations to extrapolate, with quantitative precision, a bright future for the Company and the nation, a future represented by the £1,914,600 increase in the "generall stocke" produced by the sale of pepper, silks, and other spices throughout the nation. England can secure its prosperity and safety only through the furthering of an international trade dominated by the EIC.

Mun's works depict the EIC and VOC as the engines of a worldwide commerce, but the very principles that he advances paradoxically threaten to undermine his identification of national strength with the East Indian trade in two ways: the Netherlands is more successful than England in exploiting the spice trade to generate wealth, and the EIC in 1620 had found very little success in gaining entry to the major markets of the Far East: China and Japan. As Mun's comments suggest, the VOC had supplanted the Portuguese as the principal obstacle to the prosperity that the Company's directors envisioned. During the first two decades of the seventeenth century, the Dutch consolidated their near-monopoly of the spice trade to Europe: they forced the Portuguese out of Ternate and Tidore, fought off incursions by Spanish vessels operating from the Philippines, and outspent and outmaneuvered the EIC.[31] From its inception, the EIC was beset by tensions that remained unresolved for more than a century, and these tensions, if anything, were exacerbated after James I rewrote its charter in 1609 to make it an monopolistic enterprise of indeterminate duration: conflicts existed between the majority of shareholders who were interested in profits and the governor, deputy-governor, and twenty-four directors who were more interested in establishing a network of factories and alliances from Arabia to Japan. Although individual voyages were often quite profitable (the overlapping third and fifth voyages returned to London in 1611 with profits of 234 percent) the Company was failing to realize its dreams of limitless expansion and wealth. The last opportunity that the EIC had to deal a decisive blow to the Dutch occurred two years before Mun published his treatise. In December 1618 and January 1619, an English fleet under the command of Thomas Dale (the former governor of Virginia) had a smaller Dutch fleet trapped in Jakarta; but individual English ships were under different captains with different instructions and different ideas about whether they were in the Indies to fight the Dutch or buy spices. The English frittered away the opportunity to attack decisively, and an inconclusive battle discouraged the English fleet. Dale and his flagship limped away to India, and the English factories throughout the region rapidly lost trade and influence to the VOC.[32]

FANTASIES AND FACTORIES

By the time John Fletcher's *The Island Princess* was performed in 1621, the threat posed by the Dutch to British aspirations in the Far East had become so pronounced that the erstwhile arch-villains of Elizabeth's letter to the Sultan of Aceh, the Portuguese, could be recuperated and presented as heroes. In adapting Bartolomé Leonardo de Argensola's *Conquista de las Islas Malucas* to entertain English audiences, Fletcher replaces the recent history of Dutch military conquest and economic domination with fantasies of romance, profit, and the conversion of the natives. As John Villiers argues, Argensola conceived of history as a means to celebrate the exploits of the Iberian powers, and he "boldly declares his principal aim is to glorify the achievements of the Spanish in conquering the Moluccas" in 1605.[33] This short-lived victory against the forces of Islamic and Protestant heresy was reversed quickly by the Dutch, who reconquered Ternate and Tidore. This defeat curtailed the Portuguese role in the spice trade; by 1640, the Dutch effectively controlled directly or indirectly the distribution, sale, and even cultivation of the lion's share of Moluccan spices that reached Europe. In Fletcher's play, the Portuguese captains Armusia and Dan Ruys become stand-ins for what Ania Loomba terms a "fantasy of colonial and sexual possession" by the English.[34] The emphasis in Loomba's discussion should fall on "fantasy" rather than "possession": as *The Island Princess* was being performed, and as Mun's *Discovrse of Trade* was promising unending prosperity, the EIC was being evicted from Run, Amboyna, and other islands in the Moluccas.

It is likely that many in the audience recognized Fletcher's sleight of hand: by ennobling the Portuguese, the dramatist evokes a traditionalist fantasy of benign colonization that equates winning the love of a beautiful Indian Queen with aggrandizing the valuable commodities that her body represents.[35] Fletcher's heroes, in effect, have become "good" colonists who, stripped of their Catholicism and re-enacting a conquest that the Dutch had rendered moot, provide a fantasy image of an *English* future when the merchants of the EIC can trump the VOC. In a letter that reached England in 1615 (subsequently printed in Purchas, *Pilgrimmes*), Richard Cocks wrote from Hirado in Japan that Company officials, "will hardlie beleeve how the Hollanders allready have daunted the Spaniardes and Portingalls in these partes, espetially in the Molucos, where they dailie encroche upon the Spaniardes, they not beinge able to w'thstand their proceadinges, but now stand in as much feare that in shorte tyme they will also take the Phillippians from them." The Dutch, Cocks continues, "are soe strong at sea that they care not a figg nether for Spaniard nor Portingale."[36] For the head of the English factory in Japan, the threat posed by the Dutch offers the hope that the EIC can capitalize on the disruption of Iberian trade. While Fletcher dramatizes the conquest of the Moluccas as a "fantasy of colonial and sexual possession," Cocks emphasizes the material consequences of the Dutch victories: on Portuguese shipping, as threats to the Spanish in the Philippines, and as opportunities for the English.

Even the comparatively well-financed VOC, however, operated at the end of lines of communication, supply, and commerce that stretched thousands of miles and, in practice, many months or years into the (or a hoped-for) future. The Dutch were not a colonial power in the same sense as the Spanish in the Americas, dictating terms of near-genocidal surrender to vanquished indigenes. Before 1600, nutmeg and mace were grown solely in the Bandas, six islands south of Seram that comprise only seventeen square miles. Ternate and Tidore, "minuscule volcanic islands" off the west coast of Halmahera, were the principal commercial source of cloves in Asia, and the rival sultanates on each of these islands used their strategic control of these commodities to extend their influence in the sixteenth century across the widely dispersed islands in the region.[37] One thousand miles east of Java, these sultanates governed by dynastic alliances, revenues from duties and customs, and tribute obligations rather than by military force.

As Oscar Spate notes, however, the arrival of one or two well-armed ships could and did wreak havoc on small islands and isolated ports in the Pacific, and seaborne invasions by both local forces and European interlopers occurred with regularity in the Spice Islands.[38] The Dutch seized Banda in 1621, turning the islands into slave plantations; they then used the profits from their control of nutmeg and mace to increase their naval presence in the region. In 1656, the VOC destroyed the clove crop on Ternate and Tidore in order to restrict production in areas that they controlled. In both cases, the Dutch reaped significant economic benefits by strategic military actions on small islands that could not muster large-scale defensive forces.[39] While the Dutch fleets in Southeast Asia significantly outnumbered English ships, the VOC comprised only a small fraction of the regional carrying trade: all European vessels in Southeast Asia were outnumbered ten-to-one by Chinese junks with roughly similar cargo capacities; the eight Dutch ships that docked in Japan every year after 1638 were far less significant than the eighty Chinese junks which regularly plied the waters between China and Japan.[40]

Rather than employing the language of imperial conquest, seventeenth-century English accounts of the Spice Islands emphasize the uncertain and multi-dimensional nature of conflicts – and alliances – among Europeans and indigenous peoples. John Saris, the captain of an EIC voyage in 1612–13, recognized that Ternate and Tidore – the linchpin of the Dutch monopoly of the spice trade – had been wasted by decades of civil war prior to the arrival of Europeans:

The *Portugall* at his first discoverie of [these islands in the sixteenth century], found fierce warres betwixt the King of *Ternate* and *Tydore*, under which two Kings all the other Ilands are either subiected or confederated with one of them. The *Portugall* for the better settling of himselfe, took part with neither of them, but politikely carrying himselfe kept both to bee his friends, and so fortified upon the Ilands of *Ternate* and *Tydore*, where, to the *Portugals* great advantage, having the whole Trade of *Cloves* in their owne hands, they domineered and bore chiefest sway untill the yeare 1605 wherein the *Flemming* by force displaced them, and planted himselfe: but so weakly and unprovided for future danger, that the next yeere the *Spaniard*, (who whilest the *Portugall* remayned there, was ordered both by the Pope and the King of *Spaine* not to meddle with them) came from the *Philippinas*, beat the *Flemmings* out of both Ilands, tooke the King of *Ternate* Prisoner, sent him to the *Philippinas*, and kept *Ternate* and *Tydore* under their command. The *Flemming* since that time hath gotten footing there againe, and at my being there had built him [several] Forts ... These Civill Warres have so wasted the *Nationals*, that a great quantitie of Cloves perish, and rot upon the ground for want of gathering. (Purchas, *Pilgrimmes*, II: 363)

Saris's account defines the limitations of European power in the region and describes the strategies that the Portuguese, Spanish, and Dutch employed in contending for control of the clove trade. Expeditions of a ship or two with approximately one hundred or one hundred and fifty men each were enough to constitute beach-head forces on small islands where the Europeans' overriding goal was to insinuate themselves "politikely" in order to play one side against the other in dynastic disputes and civil conflicts. The forts that the Europeans erected often could not withstand blockade or bombardment. The communities of European merchants, administrators, and soldiers in the Spice Islands during the early seventeenth century usually numbered in the dozens, although larger forces, such as the Spanish expeditionary force, could be mustered for one-shot naval operations. What European powers could do was to intervene strategically, currying favor by paying higher prices for cloves on Ternate and Tidore, or, as Saris did when he arrived at Bantam, paying "thrice the value [for seven hundred sacks of pepper] of what they were bought for" (II: 353). Even though he was well aware of this "great (though sudden) alteration in the prices of commodities," Saris willingly paid these jacked-up prices to try to buy England's way into the lucrative markets of the region, despite being warned by the Dutch against trading in the Moluccas.

Rather than the heroic tales of love and conquest depicted by Argensola and Fletcher, political change in the region was neither pretty nor high-minded. Anglo-Dutch relations had been strained since 1605–06 when the English earned the VOC's ire for buying nutmeg on Amboyna and cloves on Tidore, even as the Dutch besieged the Portuguese forts on those islands. Having booted the Portuguese out of Ternate and Tidore, the Dutch claimed that "all the people of the *Moluccas* had made a perpetuall contract with them for all Cloues [at a fixed price] in respect that they had deliuered them out of the seruitude of the *Spaniards*." Outnumbered and outgunned, Saris fell back on the rhetoric of free trade, assuring the VOC that "we would not meddle with their businesse, our coming only to trade with such as desired to trade with vs"; the Dutch asserted what amounted to monopoly rights, "holding the Countrey to be their owne, as conquered by the Sword" (II: 354). England's last stand in the Bandas occurred five years later, when Nathaniel Courthope occupied the small island of Run, defying the Dutch authorities. Acting on the orders of Jan Pieterszoon Coen, the Governor General of the Dutch East Indies, to drive the British out and enforce one-sided trading contracts with natives on the islands of Great Banda and Neira, the Dutch blockaded Run, tortured captives, and executed dissidents. Against overwhelming odds, Courthope held out for nearly three years (1617 to 1620) before being betrayed and killed while he was making the dangerous crossing from Run to Great Banda. This outrage, as the English saw it, festered for years: the English did not relinquish their claim to Run until 1664, when they agreed to Dutch control of the island in exchange for the Netherlands ceding control of New Amsterdam to Charles II.[41]

The Europeans' strategic intervention, both economic and military, in Southeast Asia, though, should not be interpreted as ironclad evidence of technological superiority in shipbuilding, cannon, or trading practices. Frequently, the Dutch gained entry into markets by providing bullion or its equivalent in munitions and supplies to cash-strapped parties in internal conflicts. It is significant, in this context, that Saris paid for pepper in Bantam with silver coins; he did not offload the pepper in Ternate where cloves lay rotting on the ground because he lacked the military and financial resources to insinuate himself into a Dutch-dominated trade. The Dutch in 1613 could not compel outgunned natives to harvest the cloves; they were not (yet) a colonial power but a trading monopoly enforcing its "perpetuall contract" to maintain a fixed price. The VOC was intent on maximizing profits and had begun to develop the strategies that led to its de facto and finally colonial control of much of the Indonesian archipelago by the late eighteenth century: it used force when necessary, often hiring local mercenaries; intervened in dynastic conflicts to secure alliances favorable to their trade; and attacked their European rivals to ensure their control of production, price, and shipping. Even at the height of their commercial empire in 1688 the Dutch had fewer than 5,000 troops stationed in their principal possessions in Southeast Asia and another 1,900 seamen, artisans, merchants, and traders; the garrisons on Ternate and Tidore were manned by fewer than three hundred soldiers.[42] Dutch successes in the Far East, as Saris recognized, resulted from picking their fights, and their alliances, very carefully.

THE ENGLISH IN HIRADO

After Saris left the Spice Islands with his cargo of pepper, he sailed northward to Japan, both "for a triall there" of trading possibilities and in response to letters from William Adams that had arrived at the VOC factory in Batavia, a port then open to English ships (1: 353). Adams, the English pilot of a Dutch ship, had been detained in Japan for several years. His letters, reprinted by Purchas (1: 125–32), emphasized the opportunities that the EIC might find in trading in Hirado. Initially distrusted by the Jesuits, who urged the Shogunate to imprison or execute Adams and his Dutch shipmates, the Englishman eventually convinced the Japanese that his intentions were peaceful and that his countrymen were not Catholic missionaries intent on spreading a faith that was coming under increasing suspicion and repression. By the time he sent letters to Batavia, he had become a trusted translator and advisor for the Shogun and, having been elevated to the rank of *samurai*, given land, servants, and a Japanese wife.[43] Adams presents himself in his letters as a spokesman for English trade: "We were a People," he tells the Shogun, "that sought all friendship with all Nations, and to have trade of Merchandize in all Countries . . . through which our Countreys on both side[s] were inriched" (II: 127). His portrait of Japan, intended for EIC officials who might stop in Batavia, is equally encouraging. According to Adams,

The People of this Iland of *Iapan* are good of nature, curteous above measure, and valiant in warre: their Iustice is severely executed without any partialitie upon transgressors of the Law. They are governed in great Civilitie, I thinke, no Land better governed in the world by civill Policie. (II: 128)

Adams's letter is clearly designed to hasten his rescue by idealizing the Japanese as potential trading partners. The Japanese, though militaristic, are "curteous," "civill," and rigorous in the impartial application of the law. The government functions both efficiently and with "Civilitie"; in short, the people of Japan embody the characteristics that the English see in themselves and identify with civilized behavior. Adams is explicit about his conflicts with Catholic missionaries at court and the opportunities that the Shogunate's suspicion of the Spanish and Portuguese offers the English. The Shogun, he tells us, "asked much concerning the warres betweene the Spaniards and Portugals, and us, and the reasons: the particulars of all which I gave him to understand, who seemed to be very glad to heare it" (II: 127). In Adams's account, both English seaman and the Japanese Emperor are seeking a "third man" to counter the influence of the Spanish and Portuguese. For Saris and the EIC, then, the lure of a well-governed nation, lying far enough north to offer a prospective market for English woolens, and apparently willing to entertain a potential trading partner at odds with Catholic Iberia, proved enticing.

After arriving in Hirado, Saris gave permission for a group of Japanese women to come aboard his ship, then realized that his cabin featured an immodest painting of Venus and Cupid that he feared might scandalize his visitors. The scene he describes discloses the complex problems of cultural translation that the ideology of trade glosses over in its eagerness to project western ideas of commerce and religion onto potential trading partners:

> I gave leave to divers women of the better sort to come into my Cabbin, where the Picture of *Venus*, with her sonne *Cupid*, did hang somewhat wantonly set out in a large frame, they thinking it to bee our Ladie and her Sonne, fell downe, and worshipped it, with shewes of great devotion, telling men in a whispering manner (that some of their owne companions which were not so, might not heare) that they were *Christians*: whereby we perceived them to be *Christians*, converted by the *Portugall* Iesuits. (11: 367)

This passage indicates that religious conversion has political and socio-economic implications as well as spiritual significance. The Japanese women translate a Christian conception of divinity into their own semiotic systems and moral codes: the wantonness of Venus and Cupid (both presumably nude) does not signify for them as it does for the English captain. This seemingly brazen lack of decorum is not inconsistent with these Japanese women's religious beliefs: the proximity of mother and child – whatever the setting, boudoir or manger, and whatever their postures – represents a spiritual authority that transcends the obligations of patriarchal and feudal obedience. The Christian women on Saris's ship may worship an image of fair-haired divinity, but their kneeling to Venus and Cupid reveals two threats to western conceptions of religious belief – from external persecution and from the destabilizing nature of transcultural contact. Saris's account of the women's shipboard visit suggests that Christianity itself is being accommodated to a cultural semiotics that reshapes western belief systems to Japanese contexts. The women whisper not because Christianity poses a spiritual threat to indigenous beliefs but because signs of obedience or deference to *any* authority besides one's master were politically dangerous in Tokugawa Japan.

The subsequent ten-year history of the English factory at Hirado (1613–23) reveals the ways in which such cultural misinterpretations hampered efforts to establish the profitable commerce that the EIC envisioned. The British were clearly at a disadvantage in trying to compete for a share of the trade to Japan, long dominated by Chinese, Portuguese, and more recently VOC merchants. Like other EIC ventures, Saris's ship brought cloth products from England, mostly woolens, that he hoped to sell. Because Japan had a climate similar to northern Europe's, officials in London reasoned, the Shogun would be willing to trade silver and luxury items for English wool. The English merchants who came ashore in Hirado, however, were not wearing the wool stuffs that they were trying to get the Japanese to buy, and, except for Saris, quickly came to realize that, in Adams's words, "such thinges as [Saris] had brought was not veri vendibel," and consequently "in respecte of the ventur by the Worshipfull Coumpani being so great, I did not see anny wayss in this land to requit the great charges therof."[44] Cocks, the merchant left in charge of the English factory at Hirado, wrote to London in 1614, confirming that the cargo they had offloaded was next to worthless: "the aboundance of lynen cloth mad in these p'tes and far better cheape then in any p'te of Christendome, & for tynne, it will not sell here for the price it cost in England; & iron [is both better] and better chepe then in England."[45] Cocks is explicit: Japanese linen is abundant and much less expensive than comparable European cloth; tin, often used as ballast on English ships, is dirt cheap; and Japanese iron is both cheaper and of higher quality than iron that the English are trying to sell. Rather than a feudal nation awed by European workmanship, Japan itself is a commercial power that regards English efforts to open trade with indifference, bemusement, or contempt.

The Dutch, Portuguese, and English considered Japan essential to efforts to establish a profitable trade in the Far East. As silver production declined in New Spain and exports to the Far East across the Pacific to the Philippines dropped, Japanese silver mining increased; given China's insatiable need for silver to fuel the world's largest economy, acquiring Japanese silver became a means for European trading companies both to supply their factories throughout the region and potentially to open trade to the Chinese mainland.[46] Whatever his limitations as an administrator and commercial representative, Cocks was astute enough to recognize the strategic significance of the VOC factory in Japan:

yf [the Dutch] fall oout w'th the Japans they will hardlie hold the Molucos any long tyme, for Japan is their storehouse from whence they p'vide in as great abundance as they will, viz. wheate, barlie, beanes, rise, beefe, pork, drid fish, wyne of the cuntrey and aquavite, at a far lower rate then they are worth in any part of Christendome; & here is iron and copper in greate aboundance to make ordinance and shot, & skillfull workmen to make or cast them yf anyone will set them a-work. I have seene triall thereof in this towne of Firando, the Hollanders having set them a-work, and at present have a greate shipp heare of 6 or 700 tonns, full laden w'th munition and victuells to goe for the Molucos, where they preveale very much against the Spaniardes, &c.[47]

The VOC invests in local industries and establishes business relationships with Japanese shipbuilders, activities tolerated by the Shogun and his court because the Dutch provided a counterweight to the Portuguese. Rather than trying to sell unwanted merchandise, the VOC profits from its economic integration with Japanese concerns as well as from trade. While the handful of Englishmen at Hirado recognized that Japanese silver could fuel English efforts throughout Southeast Asia, the EIC was wary, underfunded, and comparatively slow moving in seizing opportunities for expanding its trade. Their commercial intelligence as well left much to be desired. When Saris returned to England in 1614 he provided Company officials with a bizarre list of goods that he claimed would sell in Japan, including paintings ("som lascivious, others of stories of warrs by sea and land, the larger the better"), steel, sugar candy, wax for candles, elephant tusks, honey, pepper, and silk – the only commodity for which Cocks and his fellow merchants managed to find buyers.[48] The Company, after some debate, added many of the items that Saris suggested to the usual exports of bullion, cloth, and lead. Three years later, in Hirado, much of this merchandise lay unsold. In a letter to the Company directors, Cocks was more explicit than he had been in 1614; in order "to have the suilver of Japon to furnish all other factories in the Indies, the truth is it must be don w'th greater quantety & better comodetis then yet we have had out of England or from Bantam; for our English comodeties must have a yeare to make sale of them, except it be lead."[49] The Japanese had little interest in European manufactures, paintings, or clothing, and EIC merchants explained repeatedly for the next century that there was no market in the Far East for the items that England wanted to export.

The President of the English factory in Bantam (the administrative headquarters for the EIC in Southeast Asia), George Ball, was critical of the Company's decisions in London. Ball had sailed with Saris in 1612 and had remained at Bantam, before he was recalled in November 1618, to account for his extensive private, off-the-books trading.[50] A shrewd and opportunistic trader, he recognized that if the English factory in Hirado "were it supplyed as it should be, not with comodityes of England but of such as may be had in these partes of the world," it could be successful. Ships would have to use gold and silver to purchase silks and spices in Arabia, India, and Southeast Asia on their way to Japan, then try to turn a profit by acquiring a greater quantity of Japanese silver in order to secure cargoes of pepper, cloves, nutmeg, and mace for the return voyage. But the factory at Hirado, "supplyed as it hath beene with gallypottes, pictures, looking glasses, table bookes, threed and spectacles & such like trumpery," is doomed to fail. "What can in reason be expected," Ball asked, other "then disgrace to the warehowse, discredditt to the factors, and disanymating to their negotiations[?]"[51] Ball's advice to remedy the situation and rescue the factory from insolvency has three major points: emulate the

Dutch, forget the kinds of fantasies entertained by Cocks that Chinese intermediaries could help the EIC gain a share of the lucrative trade between Hirado and China, and resort to the one surefire method of turning a profit: piracy. While "Mr Cockes, having his imaginations leavelled beyond the moone," waits for nonexistent opportunities for trade to China, and unsold goods lie moldering in the Company's "warehowse," the factory can be made profitable by becoming a base for raiding Chinese junks and Portuguese cargo vessels in the China Sea: "the sooner you beginne with [the Chinese] in the way of force (I mean takinge) the better, & the most reasonable course of dealinge with them and the best way to enable us to keepe markett with the Fleminges."[52] Piracy, for Ball, is not only a quick way to secure goods for the factory but a means to pressure the Chinese into granting trading concessions. While this method had yet to work for the Dutch in opening trade to China, Ball's successors in Bantam sent orders to Cocks to comply with VOC requests for a vessel to join the Fleet of Defence, the joint naval force mandated by the Treaty of 1619. In 1621–22, Japan-based ships of the two companies blockaded Manila and plundered Chinese junks before tensions between England and the Netherlands scuttled the Treaty and its provisions for joint-piracy. Although raiding from Japan returned a £40,000 profit, the factory in Hirado dissolved in 1623 amid charges that Cocks and the other merchants, "men of such antique yeares . . . miserablie given over to voluptuousness," were guilty of theft, incompetence, and the failure to keep the accurate bookkeeping that Mun and other directors of the Company demanded.[53] The take from the raids defrayed some of the costs that had gone into English efforts to open trade to Japan, but did not satisfy the needs of a regular commerce that would justify further investments. The withdrawal from Japan and the massacre of English merchants on Amboyna signaled the end of the hopes that Elizabeth had expressed in her letter to the Sultan of Aceh two decades earlier.

HEYLYN'S *COSMOGRAPHIE*

While English readers thumbing through the five folio volumes of Purchas could read edited versions of the letters of Cocks, Saris, Adams, and others, there was a substantial market for shorter, one-volume digests of information on the history, geography, natural resources, commodities, and trading habits of countries and regions outside of Europe. Foreign atlases such as Pierre d'Avity's *Estates, Empires, & Principalities of the World* and Giovanni Botero's *The Travellers Breviat* were translated into English; early in the

seventeenth century the most popular handbook was Peter Heylyn's
Microcosmos: Or, A Little Description of the Great World, first published
in 1621, and it ran to eight editions by 1639.[54] At first glance, Heylyn seems
an unlikely author for a work that places geographical knowledge firmly
within an expansionist trade policy. A student at Oxford when he wrote
Microcosmos, Heylyn became a prominent royalist and Anglican clergy-
man. He served as Archbishop Laud's right-hand man in the 1630s and
wrote a laudatory biography of his benefactor after Laud was executed. The
author of controversial works in defense of the established Church, Heylyn
was ejected from his living in 1642 and – according to his own account –
literally on the run for several years, hiding with various royalist families
and churning out anti-Commonwealth propaganda. His decision in the
late 1640s "to review my *Geographie* [*Microcosmos*]; to make it more
complete and usefull to an English Reader," may have been, in part, a
financial one, but Heylyn thoroughly transforms what had been a pocket
guide into a full-fledged historical geography, enlarging all the entries, and
updating some of them, to reflect three decades of English dealings with
the "Great World."[55]

As the most popular historical geography of the second half of the
seventeenth century, Heylyn's *Cosmographie* offers a compendium of
English attitudes toward other cultures, a measure of the complex tensions
and desires that characterize descriptions of the Far East. It is hardly an
original work; although Heylyn claims to have written it after
Commonwealth officials had seized his library, whole pages are lifted
from prior works such as d'Avity's *Estates* and Botero's *Travellers Breviat*;
sections from Hakluyt and Purchas are condensed and rephrased. This
redactive, intertextual quality of the *Cosmographie* is characteristic of a
genre – the universal geography – that recycles and recombines eyewitness
accounts in order to provide snapshot views of a world potentially open to
ever-expanding trade. A significant market existed for such compendia,
and the ideology of trade that motivated writers as different as John Milton
(who planned a one-volume redaction of Purchas) and Heylyn testifies to
the ways in which the appeal of the Far East cut across the divisions of
partisan politics in seventeenth-century England.[56]

Heylyn's Preface is tub-thumpingly patriotic, asserting that as an
Englishman and a divine he has "apprehended every modest occasion, of
recording the heroic Acts of my native Soil, and filing on the Registers of
perpetual Fame the Gallantry and brave atchievements of the People
of *England*" (A3r). Heylyn seizes on Elizabeth's image of a fallen world
that can be redeemed through trade to reaffirm a heroic national identity

that transcends the "Tragedies of blood and death" (B1r) that have disfigured England in the 1640s. Downplaying his ardent royalism, he reasserts a familiar theological argument for prosperity through trade: "Nothing more sets forth the Power and Wisdome of Almighty God," he declares, "than that most admirable intermixture of Want with Plenty, whereby he hath united all the Parts of the World in a continuall Traffique and Commerce with one another" (4). For Heylyn, as for Elizabeth, such "continuall Traffique" is essential if humankind is to overcome the scarcity of post-lapsarian nature. An inclusive ideology of trade, moreover, offers the hope in 1652, on the eve of the first Anglo-Dutch War, that England can put aside the antagonisms of the Civil War by uniting against the threats posed by the Dutch, French, and Spanish. The structure of *Cosmographie* suggests where Heylyn's interests lie in rendering his efforts "usefull" to this commercial project. In a one-volume work divided into four books (one each for Europe, the Americas, Asia, and Africa), the countries of Asia receive as many pages as those of Europe and three times as many as the Americas. While his entries on Asia testify to his and his readers' fascination with trade to the Far East, Heylyn must define the "brave atchievements of the People of *England*" very carefully in a region where trade has yet to make good on its promises of profit and prosperity.

Throughout the *Cosmographie*, Heylyn's responses to the peoples he describes are governed not by skin color, religion, or geographical proximity to England, but by an archaeology of European desire. He offers few original judgments on the major trading nations of the Far East, preferring instead to appeal to what he presumes his readers want to hear about the potential of trade. Echoing Jesuit accounts of China that had themselves been reprinted, translated, and redacted many times, Heylyn lavishes praise on the Chinese for "their natural industry, and their proficiencie in Manufactures and Mechanick Arts," and reiterates the widespread view that, because China enjoys the "abundance of all things necessary to life," it is a bastion of political stability and economic prosperity (865, 866). Since English efforts to open trade to China had met with little success, Heylyn has no "brave atchievements" to report, and no tragedies like the one on Amboyna to explain away. Consequently, his entry on China is measured, even pedestrian, a derivative encyclopedia piece on a land that remains an idealized manifestation of Europeans' desire for trade.

The Dutch domination in the Spice Islands, in contrast, offers profound challenges to the *Cosmographie*'s patriotism. The United Provinces provide a disturbing image of what Interregnum Britain might become: a republic at once prosperous and commercially powerful that extends rights and privileges of the sort that Laud had ruthlessly denied. England's rival, Heylyn declares, lacks only "*a gracious Prince, unitie of Religion,* and *a quiet Government*: which if it pleased the Almighty to confer upon them, they would surpass all neighbouring States in treasure, potency, content, and worldly happiness" (396). His royalist beliefs produce a divided rhetoric that sidesteps the problem of how a nation without a monarch, an established church, and autocratic government can become so prosperous. Heylyn describes Amsterdam, for example, as "a very fair Haven Town, where divers times at one tide, 1000 ships of all sorts have been seen to go out and in … The people thereby made so rich, that if a Fleet of 300 sail should come into the Port, fraught with all kinds of commodities, in five or six days they would be ready to buy all the lading" (383). The city's prosperity is defined in terms of quantitative measures of consumer desire. Although the *Cosmographie* is a very different kind of work from Mun's *Discovrse of Trade*, it reproduces his predecessor's logic of dispassionate observation and numerical reckoning. In his terse, almost telegraphic style, Heylyn frequently suppresses main verbs; his passive construction ("have been seen") governs the spectral calculations that allow him to assert that, in less than a week, Amsterdam's inhabitants and merchants will purchase all the commodities of three hundred ships. This rhetoric of objectivity, though, is set against a moralistic language of social, moral, and political judgment. International trade and finance produce a city "inhabited by men of all Nations, and of all *Religions*; and those not only *tollerated*, and *connived* at in private, but openly and freely *exercised* without any dislike. A greater confusion (in my mind) than that of *Babel*; this being of *Religions*, that of *Languages* only" (384). For Heylyn, religious toleration is worse than the confusion of tongues at Babel, the all-purpose trope in the Renaissance for linguistic corruption, dialogic instability, and political and social fragmentation.[57] Such religious "confusion," therefore, should produce a nightmare of internecine strife of the kind that England experienced in the 1640s. But it does not. His description of Amsterdam consequently becomes a function of two opposed discursive and moral registers that present his readers with a difficult paradox: a devilish nation is prospering through what is supposed to be a godly commerce.

Although Heylyn duly notes Dutch prowess in industry and navigation, he does not voice the logical conclusion that the VOC has outstripped the EIC, nor does he mention that by 1620 Dutch vessels in Southeast Asia outnumbered English ships by eight to one. Instead of explaining England's inability to crack the Dutch monopoly of the spice trade, he instead scapegoats the Moluccans. Consistently in his entries on the peoples of Asia, Heylyn treats racial characteristics, national identities, social behaviors, and morality as functions of their willingness and ability to engage in trade with English merchants. Without their spices, the people of these islands are described as "*Idolaters . . .* [of] severall *Originals*, and different languages, but all in general fraudulent, perfidious, treacherous, inhumane, and of noted wickednesse. Few of them clothed, nor much caring to hide their shame. Not civilized by cohabitation of more modest and civill Nations" (918). Heylyn's assertive style lends a seemingly objective authority to what is at best a second-hand account. No sources are cited, and no references are made to the positive descriptions of the Bandanese (to take only one example) who resisted the VOC and aided Courthope when he was besieged on Run. In such entries, Heylyn subsumes the history of triangular rivalries, civil war, and European competition described by Saris and Cocks into essentialist judgments of national character. The same islanders who had petitioned James I to come to their aid against the Portuguese are denigrated by a logic that casts their subservience to the VOC as an intrinsic moral failure. The Moluccans seem beyond the pale of morality and civilization because, in Heylyn's eyes, they have allowed themselves to be dominated by the Dutch.

Another Asian country with a population of "*Idolaters*" ruled by Muslims receives much more favorable treatment. Heylyn carefully includes the EIC's chief trading partner – the Moghul Empire – within the circuits of civilization.[58] South Asians accordingly are described as

tall of stature, strong of body, and of complexion inclining to that of the *Negroes*: of manners Civill, and ingenuous, free from fraud in their dealings, and exact keepers of their words. The Common sort but meanly clad, for the most part naked, content with no more covering than to hide their shame. But those of greater estates, and fortunes (as they have amongst them many antient and Noble families) observe a majesty in both Sexes, both in their Attendants and Apparel; sweetning the last with oils, and perfumes, and adorning themselves with Jewels, Petals, and other Ornaments befitting. They eat no flesh, but live on Barley, Rice, Milk, Honey, and other things without life . . . Originally descended from the Sons of *Noah*, before they left these Eastern parts to go towards the unfortunate valley of *Shinaart*. (881)

Indians are spared the calumny directed at the Moluccans because the English have crucial trading interests in the Moghul Empire; India supplies the bulk of the goods that are re-exported from England to markets in Europe and the Americas. As significantly, South Asians can be assimilated within a biblical history that works in their favor: they are descended from

those virtuous sons of Noah who remained in the East when their wicked
brethren journeyed to Shinaar to build the Tower of Babel. Heylyn, in this
instance, follows Sir Walter Ralegh in implying that India was resettled
after the Flood by those sons of Noah whose descendants preserve a
Noachian virtue. If nakedness is de facto evidence of depravity in the
Moluccas, it is simply a characteristic of the lower classes in India that
can be passed over quickly in order to praise the "majesty" of the elite
orders. Skin color, religious differences, and seemingly odd customs such
as vegetarianism can be encompassed by a class-specific notion of transcultural civilization: upper-class Indians exhibit the civility, honesty, and
even aesthetic sensibilities that mirror an idealized self-image of English
virtues. This identification of Indian and English sensibilities enacts the
civilizing function that Heylyn attributes to international commerce.
Trade civilizes: it both produces and reaffirms a like-minded compatibility
between English desires and South Asian interests.

In identifying trade with civilized morality, Heylyn's *Cosmographie*
breaks down as many distinctions between Europe and the Far East as it
establishes. While Heylyn invokes racial hierarchies, defends European
technology, rails against the impediments to trade enforced by Chinese
and Indian bureaucracies, and repeatedly denounces "heathen" religious
practices, his most vitriolic attacks are aimed at other Europeans who either
compete with English trade, like the Dutch, or who frustrate English
ambitions to gain entry to the markets of Japan and China. In this regard,
he follows his sources, notably Botero and d'Avity, by abusing the Russians
at length.[59] By the middle of the seventeenth century, efforts to use Russia
as a conduit to the riches of the Orient had proved fruitless. Trade between
England and the Czar was particularly vexed, and Heylyn includes a litany
of complaints: the Russians competed with English merchants in the
Baltic; they repeatedly sought to drive prices of their timber and fur exports
as high as they could, demanding silver in return; and they persisted in
trying to open an overland trade route to China. The result is a third or
fourth-hand account of Russian perfidy that marks the Czar's subjects –
though "white" and Christian – as thoroughly other.

[They] are very perfidious, crafty, and deceitful in all their bargains, false-dealers
with all they have to do with, making no reckoning of their promises, and studying
nothing more than ways to evade their Contracts. Vices so generally known, and
noted in them, that when they are to deal with strangers, they dissemble their
Country, and pretend to be of other Nations, for fear lest no body should trust
them. Destitute of humane affections, and so unnatural, that the Father insults on
his Son, and he again over his Father and Mother: So malitious one towards an

other, that you shall have a man hide some of his own goods in the house of some man whom he hateth, and then accuse him for the stealth of them. (511)

Heylyn borrows from Botero and d'Avity the example of neighbors staging robberies and then charging each other with theft; he generalizes this story into an ethnic portrait of endemic dishonesty and malice. Familial disorder and dishonesty in trade define a violent and tyrannical state. His condemnation of the Russians harks back to the misunderstandings and distrust that accompanied the decline of the Muscovy Company's fortunes in the late sixteenth century when its merchants encountered the difficulties of trading to a country that demanded silver for raw materials and provided no easy access to the Far East.

Renaissance commentators were explicit about what they expected from the forays of the Muscovy Company. Purchas, for example, describes the "intent" of the Company's first voyage in 1553 as "the discouerie of *Cathay*, and diuers other Regions, Dominions, Ilands, and places vnknowne" (III: 212); Robert Parke, the translator of Gonzalez de Mendoza's *Historie of China*, notes in his preface that the Muscovy Company's attempt at "the discouerie of *Cathaia* and *China*" was motivated "partly of desire that the good young king [Edward VI] had to enlarge the Christian faith, and partlie to finde out some where in those regions ample vent of the cloth of England."[60] Heylyn's description of the Russians is redolent of the disappointments that confronted English merchants a century later who had to compete with German, Dutch, Swedish, Danish, Polish, Turkish, and Persian traders in Russia as well as trying to placate a court that tried to keep strict control over much of the country's international trade.[61] For Heylyn, as for Botero and d'Avity, civilization is defined by a language of "promises" and "contracts," by the ties of nation, family, friendship, and profit. The Russians fall beyond the pale of civilized behavior because their deceit in trade is emblematic of a lack of moral self-consciousness and industry. They are the antithesis of the Indians, even as they reinforce the same values and assumptions that inform the ideology of trade: skin color, clothing, customs, and even religion, are not the ultimate markers of civilized behavior – trade is.

CODA: COSMOGRAPHIES

The popularity of Heylyn's *Microcosmos* and *Cosmographie* throughout much of the seventeenth century reveals a deep-seated ideological investment on the part of his readers in both accumulated knowledge – or really strings of truisms – about the Far East and in the prospect of a godly and profitable commerce. These investments cut across political divisions between republicans and royalists in the middle of the century despite qualms about the corrupting influences of foreign luxuries and the shipping of bullion overseas. Between 1620 and the renewal of its charter by Oliver Cromwell in 1657, the East India Company fell on difficult times, sending comparatively few ships to a handful of beleaguered outposts on the coast of India and maintaining intermittent contacts with struggling English factories in the Far East. It was forced to make loans to both Charles I and to the Commonwealth government, neither of which were repaid, and, during the First Dutch War in 1652–54, while the English and Dutch navies fought to bloody standstills in the Caribbean, Mediterranean, and Atlantic, the Company saw the outnumbered English fleet suffer humiliating defeats in the Persian Gulf. Even as the political landscape altered radically in 1642 and again in 1660, the EIC represented a faith in the process of trade itself to create the seemingly endless profits that Mun attributed to the sale of spices. Ideology usually trumps experience because disappointment and defeat seemingly necessitate a rearticulation of faith in the traditional, seemingly bedrock values of nation, faith, and virtue rather than wholesale rejections of outmoded beliefs. EIC stock issued for £100 in 1657 was selling for £245 twenty years later, and up to £500 in 1683 before plummeting during the disastrous Moghul War at the end of that decade.[62] Yet even as the East India Company concentrated on trade in Gujarat, Bombay, and Madras, efforts persisted to reopen trade to the Far East and objections that Mun had answered in 1621 resurfaced. For writers of different political persuasions, China and Japan remained the ultimate goals for Europeans who sought commercial partners wealthy enough to buy large quantities of western goods and to energize the imaginary structures of faith in the production of surplus value. In the second half of the seventeenth century, the fascination with China gripped many intellectuals in western Europe, and debates that had been stirring since the Jesuits first arrived in the Middle Kingdom in the sixteenth century began to surface in some of the now-canonical works of English literature, including those of John Milton.

NOTES

1. John Keay, *The Honourable Company: A History of the English East India Company* (London: HarperCollins, 1991), 4–7.
2. On the Portuguese in the Moluccas in the sixteenth century, see Jerry Brotton, *Trading Territories: Mapping the Early Modern World* (Ithaca: Cornell University Press, 1998), 119–50.

3. The figures are from Keay, *The Honourable Company*, 4–5; see also K. N. Chaudhuri, *The East India Company: A Study of an Early Joint Stock Company, 1600–1640* (New York: Kelley, 1965); Neils Steensgaard, *The Asian Trade Revolution of the Seventeenth Century: The East India Companies and the Decline of the Caravan Trade* (Chicago: University of Chicago Press, 1974); Steensgaard, "The Growth and Composition of the Long-Distance Trade of England and the Dutch Republic before 1750," in *The Rise of Merchant Empires: Long-Distance Trade in the Early Modern World 1350–1750*, ed. James Tracy (Cambridge: Cambridge University Press, 1990), 102–52; Kenneth Andrews, *Trade, Plunder, and Settlement: Maritime Enterprise and the Genesis of the British Empire 1480–1630* (Cambridge: Cambridge University Press, 1984), 256–79; and Anthony Farrington, *Trading Places: The East India Company and Asia 1600–1834* (London: British Library, 2002).

4. Keay, *The Honourable Company*, 10–13. On the financing of overseas trade by London Companies, see Andrews, *Trade, Plunder, and Settlement: Maritime Enterprise and the Genesis of the British Empire*; and Robert Brenner, *Merchants and Revolution: Commercial Change, Political Conflicts, and London's Overseas Traders, 1550–1633* (Cambridge: Cambridge University Press, 1993). On the French effort to open trade with Aceh, see François Martin, *Description du Premier Voyage Facit aux Indes Orientales par les Francois en l'an 1603* (Paris, 1604).

5. On the dangers of shipwreck and the horrific conditions aboard ship in the period, see Josiah Blackmore, *Shipwreck Narrative and the Disruption of Empire* (Minneapolis: University of Minnesota Press, 2002); and Mike Dash, *Batavia's Graveyard* (New York: Crown, 2002).

6. Els M. Jacobs, *In Pursuit of Pepper and Tea: The Story of the Dutch East India Company*, 3rd edn (Amsterdam: Netherlands Maritime Museum, 1991), 7–14.

7. Keay, *The Honourable Company*, 13–14.

8. Jan van Linschoten, *Iohn Huighen van Linschoten his Discours of Voyages into ye Easte and West Indies* (London, 1598). All quotations are from this edition.

9. See Rajan, *Under Western Eyes*, 31–49, and Raman, *Framing "India"*.

10. See Charles Boxer, "A Note on Portuguese Reactions to the Revival of the Red Sea Spice Trade and the Rise of Acheh, 1540–1600," *Journal of Southeast Asian History* 10 (1969), 416–19, and Anthony Reid, "Islamization and Christianization in Southeast Asia: The Critical Phase, 1550–1650," in *Southeast Asia in the Early Modern Era: Trade, Power, and Belief*, ed. Anthony Reid (Ithaca: Cornell University Press, 1993), 151–78.

11. See Reid, "Islamization and Christianization," 159, and Janet Hoskins, "Spirit Worship and Conversion in Western Sumba," in *Indonesian Religions in Transition*, ed. Rita Kipp and Susan Rodgers (Tucson: University of Arizona Press, 1987), 144–58.

12. Pierre-Yves Manguin, "The Vanishing *Jong*: Insular Southeast Asian Fleets in Trade and War (Fifteenth to Seventeenth Centuries)," in Reid, *Southeast Asia in the Early Modern Era*, 197–213.

13. Reid, "Islamization and Christianization," 165.
14. Samuel Purchas, *Purchas his Pilgrimmes* (London, 1625), II: 154. All quotations are from this edition.
15. Jeyalamar Kathirithamby-Wells, 'Restraints on the Development of Merchant Capitalism in Southeast Asia before *c.* 1800', in Reid, *Southeast Asia in the Early Modern Era*, 123–48. See also Anthony Reid, *Southeast Asia in the Age of Commerce, 1450–1680*, vol. II: *Expansion and Crisis* (New Haven: Yale University Press, 1993), 17–26.
16. Michel Serres, *The Parasite*, trans. Lawrence Scher (Baltimore: Johns Hopkins University Press, 1982).
17. On Lancaster's audience with the Sultan, see Giles Milton, *Nathaniel's Nutmeg: Or, the True and Incredible Adventures of the Spice Trader Who Changed the Course of History* (New York: Penguin, 2000), 83–93.
18. Reid, "Introduction: A Time and a Place," in *Southeast Asia in the Early Modern Era*, 5.
19. Keay, *The Honourable Company*, 12–25; Milton, *Nathaniel's Nutmeg*, 93–101; Andrews, *Trade, Plunder, and Settlement*, 263–4; and K. N. Chaudhuri, *The East India Company: A Study of an Early Joint Stock Company*, 115–17, 153–54.
20. On the relationship between foreign products and food consumption in England, see Keith Sandiford, "Vertices and Horizons within Sugar: A Tropology of Colonial Power," *The Eighteenth Century: Theory and Interpretation* 42 (2001), 142–60.
21. See, Fernand Braudel, *Civilization and Capitalism*, vol. II: *The Wheels of Commerce*, trans. Sian Reynolds (1982; rpt. Berkeley and Los Angeles: University of California Press, 1992); Chaudhuri, *Asia before Europe*; Bairoch, *Economics and World History*; Frank, *ReOrient*; Pomeranz, *The Great Divergence*; and Gunn, *First Globalization*.
22. See Joseph Roach, *Cities of the Dead: Circum-Atlantic Performance* (New York: Columbia University Press, 1996); Keith Sandiford, *The Cultural Politics of Sugar: Caribbean Slavery and Narratives of Colonialism* (Cambridge: Cambridge University Press, 2000); and Charlotte Sussman, *Consuming Anxieties: Consumer Protest, Gender, and British Slavery, 1713–1833* (Stanford: Stanford University Press, 2000).
23. See Frank, *ReOrient* and Gunn, *First Globalization* for extended descriptions of these circuits of trade.
24. Mun, *A Discovrse of Trade*. Reprinted in Purchas, vol. I, book 5: 732–47. All references are to Purchas's edition of the text.
25. See, for example, Eric Roll, *A History of Economic Thought*, 5th edn (London: Faber and Faber, 1992), 63–74.
26. Keay, *The Honourable Company*, 112–13; Andrews, *Trade, Plunder, and Settlement*, 256–79. On joint-stock offerings see Chaudhuri, *East India Company*; and W. R. Scott, *The Constitution and Finance of English, Scottish and Irish Joint-Stock Companies to 1720*, 3 vols. (Cambridge: Cambridge University Press, 1910).

27. Chaudhuri, *East India Company*, 125–40. Conditions worsened significantly for the Company in the 1630s through the end of the Interregnum. See Keay, *The Honourable Company*, 120–28.

28. See Joyce Oldham Appleby, *Economic Thought and Ideology in Seventeenth-Century England* (Princeton: Princeton University Press, 1978), 37–41.

29. On the mathematicizing of economics in the early modern world, see Hadden, *On the Shoulders of Merchants*, 46–56; Buck-Morss, "Envisioning Capital", 434–67; and Crosby, *The Measure of Reality*, 199–223.

30. On timber in the seventeenth century, see Andrew McRae, *God Speed the Plough: The Representation of Agrarian England, 1500–1660* (Cambridge: Cambridge University Press, 1996); and Markley, "'Gulfes, deserts, precipices, stone', 89–105.

31. For statistics on EIC and VOC shipping during these decades see Steensgaard, "Trade of England and the Dutch before 1750," 109–10.

32. On the hostilities in 1618–19 see Milton, *Nathaniel's Nutmeg*, 281–306; on the English–Dutch rivalry in Southeast Asia in the early seventeenth century, see Keay, *The Honourable Company*, 25–39; Kristof Glamman, *Dutch–Asiatic Trade 1620–1740* (1958; rpt. 's-Gravenhage: Martinus Nijhoff, 1981); Holden Furber, *Rival Empires of Trade in the Orient, 1600–1800* (Minneapolis: University of Minnesota Press, 1976); O. H. K. Spate, *The Pacific Since Magellan*, vol. II, *Monopolists and Freebooters* (Minneapolis: University of Minnesota Press, 1983), 87–91; Steensgaard, "Growth and Composition of the Long-Distance Trade of England and the Dutch Republic before 1750," 102–52; Larry Neal, "The Dutch and English East India Companies Compared: Evidence from the Stock and Foreign Exchange Markets," in *The Rise of Merchant Empires: Long Distance Trade in the Early-Modern World, 1350–1750* (Cambridge: Cambridge University Press, 1990), ed. James D. Tracy, 195–223; and David Armitage, *The Ideological Origins of the British Empire* (Cambridge: Cambridge University Press, 2000), 100–24.

33. John Villiers, "'A truthful pen and an impartial spirit': Bartolomé Leonardo de Argensola and the *Conquista de las Islas Malucas*," *Renaissance Studies* 17 (2003), 457.

34. Ania Loomba, "'Break her will, and bruise no bone sir': Colonial and Sexual Mastery in Fletcher's *The Island Princess*," *Journal for Early Modern Cultural Studies* 2 (2002), 68–108. See also Michael Neill, *Putting History to the Question: Power, Politics, and Society in English Renaissance Drama* (New York: Columbia University Press, 2000), 311–28; and Raman, *Framing "India,"* 155–88. Argensola's history was not translated into English until 1708.

35. Heidi Hutner, *Colonial Women: Race and Culture in Stuart Drama* (New York: Oxford University Press, 2001).

36. Anthony Farrington, *The English Factory in Japan 1613–1623*, 2 vols. (London: The British Library, 1991), 1: 262.

37. Lynda Norene Shaffer, *Maritime Southeast Asia to 1500* (London: Sharpe, 1996), 32–33.

38. Spate, *Monopolists and Freebooters*, 90.

39. On the Dutch in Southeast Asia, see Philip D. Curtin, *Cross-Cultural Trade in World History* (Cambridge: Cambridge University Press, 1984), 158–66; C. R. Boxer, *The Dutch Seaborne Empire 1600–1800* (1965; rpt. London: Hutchinson, 1977); Leonard Andaya, "Interactions with the Outside World and Adaptation in Southeast Asian Society, 1500–1800," in *The Cambridge History of Southeast Asia*, vol. 1: *From Early Times to c. 1800*, ed. Nicholas Tarling (Cambridge: Cambridge University Press, 1992), 345–401; and, in the same volume, Anthony Reid, 'Economic and Social Change, c. 1400–1800', 460–507; Jan M. Pluvier, *Historical Atlas of South-East Asia* (Leiden: Brill, 1995), 25–27; and Schnurmann, "'Wherever profit leads us, to every sea and shore . . .'," 474–93.

40. Frank, *ReOrient*, 165.

41. On Courthope see Keay, *The Honourable Company*, 43–8, and Milton, *Nathaniel's Nutmeg.*

42. Jonathan Israel, *The Dutch Republic: Its Rise, Greatness, and Fall 1477–1806* (Oxford: Clarendon Press, 1995), 939–43.

43. See Giles Milton, *Samurai William: The Adventurer Who Unlocked Japan* (London: Hodder and Stoughton, 2002), and Derek Massarella, *A World Elsewhere: Europe's Encounter with Japan in the Sixteenth and Seventeenth Centuries* (New Haven: Yale University Press, 1990), 71–130.

44. Farrington, *English Factory*, 1: 103.

45. Farrington, *English Factory*, 1:225–26. The brackets indicate additions from a second version of the letter that Cocks sent on December 10, 1614.

46. See Ward Barrett, "World Bullion Flows, 1450–1800," in *The Rise of Merchant Empires*, ed. Tracy, 224–54.

47. Farrington, *English Factory*, 1: 262.

48. Farrington, *English Factory*, 1: 6. For Saris's complete list of trade goods, see 1: 209–11.

49. Farrington, *English Factory*, 1: 553.

50. On Ball, see Farrington, *English Factory*, 11: 154–56. The EIC entered an action against him for £70,000 on his return, a suit still in the courts when he died in 1625.

51. Farrington, *English Factory*, 1: 665.

52. Ibid.

53. Farrington, *English Factory*, 1: 12; 11: 925.

54. Pierre d'Avity, *The Estates, Empires, & Principalities of the World*, trans. Edward Grimstone (London, 1615); Giovanni Botero, *The Travellers Breviat, or an Historicall Description of the Most Famous Kingdomes in the World* (London, 1601; five editions by 1626); and Peter Heylyn, *Microcosmos: Or, A Little Description of the Great World* (Oxford, 1621).

55. Peter Heylyn, *Cosmographie*, 2nd edn (London, 1657), A2r. All quotations are from this edition. For the circumstances of Heylyn's revision, see the rival biographies of Heylyn, by George Vernon, *The Life of the Learned and Reverend Dr. Peter Heylyn* (London, 1682), and John Barnard, *Theologico-Historicus, or*

the True Life of the Most Reverend Divine, and Excellent Historian Peter Heylyn* (London, 1683).

56. See D. S. Proudfoot and D. Deslandres, "Samuel Purchas and the Date of Milton's *Moscovia*," *Philological Quarterly* 64 (1985), 260–65. On the popularity of accounts of China in the seventeenth century, see Lach, *Asia in the Making of Europe*, 1: 730–821.

57. On the image of Babel, see Robert Markley, *Fallen Languages: Crises of Representation in Newtonian England, 1660–1740* (Ithaca: Cornell University Press, 1993).

58. On perceptions of India during the seventeenth century, see Sinnappah Arasaratnam, *Maritime Trade, Society and the European Influence in Southern Asia, 1600–1800* (Aldershot: Variorum, 1995); Keay, *India: A History*, 320–69.

59. See d'Avity, *Estates, Empires, & Principalities of the World*, 690–91. In *Microcosmos*, Heylyn's description of Russia (183) is glossed in the margins as derived from Botero's *Travellers Breviat*.

60. Gonzalez de Mendoza, *The Historie of the Great and Mightie Kingdome of China*, trans. R[obert] Parke (London, 1588), A2r.

61. See Mark Mancall, *Russia and China: Their Diplomatic Relations to 1728* (Cambridge, MA: Harvard University Press, 1971).

62. Keay, *The Honourable Company*, 170.

CHAPTER 2

China and the limits of Eurocentric history: Milton, the Jesuits, and the Jews of Kaifeng

PROVIDENTIAL HISTORIOGRAPHY AND THE PROBLEM OF CHINA

As a prelude to the revelation of postlapsarian history in book eleven of *Paradise Lost*, Michael takes Adam to the highest hill in Paradise to show him a geographic "prospect" of "the Seat[s] of Mightiest Empire[s]" (XI 384–85).[1] Before moving westward, this catalogue begins in the Far East, evoking

> the destin'd Walls
> Of *Cambalu*, seat of *Cathaian Can*,
> *Samarchand* by *Oxus, Temir's* Throne,
> To *Paquin* of *Sinean* Kings, and thence
> To *Agra* and *Lahor* of great *Mogul*
> Down to the golden Chersonese[.]
>
> (XI 387–92)

Traditionally, source-hunting critics have assumed that such catalogues demonstrate Milton's fascination with contemporary geography.[2] In actuality, however, these lines are sonorously anachronistic. By the middle of the seventeenth century, educated Europeans knew that China and Cathay were one and the same and that the Manchus, led by a "*Cathaian Can*," had invaded China in the 1640s, established themselves in Beijing after the collapse of the Ming dynasty, and embraced Chinese cultural traditions and values.[3] By the time Milton wrote *Paradise Lost*, the "sinification" of the Qing dynasty was well underway and was widely interpreted in China and Europe as a testament to the enduring virtues of an empire that traced its history back 4,600 years.[4] But if Milton's lines reveal little about contemporary geographical knowledge, his doubling of Cambalu and Beijing, Cathay and China, underscores his and his contemporaries' continuing fascination with the Chinese. Like the voyage collections on which the poet drew, his verses in book eleven trace an archaeology of European desire – a wish list, for merchants, investors, and government officials, of exotic realms that tantalize with the promise of an infinitely profitable trade. *Paradise Lost*, like other canonical works in the seventeenth and early eighteenth centuries, suggests how widely this fascination with trade to China and the Far East extended beyond handbooks for merchants and armchair geographies in the Renaissance. Such visions of trade to China allow Milton's contemporaries – royalists and republicans alike – to imagine a return to a golden age of prosperity and social stability, even as idealized visions of the wealth and stability of the great empires of East Asia call into question some of the fundamental assumptions and values of Christian civilization. "The destin'd Walls/Of *Cambalu*," for Milton, thus serve a complex double function: they stand synedochically for the riches that will help Europeans overcome the curses of sin and scarcity and they pose a formidable challenge to Eurocentric visions of history, politics, and theology.

In this chapter, I want both to contextualize Milton's understanding of the challenges that China poses to his view of history and to defamiliarize that context. Milton's ironclad commitments to a voluntarist theology and republican politics lead him to distance himself from sixteenth and seventeenth-century Jesuit accounts that celebrated China's wealth, socio-economic stability, good government and presumed monotheistic religion. Yet no Englishman contemplating the implications of the "destined Walls/ Of *Cambalu*" could escape the near obsession in England, notably in the travel accounts edited by Samuel Purchas, with the works of Jesuit missionaries, including Matteo Ricci, Alvarez Semedo, and Martino Martini. This widely disseminated literature on China and Japan might be brusquely dismissed as, we will see, Milton was wont to do, but nonetheless it haunts (or even mocks) England's pretensions to national greatness and moral purity. Unlike the corrupt monarchies and repressive churches of Catholic Europe and Stuart England, China was a tough target for a republican polemicist to attack: it was an ancient empire that had escaped the fate of the pagan regimes of the Mediterranean and Near East and continued to prosper; it boasted a written history that, in its antiquity, narrative coherence, and moral probity apparently rivaled the Old Testament; and it seemed, to many commentators besides Jesuit accommodationists, to provide a unassailable model of sociopolitical order and economic prosperity. Although Milton shares his contemporaries' views of the potential for trade to China and the East Indies, he resists the explicit political lessons that Ricci, Martini, and English royalists such as John Webb draw in idealizing the Middle Kingdom as a model for Europe to emulate. The prospect of an empire resistant to his voluntarist critiques of

tyranny, sin, and idolatry forces Milton to distinguish between the potential benefits of trade to the Far East and the challenges that China poses to
his vision of providential history.

If Milton's scattered references to China do not coalesce into a condemnation of Chinese idolatry or a rejoinder to Jesuit enthusiasm, they
nonetheless allow us to assess the anxieties – both personal and cultural –
that threaten his interlocking commitments to Mosaic history, voluntarist
theology, and the redemptive possibilities of international trade. To safe-
guard his providentialist faith and republican virtue, Milton must sidestep,
or dismiss, three crucial intellectual traditions in the seventeenth century:
universal history, a genre that threatened to relativize Judeo-Christian
historiography; the Jesuit and Jesuit-inspired texts that maintained
China's material wealth testified to both its exemplary sociopolitical
order and moral philosophy; and the accounts of western acculturation
to the standards of Chinese civilization, particularly the assimilation of the
Jews of Kaifeng to Confucianism and the accommodation of Jesuit missionaries to the lifestyles of the mandarins they attempted to convert.
Confronted by such challenges, Milton must also deal with another threat
to English national identity: Dutch efforts to aggrandize the wealth of
China, the Spice Islands, and Japan. Like Defoe after him, he paradoxically
defends the very trade for eastern luxuries that he worries are corrupting the
republican virtue of England.

MILTON AND UNIVERSAL HISTORY

Milton's retelling of Mosaic history in the final books of *Paradise Lost*
recasts the generic postulates of seventeenth-century universal history in
order to justify his political and theological principles after the collapse of
the Commonwealth. Although books eleven and twelve share some affi-
nities with the efforts of other historians intent on discerning the hand of
providence in millennia-long cycles of moral depravity, political disorder,
and economic hardship, Milton stands willfully outside of a euhemeristic
tradition that he considers both theologically and politically suspect.
Euhemerism, in brief, is usually treated as a response to pagan accounts
of antiquity that challenged the Bible's historical and moral authority, but
it was pressed into the service of shoring up arguments for the historical
and conceptual primacy of Mosaic history against the threat posed by
China. Gerard and Isaac Vossius, Sir Walter Ralegh, Henry Isaacson,
Georg Horn, John Webb, Matthew Hale, Isaac Newton, Francis
Tallents, and Jean LeClerc respond, in different ways, to the crises of

historiography provoked by these accounts, jerry-rigging chronological schemes to subsume Egyptian, Chaldean, Greek, and Chinese chronologies within an authoritative Judeo-Christian metanarrative.[5] The pattern of history that these writers record, however, is overdetermined by their fascination with the baleful consequences of humankind's sins: the purpose of history itself becomes, as Ralegh says, "the comparison and application of other mens fore-passed miseries, with our owne like errours and ill deservings."[6] The study of pagan histories remains useful for these historians, then, because it reinforces their tendency to read postlapsarian history as the record of a world "To good malignant, to bad men benign" (*PL* XII 538).

For Milton, however, universal histories demean the Mosaic account by suggesting that the Old Testament's chronological and moral coherence requires buttressing from pagan sources. In *Of Prelaticall Episcopacy*, he dismisses the euhemerist tradition and its reliance on "those stale, and uselesse records of either uncertaine, or unsound antiquity."[7] Although Milton is hardly alone in defending the Bible's authority, he is perhaps unique among his learned contemporaries in disdaining the masterworks of Renaissance historical scholarship. There are no references in his published works and letters to widely read and cited universal histories: none to either Vossius; none to the chronologies of his ecclesiastical antagonist, Archbishop Ussher; and only one in his commonplace book (on polygamy in the Congo) to Ralegh's *History of the World*, even though Milton thought enough of Ralegh to publish the manuscript of his *Cabinet-Council* in 1658. His disdain for euhemerism may best be explained by his desire, at the end of *Paradise Lost* and elsewhere, to counter the tendency of universal histories to argue that a fallen humankind must be kept in check by ecclesiastical and monarchical authority. But while Milton may see himself as a stalwart defender of Mosaic truth against the spectres of political, theological, and hermeneutical coercion, he seems well aware that the tensions in books eleven and twelve between redemptive and degenerate history reflect larger instabilities within the historiographic tradition.[8] Above all else, universal histories deal obsessively with the spiritual degeneration of humankind as both cause and effect of the economic and environmental crises which beset a fallen earth.

In charting the fate of humankind after the expulsion from Eden, Milton, like his contemporaries, works within a Christian tradition that yokes Adam's sin to the fall of nature. Throughout the century, theologians such as Godfrey Goodman invoke God's condemnation of Adam – "Cursed be the ground for thy sake" (Genesis 3.17) – to suggest both that his disobedience corrupted nature and that God cursed nature to punish Adam. If sin marks a fall into scarcity, then a Hobbesian competition for scarce resources is both the impetus for and result of humankind's corruption. Such views of human degeneracy blur moral cause and environmental effect. Goodman claims that nature "gives man an infinite desire, intimating that she hath an infinite treasure; but our desires are therefore infinite, because wee receive no contentment at all, and so still wanting, still we desire."[9] If nature's "treasures" were infinite, he implies, then scarcity, contention, and environmental degradation could forever be held at bay. But nature, Goodman complains, has no "infinite treasure" and falls into "a generall scarcitie and penury": "we seem to sustain a continuall famine, notwithstanding our peaceable times, and our great labors (necessity so enforcing us); and therefore we can blame none but nature, nor can we thinke that she is casually distempered . . . for we see no tokens, signes, or appearance of any recovery" (370). The degeneration that Goodman describes – more work for less output – is the default condition of universal history, a condemnation of nature's false promises that marks, in moralistic terms, his and his culture's recognition of the consequences of intensification: rising prices, deprivation, and diminishing marginal returns.[10] As the corruption of nature plays itself out in economic hardship, disease, and hunger, the vision of its "infinite" resources leaves humankind with frustrated desires that both gnaw inwardly as private vices and explode externally in violence, rebellion, and disorder.[11]

For defenders of a Judeo-Christian narrative of postlapsarian history, China poses unique problems because all European accounts agreed that the Middle Kingdom had escaped or overcome the disorder, scarcity, and inflation that were considered the irrevocable marks of corruption. Ancient pagan chronologies could be condemned because they were the products of vanished empires that, seventeenth-century historians maintained, had destroyed themselves. In the Preface to his *Cosmographie*, Peter Heylyn locates the "causes of that desolation which hath hapned in the Civill State of . . . mighty Empires" in "their crying sins[:] the pride of the *Babylonians*, the effeminacy of the *Persians*, the luxury of the *Greeks*: and such an aggregate of vices amongst the *Romans* (or western *Christians*) before the breaking in of the barbarous Nations, that they were grown a scandall unto *Christianity*."[12] In contrast to these empires, China has survived, absorbed would-be conquerors, and prospered for over four thousand years. The Jesuit Gabriel Magalhães, in his influential account of the Middle Kingdom, describes the missionaries' rhetorical tactics in avoiding a direct challenge to the beliefs of their Chinese hosts, but confesses, "it must be acknowledg'd that there is not any Kingdom in the World that can boast a Train of Kings so Ancient and so well continu'd. Those of the *Assyrians*, the *Persians*, the *Greeks*, and *Romans*, have had their Periods; whereas that of *China* continues still, like a great River that never ceases rolling along the streams that fall from its first fountain."[13] China has avoided the civilization-rending sins that Heylyn describes because it has escaped moral, political, economic, and ecological "desolation"; it defies the theocentric logic that structures both degenerative and redemptive narratives of European history.

China's prosperity was axiomatic in sixteenth and seventeenth-century Europe. Throughout Milton's lifetime, first and secondhand accounts of China appeared in Latin and more than a dozen vernaculars, all reiterating that readers could "compare [China] to a Precious Gem . . . in which more Riches are found than in the whole Earth besides."[14] Magalhães declares "that the two Fountains of Trade, are Navigation and Plenty, in a Kingdom stor'd with all sorts of Commodities. *China* enjoys both these Advantages to that degree that no Kingdom exceeds it" (133–34). Such descriptions could be multiplied a hundredfold. If a fallen nature in Europe frustrates the "infinite desires" of humankind, resulting in economic hardship and sociopolitical turmoil, China offers the prospect of "infinite" resources. In one of the standard geographies of the early seventeenth century, Pierre d'Avity asserts that "all things abound there in such sort, as besides the prouision of the *Chinois*, they haue wherewithall to furnish both their neighbours, and remote countries."[15] This natural wealth reinforces Jesuit assessments of the moral and sociopolitical virtues of Chinese civilization as well as its natural resources and native industry. The laments of Goodman and Heylyn seem irrelevant to a land blessed by such abundance.

If Milton has little problem condemning the "stale, and uselesse records" that bolster ecclesiastical and monarchical authority, his rejection of Jesuit accounts of China's history implicitly testifies to his awareness of the problems they pose. In a letter dated June 25, 1656, Milton responds to Henry Oldenburg's report of the anticipation surrounding the publication of Martino Martini's *Sinicae historiae* by dismissing the notion that this detailed history – which Martini wrote in China and saw through the press after his return to Europe – will offer any insight into providential history: "Those ancient annals of the Chinese from the Flood downwards which you say are promised by the Jesuit Martini are doubtless very eagerly expected because of their novelty; but I do not see what authority or confirmation they can add to the Mosaic books."[16] Milton rejects the

significance of China's "ancient annals" on theological grounds; by attributing the excitement about Martini's history to its "novelty," he sidesteps
the implications of Chinese antiquity that Jesuit commentators such as
Martini and Matteo Ricci (who Milton no doubt encountered in Purchas)
treat forthrightly.[17] If China has preserved a cultural and moral legacy since
the Flood, and if that legitimacy is reinforced by its economic prosperity,
then its "ancient annals" have the potential to supplement – or compro-
mise – the authority of the "Mosaic books." To avoid putting history to
this kind of question, Milton denies even the role of "confirmation" to
Sino-Jesuit historiography.

Milton's response to Oldenburg is suggestive in other ways as well; it
implies a skepticism about the political and theological motives which
underlie the missionaries' descriptions of Chinese antiquity and virtue. If
Jesuit histories of China sought to reconcile Christian doctrine and
Confucianism, other European writers extrapolated Ricci's accommodationist tendencies by projecting onto the Chinese sociopolitical system
idealized visions of their own assumptions and values.[18] In England,
China became an intellectual rallying point for supporters of the Stuarts
and a favorite topic for royalists seeking preferment: the translators of Jesuit
accounts and armchair historians of China were, to a man, ardent monar-
chists. Heylyn, as we have seen, was a committed defender of the established Church. John Webb, a prominent architect and royalist, dedicated
his treatise on China to Charles II, recommending the Middle Kingdom as
a model for England to emulate. Isaac Vossius spent the last years of his life
at Charles II's court, and John Ogilby, who translated five massive folios on
Asia between 1669 and 1673, was Master of the Revels for Ireland, and later
held a variety of court appointments.

In this context, Milton's brusque dismissal of "the Jesuit Martini"
underscores his rejection of the ideological lessons that his political antagonists were drawing from missionary accounts. As David Porter demonstrates, seventeenth-century descriptions of Chinese cultural and linguistic
authority adapted the vocabularies of property ownership and divine right
to a transcultural rhetoric of sociohistorical legitimation.[19] John Webb in
*An Historical Essay Endeavoring a Probability That the Language of the
Empire of China is the Primitive Language* idealizes Chinese culture as an
embodiment of royalist virtues, but his idealization also intervenes in
complicated debates about the biblical account of Genesis and Chinese
history. Following the arguments of, among others, Sir Walter Ralegh and
Heylyn, Webb argues that, after the Flood, Noah's Ark came to rest on the
border of what is now India rather than in Armenia. He then extends

Martini's conjecture that China was first inhabited by Noah's descendants by arguing that after settling India, Noah and some of his sons migrated to the east, to China, irrevocably separating themselves from those who went west to the plains of Shinaar and subsequently built the Tower of Babel. Therefore, he reasons, the descendants of Noah in China escaped the sin of pride and the punishment of the confusion of tongues at Babel, and retain the "primitive language" which Adam and Eve spoke in the Garden of Eden. Webb goes on to identify Noah with "Jaus" or "Yaus," the patriarch of Chinese culture. His *Historical Essay* is copiously annotated with marginal glosses to a wide variety of works: Renaissance studies of ancient history such as Ralegh's *History of the World*; Jesuit reports from China, including the historical and linguistic studies by Ricci and Martini; and speculative, armchair pronouncements on Chinese historiography by Isaac Vossius, and Athanasius Kircher.[20] This is euhemerism taken to a sinocentric extreme.

Webb's seemingly fanciful rewriting of ancient history to place Noah in China is less an argument about biblical geography (an important genre in seventeenth-century hermeneutics) than an attempt to project onto a still thriving empire the very ideals of moral and political legitimation and patrilineal descent. China preserves the pristine virtues of the world after it had been cleansed of evil by the Flood and consequently preserves the pristine morality that inheres, as Porter demonstrates, in the idealization of a "primitive language." Deliberately isolating itself from contact with other cultures, China resists their corruption and relies on its own wealth to maintain its moral and socioeconomic virtues. The "ancient annals" that Milton downplays become, in Webb's mind, the repositories of an uncorrupted theology and an unbroken history of legitimate succession. A Jesuit-inspired portrait of China becomes Webb's standard against which the claims of other countries to good government and morality must be measured:

if any Monarchy in the world was constituted according to political principles, and dictates of right reason, it may be boldly said that of the *Chinois* is. For therein every thing is found disposed in so great order; as that whereas all matters are under the rule and power of their *Literati*, or wisemen, so also hardly any thing is transacted throughout the whole Empire which depends not upon them; neither can any man attain to any degree of Honour, that is not very richly learned in their Letters and Sciences. In a word, their Kings may be said to be Philosophers, and their Philosophers, Kings; and they order every thing . . . in such manner, as may most conduce to good government, concord, peace, and quietness in families, and to the exercise of vertue[.][21]

China becomes, for Webb, a realm of royalist wish fulfillment, defined by its interlocking sociopolitical ideals: monarchical authority, patrilineal legitimacy, classical learning, and individual and familial honor. The Emperor exercises power through the efforts of an autocratic meritocracy, gentlemen-scholars selected through a rigorous examination system for their virtuous command of "Letters and Sciences." For Webb, frustrated in his desire to be appointed Surveyor of the Works, the prospect of a ruling elite selected by merit rather than the vagaries of patronage must have seemed a dramatic confirmation that China, unlike England, was ordered by the "dictates of right reason." In this system, personal honor manifests itself in a network of affiliations and loyalties to Emperor, class, and family. Webb manipulates his Jesuit sources to promote an idealized vision of a royalist order that provides both stability and an objective, depoliticized means to recognize and reward learned and virtuous individuals. In short, Webb locates Noachian principles of justice and temperance not in a pristine Christianity, as Milton does, but in an ethico-political system of timeless Confucian values.

If the example of China gives English royalists a means to reinforce their sociopolitical views, the empire's prosperity offers a more general hope that the age-old dream of an unfallen – and therefore infinitely exploitable – nature is not a lost ideal but an attainable and profitable reality. Extrapolating from Linschoten's account of twice-yearly harvests in parts of China and much of South and Southeast Asia, Ralegh projects onto the East the idealized traces of a lost paradise of universal abundance. Insisting that "Paradise was a terrestriall garden," Ralegh devotes a long discussion in his *History of the World* to locating Eden in a region south of Armenia where, even in its fallen state, the land retains vestiges of its originary fertility: "so great is the fertilitie of the ground," he asserts, "that the people are constrained twice to mow downe their cornfields, and a third time to eat them up with sheep."[22] If historical time is itself a consequence of the Fall, then Eden can be described only as a back formation – as the *negation* of a postlapsarian nature marked by economic competition and ecological devastation. The fertility of the land therefore allows readers to imagine the lost reality of Eden and confirms Ralegh's historico-theological narrative.

But for countless armchair geographers and their readers in the seventeenth century, glowing descriptions of China's fecundity raised the possibility that paradise has not been lost irrevocably but transplanted to the Far East. This displacement transforms the rhetoric of prophetic faith into the dialectically related discourses of fear and desire. The same accounts that idealize Chinese virtues and, by implication, castigate European vices also animate a faith that trade to China can bring the material benefits of such abundance to the markets of Europe. In celebrating the fertility of China, d'Avity borrows from his Jesuit sources to invoke a vision of paradise regained that is reminiscent of Ralegh's Eden: "the land doth beare fruit three or foure times a yeare, . . . [and] brings forth all manner of greene things, and great store of diuers fruit like vnto those that grow in Spaine, besides many others which are not knowne here, for that they differ from ours, and all these fruits (as they say) are exceeding good."[23] D'Avity refigures conceptions of the "terrestriall garden" of Renaissance myth by characterizing paradise in terms of consumption. The "great store of diuers fruits" provides an incentive not to lament humankind's Fall into sin and scarcity but to seek ways to gain access to those "exceeding good" products unknown to Europeans.

In descriptions such as d'Avity's, China threatens to transcend the theological and sociopolitical assumptions that govern the moral vision of *Paradise Lost* and countless other European texts. For Milton, the unequal distribution of resources is a consequence of ambition, greed, and luxury. Even after the expulsion from Eden, Michael tells Adam, "th' Earth shall bear/More than anough, that temperance may be tri'd" (XI 804–05). Temperance is the virtuous individual's response to corruption and scarcity. But in an empire in which "all the ground that . . . can yeeld any kinde of fruit receiuing seede, is husbanded," and "euery one enioyeth the fruits of his labour," the consumption of what would be luxury goods in Europe becomes a "natural" benefit of living in a fertile and prosperous country.[24] In this regard, the prospect of another Eden, a demi-paradise in the Far East, leads Webb to question which nation – strife-ridden England or serene and wealthy China – can best lay claim to being God's instrument for the temporal and spiritual salvation of humankind. For Milton, particularly after the Restoration, the example of a heathen empire seemingly impervious to the consequences of sin and corruption is best passed over quickly as an enigma that lies outside his vision of prophetic history. China, in fact, might be dispensed with entirely, were it not for his conviction, shared by most educated Europeans, that the path to economic salvation led almost invariably to the "destin'd Walls/Of *Cambalu*."

TRADE AND RIVALRY

For many English writers in the seventeenth century, trade to the Orient seemed preferable to colonization because it did not involve vast military or administrative expenditures. For officials in the East India Company, such as Thomas Mun, the troubled Portuguese seaborne empire was a negative example of the overly expensive and counter-productive use of force. The very limitations of English economic and military power in the Far East led many observers, well into the eighteenth century, to advocate peaceful trade as a viable strategy to compete with European rivals in some Asian markets and outflank them in others, thereby securing maximum profits while minimizing financial and military risks. Rather than a national identity predicated on heroic models of military prowess, self-discipline, and unquestioned obedience – the stock-in-trade of the epic tradition – the prospect of an English trading empire extending to "Cambalu" and Southeast Asia suggested alternative paths to greatness. Belief that England's future prosperity rested on the Asian trade cut across many of the political and religious divisions of mid-century England.

This kind of peaceful trade rather than the brutality of colonization offers Milton an attractive option to the violence of postlapsarian history, the "infinite/Man-slaughter" that becomes "the highest pitch/Of human Glory" in a fallen world (XI 692–4). From an early age, he seems to have been fascinated by the possibilities of trade to the Far East. As early as 1626, when he may have been writing *A Briefe History of Moscovia*, Milton confesses to a fascination with those authors, however tiresome, who "yet with some delight drew me after them, from the eastern Bounds of *Russia*, to the Walls of *Cathay*."[25] Although *Moscovia* simply redacts well-known narratives from Hakluyt and Purchas, it is significant because it suggests that Milton, like his contemporaries, treated Russia as merely a way station on the route to China. Purchas, for example, describes the "intent" of the first voyage of the Muscovy Company in 1553 (which Milton summarizes) as "the discouerie of *Cathay*, and diuers other Regions, Dominions, Ilands, and places vnknowne"(*Pilgrimmes*, III: 212), and Robert Parke, the translator of Gonzalez de Mendoza's *Historie of China*, adds that this attempt at "the discouerie of *Cathaia* and *China*" was motivated "partly of desire that the good young king [Edward VI] had to enlarge the Christian faith, and partlie to finde out some where in those regions ample vent of the cloth of England."[26] This desire was still motivating English ventures into the Pacific two centuries later. Although Milton devotes much of his time in *Moscovia* to retelling the stories of English efforts to open trade to Moscow, he excerpts from Purchas a long narrative of a Russian mission to China in 1618–19, concisely presenting what he considers essential information about that empire:

The People are Idolaters; the Country exceeding fruitfull ... Next to the [Great] Wall is the City *Shirokalga* ... [which] abounds with rich Merchandize, Velvets, Damasks, Cloth of Gold and Tissue, with many sorts of Sugars ... [In Beijing] The People are very fair, but not warlike, delighting most in rich Traffick. (VIII: 509–10)

This paradox – idolatry and prosperity – informs Milton's later accounts of the Far East. It is significant, even in this redaction, that Milton erases what we now would think of as racial distinctions between western Europeans and the inhabitants of China and emphasizes their wealth and desire for trade rather than their military prowess. The "rich Traffick" of Beijing provides an incentive for the young historian to encourage his countrymen to seek the "rich Merchandize" on which dreams of national prosperity are made. They also serve, it seems, who sail and trade.

Milton's *Moscovia* is characterized by its ideological shorthand: it pares down seventeenth-century geographies and travel narratives to promote a familiar ideology of trade: merchants are doing God's work and turning a substantial profit for themselves and their countrymen in the process. Its significance lies precisely in its commonplace articulation of the value of Asian commerce for Commonwealth England. In 1648, Samuel Hartlib noted in his daybook that "Milton is writing not only a Vniv. History of Engl., but also an Epitome of all Purcha's Volumes."[27] The key word in this intriguing notation is "all." Most of the narratives in Purchas's five folio volumes are edited reports from European missions devoted to exploring trade routes and seeking new markets in Asia, Africa, and the Americas; over half of these deal with China or the Far East, and Purchas includes all of the published accounts of the Jesuit missionaries.[28] Rereading Purchas in 1648, Milton would have found ample justification for seeing international trade as a means to unify and enrich England in the aftermath of the Civil War. Purchas, significantly, begins his *Pilgrimmes* with a theological defense of trade as the lifeblood of national prosperity and international harmony:

mutuall Necessitie [is] the Mother of mutuall Commerce ... the superfluitie of one Countrey, should supply the necessities of another, in exchange for such things, which are here also necessary, and there abound; that thus the whole World might bee as one Body of mankind, the Nations as so many members, the superabundance of in each, concocted, distributed, retained or expelled by merchandising ... where by not without mutuall gaine One may releeue others Wants. (I: 5)

Purchas's bodily metaphors evoke an integrated, holistic, and self-regulating system of international trade. His rhetoric of "superabundance" encodes a belief that trade can take place with "mutuall gaine," that all nations can profit by exchanging their "superfluitie[s]" with others for "necessities." Trading "Nations," at least in theory, are leveled to interdependent "members" so that international competition is displaced into an idealized image of mutual profit. Put simply, this redistribution of "superabundance" provides a theologically sanctioned means to overcome the material consequences of the Fall by pursuing wealth through an ever-enriching trade.

In practice, however, as I suggested in the previous chapter, international trade in Milton's lifetime provoked numerous wars, piracy, cutthroat competition, vast profits, and vast losses of men, ships, and capital. As Latin Secretary during the early 1650s, Milton was involved in the diplomatic maneuvering that preceded the First Dutch War; his correspondence for the Commonwealth reveals England's desire to recapture a share of the spice trade in Southeast Asia. In his official capacity, Milton twice raises the issue of reparations for the Dutch seizure of Amboyna in 1623 and the execution of English merchants on the island, denouncing "that cruel and bloody Business . . . for which no Satisfaction at all hath been given."[29] The stakes for the Commonwealth were immense; EIC officials, throughout the seventeenth century, claimed that "all other Foreign Trade in Europe, doth greatly depend upon *East-India* Commodities; and if we lose the Importation of them into *Europe*, we shall soon abate in all our other Foreign Trade and Navigation: and the Dutch will more then proportionably increase theirs."[30] Even though Cromwell, like Charles I before him, did little to aid the Company directly, the belief persisted that England's economic and military security depended on a healthy share of the re-export trade. In June 1652, Milton specified English demands for reparations from the Dutch for "our due part lost of the fruits in the *Molucca* Islands, *Banda* and *Amboyna*, from . . . the year 1622. to the present year 1650. for the yearly Revenue of 25000 *lib.* amounts in 28 years to 700000:00:00." Including English losses in the Indian Ocean, the total damages demanded by the English reach £1,681,816 and, he adds, "*The Interest from that time will far exceed the Principal.*"[31] These figures give some sense of the profits that the EIC hoped to realize from a "due part" of the trade in the Spice Islands, even as its calculations reduce agricultural and climatological uncertainties, political conflicts among states, and complex negotiation of prices in the region to the abstractions of supposedly predictable profits. In the diplomatic negotiations of 1652, these islands are not distinct nations, in the sense that Purchas describes, but tributary states, small and vulnerable harbingers of the eighteenth and nineteenth-century colonial future. The Dutch refused the English demands and in 1652–53 the two countries fought the first of three naval wars within a twenty-year period.[32]

English anxieties about the Dutch monopoly in the East Indies are reflected in a key passage in *Paradise Lost*, one often misread as an orientalist condemnation of the East rather than a thinly veiled indictment of a European archrival. In book two, Satan's "solitary flight" from Hell is described in an epic simile:

> As when far off at Sea a Fleet descri'd
> Hangs in the Clouds, by *Equinotical* Winds
> Close sailing from *Bengala*, or the Isles of
> Of *Ternate* and *Tidore*, whence Merchants bring
> Thir spicy Drugs: they on the Trading Flood
> Through the wide *Ethiopian* to the Cape
> Ply stemming nightly toward the Pole. So seem'd
> Far off the flying Fiend[.]
>
> (II, 636–43)

Balachandra Rajan is right to suggest that the "spicy Drugs" stand as "a synecdoche for the entire range of conspicuous consumption" that Milton condemns.[33] But even after the First Dutch War, the Dutch held a near monopoly on the spice trade from the East Indies; the "Merchants" bringing drugs from Ternate and Tidore, seventeenth-century readers would assume, are bound for the United Provinces. The fleet sailing westward across the Indian Ocean and around the Cape traces a course of both conspicuous consumption identified with the VOC's economic power and of frustrated English desires for a share of that trade. Satan, then, is identified in these lines not with the natives of two small islands (who had appealed to James I for protection from the monopolistic practices of the VOC) but with England's commercial rival, the rapacious and imperialistic enemy that had perpetrated "that cruel and bloody Business of *Amboyna*." The Dutch have perverted a godly commerce to corrupt and corrupting ends.

The paradox of his denigrating conspicuous consumption while protesting the Dutch monopoly of the spice trade, in an important sense, defines the ambiguities of Milton's response to trade to the East Indies. As his diplomatic correspondence suggests, national prosperity depends, to a great extent, on profiting from a lucrative international trade in what Purchas calls "superfluitie[s]." To follow the logic of Purchas's description of "mutuall Commerce" and "mutuall gaine" is to recognize that the luxury items of the Far East – peppers, cloves, nutmeg, porcelain, and tea – become "necessities" in Europe: spices as a means to preserve as well as to flavor meat, tea as a medicinal stimulant. "Superabundance" thus can be converted to surplus value, to capital, for investment in ships, infrastructure, and military garrisons *only* through international trade, only by fulfilling the "Wants" of other nations. Trade has an alchemical allure: it allows England to rid itself of its "superfluitie[s]" – the woolens that the Muscovy Company was hoping to peddle in 1553, for example – in exchange for another country's surplus goods. Once they reach England, however, these luxury items become "necessities" to fulfill "Wants" at home or, increasingly in the seventeenth century, the "Wants" embodied in the re-exportation markets of Europe and the American colonies. Surplus value is converted to use-value. An increase in trade, in Purchas's bodily metaphor, therefore does not lead necessarily to luxury and excess because, in theory, use-value becomes elastic: the more England exports, the more imports it can absorb (or re-export for more commodities) so that its "infinite desires" are always in the process of being excited and satisfied. But, in practice, as Milton suggests in *Paradise Lost*, the very means to promote national prosperity is through a trade in goods that foster "luxury and riot" (XI 715). The profits from international trade paradoxically allow England to increase its national wealth while condemning it to the vice and instability, the by-products of "luxury," that characterize a fallen world. If the exchange of "superfluitie[s]" promises national redemption and threatens that "all shall turn degenerate, all deprav'd" (XI 806), then Milton comes close to suggesting that the Anglo-Dutch rivalry on "the Trading Flood" becomes a zero-sum game in which one country can gain only from the other's losses.

In the seventeenth-century European imagination, however, China promises a "superabundance" of goods that transcends the grim logic of scarcity. Gaspar da Cruz describes China's trade in the sixteenth century in a manner guaranteed to entice readers of Purchas to imagine with "some delight" crossing "the destin'd Walls" of the Ming Empire: "that which the *Portugals* doe carrie," says Cruz, "and some that they of *Syam* doe carrie, is so little in comparison of the great trafficke of the Countrey, that it almost remayneth as nothing, and vnperceiued . . . [T]he great plentie and riches of the Countrey doth this, that it can sustayne it selfe alone" (III: 173). The self-sufficiency of China – its barriers to more than token trade with Europe – itself serves as an inducement to seek ways to open the Middle Kingdom to "mutuall Commerce."[34] Drawing on the journals of Matteo Ricci, d'Avity enumerates the Chinese goods that find their way to the Portuguese trading post at Macao:

The inhabitants draw out of diuers mines, great store of gold siluer, and other mettals. They carrie out of China, much pearle, porcelaine vessel, rich furres, flax, wooll, cotton, silke, and all sorts of stuffe, as also, much sugar, honie, wax, rhubarbe, camphire, vermillion, woad for Diers, and Muske, whereof they haue aboundance.[35]

This list of natural and manufactured goods testifies both to the richness of the country and the industriousness of its people. This vast wealth is invariably converted by European writers into cash equivalents: all of the major texts on China that appeared after Mendoza's 1585 history list the Emperor's tax revenues, usually broken down by province and by form of payment. In a land in which, as Magalhães says, "the great quantity of Gold which is found in all the Mountains is such, that instead of Coining it into Money, to buy Necessaries; it is it self a Commodity" (133–34), the Emperor's "reuenues," according to d'Avity, "doe amount to one hundred and twentie million [crowns] of gold yearely, which is so greate a summe, as that great and sparing Emperour *Vespasian* neuer gathered so much together in his whole life" (727). The Emperor's revenues from an adult male population of fifty-eight million (excluding Mandarins, government officials, and members of the extended royal household) dwarfed the taxes collected by European monarchs. Throughout seventeenth-century histories and geographies, such as Ogilby's translation of Olfert Dapper's *Atlas Chinensis*, English readers encountered imaginatively an empire richer, more populous, and larger than any in Europe. Yet China exists in an idealized and virtual space where fixed rents, unpaid debts, corrupt courts, and financially strapped monarchs give way to visions of infinite resources, infinite wealth, and infinite profits. For Milton, then, the "seat of Mightiest Empire" was overdetermined by a century of travel literature that depicted trade to China as a means to unending prosperity. To imagine the revolution of the saints was, in some measure, to dream that the "destin'd Walls" of this infinitely wealthy and fertile country were within the reach of virtuous and enterprising merchants.

JEWS AND JESUITS IN LATE MING CHINA

To write an "Epitome" is to leave out much of the original text, and Milton's familiarity with Purchas inevitably would have presented him with material that could be neither assimilated easily to his view of providential history nor simply ignored. In Purchas's abridgment of Ricci's narrative Milton and his contemporaries encountered an episode difficult to turn to the purpose of promoting England's overseas trade – the story of the Jews of Kaifeng being assimilated to Chinese civilization. Because this account epitomizes, in many respects, the anxieties of European marginalization in a sinocentric world, it is worth quoting at length:

A certaine *Iew* at *Pequin* hearing of the *Iesuites* there, came to see and conferre with them, imagining them to be *Iewes*. This *Iewe* was borne at *Chaifamfu*, the Mother-citie of the Prouince *Honan*, his name was *Ngai*, his countenance not resembling the *Chinois*; hee neglecting *Iudaisme*, had addicted himselfe to the *China* studies, and now came to *Pequin* to the examination, in hope of proceeding Doctor ... Seeing the *Hebrew* Bible, hee knew the Letters, but could not read them. He told them that in *Chaifamfu* were ten or twelue Families of *Israelites*, and a faire Synagogue, which had lately cost them ten thousand Crownes; therein the *Pentateuch* in Rolls, which had bin with great veneration preserued fiue or six hundred yeers. In *Hamcheu* the chiefe Citie of *Chequian*, hee affirmed, were many more Families with their Synagogue; many also in other places but without Synagogues, and by degrees wearing out ... His Brother, hee said, was skilfull in *Hebrew*; which he in affection to the *China* preferment had neglected; and therefore was hardly censured by the Ruler of the Synagogue.
   ... After this, three *Iewes* came from thence to *Pequin*, and were almost perswaded to become *Christians*. These complayned, that through ignorance of the *Hebrew*, their Religion decayed, and that they were likely all of them in a short time to become *Saracens* or *Ethnikes* [Confucians] ... And that their *Iewish* Religion was indeed languishing, appeared by this, that they both worshipped the Popish Images, and complayned that in their Synagogue and priuate houses they had none. (III: 399–401)

The fall of God's chosen people is, of course, a familiar topos in seventeenth-century theology. But the assimilation of "Ngai," the Chinese Jew Ai T'ien, and his compatriots is not troped as a descent into self-destructive sins.[36] Instead, Ricci's account and those of subsequent Jesuits who visited Kaifeng and examined the Chinese Torah describe a slow process of acculturation, a "languishing" of Judeo-Christian belief despite the fact that these colonies of Jews have maintained their way of life for centuries "with great veneration." The scrolls of the Old Testament remain intact, and the Jews are prosperous; but, at least according to Ricci, their faith languishes, and they are prone to worship "Popish Images" (a sentence interpolated by Purchas). This account of assimilation, of Ai T'ien's "addict[ion] to the *China* studies," can be read, in one respect, as a warning to Christians not to backslide from the true faith. In another, despite Purchas's efforts to belittle the Jesuits' policy of "conforming to *Confutius* Ethikes, and *China* Literature, Habite, Names and officious Rites" (III: 401), Ai T'ien's assimilation to a prosperous and virtuous culture marks a limit to the power of Judeo-Christian monotheism in China and to the metanarratives of Mosaic and redemptive history.

Like much of what Ricci and the Jesuits have to say about their contacts with the Chinese, the account of their meeting with a Jew from Kaifeng is characterized by misinterpretations. Ai T'ien had attained the prestigious literary licenciate's degree, *chü-jen*, in 1573 and possibly held the post of supervisor of schools and served as district magistrate. He had traveled to Beijing in search of a better job in the imperial civil service; intrigued by reports of Europeans living in the city, he assumed that the Jesuits were Jews and sought them out. Ai T'ien's brothers were rabbis, and the invitation that he extended to Ricci in 1605 to return to Kaifeng and serve as a rabbi needs to be contextualized: in 1489 at least seven men in the Kaifeng congregation were designated by the Hebrew letter *resh*, indicating that they were "rabbis," that is "'they were well versed in the Law, and encouraged others to do good."[37] Ai T'ien presumably may have been inviting Ricci to join a community of scholars rather than accept a mantle of spiritual authority. Rather than a dozen families forgetting their language and heritage, as Ricci and subsequent Jesuits portrayed them, the Jews of Kaifeng maintained aspects of their religious and cultural heritage while accommodating themselves to the laws, intellectual traditions, and sociopolitical conditions of late Ming and early Qing China. Although the Kaifeng synagogue was destroyed in a flood in 1642, and not rebuilt for twenty years, there seem to have been between 200 and 250 families in a community that survived until the early twentieth century. The survival of this community provides a dialectical model of cross-cultural engagement – a dynamic matrix of cultural assimilation and religious identity – of a sort that was alien to the religious and intellectual traditions of counter-reformation Europe. The Jesuits could describe the Jews they met only in generic narratives of a fall from the true faith.

Ricci's initial characterization of the Jewish community in China was seconded by the Jesuits Julius Aleni, who spent time in Kaifeng, and Alvarez Semedo; all three men convert a complex process of cultural interaction and assimilation into a straightforward tale of monotheists abandoning the faith of their fathers. Semedo declares that although "anciently there was greater store of [Jews in China], they have been diminished little by little, many of them turning *Moors*." The tiny community, as he characterizes it, that remains in Kaifeng is of interest primarily because its members "have no knowledge at all of *Christ*, so that it seemeth, they were entred into *China* before he came into the World; or at least, if they have ever heard of him, the memorie of it is quite lost: and therefore it would be of great consequence to see their *Bible*: for perhaps they have not corrupted it, as our Jews have done, to obscure the glorie of our *Redeemer*."[38] Rehashing the belief that the Jews of Europe had edited the Old Testament to erase unambiguous references to the coming of Christ, the Jesuits became eager, for a time, to read the Chinese Torahs in the hopes that they could re-establish an "authentic" text that would validate their beliefs and invalidate Protestant heresy. But Jews like Ai T'ien themselves posed problems which the Jesuits could not solve: while the synagogue in Kaifeng had been in existence for centuries, rumors of large colonies of Christians in China – rumors that the Jesuits tried for years to track down – proved unsubstantiated. Christianity, allegedly introduced to China by Saint Thomas, had failed to take root; Judaism, at least on a small scale, persisted.

More disturbingly, the experience of the Jews in China, as Erik Zürcher suggests, presents Jesuits and their readers with the possibility that Christianity is but "a marginal religion in its Chinese context," much like Judaism and Islam. Without exception, Christian converts in seventeenth-century China, at least those among the *literati*, "were convinced Confucianists, and remained so after their conversion." Christianity added "a new dimension" to their Confucianism.[39] The Jesuits, to a man, sought to straitjacket a complex and multifaceted set of Chinese intellectual traditions into single concepts that then could be assimilated to their own theology. Ai T'ien and other Chinese Jews were far less rigid in their thinking, more in tune with the social and ethical postulates of their homeland. On a stele outside the synagogue in Kaifeng, an inscription dated 1489 reads:

Confucianism and our doctrine may differ from each other, while being in agreement on the main points. As regards the way to establish the mind and to regulate the conduct they [both] amount to revering the Way of Heaven, honour-ing our ancestors, esteeming the relation between ruler and subject, being filial towards our parents, living in harmony with wife and children, observing the right distinctions between superiors and inferiors, and the right relations between friends.[40]

Accommodation, this inscription implies, is a strategy of retaining aspects of an ethnic or religious identity precisely by aligning one's behavior, and to some extent one's beliefs, with the principles of Confucian thought that emphasize morality, duty, stability, and filial and familial devotion. In this respect, Ai T'ien and his community have developed a conscious strategy, as larger Islamic communities had done, of maintaining a dual identifica-tion with state and religious institutions. His offer to Ricci to join the Kaifeng community, in this context, reveals less an ignorance born of centuries of isolation from the West than a sophisticated understanding of religious difference in late Ming China.

In important ways, the Jesuits' narrative of Jewish colonies in late sixteenth-century China resists typological interpretations that could be used to promote English designs to open trade to China. The image of the Jew turned Mandarin could be read as an inverted type of the upright individual who is essential to redemptive history. In books eleven and twelve of *Paradise Lost*, as numerous critics have noted, Noah serves as the archetype of the "one just Man" who heeds God's word and rejects a world of "triumph and luxurious wealth" (XI 818, 788).[41] Milton's self-identification with this "only Son of light/In a dark Age" (XI 808–09) allows the poet to distance himself from a sinful world; to a great extent, his sense of redemptive history depends crucially on the individual's aloofness from systemic corruption. One of the important lessons that Adam learns from Michael is that there is no secular analytic that can be developed, no moral course that can be charted, within history to overcome "pleasure, ease, and sloth/Surfeit, and lust" (XI 794–95). The only bulwark against such inevitable corruption is faith. If, as Amorose suggests, the "true object of prophetic history-writing is to move mankind beyond history," then the typological image of "one just Man" encodes a radically Protestant belief in a future revelation that lies outside of historical time.[42]

In Purchas's redaction of Ricci, however, the image of the Chinese philosopher-civil servant emerges as a competing figure of the just and temperate man. In contrast to Noah as the archetype of the Miltonic iconoclast, the Mandarin attains his position by dedicating himself to a systemic morality and hierarchical sociopolitical order. He masters a classical corpus of knowledge, preserving and legitimating a millennia-old tradition by rote examination rather than by individualistic interpretation. Unmarked by the characteristic vices of worldly dissolution, he practices temperance and justice from within an economy of abundance. In this regard, Webb's appropriation of Noah as the patriarch of China removes Milton's "one just Man" from the context of Mosaic history and locates in his example of righteousness the origin of the philosophy to which Ai T'ien, thousands of years later, is "addicted." Following Ralegh, Webb generalizes what he considers a fundamental principle of civilization: "from the East came the first knowledge of all things, and that the East parts of the world were the first civilized, having *Noah* himself for an Instructer, whereby the farther East to this day, the more Civil, the farther West the more Savage" (21). In its antiquity and prosperity, China redefines the basis of virtue and salvation; it incorporates each "just Man" into the elite fraternity of the "*Literati.*"[43]

THE POLITICS OF ACCOMMODATIONISM: CHINESE VIEWS

Paradoxically, Milton (like Defoe sixty years later) must dismiss the threat that China poses to his view of providential history in and through the literature of Jesuit accommodationism. Like others in England, he reads the Jesuits' self-characterization of their mission as an effort to assimilate Confucianism to Christianity, ironically: the Catholic missionaries surrender the essentials of their faith to appease idolaters. Yet this spectacle produces a complex double response: smug superiority at the folly of the Jesuits and a nervous fascination with the prospect of western Christians going native. In this sense, Milton intuitively recognizes the risk embodied by both the Jews of Kaifeng and their missionary chroniclers: accommodation cuts both ways. The assimilation of the Jesuits raises two disturbing possibilities: either that Webb and the royalists are right and China represents a virtue to which England only can pretend, or that the Middle Kingdom embodies the ultimate temptation of postlapsarian history, that its "destined Walls" beckon only to assimilate God-fearing Protestants to lives of luxury, sin, and the surrender of individualistic faith to systemic secularism. Like Purchas, Milton apparently reads Jesuit accounts against themselves, finding in the missionaries' strategic decisions to adopt Chinese dress and manners a relinquishing of all pretenses to be anything but idolaters.

In one sense, such Protestant skepticism is encoded in the ambiguities that Ricci, Martini, and others encountered in China. While Jesuits assert that they control their intellectual commerce with the Chinese, their defenses of accommodationism betray an underlying anxiety about the risks of their own assimilation and the tenuousness of their own position. Writing in 1668, Magalhães acknowledges that their wealth, historiographic tradition, and "other Excellencies ... infuse into the *Chinese* a Pride most Insupportable. They put the highest value imaginable upon their Empire and all that belongs to them; but as for strangers, they Scorn 'em to the lowest pitch of Contempt."[44] Confronted by such invincible convictions, the Jesuits worked hard to assure potential converts that Christianity was not an alien doctrine but dovetailed with many of their own beliefs. In justifying his approach in his Chinese text *Tienzhu shiyi* [*The True Meaning of the Master of Heaven*], a handbook of sorts for recent converts, Ricci states that "rather than attack" Confucian philosophy, he tries "to turn it in such a way that it is in accordance with the idea of God, so that we appear not so much to be following Chinese ideas as interpreting Chinese authors in such a way as they follow our ideas."[45] Yet even in justifying his efforts to simplify the complexities of intercultural exchange, he acknowledges the limitations of his methods. As early as 1595, Ricci admitted that his "fame" rested on a host of extra-theological factors: his prodigious feats of memory, his collection of clocks and prisms, his ability to read and write Chinese, his mathematical skills, and his reputation as an alchemist. This "indivisible amalgamation of science, technology, philosophy, and ethics," as Jacques Gernet calls it, took precedence over Christian theology; Ricci wrote that the Chinese "who come" to hear him preach or be taught the rudiments of Christianity "are the least numerous" of his visitors.[46] Much later in the seventeenth century, Magalhães expressed his frustration with the Chinese lack of interest in western theology:

I have many times observ'd, that when I have been discoursing with the Learned concerning the Christian Religion, and the Sciences of *Europe*, they ask'd me whether we had their Books? To which when I answer'd No, they reply'd altogether surpris'd, wavering and scandaliz'd, If in *Europe* you have not our Books and our Writings, what Learning or what Sciences can you have? . . . it is impossible to imagine the high Idea which not only the great Lords and Learned Men, but also the Vulgar People have conceiv'd of this Empire.[47]

For Magalhães, the only explanation for this self-absorption is the sin of pride. Yet his acknowledgment that the Chinese are incredulous about the lack of "their Books" in Europe testifies to the difficulties that hampered the Jesuits in "discoursing with the Learned." The comparatively few Chinese *literati* who converted to Christianity offer a very different perspective on the Jesuits' efforts than the accounts published in Europe. Ironically, Chinese descriptions of what they understood Christianity to mean confirm the suspicions of English Protestants like Purchas, Milton, and Defoe: Christianity was being assimilated to indigenous traditions.

The Chinese perceived the Jesuits and other Christian missionaries within the established tenets of Chinese philosophy. What limited success the Jesuits had seems to have been derived from their ability to ally themselves with an established Chinese intellectual and ethical tradition against the perceived threats posed by Buddhist theology. Xu Zhijiang in his *Tianxue Chuangai* [*A General View of the Transmission of the Doctrine of Heaven*] (1663) declared that the doctrine taught by the Jesuits "was in no way different from Confucianism," and elaborated its fundamental tenets: "the doctrine of the Master of Heaven consists in serving Heaven, overcoming one's egoistical inclinations, loving mankind, repenting of one's errors and proceeding in the path of goodness."[48] Under questioning from suspicious magistrates in 1637, a convert from Fujian concisely summarized a popular defense of the Jesuits: "In China since Confucius, it has no longer been possible to imitate Confucius. By coming to China, [the doctrine of the Master of Heaven] teaches men to act rightly and this causes each person to imitate Confucius."[49] In assembling a number of similar statements that suggest a conflation of Jesus and Confucius, Gernet demonstrates convincingly that the Chinese understood Christianity not in eschatological, spiritual, or even metaphysical terms but within the context of a traditionalist value system of ethical duty, service, moderation, and self-discipline. Ricci and the Jesuits do not introduce a new doctrine of salvation but preach what their "converts" perceive as a return to the originary values of Chinese cultural and national identity. The missionaries become the agents for a cultural nostalgia during the years before and after the Ming-Qing cataclysm.[50]

Although in 1610 the Jesuits claimed that they had made 2,500 converts in China, by Ricci's death in 1615 Christianity already was starting to meet growing hostility among the *literati*. According to Gernet, there were no conversions after 1620 "among important men of letters or high-ranking administrators."[51] The noted philologist Zhang Erqi (1612–78) praised the missionaries for helping to combat Buddhism, but derided their "comments on the Master of Heaven" as "altogether inadequate as a true idea of Heaven," and claimed that they even outdo the Buddhists in "extravagance and nonsense" when they discuss "paradise and hell."[52] Even more sympathetic commentators find the very basis of Christian doctrine – eternal salvation for the faithful – an absurdity. In his *Xifang Yaoji* [*Essential Ideas about the Countries of the West*] (1697), Zhang Chao, who collaborated on translating texts with several missionaries, including Magalhães, praises the Jesuits for their knowledge of "astronomy, the calendar, medicine, and mathematics" and their "loyalty, good faith, constancy, and integrity," yet concedes "that it is a pity that they speak of a Master of Heaven, an incorrect and distasteful term which leads them into nonsense." If only the missionaries could "leave [that idea] alone and not talk about it, they would be very close to ... Confucianism."[53] Such comments call into question the very nature of what the Jesuits mean by "conversion."

Ricci's efforts to use Christian iconography and paintings to impress potential converts led to the widespread belief among the Chinese that the Virgin Mary was a representation of the Judeo-Christian God; he had little success in explaining the significance of the crucified Christ to Chinese friends who found the image distasteful, even apparently sadistic.[54] Consequently, the doctrine he preached was shorn of some of the fundamental precepts of Christian belief – the resurrection, the Trinity – and he had to explain what was left of Catholic theology in a borrowed "neo-Confucian or Buddhist vocabulary, which evokes concepts quite incompatible with those of eternal salvation and redemption."[55] The Jews of Kaifeng used *Dao* – "nature's mode of action" – to translate the Old Testament "God," and rendered Jahweh as *shangdi*, "Sovereign on High" rather than *tianzhu*, "Master of Heaven," as the Jesuits did. The assimilated Jews understood far better than the Jesuits the nuances of meaning and the significance that would be attached to the analogies on which the theory and practice of accommodation rested. The Jesuits in China, Lionel Jensen argues, were a "self-constituting intellectual community": even as they translated Chinese texts into the idiom of western monotheism, they were translating themselves into the complex cultural semiotics of Ming China, "a form of sinification, of becoming Chinese" that depended on "a meticulous cultural imitation" of the literati.[56]

Ricci and his fellow Jesuits apparently had little trouble, by their own accounts, in separating their religious zeal from their cultural assimilation into the daily life of Ming China. But this very separation suggests a misunderstanding of the conditions of their assimilation, of the ways in which they were perceived by their hosts. In Nanjing and after 1601 in Beijing, Ricci was a guest at "an endless succession of dinner parties, often three or more a day," engaging in theological discussion between courses and exhausting himself with social obligations.[57] In his mind, social acceptance by the Chinese was a means to an end, and, like all over-eager newcomers trying to fit in, he and his fellow Jesuits interpreted the complex semiotics of social and intellectual prestige accorded the *ru* in the familiar terms of their own order. As Jensen observes, *ru* signifies in multiple ways to designate both individuals (examination candidates, scholar-officials, members of private academies, local intellectual groups, some members of the gentry) and various aspects of what were perceived to be essential characteristics of Chinese civilization (civility, traditional values and ethics, the practices and preservation of legitimacy, and orthodox interpretations of foundational customs, rites, and principles).[58] In 1584, shortly after he arrived in China, Ricci adopted the dress and shaved head of a Buddhist monk, unaware of the sociocultural stigma that most educated Chinese attached to the semiotics of the Buddhist faith. A decade later, he described his appearance to a friend in Macao: "We have let our beards grow and our hair down to our ears; at the same time we have adopted the special dress that the literati wear on their social visits ... which is of purple silk, and the hem of the robe and the collar and the edges are bordered with a band of blue silk a little less than a palm wide; the same decoration is on the edges of the sleeves which hang open [and] a wide sash of the purple silk trimmed in blue . . . is fastened around the same robe."[59] Ricci's attention to the details of his silk robes suggest that he is already assimilating the cultural values of the men he wants to convert. His assumption that hairstyles, clothes, and sedan chairs are mere trappings that make the real work of conversion easier is, at the very least, naive. For Protestant readers in England, such mummery was perceived as a capitulation to another form of near-papist idolatry. Purchas summed up many of his coreligionists' attitude toward the Jesuit practices of accom-modation by claiming that they appealed only to Chinese "Couetousness and Curiosity," and he accused the missionaries of trying to convey the gospel by means of "merchandise, money, & gifts, Mathematicks, [and] Memoratiue-art." The Jesuits engaged in a perverse parody of godly commerce, "a mutuall exchange in many things, of *Romish* for *Chinois* Beades, Shauing, Vests, Songs, Mumsimus, Tapers, Censers, Images, Legends, Monkes, Nunnes, Processions, Pilgrimages, Monasteries, Altars, hee and shee Saints, and other things innumerable pertayning rather to *bodily exercise which profiteth little*, then to *Godlinesse*" (III: 401). In an important sense, the spectacle of Jesuits in mandarin robes marks their assimilation by a culture with little regard for the monologic metaphysics of the Master of Heaven.

Like other European encounters in China in the seventeenth century, the Jesuits' experiences of acculturation were mediated through the irreducibly complex networks defined by technologies, material objects, linguistic traditions, and social behaviors. These interactions never can be reduced to the triumphalist narratives of Eurocentric modernity that assume rather than demonstrate the superiority of the Europeans and their assorted gadgets; instead the Jesuits' encounters suggest a willful misreading of the significance of their decisions to ape the dress, hairstyles, and manners of the local elites. In his historical account of the fall of the Ming dynasty, Martini provides both a narrative of events as the Jesuits pieced them together and an invaluable record of his own experiences; his description offers sharp contrasts to the armchair history of the 1640s in China by Juan de Palafox y Mendoza, who had never been to the country.[60] Martini recounts at length his fashion makeover from Chinese mandarin to Manchu retainer:

I dwelt in a very fair house of the City *Venxus*, the whole Town then being in a tumult by reason of the feare and flight of most of the Citizens. As soone as I understood of the approach of the *Tartars*, I fixed over the fairest gate of the house, a red paper very long and broad, with this Inscription upon it. *Here dwells the European Doctor of the Divine Law.* For I had observed the *China* Governours when they take any journy to affixe such Inscriptions upon the houses where they happen to lodge, that all men may take notice what great persons are there. Likewise at the entrance of the greater Hall, I set out my greatest and fairest-bound books: to these I added my Mathematicall Instruments, prospectives, and other optick glasses, and what else I thought might make the greatest show; and withall I placed the picture of our Saviour upon an altar erected for that purpose. By which fortunate stratagem I not only escaped the violence and plunder of the common Souldier, but was invited, and kindly entertained by the *Tartarian* Vice-Roy: Who demanded of me whether I would with a good will change my *China* habit, and cut off my hair. To which I readily consented; and so he commanded me to be shaven there in his presence; and I telling him, that a shaven head would not so well suite with a *China*-Garment, he pluk't off his own boots, and made me draw them on, put his *Tartar* bonnet on my head, seated me at his Table, and accommodating me with his Passe, dismissed me to my ancient quarters in the noble City *Hancheu*, where we had a stately Church and Colledge[.][61]

To survive the arrival of the Manchu invaders, Martini relies on both Chinese customs (the banner over the door) and his scientific instruments, books, and other items to which he attaches almost totemic significance. But the Viceroy apparently takes less notice of the artifacts of the Christian religion or western technoscience than he does of the missionary's Chinese clothes and hair. To preserve both his person and ultimately his mission, the Jesuit "readily" agrees with "good will" to cut his hair, change his clothes, put on Manchu boots, and wear a "*Tartar* bonnet." While Martini is glad to transform his appearance in order to continue proselytizing under the new Qing regime, his eagerness to conform to Manchu codes of dress signals, to the Viceroy, his *political* allegiance to the new rulers of China. Despite the apparent gestures of friendship that Martini attributes to the Viceroy, he does not emphasize the price of his acquiescence, nor does he trouble himself with the uncertainties that his display of religious icons might occasion. Does the altar that Martini has built to display a picture of Christ impress the Manchus as a representation of God the Son or is it read within the context of Chinese and Manchu ancestor worship? We can guess how Purchas would answer this question. For Milton and his contemporaries, committed politically and theologically to the Commonwealth's emphasis on plain and modest dress, the spectacle of Jesuits in silk means that the missionaries have conceded the game by assimilating themselves to a new regime of heathens.

AN ATLAS "LARGER AND MORE CORRECT"

Several months after he wrote to Oldenburg dismissing the efforts of "the Jesuit Martini," Milton asked Peter Heimbach, then in Amsterdam, to find "the lowest price" available for a new atlas. Heimbach's response gave the bargain-hunting Milton pause:

You write that they ask 130 florins: it must be the Mauritanian mountain Atlas, I think, and not a book, that you tell me is to be bought at so huge a price. Such is now the luxury of Typographers in printing books that furnishing a library seems to have become as costly as furnishing a villa. Since to me at least, because of my blindness, painted maps can hardly be of use, vainly surveying as I do with blind eyes the actual globe of the earth, I am afraid that the bigger the price at which I should buy the atlas the greater would seem my grief over my deprivation. Be good enough to take so much farther trouble as to be able to inform me, when you return, how many volumes there are in the complete work, and which of the two issues, that of the Blaeu or that of Jansen, is the larger and more correct.[62]

Conventional wisdom has it that Milton, throughout his life, exhibited a disinterested, even apolitical love of maps and geography. Cawley, for example, notes several coincidences in spelling between Milton's poem and Heylyn's *Cosmographie* to argue that, despite their political differences, Heylyn was the poet's "favorite geographer."[63] If the idea of Milton's patronizing an arch-royalist and unrepentant Laudian propagandist seems unlikely, then the fact that Heylyn's work was published with only four maps, one each for Europe, Asia, Africa, and the Americas, makes Cawley's assertion that the blind poet consulted the *Cosmographie* to refresh his memory while writing *Paradise Lost* improbable. Milton's request to Heimbach is specific: find out which atlas is "larger and more correct." The atlases of Blaeu and Jansen were multivolume works of staggering complexity and expense. Blaeu's *Atlas Maior* ran to twelve volumes and was finally complete in 1663; it was the most expensive book published in the seventeenth century.[64] One of its crucial selling points was that it included, as volume eleven, Martini's *Atlas Siensis* (Amsterdam, 1655), the result of the missionary's years traveling through China, on the Emperor's orders, to update traditional Chinese maps.[65] Although Milton jokes ruefully about the price (approximately £80), he still seems to want the best atlas that money can buy.

In his famous nineteenth sonnet on his blindness, Milton concludes that "God doth not need/Either man's work or his own gifts" because "Thousands at his bidding speed/And post o'er land and ocean without rest."[66] These thousands cannot be identified solely with an infinite host of angels conveying God's word; they do not fly through the air or soar to the heavens, but "post" over land and sea. In fact, this seemingly personal sonnet is shot through with images of trade and communication that were essential to international commerce. In describing his "soul more bent/To serve therewith my maker, and present/My true account," Milton aligns his writing metaphorically with the practices of bookkeeping, and the thousands doing God's bidding easily can be imagined as merchants engaged in a divinely sanctioned commerce. The goal of those thousands was the kind of wealth that, since the sixteenth century, had been identified with China.

"Vainly surveying the actual globe of the earth," Milton's concerns in mid-career seem as much economic as geographic. In 1656, the English were still shut out of the lucrative trade to the Spice Islands, and remained spectators while the Dutch, Portuguese, and Russians sent embassies to Beijing to seek to open China to large-scale foreign trade. Detailed and accurate maps and up-to-date descriptions of Asian nations, such as those offered in Martini's *Atlas Siensis*, outstrip what Milton could learn from the encyclopedic compilations of d'Avity and Heylyn. Dutch maps were particularly prized in England, artifacts that testified to the Netherlands' abiding commitment to prosperity through an international trade that sought to control the flow of spices to European markets. If Milton's letter to Heimbach suggests something of the poet's lifelong curiosity about the exotic East, it also indicates his determination to pursue useful knowledge even after the onset of his blindness. Characteristically, however, Milton's comments about why he wants a top-drawer atlas are sparing. But to reread his references to the Far East in the context of his inquiries to Heimbach is to recognize that the implications of China's "ancient annals" and wealthy idolaters reverberate throughout Milton's work. As we will see in the next two chapters, in the late seventeenth century "the destin'd Walls/Of *Cambalu*" mark the limits of what Europe could imagine about its past, its cultural and religious significance, and its economic prospects for the future.

NOTES

1. John Milton, *Paradise Lost*, ed. Merritt Y. Hughes (New York: Odyssey Press, 1962). All quotations are from this edition.
2. See, for example, Robert Ralston Cawley, *Milton and the Literature of Travel* (Princeton: Princeton University Press, 1951). John Michael Archer follows Cawley (incorrectly in my view) in claiming that Heylyn was Milton's favorite geographer; see Archer, *Old Worlds: Egypt, Southwest Asia, India, and Russia in Early Modern English Writing* (Stanford: Stanford University Press, 2001), 77, 88.
3. On the popularity of accounts of China in the seventeenth century, see Lach, *Asia in the Making of Europe*, I: 730–821; Jonathan D. Spence, *The Chan's Great*

Continent: China in Western Minds (New York: Norton, 1998), 19–80; and Julia Ching and Willard Oxtoby, eds., *Discovering China: European Interpretations in the Enlightenment* (Rochester, NY: University of Rochester Press, 1992).

4. On the "sinification" of the Manchu elites, see Robert Oxnam, *Ruling from Horseback: Manchu Politics in the Oboi Regency 1661–1669* (Chicago: University of Chicago Press, 1975); Lawrence Kessler, *K'ang-Hsi and the Consolidation of Ch'ing Rule 1661–1684* (Chicago: University of Chicago Press, 1976); Frederic Wakeman, Jr., *The Great Enterprise: The Manchu Reconstruction of Order in Seventeenth-Century China*, 2 vols. (Berkeley and Los Angeles: University of California Press, 1985); and Timothy Brook, *The Confusions of Pleasure: A History of Ming China (1368–1644)* (Berkeley and Los Angeles: University of California Press, 1998).

5. See Gerard Vossius, *De Theologia Gentili et Physiologia Christiana* (1641; rpt. New York: Garland, 1976); Isaac Vossius, *Dissertatio de vera aetate mundi* (The Hague, 1659); Sir Walter Ralegh, *The History of the World* (London, 1614); Matthew Hale, *The Primitive Origination of Mankind, Considered and Examined According to the Light of Nature* (London, 1677); Henry Isaacson, *Saturni Ephemerides* (London, 1633); Georg Horn, *Arcae Noae sive historia imperiorum et regnorum a condito orbe ad nostra temporum* (Leiden, 1666); John Webb, *An Historical Essay Endeavoring a Probability that the Language of the Empire of China is the Primitive Language* (London, 1669); Francis Tallents, *A View of Universal History* (London, 1695); and Jean LeClerc, *Compendium Historiae Universalis: A Compendium of Universal History from the Beginning of the World to the Reign of Charles the Great* (London, 1699). On Newton see Kenneth Knoespel, "Newton in the School of Time: The *Chronology of Ancient Kingdoms Amended* and the Crisis of Seventeenth-Century Historiography," *The Eighteenth Century: Theory and Interpretation* 30 (1989), 19–41.

6. Ralegh, *History of the World*, A2r. On universal history, see Arnaldo Momigliano, *On Pagans, Jews, and Christians* (Middletown, CT: Wesleyan University Press, 1987), 11–57; Arthur B. Ferguson, *Utter Antiquity: Perceptions of Prehistory in Renaissance England* (Durham: Duke University Press, 1993); Paolo Rossi, *The Dark Abyss of Time: The History of the Earth and the History of Nations from Hooke to Vico*, trans. Lydia G. Cochrane (Chicago: University of Chicago Press, 1984); Donald Wilcox, *The Measure of Times Past: Pre-Newtonian Chronologies and the Rhetoric of Relative Time* (Chicago: University of Chicago Press, 1987); Kenneth Knoespel, "Milton and the Hermeneutics of Time: Seventeenth-Century Histories and the Science of History," *Studies in the Literary Imagination* 22 (1989), 17–35; and David Katz, "Isaac Vossius and the English Biblical Critics, 1670–1689," in Richard H. Popkin and Arjo Vanderjagt, eds., *Scepticism and Irreligion in the Seventeenth and Eighteenth Centuries* (Leiden: Brill, 1993), 142–84.

7. *Complete Prose Works of John Milton*, ed. Don M. Wolfe, 8 vols. (New Haven: Yale University Press, 1953–82), I: 624.

8. On Milton's historical vision see David Loewenstein, *Milton and the Drama of History: Historical Vision, Iconoclasm, and the Literary Imagination* (Cambridge: Cambridge University Press, 1990); Thomas Amorose, "Milton the Apocalyptic Historian: Competing Genres in *Paradise Lost*, Books XI–XII," *Milton Studies* 17, ed. Richard S. Ide and Joseph Wittreich (Pittsburgh: University of Pittsburgh Press, 1983), 141–62; Knoespel, "Milton and the Hermeneutics of Time," 17–35; Achsah Guibbory, *The Map of Time: Seventeenth-Century English Literature and Ideas of Pattern in History* (Urbana: University of Illinois Press, 1986), 169–211; Marshall Grossman, *"Authors to Themselves": Milton and the Revelation of History* (Cambridge: Cambridge University Press, 1987); Gary D. Hamilton, "The *History of Britain* and its Restoration Audience," in *Politics, Poetics, and Hermeneutics in Milton's Prose*, ed. David Loewenstein and James Grantham Turner (Cambridge: Cambridge University Press, 1990), 241–55; Jeffrey S. Shoulson, *Milton and the Rabbis: Hebraism, Hellenism, and Christianity* (New York: Columbia University Press, 2001), 189–95, 200–02; and Archer, *Old Worlds: Egypt, Southwest Asia, India, and Russia in Early Modern English Writing*, 63–99.

9. Godfrey Goodman, *The Fall of Man, or the Corruption of Nature* (London, 1616), 369.

10. On universal histories as efforts to contend with crises of intensification, see Markley, "Newton, Corruption, and the Tradition of Universal History," 121–43. See also Harris, *Cannibals and Kings*, and Goldstone, *Revolution and Rebellion*.

11. Blair Worden, "Politics and Providence in Cromwellian England," *Past and Present* 109 (1985), 55–99; Laura Lunger Knoppers, *Historicizing Milton: Spectacle, Power, and Poetry in Restoration England* (Athens: University of Georgia Press, 1994); Michael Lieb, *Milton and the Culture of Violence* (Ithaca: Cornell University Press, 1994); David Norbrook, *Writing the English Republic: Poetry, Rhetoric, and Politics, 1627–1660* (Cambridge: Cambridge University Press, 1999); David Loewenstein, *Representing Revolution in Milton and His Contemporaries: Religion, Politics, and Polemics in Radical Puritanism* (Cambridge: Cambridge University Press, 2001); John Coffey, "Pacifist, Quietist, or Patient Militant? John Milton and the Restoration," *Milton Studies* 42 (2002), 149–74; and Sharon Achinstein, *Literature and Dissent in Milton's England* (Cambridge: Cambridge University Press, 2003).

12. Peter Heylyn, *Cosmographie* 2nd edn (London, 1657), B1r.

13. Gabriel Magaillans [Magalhães], *A New History of China* (London, 1688), 60–61. On Magalhães, see Donald Lach with Edwin van Kley, *Asia in the Making of Europe*, vol. III: *A Century of Advance* (Chicago: University of Chicago Press, 1993), 362, 424. Lach and van Kley call his account "perhaps the most comprehensive and perceptive general description of China published during the second half of the century" (242). Originally composed in Portuguese in 1668 and brought to Europe by Philippe Couplet, Procurator of the Jesuit Missions in China, it was translated into French (1688; reissued 1689, 1690) and English by John Ogilby, whose name does not appear on the

title page. See also David E. Mungello, *Curious Land: Jesuit Accommodation and the Origins of Sinology* (Stuttgart: Steyler Verlag, 1985), 90–105.

14. [Olfert Dapper], *Atlas Chinensis*, trans. John Ogilby (London, 1671), 465. Ogilby misattributes Dapper's work to Arnoldus Montanus.

15. d'Avity, *The Estates, Empires, & Principalities of the World*, 727.

16. *Works of John Milton*, ed. Frank Allen Patterson, *et al.* (New York: Columbia University Press, 1931–38), vol. XII, ed. Donald Lemen Clark, 79.

17. See Edwin J. van Kley, "Europe's 'Discovery' of China and the Writing of World History," *American Historical Review* 76 (1971), 358–85, and Rossi, *Dark Abyss of Time*, 141–67. On the influence of Chinese thought in seventeenth-century Europe see Yuen-Ting Lai, "Religious Scepticism and China," in *The Sceptical Mode in Modern Philosophy: Essays in Honor of Richard H. Popkin*, ed. Richard A. Watson and James E. Force (Dordrecht: Martinus Nijhoff, 1988), 11–41, and, for the complex semiotics of European representations, and mis-representations, of Chinese traditions, see Lionel Jensen, *Manufacturing Confucianism: Chinese Traditions and Universal Civilization* (Durham: Duke University Press, 1997).

18. On Jesuit accommodationism, see Mungello, *Curious Land: Jesuit Accommodation and the Origins of Sinology*; Bernard Hung-Kay Luk, "A Serious Matter of Life and Death: Learned Conversations at Foochow in 1627," in Charles E. Ronan S. J. and Bonnie B. C. Oh, eds., *East Meets West: The Jesuits in China, 1582–1773* (Chicago: Loyola University Press, 1988), 173–206; Yu Liu, "The Jesuits and the Anti-Jesuits: The Two Different Connections of Leibniz with China," *The Eighteenth Century: Theory and Interpretation* 43 (2002), 161–74; and Franklin Perkins, *Leibniz and China: A Commerce of Light* (Cambridge: Cambridge University Press, 2004). Jensen, *Manufacturing Confucianism*, 77–133, offers an important analysis of the ways in which Jesuits adapted, promulgated, and altered heterogeneous collections of texts and practices to produce a westernized redaction, "Confucianism."

19. David Porter, *Ideographia: The Chinese Cipher in Early Modern Europe* (Stanford: Stanford University Press, 2001).

20. Rachel Ramsey, "China and the Ideal of Order in John Webb's *An Historical Essay*," *Journal of the History of Ideas* 62, 3 (2001), 483–503; Mungello, *Curious Land*, 127. On Vossius, see Katz, "Isaac Vossius and the English Biblical Critics 1670–1689," 142–84. See Athanasius Kircher, *China Illustrata* (Amsterdam, 1667). Martini had been a pupil of Kircher's before leaving Rome in 1643 for his first trip to China.

21. Webb, *An Historical Essay Endeavoring a Probability That the Language of the Empire of China is the Primitive Language*, 92–93.

22. Ralegh, *History of the World*, 56.

23. D'Avity, *Estates, Empires, & Principalities of the World*, 719.

24. Gaspar da Cruz, *A Treatise of China*, abridged in Purchas, *Pilgrimmes*, III: 175. All quotations from Purchas are from this edition.

25. *Complete Prose Works*, vol VIII., ed. Maurice Kelley (New Haven: Yale University Press, 1982), 475. On the dating of *Moscovia*, see D. S. Proudfoot

and D. Deslandres, "Samuel Purchas and the Date of Milton's *Moscovia*," *Philological Quarterly* 64 (1985), 260–65. Those who date *Moscovia* to the late 1640s include William Riley Parker, *Milton: A Biography*, 2 vols. (Oxford: Clarendon, 1968), I: 325–26; Nicholas von Maltzahn, *Milton's History of Britain: Republican Historiography in the English Revolution* (Oxford: Clarendon Press, 1991), 28–31; and Barbara Lewalski, *The Life of John Milton: A Critical Biography* (Oxford: Blackwell, 2000), 212. See also John B. Gleason, "The Nature of Milton's *Moscovia*," *Studies in Philology* 61 (1964), 640–49.

26. Gonzalez de Mendoza, *The Historie of the Great and Mightie Kingdome of China*, trans. R. Parke (London, 1588), A2r.

27. Cited in George Henry Turnbull, *Hartlib, Drury, and Comenius: Gleanings from Hartlib's Papers* (Liverpool: University Press of Liverpool, 1947), 40–41.

28. See David Armitage, *The Ideological Origins of the British Empire* (Cambridge: Cambridge University Press, 2000), 65–95.

29. *A Declaration of the Parliament of the Commonwealth of England, Relating to the Affairs and Proceedings between this Commonwealth and the States General of the United Provinces of the Low-Countries, and the present Differences occasioned on the States part*, in *Works of Milton*, ed. Patterson *et al.*, XVIII: 13.

30. Sir Josiah Child, *A Treatise Wherein is Demonstrated . . . that the East-India Trade is the Most National of All Trades* (London, 1681), 26.

31. *A Summary of the particular real damages sustain'd by the English Company, in many Places of the East-Indies, from the Dutch Company in Holland* [June 1652], *Works of Milton*, ed. Patterson *et al.*, XIII: 133–35.

32. On the First Anglo-Dutch War, see Charles Wilson, *Profit and Power: A Study of England and the Dutch Wars* (London: Longmans, 1957), 25–47; and Jonathan I. Israel, *Dutch Primacy in World Trade, 1585–1740* (Oxford: Clarendon, 1989), 174–76; 209–13. On Amboyna see the notes in chapter four below.

33. Rajan, *Under Western Eyes*, 53–4. See also Pompa Banerjee, "Milton's India and *Paradise Lost*," *Milton Studies* 37 (1999), 142–65.

34. On the difficulties of trading to Qing China see John E. Wills, Jr., *Pepper, Guns, and Parleys: The Dutch East India Company and China, 1662–1681* (Cambridge, MA: Harvard University Press, 1974), and Wills, *Embassies and Illusions: Dutch and Portuguese Envoys to K'ang-hsi, 1667–1687* (Cambridge, MA: Harvard University Press, 1984).

35. See d'Avity, *Estates, Empires, & Principalities of the World*, 728, for an inventory, taken from Ricci, of the tax payments made to the Emperor at the turn of the seventeenth century. See Purchas, *Pilgrimes*, III: 370–411, for an abridgment of Ricci's journals.

36. On Ricci and Ai T'ien, see Michael Pollak, *Mandarins, Jews, and Missionaries: The Jewish Experience in the Chinese Empire* (1980; rpt. New York and Tokyo: Weatherhill, 1998), 1–12. Ai T'ien's genealogy is discussed in D. D. Leslie, "The Chinese–Hebrew Memorial Book of the Jewish Community of K'aifeng," part three, *Abr-Nahrain* 6 (1965–66), 1–52. See also Chen Yuan, "A Study of the Israelite Religion in Kaifeng," in Sidney Shapiro, ed. and trans., *Jews in Old*

China: Studies by Chinese Scholars, ed. and trans. Sidney Shapiro, rev. edn (New York: Hippocrene Books, 2001), 15–45, and, in the same volume, Yin Gang, "The Jews of Kaifeng: Their Origins, Routes, and Assimilation," 217–38. Manasseh ben Israel, the noted Amsterdam rabbi, invoked accounts of the Jews in Kaifeng to bolster his campaign to get Cromwell and Parliament to allow Jews officially back into England. His 1650 work, *Spes Israel*, was translated into English by Moses Wall, "at the instigation, it is said, of John Milton" (Pollak, *Mandarins, Jews, and Missionaries*, 43).

37. Quoted in Leslie, "Chinese–Hebrew Memorial Book of the Jewish Community of K'aifeng," 45.

38. Alvarez Semedo, *The History of that Great and Renowned Monarchy of China* (London, 1655). On Semedo, see Mungello, *Curious Land*, 74–90.

39. Erik Zürcher, "Jesuit Accommodation and the Chinese Cultural Imperative," in D. E. Mungello, ed., *The Chinese Rites Controversy: Its History and Meaning* (Nettetal: Steyler Verlag, 1994), 31–64.

40. Quoted in Zürcher, "Jesuit Accommodation and the Chinese Cultural Imperative," 33.

41. See Mary Ann Radzinowicz, "'Man as a Probationer of Immortality': *Paradise Lost* XI–XII," in *Approaches to Paradise Lost: The York Tercentenary Lectures*, ed. C. A. Patrides (London: Edward Arnold, 1968), 31–51; Michael Cavanagh, "A Meeting of Epic and History: Books XI and XII of *Paradise Lost*," *ELH* 38 (1971), 206–22; Michael Wilding, *Dragon's Teeth: Literature in the English Revolution* (Oxford: Clarendon, 1987), 243–48; William Walker, "Typology and *Paradise Lost*, Books XI and XII," *Milton Studies* 25, ed. James D. Simmonds (Pittsburgh: University of Pittsburgh Press, 1989), 245–64; and Claude N. Stulting, Jr., "'New Heav'ns, New Earth': Apocalypse and the Loss of Sacramentality in the Postlapsarian Books of *Paradise Lost*," in *Milton and the Ends of Time*, ed. Juliet Cummins (Cambridge: Cambridge University Press, 2003), 184–201.

42. Amorose, "Milton the Apocalyptic Historian," 145.

43. See Lin Jinshui, "Chinese Literati and the Rites Controversy," trans. Hua Xu and ed. D. E. Mungello, in Mungello, *The Chinese Rites Controversy: Its History and Meaning*, 65–82.

44. Magalhães, *New History*, 61.

45. Cited in Jacques Gernet, *China and the Christian Impact: A Conflict of Cultures*, trans. Janet Lloyd (Cambridge: Cambridge University Press, 1985), 27.

46. Quoted and translated in Gernet, *China and the Christian Impact*, 18.

47. Magalhães, *New History*, 63–4.

48. Quoted and translated in Gernet, *China and the Christian Impact*, 36.

49. Ibid.

50. See Ray Huang, *1587, A Year of No Significance: The Ming Dynasty in Decline* (New Haven: Yale University Press, 1981), and the accounts translated in Lynn Struve, ed., *Voices from the Ming-Qing Cataclysm: China in Tigers' Jaws* (New Haven: Yale University Press, 1993).

51. Quoted in Gernet, *China and the Christian Impact*, 43.

52. Quoted in Gernet, *China and the Christian Impact*, 39. On Zhang Erqi, see Arthur W. Hummel, ed., *Eminent Chinese of the Ch'ing Period (1644–1912)*, 2 vols. (Washington, D.C.: Government Printing Office, 1943), 34–35.

53. Quoted in Gernet, *China and the Christian Impact*, 39–40.

54. Jonathan Spence, *The Memory Palace of Matteo Ricci* (New York: Penguin, 1984), 245–47.

55. Gernet, *China and the Christian Impact*, 48.

56. Jensen, *Manufacturing Confucianism*, 35, 40, 41.

57. Spence, *Memory Palace of Matteo Ricci*, 160.

58. Jensen, *Manufacturing Confucianism*, 52–53.

59. Quoted in Spence, *Memory Palace of Matteo Ricci*, 115. See also the excellent discussion in Jensen, *Manufacturing Confucianism*, 39–48.

60. Juan de Palafox y Mendoza, *The History of the Conquest of China by the Tartars* (London, 1671).

61. Martinus Martini, *De Bello Tartarico Historia* (Amsterdam, 1655), translated and incorporated in Semedo, *History*, 255–308. The quotation is on 284.

62. Letter to Heimbach, November 8, 1656, in *Works*, ed. Patterson *et al.*, XII: 83, 85. I have modified the translation from the Latin text on 82 and 84.

63. Cawley, *Milton and the Literature of Travel*, 13, 22–23.

64. On Blaeu, see Cornelius Koeman, *Joan Blaeu and His Grand Atlas* (Amsterdam: Theatarum Orbis Terrarum, 1970).

65. See Theodore N. Foss, "A Western Interpretation of China: Jesuit Cartography," in Ronan and Oh, eds., *East Meets West*, 209–51, and Walter Mignolo, *The Darker Side of the Renaissance: Literacy, Territoriality, and Colonization* (Ann Arbor: University of Michigan Press, 1995), 219–26.

66. *The Complete Poetical Works of John Milton*, ed. Harris Francis Fletcher (New York: Houghton Mifflin, 1941), 134.

CHAPTER 3

"Prudently present your regular tribute": civility, ceremony, and European rivalry in Qing China

CIVILITY AND CIVILIZATION IN CHINA

"Civility" is a term that has little purchase in the critical vocabulary of early modern studies, yet it is almost ubiquitous in seventeenth and eighteenth-century discussions of social and personal identity. As a marker for the accomplishments of upper-class self-presentation and self-definition, "civility" encompasses a range of attributes and behaviors that contribute to the development, however vexed and contradictory, of modern notions of identity.[1] Much of the recent scholarship on the interlocking structures of thought, belief, emotion, sensation, and perception that fall under the rubric of "sensibility" and "character" in the long eighteenth century has focused on the development of gendered and class-based notions of the experiential self in literary, medical, and philosophical texts produced in western Europe and North America.[2] If these texts are often self-consciously introspective, they are also culturally as well as psychologically insular. Ironically, many postcolonial critics tend to reproduce aspects of this insularity by assuming that when the peoples of the rest of the world appear in the fiction, drama, and non-fiction of the early modern era, they serve merely as stage props for one-sided portrayals of European colonization and conquest. Admittedly, in many such works, the native peoples of the Americas typically are depicted as either noble savages, whose virtues parody those of their European oppressors (Oroonoko, particularly in Southerne's play), or pathetic victims of the white man's betrayal (Yarico jilted and sold into slavery by her lover, Inkle).[3] Those critics who, quite rightly, emphasize the silencing of the victims of European imperialism, though, ignore the vast literature on China available to early modern readers – a body of work that challenges, in the twenty-first century as well as the seventeenth and eighteenth, Eurocentric narratives of Enlightenment or modernity that ignore whatever texts they cannot easily assimilate.[4] Paradoxically, even critics intent on demystifying ideologies of class, gender, and race that identify the victims of colonialism with "feminine" powerlessness often leave undisturbed our Eurocentric fascination with literary representations of the internalized costs (moral self-questioning) and benefits (self-congratulation on our sensitivity to suffering) of our domination.[5]

In the previous chapter, I suggested that in the late sixteenth and early seventeenth centuries, China functions as the locus for dreams of attaining a golden age of prosperity and abundance. I now want to flesh out the depiction of European–Asian relations in the 1650s and after by exploring the ways in which concepts of civility emerge as crucial means to mediate – and to mystify – differences of language, race, and nationality in texts written by European emissaries who trekked to Beijing in efforts to open trade with the first Qing Emperor. This undertaking, for twenty-first-century critics as well as readers in the 1600s, poses a crucial set of challenges to Eurocentric conceptions of culture, personal and national identity, and both progressivist and providentialist history. The accounts of China that I examine in this chapter provide a means to explore the ideological power of civility because their authors, Jan Nieuhoff and Evret Ysbrants Ides, were attached to trade missions authorized to negotiate with an empire at once alien and civilized, non-Christian yet undeniably richer than the powers of Europe. Civility is the semiotics that Nieuhoff and Ides use to override linguistic, religious, and cultural differences, to convince themselves that a mutual understanding of economic, social, and military interests exists between European merchants and Chinese and Manchu authorities. The complicated semiotics of civility include class and gender-inflected practices, values, and assumptions that forge imagined communities of sympathetic interest across the divides of religion, language, skin and hair color, fashion, cuisine, architecture, and musical and artistic styles. Civility is performative: it becomes the means to promulgate the fiction (to themselves, their employers, and their readers in Europe) that like-minded gentlemen, of whatever background, will see eye-to-eye on the fundamental values that underlie the economics of class and gender privilege.

In Nieuhoff's and Ides's accounts, civility takes the form of manners, dress, comportment, courtesy, hospitality, domestic order, and imputed honor that the Europeans regard as crucial demonstrations of transcultural "understanding" – an understanding that mediates religious differences or, in the case of Jesuit accommodationists like Matteo Ricci, allows for a willful misreading of the nature and extent of such differences.[6] In this regard, the differences between China and the West that the European writers note do not reflect what they perceive as their innate cultural or racial superiority to the Chinese but variations of an "essential" cultural identity based on shared codes of upper-class interest and desire. The members of the Manchu and Chinese upper-classes who greet, entertain, guide, and scheme against the Europeans resemble the writers themselves; they both mirror the desires of Europeans for trade, profit, and political alliances and – precisely because they are granted an interiority of civilized self-interest – frustrate and even compete with those desires. The China that emerges in Nieuhoff's and Ides's accounts, then, exists as the idealized projection of complex social codes that embody, with subtle differences, European self-perceptions, desires, and anxieties. In different ways, both writers champion a transcultural identity of upper-class honor and civility by suppressing both the differences between European and Chinese cultures and the dialogic instability of the values that define gentlemanly trust.

EUROPEAN PERCEPTIONS OF CHINA

Nieuhoff's description of China draws on, exploits, and often mimics a rich tradition of Jesuit writing. As David Mungello, Lionel Jensen, and David Porter have demonstrated, Jesuit efforts to convert the Chinese were part of a complex process of cultural exchange from which both Christian missionaries and Chinese and Manchu *literati* drew their own interpretations. To promote Christianity, as we have seen in chapter two, the Jesuits downplayed the differences between Catholicism and Confucianism, idealizing those precepts that exalted the principles of social order and stability and, in the process, forged a coherent, hybrid account, "Confucianism," out of heterogeneous teachings and practices that they observed in China.[7] Matteo Ricci and Martino Martini, as we have seen, employed these accommodationist strategies to encourage wealthy and educated Chinese to accept the sacrament, even as they adopted the dress, hairstyles, and culinary habits of their hosts.[8] Within Catholic Europe, accommodationism was a risky strategy. The Jesuits were accused by their Franciscan and Dominican rivals of sanctioning idolatry under the cover of accepting Confucianism as a monotheistic analogue of Christianity; these accusations led to the Rites Controversy that ultimately required the intervention of the Pope to sort through which Chinese practices could be tolerated by Christian missionaries and which could not.[9] If the Rites Controversy increased the popularity of all sorts accounts of China among European readers, it also emphasized the secular and cultural components of these missionary treatises.

The accommodationist principles of Jesuit cultural anthropology both inform and were extended later in the seventeenth century by emissaries from the VOC and the Czar who sought to find common ground with Manchu and Chinese elites to promote their efforts to regularize trade. The accounts of these missions, Nieuhoff's *An Embassy from the East-India Company of the United Provinces, to the Grand Tartar Cham Emperour of China, Delivered by their Excellencies Peter De Goyer, and Jacobs De Keyzer, At his Imperial City of China* (London, 1669; translation of the Dutch edition of 1665) and Ides's *Three Years Travels from Moscow Over-Land to China* (London, 1706; translation of the Dutch edition of 1704), borrow liberally from Martini, in particular, and voice (often in derivative language) enthusiastic descriptions of China, its resources, and its people that have their ultimate source in Ricci's journals.[10] Paradoxically, these secular traders are freer than their missionary counterparts to disparage "pagan" temples and "heathen" practices because they do not have to worry about trying to reason their converts into Christianity; but such criticism seems almost formulaic. It is not until Defoe's *Farther Adventures* in 1719 (the subject of chapter five) that Chinese economic structures, religion, culture, technology, and politics are castigated for being vastly inferior to their European counterparts. The Europeans' overwhelming desire to secure trade with China demands that they not only accommodate their behavior to Chinese and Manchu customs but resign themselves to the ceremonial performance of tributary rituals, literally kowtowing to the Emperor. This form of symbolic submission is described by both writers in great detail but understood poorly. Animated by the hope of securing trading privileges with Beijing, Nieuhoff and Ides present their audiences with the Emperor as indications of mutual respect rather than as ceremonies that establish symbolically the tributary status of their governments to the Qing Empire.[11]

The desire to gain access to the seemingly infinite wealth of China was stoked by the diffusion of Jesuit descriptions that implicitly and explicitly suggested that China, even after the Manchu conquest, could serve as a model of rectitude and prosperity for a Europe beset by religious wars and dynastic conflicts. This idealization of an orderly Empire administered by philosopher-scholars becomes a means for writers to gloss over the complicated and bloody history of the end of the Ming dynasty so that dreams of mass conversions and infinitely profitable trade can persist in the face of a complex and recalcitrant reality.[12] At a time when England has fallen into chaos, China represents an idealized conception of how a complex society can function without succumbing to the sins which have destroyed other empires.[13] The Chinese are characterized, says Peter Heylyn, by "their natural industry, and their proficiencie in *Manufactures* and *Mechanick Arts*," and the country itself is "very rich and fertile, insomuch that in many places they have two, and in some three harvests a year: well cultivated, and sowed with all manner of grain, and planted with the best kind of fruit; which do not only come to a speedy maturity, but to more excellencie and perfection than any of these Western parts." China receives from a benevolent Nature blessings denied other nations since the golden age. Because China enjoys the "abundance of all things necessary to life" it can feed its incredibly large population of two hundred million.[14] For Heylyn, the "abundance" of the country is a measure of both the opportunities it offers Europeans for trade and the sociopolitical stability that underwrites its claims to cultural and morality authority. This idealization rests on the enabling fictions of political economy that prompted European embassies to Beijing in the seventeenth and eighteenth centuries: the notion that humankind, through trade, can achieve a kind of exponential growth in prosperity, repairing the damage done by sin and transcending the ecological constraints of a fallen nature.

Such economic idealizations override the recent history of the empire. For the most part ignoring the fall of the Ming, John Webb reiterates century-old truisms that link the empire's prosperity to the fertility of the land:

> The Kingdom of *China* alone, we may see so adorned with innumerable, and those most flourishing Cities, that if we should say, it were one entire Province, we should hardly say amiss. It is so furnished with frequent Towns, Castles, Villages, and places dedicated to their superstition; that if that wall of three hundred leagues in length, memorable in all Ages, were extended from Sea to Sea, all throughout how great, how large soever, might not undeservedly be said to be one City, in which is found such infinite plenty of whatever is necessary for the life of mankind; as that, that which the wise industry of Nature hath here and there amongst other kingdoms of the World dispersed, may all be summarily seen to be contained within this one only.[15]

China is so wealthy that it apparently has little motivation for the kind of international trade on which the Europeans pin their dreams of wealth. Webb's account of its historical origins informs his praise of China and allows him to generalize his anti-Miltonic principle of the history of civilization: "from the East came the first knowledge of all things, and that the East parts of the world were the first civilized, having *Noah* himself for an Instructer, whereby the farther East to this day, the more Civil, the farther West the more Savage."[16] For Webb, civility becomes the expression of internalized moral principles, of a moral and ethical psychology that preserves the "first knowledge" of Noachian rectitude. He downplays the distinction that

Jesuit accommodationists sought to defend against their critics in Europe: Confucianism described the secular values of an ordered and enlightened culture, and Christianity the revealed word of God that provided the ultimate theological authority for individual and social morality. In its place, Webb champions as a model for European monarchies to emulate.[17]

Significantly, for other writers besides Webb, China's "infinite plenty" is seen as the basis for an ordered society which has found ways to overcome conflicts brought about by competition for scarce resources. China's status as an exemplary civilization, its image as a model of moral and cultural continuity – even after the Manchu conquest – at a time when much of Europe, and particularly England, was in turmoil, depends on its seemingly infinite resources. The equation made by Sir Walter Ralegh, Godfrey Goodman, and other writers, between sin and scarcity is inverted: China's material wealth underwrites and is underwritten by its moral and sociopolitical order.[18] This wealth, for European readers, was mind boggling. In the second edition of Nieuhoff's account, which included narratives of subsequent embassies, the Dutch editor, Olfert Dapper, describes, as Ricci had done fifty years earlier, China's vast wealth:

Great Revenues are sent yearly to the Emperor out of the fifteen Provinces; for none in the whole Realm possesseth one Foot of Land without paying Tribute: Nay, they say, that besides the common Charges bestow'd on the *Mandarins*, Governors and Soldiers, the Emperor hath sixty Millions of *Ducats* brought yearly into his Treasury: The whole Sum of his Revenue is reckon'd to a hundred and fifty Millions of Crowns.[19]

At a time when England's revenues and expenditures were less than 10 percent of China's, such figures redefine standards of wealth. Imperial revenues (Dapper's figures, borrowed from Ricci, date from the last years of the Ming dynasty) are broken down by province and commodity so that European readers get a precise sense of the size of the empire's economy:

All the fifteen Provinces, produce Annually 32207447 Bags of Rice for Tribute, every one containing as much as would plentifully feed a hundred Men a whole day; 409949 of Raw Silk, 712436 Rowls of Hempen Cloth, 630770 Bales of Cotton, 191730 Rowls of Silk-Stuffs, 1794261 Weys of Salt, every Wey containing a hundred twenty four Pound, together 187688364. 2418627 Bundles of Hay and Straw for the Emperor's Horses. Some reckon that the yearly Revenue amounts to 50000000.[20]

Most twenty-first century readers no doubt find the absence of commas within these strings of numbers disconcerting; 50,000,000 is much easier to understand at a glance than "50000000." Imagine, then, how much

stranger and more enticing numerical representations would appear to
English or Dutch readers in the 1600s. At a time when Charles I was
signing a secret treaty with France to prop up his impecunious royal
household, Dapper describes the last years of the Ming dynasty – an era
during which the Emperor could no longer afford to defend his northern
and western borders – in figures that beggar the European imagination:
"The last *Chinese* Emperor call'd *Soungchung*, hath from the Year 1623. till
1640. receiv'd yearly the following Revenues, *viz.* 4756800 *Tail* of Gold;
one *Tail* of Gold is ten of Silver; in Silver, 3652120 *Tail*; in Pearls, the value
of 2926000 *Tail*; in Precious Stones, the value of 1090000 *Tail*; in Musk
and Ambergreece, to the value of 1215000 *Tail*" in addition to the revenues
in produce from his own lands.[21] This list of figures comes near the end of
three large folio pages which are little more than an accounting of expected
revenues, the representation for European readers of figures derived from
imperial memoranda. The overkill that these numbers represent describes a
kind of socioeconomic sublime – wealth that strains or exceeds the very
bounds of representation. In this respect, these numbers are not objective
representations of exact quantities, an oriental version of Thomas Mun's
calculations, but semiotic indicators that shade from, and mediate
between, the promise of precise quantification and the infinite desires
that such extravagant figures provoke.[22]

For Heylyn, Dappert, and their contemporaries, the prospect of commerce with the Middle Kingdom holds out the possibility that regularizing
trade relations will allow Europeans to exploit the inexhaustible wealth
of China and thereby to recover the sociopolitical stability that such riches
make possible. Paradoxically, however, this idealization calls into question
the values and assumptions that sustain the Eurocentric fiction of
a mutually beneficial trade. If China is as prosperous as these writers
contend, what motivations can its rulers have to allow Europeans large-
scale access to its fantastic wealth? The efforts of the Dutch and Russian
embassies to address this question reveal deep fissures within seventeenth-
century ideologies of trade, fissures that transcultural conceptions of civility attempt to bridge.

NIEUHOFF'S EMBASSY AND THE POLITICS OF CIVILITY

In 1655–56, Jan Nieuhoff accompanied two ambassadors from the Dutch
East India Company who sought an audience with the Shun-chih Emperor
to negotiate "*a Free and Mutual Commerce*" with China.[23] This embassy,
from the start, had its work cut out for it. The Dutch had raided the Fukien

coast between 1622 and 1624, and had been frustrated by the Portuguese at Macao from extending their trading base on Taiwan to the mainland. A mission to open trade in 1652 in Canton with the Feudatory Princes Shang K'o-hsi and Keng chi-mao met with some initial encouragement, but, in the following year, officials in Beijing refused to allow the Dutch to land.[24] Despite these frustrations, the Dutch, after their failure two years earlier, understood enough about politics in the Forbidden City to recognize that they had to assume the role of a tributary nation in order to open trade negotiations, even as they promoted themselves as a potentially rich trading partner and a powerful ally of the Emperor against the Ming pretender, Cheng Ch'eng-kung (English: "Coxinga"), who raided Dutch and Chinese shipping in the waters around Taiwan, and eventually invaded the island in 1661–62. Accordingly, they carried with them to Beijing "for the great *Cham*" various "Presents," including "several rich piece Goods, as Cloth, Kersies, and other Woollen Manufactures, of Fine Linnen, of Mace, Cinamon, Cloves, Nutmegs, Corral, little Trunks of Wax, Perspective Glasses, Looking Glasses, great and small Swords, Guns, Feathers, Armour, and several other Wares" (25). This catalogue of seemingly miscellaneous items discloses what the Dutch considered appropriate gifts for the Qing Emperor and Court officials.[25] It can be subdivided into three categories: textiles produced in the Low Countries, spices from the VOC-dominated Moluccas, and artifacts of European manufacture intended for elite consumption. The odd intrusion of "Feathers" into this list of European military hardware is revealing because it helps to contextualize the swords, guns, telescopes, and armor sent to China. These weapons are not examples of superior western technology but showpieces intended either for display or as symbolic tributes to the Qing military prowess in conquering most of China.[26] The Dutch expect their gifts to mediate a diplomatic and commercial relationship among equals. For lesser officials, gifts of "fine Linnen" and other clothing seems intended to demonstrate the potential value of European goods; silks and spices advertise the usefulness of Dutch ships, with their vast cargo capacities, as a cost-effective means of transport in the country trade between China and Southeast Asia. In brief, these gifts "for the great Cham" encode the merchants' perceptions of the values that inform and the desires that motivate the new Qing dynasty.

The Dutch embassy had to contend, however, with the efforts of the Portuguese in Macao and the Jesuits in Beijing to undermine the de Goyer and de Keyzer mission. Earlier in the seventeenth century, the Dutch had forced the Portuguese out of the Spice Islands, raided the South China coast, and, in 1622, launched an assault against the Portuguese stronghold of Macao. In 1615, Catholic missionaries had been expelled from Japan or driven underground, and in 1638, after thousands of Japanese Christians had been tortured, executed, or forced to recant, the Dutch aided the Shogun in putting down a peasant rebellion that included Christian converts.[27] The lucrative trade between Macao and Japan was severed, and the Dutch became the only European nation to retain (very limited) trading privileges with Japan. By the middle of the seventeenth century, Portuguese trade in the Far East depended on Macao: spices and cloth from India and European bullion were marketed in Canton in exchange for Chinese luxury goods, particularly porcelain, silk, and tea, that brought high prices in Goa, the middle east, western Europe, and even Brazil. Because the entrepôt at Macao relied on the sufferance of the Chinese and later Manchu authorities in Canton, the Dutch embassies in the 1650s represented a grave threat to Portuguese economic and missionary interests.

The first Dutch mission to the Qing Court in 1653–54, led by Frederik Schedel, had been resisted by the Portuguese, and foundered when the Dutch were unable to present the necessary credentials; they carried letters from the Governor of Batavia in present-day Indonesia, not from the Stadholder in the Netherlands, and were unprepared for the Manchu authorities' insistence on the protocols demanded of tributary embassies. Nieuhoff, nonetheless, is unambiguous in blaming the machinations of the Jesuits for this mission's failure:

The Governour and Council in *Maccoa*, to stifle in its birth the progress of this negotiation did endeavour not only to corrupt *Haitonu* ["a Mandarin Admiral"] with Presents and contrary Arguments, but they sent likewise a considerable Embassy to *Canton* ... to acquaint the Governour that [the Dutch] were of a cunning nature, deceitful in all things, and without any Country or Habitation of their own; and that they got their livings by Stealth and Piracy: That they had a number of Ships and Guns, had made themselves very considerable at Sea, and were now only endeavouring to get sure Footing in *China*, that so by that means they might enrich themselves ... they had made a Peace with the Pyrat *Coxinga*, and for that reason were to be looked upon no otherwise then as Enemies to the *Tartar* Crown. (22)

By ventriloquizing the Portuguese and Jesuits' standard accusations, Nieuhoff sets the stage for his account of the difficulties that dogged the de Goyer and de Keyzer mission. Following Schedel's failure, the Dutch had to counter claims that they were pirates, convince the Manchu and Chinese authorities that they had goods worth trading, and establish a relationship of mutual trust with officials in Canton and Beijing. Paradoxically, however, they had to rely, to some extent, on the Jesuits at

Court as mediators, even as they tried to circumvent the missionaries' influence, particularly that of John Adam Schall von Bell, the most influential of the Jesuits. For their part, the Jesuits, in concert with Portuguese authorities in Macao, sought from the start to frustrate Dutch efforts to establish trade with the new dynasty. The complex politics of religious conflict in Europe were played out in the audience chambers and teahouses of imperial Beijing.

Nieuhoff begins his account by promising "to make a more exact discovery of the *Genius* and Manners of the People, and Customs of [China,] supposed by all Geographers to be the richest in the World, and where any Stranger formerly durst never attempt" (3). Throughout his narrative, Nieuhoff strives for an almost mathematical accuracy in his detailing of census figures and taxes, although his description of the country itself, interpolated in his history of the embassy, draws heavily on previous Jesuit writers. Nieuhoff reiterates the truism that China is an empire that "exceed[s] all other parts of the world for the number of most rare Edifices and Rich Cities, so they are likewise no less abounding in People; for the most populous Country of all *Europe* stands not in competition with this" (8). To establish the accuracy of his account, Nieuhoff details precise figures for the population – 58,940,284, adult males, according to the official tax census, which excludes scholars, large landholders, and court officials – gross and net revenues of the Crown, and annual taxes, figured in bags of rice, bales of hay, and so on (8).[28] These figures validate the Dutch view that China's wealth is, to all intents and purposes, inexhaustible. England's population in the 1650s, by comparison, was under six million.

If the opulence of the country fascinates the Dutch envoys and whets their desire to establish a profitable trade, its natural resources make it seem a storehouse of plenty. Nieuhoff contends that China is capable of feeding its population and satisfying the Europeans' infinite desire for all sorts of goods and products:

this may be affirmed for truth in general, that all things necessary for the sustenance of Man, as well as for delight, are to be had [in China] in great abundance, without being beholden to their Neighbours. And thus much I dare from my own knowledge affirm, that whatsoever is to be had in *Europe*, is likewise found in *China*; and if in truth there want any thing, Nature hath supply'd that single defect with divers other things beyond those we have in Europe. (244)

This passage has analogues in Martini and Alvarez Semedo, both of whom, in turn, may be echoing Trigault's edition of Ricci's journals.[29] Nieuhoff's truisms, confirmed by his "own knowledge," are indicative of the reluctance of Europeans writers to compare their cultures directly to the Chinese or to use China to reflect unfavorably on the limitations of European economic and military power. The nation's wealth, therefore, is cast in terms of consumption – "delight" – rather than military power, with sixty million households imagined to be full of potential consumers for "fine Linnen" and cheap woolens.

Nieuhoff's descriptive strategy helps to blunt the significant moral and conceptual problems posed by the Manchu conquest of China in the 1640s, and the ongoing efforts at the time of the embassy to pacify the southern part of the country by defeating the remnants of the Ming armies and putting an end to the rampages of Coxinga.[30] Although his comments on the pacification of China are few, his recognition of the effects of the Manchu conquest reveals something of the conceptual problems that the Qing dynasty poses for European commentators. According to Nieuhoff, the "ancient *Greeks* and *Romans,* who formerly subdued whole Countries, never dealt so Barbarously by those whom they Conquered, as these unmerciful Tartars, who by their cruel usage in this last Invasion, have not only laid waste abundance of noble Cities, Towns, and Villages (which are now places for Birds and Beasts to roost in) but they have likewise made Slaves of the best of the natives" (49). The comparison of the Qing dynasty to the Greek and Roman empires underscores the barbarity of the new rulers of China, but it also testifies to their military power and organizational effectiveness: the very people – "the natives of China" – who, for more than a century, had been the subject of European dreams of untapped consumer desire have been reduced to "slavish labour" by a superior force.

Yet if the Manchu conquest threatens to undermine the vision of China offered in Jesuit accounts of late Ming China, the advent of the Qing dynasty does not disrupt Dutch prospects for trade but allows Nieuhoff to imagine an implicit dialectic at work in Beijing: traditional Chinese virtues balanced by a more hospitable attitude toward international commerce. The Qing victory offers the Dutch the hope that they can capitalize on the political change to develop an extensive and lucrative trade. As a relatively new world power, the Dutch find themselves in a roughly analogous position to the Manchu conquerors – a dynamic political force eager to take advantage of its victory over a sclerotic, though wealthy, empire (Spain). In this respect, the Manchus represent something of a mirror image for the Dutch in their quest for legitimacy, power, and profit, even though Nieuhoff is careful to emphasize the effects of sinicization on the Qing. They will, he suggests, integrate themselves into a dominant Chinese culture, while presumably looking favorably on trade with VOC factories in Southeast Asia.

Like his Jesuit predecessors, Nieuhoff emphasizes China's self-absorption and defensive military posture; rather than a threat to Dutch ambitions in Asia, China emerges as part storehouse, part trading partner-in-waiting. Significantly, it is "Nature" which grants to China an "abundance" of riches that exceeds the endowment of Europe, and this abundance, for Nieuhoff, as well as for his Jesuit contemporaries, structures his perceptions of the civil order and polite behavior of the upper classes. He devotes much of his time to recording his observations of the country and its people. Describing a reception for the Dutch in one of the regional capitals, Nieuhoff declares that

It is almost incredible for any body to believe (unless they had seen it) in what State and Pomp these Idolaters and Heathen Princes live, and with what good orders their People are Governed; for as well high as low Offices, in the Courts of the Vice-Roys (which are betwixt two and three thousand) manage their Affairs with so much quietness and expedition, that all things were dispatched, and with like dexterity as in a private Family. Amongst others that dined at [our] Tables, were the Vice-Roys Children, who were so civilly Educated, that I never saw any in *Europe* better brought up. (41)

The image of the state as a family externalizes and extends bourgeois virtues of domestic order into the civil and political realm. Nieuhoff's amazement at the "State and Pomp" of the Viceroys' court is, in part, the result of its size. Political ritual takes place on a scale that dwarfs similar ceremonies in Europe; two to three thousand people organized hierarchically in displays of obedience to feudatory princes, and thus to the Emperor, suggest a qualitative as well as quantitative difference between statecraft in Qing China and Europe. To maintain such order with "quietness and expedition," Viceroys and the elite classes more generally must have access to resources – money, estates, patronage, and positions – that can satisfy thousands of retainers. The key to order, then, is not force but the ability to deploy the resources necessary to maintain a decorum that encompasses political loyalty, bureaucratic efficiency, obedience, and even the politeness of children. In this respect, modifiers such as "civilly" work synedochically to gesture toward an overarching ideology of civility – an ideal of hier-archically organized domestic and political order that unites the Viceroys, their families, and their awestruck Dutch guests – sympathetically, "natu-rally" across linguistic and cultural differences. The Chinese/Manchu Courts, in Canton as well as Beijing, gratify the Dutch desires for order

FIGURE 2. Harbor of Canton, from Jan Nieuhoff, *An Embassy from the East-India Company of the United Provinces, to the Grand Tartar Cham Emperor of China* (1669). Reproduced by permission of the British Library.

and abundance, paradoxically embodying and transcending the mercantile values of thrift (now metamorphosed to "expedition") that promise a fantastically profitable trade.

The order, wealth, and potential profitability of China are coded culturally and artistically in the hundreds of plates that are included in Nieuhoff's *Embassy*. In their detail and sophistication, they depict a socionatural order emblematic of the industry of the Chinese people and the authority of its new Qing dynasty. The engraving of Canton (figure 2) depicts Dutch ships anchored in a port and surrounded by dozens of smaller vessels dedicated, it seems, to trade and transportation. In an important sense, these junks and skips stand emblematically for "all things necessary for the sustenance of Man, as well as for delight" because they represent internal networks of production and commerce – a riverine cornucopia that is in constant motion in the harbor of Canton. In 1703, the Scots merchant Alexander Hamilton declared, "there is no Day in the Year but shews 5000 Sail of trading *Jonks*, besides small Boats for other Services, lying before the City."[31] In the background, the city walls extend horizontally across the plate; the parallel lines of their base and ramparts

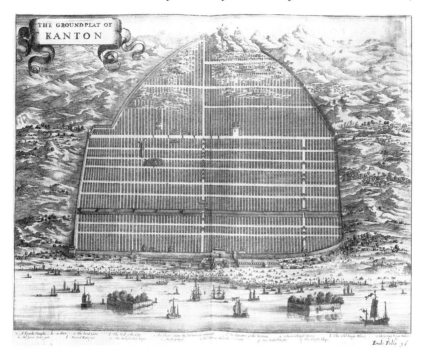

FIGURE 3. Ground plan of Canton, from Jan Nieuhoff, *An Embassy from the East-India Company of the United Provinces, to the Grand Tartar Cham Emperor of China* (1669). Reproduced by permission of the British Library.

seem to stretch off the page as though they were visual analogues of the Europeans' favorite adjective to describe Chinese trade: infinite. Behind the walls lie not only the porcelain, tea, and silks that are the objects of the Dutch mission, but also the "infinite" possibilities for Chinese consumption of European and Japanese silver, South Asian textiles, and Southeast Asian spices.

The ground plan of Canton (figure 3) reveals "behind" the wall of the city a stylized, geometric representation of the vast size and orderly structure of a Chinese city. This plate is neither a realistic representation of a cityscape nor a map: the plan employs its surrealistic geometry and weird perspective to model a demographic, economic, and sociopolitical ideal. In its size and regularity, the alien city is "other" not because it fails to live up to European conceptions but because it projects an unvariegated commitment on the part of its inhabitants to live up to Confucian ideals of good government and social order. In calculating the population of Canton at the beginning of the eighteenth century "by the Quantity of Rice daily expended in it," Hamilton reports that local merchants "reckon 10000 *Peculs* is the daily Import of that Grain. It is also reckoned, that every Person consumes one *Pecul* in 3 Months, so that by that Calculation, there must be above 900000 People in it, and the Suburbs one Third of that Number."[32] In size and appetite, Canton rivals London and Paris, its inhabitants rendered numerically as engines of consumption for the imports that the Dutch, Portuguese, and (by the end of the seventeenth century) English are vying to deliver.

It seems that almost everywhere Nieuhoff and his compatriots visit between Canton and Beijing the ideals of sociopolitical order and consumer desire become inseparable from the merchants' perceptions of China. Yngtak, for example, is "beautified with stately Houses, and Magnificent Idol Temples; surrounded with pleasant Hills, delightful in Prospect, the Suburbs well and sufficient" (51). Underlying this description and others like it is the implicit assumption that the Chinese and Dutch share fundamental values about architectural beauty, urban design, the significance of religious houses of worship, and the aesthetics of landscape. Although Nieuhoff, unlike Webb and Jesuits such as Ricci, does not believe the Chinese are monotheistic, his references to "Idol Temples" and "Heathenish priests" marginalize the otherness of Chinese religion; paganism and idolatry become adjectival modifications of an underlying social identity between civilized idolaters and European Christians. In this respect, Chinese culture mirrors and reinforces European self-perceptions; the presuppositions of upper-class identity across cultural differences naturalize hospitality, grandeur, and luxury as essential, transcultural qualities of nobility and privilege.[33] The problems posed by the oxymoron "heathen civilization" are thus mediated by Nieuhoff's subordinating of religious differences to his eagerness to interpret the semiotics of civility as evidence of like-minded attitudes among Chinese and Manchu elites toward socioeconomic privilege and "free trade."

To put it more prosaically, Nieuhoff has a tough time describing cultural difference – if we assume that such differences define distinct national and racial identities. The accommodationist tradition of Jesuit missionaries who emphasized the similarities between Christianity and Confucianism creates for seventeenth-century writers and travelers a tendency to search for similarities among upper-class Chinese, Manchus, and Europeans that extends to the description of physical characteristics as well as social behavior. Surprisingly for those of us who are products of centuries of institutionalized racism, Nieuhoff, like almost all other seventeenth-century European writers on China, barely registers what we have been trained to perceive as essential racial differences:

The Chinese ... are almost as White of Complexion as the People of Europe; though indeed some of them who live in the Southern Countries, somewhat near the Line, are so scorched with the Heat of the Sun, that they become of a Swarthy colour ... Their Eyes are little, somewhat long, yet inclined to round, black of colour. Their Noses little, and not rising very high, but their Ears are of the largest size; but in the other parts of the Face, they differ very little or nothing from those of *Europe*. (208)

Significantly, whiteness does not register as an essential determinant of race; neither does what most of us would consider the distinctive shape of the eyes of people of Chinese origin. Skin color, for Nieuhoff, is a product of climatic conditions so that the white "Complexion" of the northern Chinese unmarks them as racially other. Alternately, if Nieuhoff assumes that all civilized people are white, then whiteness becomes a function of dress, taste, decorum, and wealth – a term of approbation that can be applied to any civilized people.[34] Big ears aside (a characteristic that does not signify in twenty-first century discourses of race), the Chinese seem indistinguishable from Europeans. Or, perhaps more accurately, the differences that will come to figure so prominently in nineteenth and twentieth-century stereotypes of the Chinese do not register as determinants of sociocultural identity. Racial characteristics are subsumed within other modes of perception, other symbolic economies beholden to the transnational identity of elite merchants, governors, and civil servants.

If civility serves as the common denominator between European and Chinese men, then Nieuhoff's descriptions of upper-class women become a crucial means to invoke and dramatize a host of explicit and implicit sociopolitical values that make commerce between the two cultures seem natural, almost inevitable. To a great extent, the similarities between Dutch and Chinese men of rank and wealth are forged over the bodies of Chinese women, who, Nieuhoff tells his readers, "are for the most part Handsome, Complaisant, and Ingenious, and exceed in beauty of Body all other Heathenish Women: Their Complexion tending to Whiteness, with Brown Eyes; all their Natural Beauties and peculiar Excellencies, they set off with Gold and Painting" (208). As the objects of transcultural masculine desire, these women embody the tacit agreement of Chinese and Dutch tastes; the artificial beauty of jewelry and painting confirms shared systems of cultural value – the semiotics of feminine attractiveness – among men. Like European women, the Chinese know how to wear make-up, accessorize, and appear "Complaisant" around strange men; they embody and reflect the naturalized values of the performance of femininity familiar to Nieuhoff and his European readers. The author, though, goes beyond describing the women's physical characteristics to touch on the dynamics of gender relations – their deference to men – and on their internal qualities of mind; the women are "Ingenious" as well as beautiful, testimony to the sophistication of a near-exemplary culture that reflects to Nieuhoff the masculinist postulates of his own. The women's appearance and behavior assure him, in other words, that the differences that distinguish them from their European counterparts are not absolute; their "tending" to "Whiteness" effectively unmarks the cultural specificity of their class and gender identity. In this respect, the author's qualifications in this description – "for the most part," "heathenish," and "tending to Whiteness" – distance him from his own fascination with the women's "peculiar Excellencies," excellencies, one is tempted to infer, that make them superior to European women. As with other comparisons between aspects of Chinese and European culture, this description of upper-class women forges an identity of interest – an overdetermined "exchange" of mutually inflected values – over another body, that of "other Heathenish Women," who presumably lack the beauty and grace which women in Beijing and Amsterdam share.

Looking into the face of a wealthy and upper-class culture, Nieuhoff can get a purchase on gradations of cultural difference only by narrative and ideological modes of triangulation, by seeking to define his embassy's common interests with the Manchu Court as an alliance against what Michel Serres calls the "third man" or parasite, the noise which paradoxically must be excluded for any successful act of communication to take place but against which, and only against which, meaning can emerge.[35] Parasites are always unstable, mediated constructs: different efforts to affirm an identity of commercial and social interests with the Chinese and Manchu elites both produce and are produced by different perceptions of the "third man," by different threats to a successful and always idealized linguistic, cultural, and economic commerce. Parasites, at different times and in different contexts, assume different forms for Nieuhoff; his comparisons between Europeans and Chinese and between Europeans and Manchus – whether men or women – are mediated irrevocably by different incarnations of the parasite: beggars, the common people, the defeated Chinese forced to serve as menial labor for their Manchu conquerors, and, significantly, the Europeans against whom the Dutch ambassadors struggle.

THE DUTCH AND THE JESUITS IN BEIJING

In seeking to reach a trade agreement with court officials, the Dutch ambassadors were frustrated by the machinations of the Portuguese, who characterized their European rivals as "deceitful in all things, and without any Country or Habitations of their own; and that they got their livings by Stealth and Piracy" (23). Battling this sort of ethnic-commercial stereotype throughout their efforts to begin negotiations, the Dutch were further undermined by the Emperor's translator, the Jesuit Adam Schall. The German-born Schall had arrived in Macao in 1619 and had helped defend the city against the unsuccessful Dutch siege in 1622.[36] Once in China, he established himself as a key advocate for the Jesuit mission in the final years of the Ming dynasty, and used his considerable skill as an astronomer and instrument maker to lead the efforts to reform the Chinese calendar. By producing more accurate predictions of eclipses of the sun and moon than rival Chinese and Islamic astronomers, Schall quickly won the support of the new Qing dynasty and was appointed Director of the Institute of Astronomy in 1644. Other honors followed, and Schall became a confidant of the young Shun-chih Emperor who ascended to the throne in 1651 and reigned for ten years. By 1658, he was awarded a post as Grand Officer of the Imperial Banquets, raising him "to the rank of mandarin of the highest division of the first class, equal to the Emperor's chief councilors and the greatest princes of the imperial family."[37] Schall's commitment to promoting the interests of the Portuguese in Macao as well as those of the Jesuits made him an extremely powerful adversary for the Dutch.

The Jesuits had learned enough from the failure of Schedel's mission to come prepared to secure, through various gifts and bribes, the good will of at least some Qing officials. If Nieuhoff testifies to the anxieties of triangulated communication and desire by blaming the troubles of the mission on the machinations of the Portuguese and their Jesuit allies, it is significant that the Jesuits regard the Dutch with the same distrust and hostility with which the Dutch regarded them. Advertised on the title page of Ogilby's 1669 translation as "An Epistle of Father John Adams their Antagonist, concerning the whole Negotiation," the separately paginated account of the clerical counter-offensive, "Written by a Jesuite," revels in the efforts of "four of us Brethren of the Society of Jesus then living at Court, [who] resolved to leave no *medium* un-essayed to overthrow those *Hollanders* designs, and with all diligence and vigilancy to vacuate their undertakings" (2). The author accuses the Dutch of the same kind of bribery that the Dutch level at the Portuguese, reiterates charges that the Dutch are "Universal Robbers," and describes them as rebels against their "lawful Soveraign" (a charge that John Dryden and other English writers leveled against them during the three Dutch wars) and apostates against the true Church (4). The fears that the Jesuits play on are not those of conquest or colonization but of piracy; they repeatedly invoke memories of the VOC's raids on the Fokien coast in the 1620s and argue that the Dutch on Taiwan are aiding Coxinga, who had attacked coastal provinces for more than a decade. In their efforts to undermine the Dutch mission, the Jesuits turn the embassy's gifts from the East Indies against them, claiming that the fact that they offer no goods of their own confirms that they are "the Arch-Pirates of all Seas" (4). Ironically, the very success of the Dutch maritime empire is used as evidence of their rootlessness and their alienation from the values of civilized order conferred by the ownership and productivity of land.

To combat Schall's insinuations, the Dutch started their own disinformation campaign against the Portuguese in Macao, apparently convinced that the recalcitrance of the Chinese to trade was the product of underhand competition by their European rivals. Nieuhoff claims that "the Embassadours were well enough informed of the designs and practices of Father *Adam* and some other *Jesuites*, who had been bribed under hand by the *Portugesses*, to oppose the *Hollanders* in this their design of Free Commerce in *China*; therefore they endeavoured to perswade the *Tartars* that the *Hollanders* under colour and pretence of *Merchandizing*, designed nothing less but to get footing first of all in their Countrey, and afterwards to Plunder and carry away whatsoever was Portable" (123). Nieuhoff's confidence in the persuasive force of civility – in his and his countrymen's ability to interpret signs of interest and friendship – hinders him from recognizing the relative lack of court interest in either the prospects of a long-term trade agreement with the Dutch or, more broadly, in commercialized values that the Dutch take as a given of civilized behavior and desire. The Dutch zeal to establish trade seems to blind them to the possibility that Schall has a better understanding than they do of the complex semiotics of the Qing Court. In his mandarin robes, friendship with the Shun-chih Emperor, and conviction that accommodating the rites of Confucianism and ancestor-worship is a way station on the road to promulgating the true faith, Schall, who was fluent in Chinese, possesses an understanding of the complexities of Ming and Qing China in ways that Dutch-speaking emissaries can only envy, not emulate or appropriate.

The differences between Dutch and Chinese views of the forms and implications of appropriate behavior may be gauged by looking at the diplomatic correspondence of the Dutch and the memorials of the

Emperor in 1655 and 1656. The VOC's attempt to establish an ideological basis for cross-cultural negotiation is translated by Manchu and Chinese officials into their own idiolects of power, civility, and desire. The Dutch ambassadors carried a letter to the Shun-chih Emperor from John Maatzuiker, the Governor General of the VOC in Batavia, who couches his appeal for trade with Beijing within (for Europeans) familiar theocentric arguments for international commerce:

The Lord Creator, who made this earth, divided it into ten thousand nations. Some nations raise only natural products; other nations produce manufactures. The former have something which the latter have not; the latter have something which the former have not. The Lord Creator wishes people to exchange what they have with each other so that they can respect and admire each other, and be in harmony. Therefore most of us [the Dutch] sail abroad and travel to the remotest regions, and everywhere we have friendly relations with the native rulers.

Now we hear that the Emperor of Ta-Ch'ing has won a great victory and has ascended the throne of the Middle Kingdom. This is by the grace of the Lord of Heaven who has given your Majesty this supreme mandate. We, therefore, seek to congratulate [your Majesty] and to petition Your Majesty for permission to allow our people to trade at any of the ports where our ships may anchor, for mutual trade is the will of God as well as the custom of all nations.[38]

Maatzuiker's letter seeks to forge relations with China by describing trade as a means to overcome a postlapsarian scarcity of resources, the effects of humankind's expulsion from Eden. His rhetoric recalls that of Queen Elizabeth writing to the Sultan of Aceh a half century earlier, and his reasoning is very close to that of Samuel Purchas in his paean to international trade.[39] God sanctions trade, the Governor General suggests, because it alone can repair the damage done by the Fall; the free exchange of goods promises a return to the golden age in which the surpluses of one country supply the deficiencies of another. The profits of far-flung trade – the mutual exchange of surplus wealth – signify a heavenly approbation. Within this ideology of a divinely sanctioned commerce, the Qing Emperor becomes, like European monarchs, God's envoy on earth, and it is precisely this theological guarantee which promotes, according to Maatzuiker, both a mutually advantageous trade and an equality of exchange – an equality premised on reciprocal desires.

Although the Dutch, by 1655, recognize that they must present the Emperor and the feudatory princes who rule Kwangtung province with "tributary gifts," their rhetoric insistently suggests that they consider these gifts as preliminary means to open substantive negotiations for "mutual trade." Because they see the desire for trade as a "natural" – indeed fundamental – mark of gentlemanly civility, they are unable to grasp the significance of the very ceremonies in which they participate. Nieuhoff, for example, repeatedly interprets the ceremonies of tributary relations – kowtowing to the Emperor – as a semiotics of civility, of a mutual desire to negotiate the specifics of Dutch trading privileges. In this regard, the ideology of "free trade" to which Maatzuiker gives voice underwrites Nieuhoff's belief that a transcultural civility will result in face-to-face negotiations with appropriate officials that, in turn, will guarantee, in unambiguous, diplomatically binding language, the rights of the Dutch to descend on Beijing once every five years and to enjoy unlimited trade with coastal ports.[40]

The response of the Emperor and court officials to the Dutch embassy, however, testifies to the gaps in understanding between the parties. The Beijing Court interprets European desires in the context of the elaborate bureaucratic system of tributary relations that the Qing Emperor had appropriated from the Ming dynasty. Although the Shun-chih Emperor seems to have understood the potential value of the Dutch as an ally against Coxinga, in August and October of 1656 he issued memorials that cast the United Provinces as simply another tributary state to be mollified:

We consider your country ... to be distantly located on Our western border, separated from Us by remote and dangerous oceans. Since ancient times your country has never embraced Chinese culture. Nevertheless, from afar you know and long for Our virtue and civilization, and respect and admire Us, your Sovereign and Father ... Concerning your petition for entering and leaving [China] for your convenience in paying Us homage and presenting tribute and for the exchange of goods: Although this will circulate money and commodities which would be to the profit of our merchants and people, we are afraid that the distance is so great and the winds and waves so dangerous, that it will be very toilsome to the tribute-bearers who travel in boats and carts and suffer the hard-ship of long journeying ... Therefore, we order that your country should present tribute every eight years, the officers and servants should not be more than 100 men, only twenty of whom shall be allowed to go to [the] Imperial Capital.

You should understand the kindness with which We will cherish and protect you and carefully perform the duties of a prince of the feudal territory. Prudently present your regular tribute. Reverently receive this gracious order.[41]

The Emperor recasts the theocentric rhetoric of mutual exchange into a hierarchical language of tribute. The ambassadors' desire for trade is transformed into a desire to subject themselves – politically and culturally – to Chinese "virtue and civilization." The Dutch are recast in the image of successive waves of "inferior" peoples who willingly emulate the values and wisdom of a superior civilization. Although the Emperor's response, limiting Dutch trade to one tributary mission every eight years, seemed designed to restrict European access to Chinese markets and to avoid the costs of transporting, housing, and entertaining yet another tributary embassy, his formulaic insistence on ceremony is a significant indication of the court's comparative lack of interest in expanding European trade. For the Dutch and the British, the China trade is imagined as the linchpin of a worldwide commerce: consumption at home and the lucrative re-export trade to the rest of Europe and to the Americas. For the Qing Court, in contrast, the Dutch offer another means to acquire silver bullion in exchange for porcelain, silks, and tea.

In the Forbidden City, the ceremony of having tributary missions kowtow to the Emperor is an essential ritual of obeisance, fundamental to barbarians' formal recognition of China's cultural and political superiority. Even if such symbolic theater masks serious divisions within the court about how to respond to European overtures, civility, for Chinese and Manchu officials, is defined as a demonstration and extension of the "good orders [by which] their People are governed" (41). What Nieuhoff fails, or refuses, to realize is that the Dutch mission is subject to the same hierarchical principles of order as are the servants, retainers, and soldiers arrayed in row after row in depictions of the Emperor's court. Their limited understanding of protocols and politics in China led the Dutch to misinterpret their standings at court. By lavishing gifts on officials in Canton, they secured some help in presenting their case to the Shun-chih Emperor. In his translation of the Jesuit's account of the embassy, Ogilby includes a version of Maatzuiker's letter to the Emperor, that, the author claims, "came at first unsealed, and without any manner of Glorious or Majestick Title, as if [Maatzuiker] had writ to one of his Familiar Friends and equals; but the *Chineses* in *Canton* did so dress it up, and adorn it, that it appeared with much reverence and ability" (12). Even with this help, the Dutch had difficulty perceiving the significance of court ritual: the Dutch were granted permission to proceed to Beijing not because the Emperor sought a mutual commerce but because the ambassadors were willing to begin a long process of gift-giving that presumably, from the court's perspective, would culminate with the barbarians performing the proper tributary rituals. To ignore such ceremonial decorum was to be barred from the Forbidden City. While Nieuhoff was in Beijing, a Russian embassy arrived to open trade talks, and appeared before the Board of Rites. The Russian ambassador, however, unlike his Dutch counterparts, "insisted on using the ceremonials of his own country . . . and did not kneel or kowtow." Because the "ambassador [proved] ignorant of our ceremonies," the official memorial continues, "it is improper to give him audience. [His] tribute is refused and he is ordered to return to his own country."[42] The Dutch did not fare much better. A letter from Father Balion, a Jesuit in Beijing, depicts the ambassadors as "highly discontented," much like the Russians: "The *Hollanders* may not come into the Kings presence (nor the *Muscovites*) because they will not submit themselves to those Ceremonies of reverence, accustomed in this Place. They are Novices, and ignorant in Affairs, and obstinate in refusing to accommodate themselves to the customs of the Countrey" (17). The Jesuits' understanding of Chinese civility, based on years of experience, remains foreign to the "*Hollanders*" who resist the acculturation that the missionaries see as fundamental to the ultimate success of their mission.

Despite their efforts, the Dutch found themselves unable to overcome the ideological differences between their views of "mutual trade" and the Emperor's and his court's assumptions that the red-haired barbarians would be content to trade at designated intervals in China while maintaining strict policies of non-aggression toward the Middle Kingdom. According to Nieuhoff, the Dutch were baffled by what they perceived as irrelevant questions posed by various officials and needless delays. A good deal of time and energy seems to have gone into trying to convince their hosts that they were not pirates:

the Mandarins . . . could not believe that the *Hollanders* had any firm Countrey, but lived and dwelt upon the Sea, or at least in Islands: Therefore, for a more clear demonstration, they desired to let them see a Map of our Countrey; whereupon the Embassadours produced a Map of the Seven United Provinces, with the Territories thereunto belonging, which they took with them to shew the Emperour. (115–16)

The result, as the Emperor's memorial makes clear, is to resituate the Netherlands from the center of Eurocentric commerce to the far western fringes of a sinocentric world. In their efforts to use cartography to bolster their status as a worthy trading partner, however, the Dutch embassy encounter further difficulties when their hosts

asked likewise after the government of *Holland*, and the power of those that had sent them; whereupon the Embassadours returned for an answer that *Holland* was never Governed by any one single person, but by a select number of the chiefest of the Countrey. They specified also the names of the Councils by which *Holland* was governed and said that besides this high Council, there was yet another Council which had received their Power and Authority from the Supreme Council, and from the Prince of their Countrey, to govern *Indian* Affairs . . .

But in regard these Commissioners could not well understand nor apprehend this form of our Government (because the *Tartars* and *Chineses* know no other then Monarchical) neither could they tell what the name of Prince signified; the Embassadours had no little Puzzle to work them into a good opinion of our State, therefore they were forced to make use of the name of the Prince of *Orange*, as if they had been sent by his Highness . . .

These Gentlemen [the court officials] were of opinion that the Dignity and Majesty of the Emperour would be much lessened, if he should give Audience to such as were not related to their Prince. (116)

Finding the Manchu and Chinese officials unable to comprehend the idea of a republic run by a Council and the Dutch East India Company that operated as a joint-stock company, the Dutch ambassadors concoct an elaborate series of partial explanations and half-truths that transform the Prince of Orange into an autocratic monarch and the merchants sent from Batavia into a branch of his royal bloodline. The ambiguity, "for the *Tartars* and *Chineses*," of the Dutch use of the title "Prince" becomes emblematic of a larger problem of cross-cultural translation that invoking supposedly transcultural standards of civility cannot overcome. The appellation "Gentlemen" that Nieuhoff uses to describe the officials in Beijing does not bring them within a common semiotics, necessary to the kinds of negotiation that the Dutch want to pursue, but calls attention to Nieuhoff's (and Ogilby's) efforts to translate foreign hierarchies into familiar terms.

These kinds of misunderstandings persisted throughout the ambassadors' residence in Beijing. After their audience with the Emperor, the Dutch expected full-scale negotiations to get underway, and were disappointed by the imperial edict that restricted their trade to one ship every eight years and limited this visit to a company of one hundred men. Overstaying their welcome, the Dutch tried to continue what they perceived as negotiations, even after they had received orders to leave the capital. Soon, however, one of their two translators, Paul Durette or Duretti, was murdered in his own lodgings. Without one of their two translators, the Dutch found communication with the Chinese Council and the Manchu Court increasingly difficult. Receiving no satisfaction from the authorities in finding and punishing those responsible for the murder, and having spent 160,099 guilders in Beijing, the Dutch abandoned their mission and returned to Batavia. All told, Nieuhoff calculates, the expedition cost (in British pounds) £5,555 in bribes and £4,327 in other expenses (145). Rather than leaving as strong-armed, commercial imperialists – a role the Dutch East India Company was used to playing in the Indonesian archipelago – the Dutch retreated to their Company headquarters in Batavia unsure of whether they had won an important entry to a lucrative trade that would soon be expanded or had been shunted aside by a factionalized court.

Despite the setbacks and uncertainties of their embassy, Nieuhoff remained undaunted. "Something [may] be done," he asserts, "to the advantage of our Traffick, by sending a few Presents more to the Emperour; which several of the Grandees of Peking did more then hint to our Embassadours: Beside, the Great Cham having Wars with that Arch Pyrate Coxinga, if we should but propose to assist his Imperial Majesty with our Ships, . . . I make no doubt but he should quickly consent to give us a Free Trade in his Dominions" (146). Nieuhoff misinterprets Chinese expectations of a continuing tributary relationship ("a few Presents more") as an invitation to bribe the Emperor into allowing the Dutch something like favored-nation trading status. His policy recommendations – more gifts and an alliance against Coxinga – thus extend strategies that have failed in the previous Dutch mission to secure "Free Trade." However dubious such recommendations may seem, Nieuhoff was hardly a novice and had an impressive track record of service. He had held posts in Brazil, and his accounts of his travels in the Americas and elsewhere in Asia were translated and reprinted in several languages.[43] In 1659, he was sent by the VOC as an emissary to Coxinga, to ascertain whether the "Arch-pirate" harbored hostile intentions towards the Dutch factory on Taiwan. Given his experience and long service to the Company, his assessments of the prospects of trade to China deliver precisely the kind of news that the directors of the VOC were eager to hear.

Nieuhoff's optimistic close to the narrative of his trip to Beijing depends on his determination to repress the costs – monetary and political – that such a "free" trade entails. The Dutch can secure concessions for limited commerce with China, it seems, only by embroiling themselves in conflicts with Portuguese and Jesuits in China and participating in a tributary economy that reinforces the power of the Emperor and the court – the very absolutist control of international trade that frustrates the Dutch East India Company's desire for duty-free, unencumbered commerce. Nieuhoff's certainty that China can be opened to commerce, then, is based less on his experiences in Beijing than on his interpellation within ideologies of trade and civility that encourage him to interpret setbacks for the embassy as the work of underhand third parties or the unfortunate result of misunderstandings that can be resolved or overcome. The Portuguese, he intimates, can be run out of Macao the way they had been out of the Spice Islands. His appeal to the Emperor's political interests, then, is also an invocation of shared standards of gentlemanly courtesy, of civility – even in the face of evidence, including the murder of an interpreter, that "Free trade" always has incalculable costs.

IDES AND THE RUSSIAN MISSION TO KANGXI

The experience of European emissaries later in the century with the Kangxi Emperor suggests both changes in the domestic political situation in China, which had complex effects on Sino-European relations, and the continuity in ambassadors' perceptions of the ways in which cultural differences can be subsumed within and translated into elaborate codes of civility. In 1692, Peter the Great, Czar of all the Russias, sent an embassy under the direction of a German (or possibly Dutch) ambassador, Evret Ysbrants Ides, to Beijing. Ides's report, published in Dutch and translated into English in 1706 under the title *Three Years Travels from Moscow Over-Land to China*, is part travelogue, part catalogue of the Czar's "Dominions out of Europe, [which] are for the most part unknown" (A2v), and part sociocultural portrait of China at the end of the seventeenth century.[44] This embassy, the first after a series of border skirmishes in the 1680s that resulted in a 1689 treaty favorable to Beijing, marks Russian efforts to formalize trade and diplomatic relations with the Manchu Court. Ides's history of his embassy is unusual for its time in that it sets Chinese civilization in an anthropological context of the various peoples and cultures that he and his train encountered in riding, sledding, and rafting across Siberia, through Tartary, to China. These Asiatic cultures, almost without exception, serve as the "third men" who become negative standards against which the similarities of European and Chinese interests are defined and celebrated. The "*Ostiacks*" in central Siberia, for example, "are so horrid lazy, that they don't desire to get any more than will barely suffice them annually for Winter . . . They are all of a middle stature, most of them Yellowish or Red haired; and their Faces and Noses disagreeably broad; they are weak and unable to labor hard, not at all inclined to Wars, and utterly uncapable of Military Exercises" (20). The Ostiacs, of course, are also idolaters, who fall into ecstasies of religious fervor at the sight of a "*Nurenberg-Bear in Clockwork*" (20). Taken together, the national characteristics of this semi-nomadic people – laziness, unattractive physical features, disinclination to labor and military exercise, and idolatry – define a conceptual as well as geographic space that the Russian embassy must traverse to reach a like-minded civilization. This deprecation of the Ostiacs is emblematic of an inability to understand the nomadic peoples of central

Asia who resist the hierarchical imposition of agricultural regimentation, feudal land ownership, and their attendant disciplinary modes of compulsory labor, conscripted military service, and fixed settlement. Even their generosity is incomprehensible. Adam Brand, Ides's secretary, describes "the extraordinary Liberality and Hospitality of the Inhabitants" who would "bring us Provisions and sometimes Furs, without the least reward or recompense."[45] In different ways, Ides's and Brand's descriptions of the peoples of Siberia reinscribe European standards of civilization and provide a framework for their assessments of Manchu government and Chinese culture.

After a year's trek across Siberia, and detailed observations of the "barbaric" customs of the various other peoples he encountered, Ides was met by one of the Emperor's emissaries, north of the Great Wall. This meeting marks a return to civilization, to shared codes of social conduct, and to a recognizable – that is, hierarchical – political and socioeconomic order:

> the *Mandarin*, who was an agreeable well bred Man, very civilly envited me to take a Meal with him … accepting which I was very well received, with particular expressions of kindness, and splendidly treated … His Men and Soldiers were all disposed in the best order, each as perfectly and respectfully knowing and taking his Station as is possible in *Europe*. What alone was very uneasie to me, was that I was obliged to sit with him on the Tapistry, with my Legs across and under me. (53)

Even more than Nieuhoff, Ides notices and reports specifics of upper-class behavior and dress as well as details of architecture, embroidery, and social rituals. Knowing that the Russians had been defeated by Qing forces, Ides seems ready, even eager, to acknowledge the attractions if not the superiority of Manchu and Chinese culture. The mandarin exemplifies transcultural standards of civility, privilege, and hospitality. He commands servants and soldiers with an order that matches or exceeds the social decorum of European courts; his control presents an idealized tableau of hierarchical social relations. The order of his entourage extends to, and, in effect, depends on, the internalized senses of inferiority and duty that make his "Men and Soldiers" models of deferential comportment. In this respect, the mandarin's court embodies what Ides takes to be (or presents to the Czar as) universal sociopolitical ideals – a civility that depends on an unshakeable system of hierarchical class relations. Cultural differences in this description (and throughout Ides's stay in China) are reduced to odd customs such as sitting cross-legged on the ground or, later, eating with chopsticks. Although Ides, like Nieuhoff, must rely on translators, they are seldom in evidence in his descriptions. An intuited "language" of mutual values and presumed sympathetic understanding inheres in the semiotics of social prestige and privilege that, he asserts, transcends cultural differences.

Racial differences similarly are noted and contained within an ideology of civility. Writing more than thirty years after Nieuhoff, Ides recognizes the ethnic identities of the Manchu officials he meets, but subsumes their difference from the Chinese within the semiotics of upper-class deportment. Having admired the Great Wall and crossed into China, Ides is welcomed by the Governor of the Province, "a very great Nobleman, by birth a *Mongolian*, or *East Tartar*: and a very affable well bred Man ... [who] gave us a noble Entertainment" (65–66). Ides tucks the nobleman's "birth" into a dependent clause, then returns to his description of his host's "affable" nature.[46] If the Nobleman is by birth ethnically distinct from the Chinese, he is also "well bred," presumably acculturated to the traditions of the Chinese, and therefore capable of hosting a "noble Entertainment." Nieuhoff, in the 1650s, had noted the devastation wrought by the Manchu invasion and observed Chinese being treated like slaves as the Dutch embassy moved upriver towards Beijing: north of Canton, "we saw into what a miserable condition the Chineses were reduced by the last War of the Tartars, who put them upon this slavish labour of Towing and Rowing their Boats, using them worse then Beasts at their pleasure, without any exception of persons, either young or old" (48). But for Ides and Brand, such effects of war and devastation are no longer evident. Instead, the same kind of transcultural standards that Nieuhoff uses to elide differences among the Dutch, the Manchu, and the Chinese elites are employed to erase the traces of the civil wars of the 1640s and 1650s. In this sense, for Ides, civility becomes the means to mediate cultural differences that otherwise would threaten to disjoin Chinese, Manchus, and Europeans; it is the symbolic currency that reassures all parties involved that dress, manners, and carriage reflect similar values, a similar social psychology of privilege and gentlemanly sensibility. Civility is defined in these diplomatic encounters as a willingness to grant to alien cultures an interiority of gentlemanly taste, sophistication, aesthetic appreciation, and sociopolitical authority. It is the mark of a psychology of mutual and mutually reinforcing desires that elevates the Governor and others of the Chinese and Manchu elites to the transcultural status of gentlemen.

Because Ides, like Nieuhoff, does not speak Chinese (or, according to Brand, even Latin), the civility to which he grants such significant, if implicit, power, is not primarily a function of a Eurocentric language of sensibility or fellow feeling. In literary texts of the period, non-Europeans can lay claim to a depth and nobility of feeling only by ventriloquizing a discourse that recalls (as in Oroonoko's case) the rhetoric of an ancient Roman honor – the ur-texts of western self-definition – or that anticipates the self-consciousness of feeling characteristic of later sentimental heroes. Linguistic and cultural differences, as in Dryden's heroic tragedies, are subsumed within an anti-experiential value system that reveals far more about late seventeenth-century political anxieties in Europe than it does about Asian or Amerindian cultures.[47] Civility, however, must be understood as a complex intersection and overlapping of semiotic systems that often displace or marginalize the languages of interiority that figure so prominently in literary representations of psychological experience. The effects of civility as a means to enact transcultural assumptions about class and gender can be gauged in Ides's account of a Chinese play that he saw at the Emperor's Court:

First entered a very beautiful Lady, magnificently dressed in Cloth of Gold, adorned with Jewels, and a Crown on her Head, singing her Speech, with a charming Voice, and agreeable motion of the Body, playing with her Hands, in one of which she had a Fan. The Prologue thus performed, the Play followed, the Story which turned upon a *Chinese* Emperor long since dead, who had behaved himself well towards his Country, and in honour of whose Memory the Play was written. Sometimes he appeared in Royal Robes, with a flat Ivory Scepter in his Hand, and sometimes his Officers shewed themselves with Ensigns, Arms, and Drums, &c. and by intervals a sort of Farce was acted by their Lacqueys, whose antick Dress, and painted Faces were as well as any I have seen in *Europe*; and as far as was interpreted to me, their Farce was very diverting, especially part of it, which represented a Person who had in his Marriage been cheated with a debauched Wife, and fancying her constant to him, had the mortification to see another make Love to her before his Face. (63)

Ides's attention is captured by the Prologue and the farcical scenes. The emissary notes carefully the dress, voice, dance, and hand movements of the female singer, paying particular attention to her dress and "Crown," the markings of her social class. Ides is enthralled by her "charming Voice, and agreeable motion of [her] Body," by her performance of an ideal of femininity that exists independently of the "meaning" of her Prologue. Significantly, the "Story" of the play matters less to Ides than the props and trappings of political power and social prestige – the scepter, the "Ensigns, Arms, and Drums" – that stand synedochically for the particulars of monarchical authority and cultural and national identity in imperial China. These props also, for the European emissary, function as performative indications of a transcultural, militaristic, and hierarchical authority. There is no narrative, no plot summary, in the ambassador's description of an Emperor, "long since dead," only "sometimes" spectacles that focus his attention on the representation of imperial power and historical memory. Ides remains silent as well about the ambiguities of a play celebrating Chinese martial prowess performed before a largely Manchu Court, about, that is, the "sinification" of the conquerors. The comic subplot, however, does fascinate him, so much so that he mentions – for one of the few times in his narrative – his need to rely on translators. These scenes, which seem as though they might have been lifted from a Restoration sex farce, entertain Ides precisely because the comedy of infidelity depends on values – the patrilineal subordination of women, a social hierarchy in which servants ape their betters – that he accepts as natural, even universal. The "mortification" of the stage-cuckold, in effect, restages and confirms a structure of masculinist values that translate across linguistic and cultural divides. Ides's description of the play, in this respect, is framed by familiar, dualistic views of women as either graceful beauties or debauched and deceitful wives. These farcical scenes of painted "Lacqueys," then, both parody the pretensions of power that the main plot represents seriously and reinforce "natural," transcultural hierarchies of class and gender that, in the ambassador's mind, reveal the similarities among European, Chinese, and Manchu perceptions of civilized behavior and political order.

Ides's descriptions of banquets, plays, costumes, and the architecture of the Court ultimately overwhelm the ostensible diplomatic purpose of his mission. When he is granted an audience with the Kangxi Emperor, he performs the kowtow without remarking on how this ceremony of submission is perceived by the court, nor does he discuss the improprieties in the Czar's letter to the Emperor that led to the Russians' tribute and memorial being returned.[48] Ides's description of a China filled with likeminded and hospitable gentlemen provides a narrative means to minimize the tensions that still existed between the two empires and to distance himself from the negative implications of the Emperor's characterization of Russia: the country has "many able men, but they are narrow-minded, obstinate, and their argument is slow." Their refusal to adhere to proper ceremonial forms brands Russia as a potential enemy "that after many generations . . . [again] might cause trouble."[49] Although the Russians were allowed to send a two-hundred-person caravan every three years, their trading privileges were limited and they could remain in Beijing only eighty days.

Like Nieuhoff, Ides is a better anthropologist than political analyst. The specificity of his comments on the Emperor are limited to a physical description of his person: "This Monarch was then aged about 50 Years, his Meen was very agreeable, he had large black Eyes, and his Nose was somewhat raised; he wore small black *Mustachio's*, but had very little Beard on the lower part of his Face; he was very much pitted with the Small Pox, and of a middling stature" (72). Although this description and others like it satisfy – and whet – European desires for information about China, they suggest that the writer's fascination with the physical performance of civility cuts in two ways: the Emperor's "agreeable" aspect implies a shared, even sympathetic, basis for the interpretation of his character but it also calls attention to how tenuous any impression of his character must be for Europeans unfamiliar with the complex semiotic systems they are trying to read. The ideal of civility that Ides invokes seeks, then, to transcend the difficulties of cross-cultural interpretation by depicting Kangxi's court as a realm of undifferentiated privilege, marked by a camaraderie among upper-class European, Manchu, and Chinese men that substitutes polite-ness for analysis and that underwrites Ides's faith in the success of his mission. Kangxi becomes emblematic of the idealized virtues attributed to the Middle Kingdom.

If Ides's audience with Kangxi serves as the climax to his narrative, it also points to the limitations of a single, ritual encounter as a means to forge the kinds of cross-cultural ties that the Europeans want to establish. Paradoxically, such brief descriptions leave so many gaps that they provoke a desire for the kind of supplement that only a handful of Jesuits in Beijing were in the position to provide for European readers. In this context, it is revealing to contrast Ides's portrait of Kangxi to that in the full-length biography of the Qing Emperor by the Jesuit Joachim Bouvet. Published a few years before Ides's account of his mission, Bouvet's *History of Cang-Hy* depicts the Emperor as a living embodiment of assumptions and values of cross-cultural civility.

According to Bouvet, the Emperor is distinguished by "many Noble Qualifications" and his "Natural Genius is such as can be parallell'd but by a few, being endow'd with a Quick and piercing Wit, a vast Memory, and Great Understanding . . . which makes him the fittest Person in the World, not only to undertake, but also to accomplish Great Designs."[50] For Bouvet, the absolute authority which the Emperor wields is matched by the devotion of his subjects, who are "equally charmed with his Love and Justice, . . . and with his vertuous Inclinations; which as they are always guided by the Dictates of Reason, so, they render him an Absolute

Master of his Passions" (2). Even as Bouvet trumpets the success of Jesuit advisors who "have imprinted into his Mind so advantageous an *Idea* of the *European* Kingdoms" that he no longer is in thrall to age-old Chinese xenophobia and contempt for foreigners, he praises the Emperor for having devoted himself "to re-establish[ing] a good Order, and to suppress[ing] such Abuses as were crept into the Government, during the Licentiousness of [China's] intestine Wars" by trying to "re-establish the antient Vigour of the Laws, and introduce Plenty among his Subjects," and by spending "Millions" in public works projects "to keep the Rivers, Channels, Bridges, and Banks and such like Things, which serve for the Conveniency of Commerce, and Ease of the People, in good Repair" (14, 23, 33). Kangxi thus fulfills several traditional requirements for embodying the principles that should govern an exemplary monarch: he restores the greatness of a war-weary empire; he continues the policies praised by Jesuit writers that allow a reinvigorated China to enjoy its wealth and prosperity; and as, Bouvet claims, he rejects Chinese ancestor-worship and offers "publick Prayers and Sacrifices ... to the Supream Lord of Heaven and Earth" (28). This idealized portrait replaces Dutch fantasies of unending trade with the fantasy of (nearly) imminent conversion by the Emperor to Christianity – a staple of missionary literature on the Middle Kingdom. As the agent for a restoration of the purity of an ancient, monotheistic religion as well as social order and political integrity, Kangxi cements his role, for Bouvet, "beyond all Dispute" as politically "the most potent Prince in the World, both in respect of his vast Revenues, and the great extent and Goodness of his Territories" and morally as "the most Exact pattern of Frugality and Modesty" (29–30). But idealizing the Qing Emperor in this fashion carries with it the danger that the imperial virtues which obtain in Beijing represent an absolute standard of kingship; the Europeans seem to be the ones who have fallen short of Chinese and Manchu standards of sociopolitical and moral value. The Emperor embodies precisely those qualities that European monarchs should emulate. In war-torn Europe at the end of the seventeenth century, Kangxi provides a historical precedent for imagining an end to war, civil unrest, dynastic tensions, and bloody but inconclusive military campaigns. Where Elkannah Settle in *The Conquest of China by the Tartars* (1676) has to resort to absurd fictions to imagine a peaceful solution to England's looming succession crisis, Bouvet can write the biography of a living Emperor.[51]

The movement of Ides's narrative – from civilized Europe across a barbaric, pagan Siberia, to a rich and populous China – might stand emblematically for European expectations in the seventeenth century as ambassadors trekked to China, intent on translating the accommodationist principles of Jesuit missionaries into concrete economic gains. Nieuhoff and Ides, no less than Heylyn and Webb, find in their images of China an idealized reflection of the values – cultural, social, and political – that they bring with them. If each of these writers describes an interiorized civility in those he takes as his Chinese and Manchu counterparts, this civility might be seen as the ongoing reinscription of European anxieties about the coherence of the western, Christianized self cast into the role of tributary barbarian kowtowing to the Emperor in Beijing. The ideology of privilege that Nieuhoff and Ides repeatedly invoke mystifies the political realities of seventeenth-century China, allowing these travelers, like other Europeans, to discover in the crowded markets and opulent palaces of Canton and Beijing sure signs of the empire's inexhaustible wealth.

In practice, however, such wealth was itself guarded by thousands of merchants and officials whose desire for profit conflicted with the Europeans' expectations of a "free" and immensely lucrative trade. On his trip to Canton in 1703, Hamilton sought to capitalize on a newly regularized commerce between English factories in India and Canton, after six decades of desultory efforts by the British to open trade to China. After months of frustrating delays and negotiation, Hamilton was forced to sell his cargo for approximately 80 percent of its market value; factoring in duties and other payments to officials, he ultimately realized only half of what he expected. Disgruntled with the Chinese, he resorts to tactics familiar to his mostly Protestant readers – attack the Jesuits. "The *Christian* Missionaries," Hamilton sneers, "have converted many by the Indulgence of several Emperors, particularly of the *Chunghee*, and those Apostles indulge their Proselytes in many Things opposite to the System and Canons of the Western *Christianity*, as Polygamy, Concubinage, and the Invocation and Adoration of *Pagan* Saints, as well as *Christian*, in their Apotheosis, which has caused no small Disturbance at *Rome*."[52] Hamilton's frustration is taken out on a convenient target, although he is all too aware of the difficulties of negotiating with the Hong merchants of Canton from a position of relative weakness. Yet despite the elusiveness of the free trade sought by the Dutch East India Company and Peter the Great, and the experience of merchants such as Hamilton, Nieuhoff, Ides, and Jesuit writers like Bouvet continued to reinscribe for their readers an idealized China – an empire that seems almost and always primed to reward those merchants who are civil and persistent enough to open its ports to an infinitely profitable commerce.

NOTES

1. Jorge Arditi, *A Genealogy of Manners: Transformations of Social Relations in France and England from the Fourteenth to the Eighteenth Century* (Chicago: University of Chicago Press, 1998); Steven Shapin, *A Social History of Truth: Civility and Science in Seventeenth-Century England* (Chicago: University of Chicago Press, 1994), 3–42, 114–19; Anna Bryson, *From Courtesy to Civility: Changing Codes of Conduct in Early Modern England* (Oxford: Clarendon Press, 1999), 153–59.

2. See particularly Janet Todd, *Sensibility: An Introduction* (London: Methuen, 1987); John Mullan, *Sentiment and Sociability: The Language of Feeling in the Eighteenth Century* (Oxford: Clarendon, 1988); Ann Jessie van Sant, *Eighteenth-Century Sensibility and the Novel: The Senses in Social Context* (Cambridge: Cambridge University Press, 1993); Nancy Armstrong and Leonard Tennenhouse, *The Imaginary Puritan: Literature, Intellectual Labor, and the Origins of Personal Life* (Berkeley and Los Angeles: University of California Press, 1992); and Deidre Shauna Lynch, *The Economy of Character: Novels, Market Culture, and the Business of Inner Meaning* (Chicago: University of Chicago Press, 1998).

3. On Southerne's play see Laura J. Rosenthal, "Owning Oroonoko: Behn, Southerne, and the Contingencies of Property," *Renaissance Drama* 23 (1992), 25–38 and Felicity A. Nussbaum, *The Limits of the Human: Fictions of Anomaly, Race, and Gender in the Long Eighteenth Century* (Cambridge: Cambridge University Press, 2003), 151–88; on Inkle and Yarico, see Peter Hulme, *Colonial Encounters: Europe and the Native Caribbean 1492–1797* (New York: Routledge, 1986), 225–63.

4. For critiques of the circular logic of modernity, see Bruno Latour, *We Have Never Been Modern* and Joseph Rouse, "Philosophy of Science and the Persistent Narratives of Modernity," *Studies in the History and Philosophy of Science* 22 (1991), 141–62. See also Robert Markley, "The Rise of Nothing: Revisionist Historiography and the Narrative Structure of Eighteenth-Century Studies," *Genre* 23 (1990), 77–101, and *Fallen Languages*.

5. For representative views, see Moira Ferguson, *Subject to Others: British Women Writers and Colonial Slavery, 1670–1834* (New York: Routledge, 1992); Firdous Azim, *The Colonial Rise of the Novel* (New York: Routledge, 1993); Laura Brown, *Ends of Empire: Women and Ideology in Early Eighteenth-Century English Literature* (Ithaca: Cornell University Press, 1993); Nussbaum, *Torrid Zones*; Joseph Roach, *Cities of the Dead: Circum-Atlantic Performance* (New York: Columbia University Press, 1996); and Srinivas Aravamudan, *Tropicopolitans: Colonialism and Agency, 1688–1804* (Durham: Duke University Press, 1999).

6. On the Jesuits in China, see Arnold H. Rowbotham, *Missionary and Mandarin: The Jesuits at the Court of China* (Berkeley and Los Angeles: University of California Press, 1942); Gregory Dunne, S. J., *Generation of Giants: The Story of the Jesuits in China in the Last Decades of the Ming Dynasty* (Notre

Dame: Notre Dame University Press, 1962); Mungello, *Curious Land*; and Jensen, *Manufacturing Confucianism*, 77–133.

7. In addition to Mungello, *Curious Land* and Jensen, *Manufacturing Confucianism*, see Spence, *Memory Palace*.

8. On Martini see Mungello, *Curious Land*, particularly 107–33, and van Kley, "News from China," esp. 563–68. Martini's Latin works on China are: *De Bello Tartarico Historia* (Amsterdam, 1655); *Novus Atlas Siensis* (Amsterdam, 1655; published as volume eleven of Joan Blaeu's *Atlas Major*); and *Sinicae Historiae Decas Prima, Res a Gentis Origine ad Christum Natum in Extrema Asia, sive Magno Sinarum Imperio Gestas Complexa* (Amsterdam, 1659).

9. On the Rites Controversy, see George Minamiki, S. J., *The Chinese Rites Controversy from Its Beginning to Modern Times* (Chicago: Loyola University Press, 1985), 25–66.

10. Ricci's journals were edited and augmented by Nicholas Trigault, who arrived in Beijing some months after Ricci's death in 1611; they were published as *De Christiana Expeditione apud Sinas* (Augsburg, 1615) and widely translated in the seventeenth century. See Mungello, *Curious Land*, 45–49, and Willard Peterson, "Learning from Heaven: The Introduction of Christianity and Other Western Ideas into Late Ming China," in *Cambridge History of China*, vol. VIII, part 2: *The Ming Dynasty, 1368–1644*, ed. Dennis Twitchett and Frederick W. Mote (Cambridge: Cambridge University Press, 1998), pp. 810–14. The standard English translation is by Louis J. Gallagher, S. J., *China in the Sixteenth Century: The Journals of Matthew Ricci 1583–1610* (New York: Random House, 1953).

11. On the tribute system in China see Wills, *Embassies and Illusions*, 42–44; and more generally Wills, *Pepper, Guns, and Parleys*; Spence, *The Chan's Great Continent*; and James Hevia, *Cherishing Men from Afar: Qing Guest Ritual and the McCartney Embassy of 1793* (Durham: Duke University Press, 1995).

12. On China in the seventeenth century Frederic Wakeman, Jr., *The Great Enterprise: The Manchu Reconstruction of Order in Seventeenth-Century China*, 2 vols. (Berkeley and Los Angeles: University of California Press, 1985); Huang, *1587, A Year of No Significance*; Denis Twitchett and John K. Fairbank, gen. eds., *The Cambridge History of China*, particularly VIII, part 2 Twitchett and Mote, ed. *The Ming Dynasty, 1368–1644*; Timothy Brook, *The Confusions of Pleasure: A History of Ming China (1368–1644)* (Berkeley and Los Angeles: University of California Press, 1998); and Roger V. Des Forges, *Cultural Centrality and Political Change in Chinese History: Northeast Henan in the Fall of the Ming* (Stanford: Stanford University Press, 2003); Oxnam, *Ruling from Horseback*; and Lawrence D. Kessler, *K'ang-Hsi and the Consolidation of Ch'ing Rule 1661–1684* (Chicago: University of Chicago Press, 1976). On China's place in the "general crisis" of the seventeenth century, Goldstone, *Revolution and Rebellion*, 349–89.

13. Heylyn, *Cosmographie*, 2nd edn (London, 1657), B1r.

14. *Cosmographie*, 865, 866. Heylyn in these instances is following Ricci; see *China in the Sixteenth Century*, 10–11.

15. Webb, *Historical Essay*, 86.

16. Webb, *Historical Essay*, 21. See chapter two above.

17. See Ramsey, "China and the Ideal of Order in Webb's *An Historical Essay*," 483–503.

18. Ralegh, *History of the World*; Goodman, *The Fall of Man*.

19. [Olfert Dapper], *Atlas Chinensis: Being a Second Part of a Relation of Remarkable Passages in Two Embassies from the East-India Company of the United Provinces, to the Vice-Roy Singlamong and General Taising Lipovi, and to Konchi, Emperor of China and East-Tartary*, trans. John Ogilby (London, 1671), 438. This collection is misattributed on the title page to Arnoldus Montanus, who put together a compilation of Dutch writings on Japan which Ogilby had translated and published the previous year (see chapter seven below).

20. Dapper, *Atlas Chinensis*, 438.

21. Dapper, *Atlas Chinensis*, 440. Three Chinese "tails," or "taehls," or "taels" were worth approximately one £.

22. For the western belief in the objectivity of mathematics, see Theodore Porter, *Trust in Numbers: The Pursuit of Objectivity in Science and Public Life* (Princeton: Princeton University Press, 1995).

23. Jan Nieuhoff, *An Embassy from the East-India Company of the United Provinces, to the Grand Tartar Cham Emperor of China; Delivered by their Excellencies Peter de Goyer, and Jacobs de Keyzer, At his Imperial City of Peking* (London, 1669), 3. This edition was "Englished" by John Ogilby, one of four book licenses granted at the time by the King, and uses the same 150 plates – maps and illustrations – as the Dutch edition. All quotations are from this translation.

24. See Wills, *Embassies and Illusions*, 42–44, and Lach and van Kley, *Asia in the Making of Europe*, III: 1685.

25. On the significance of diplomatic gifts, see Cynthia Klekar, "'Prisoners in Silken Bonds': Obligation, Trade, and Diplomacy in English Voyages to Japan and China," *Journal for Early Modern Cultural Studies*, 6 (2006).

26. On Chinese technology in the seventeenth century, see the classical 1637 work by Sung Ying-Hsing, *Chinese Technology in the Seventeenth Century: T'ien-Kung K'ai-Wu*, trans. E-Tu Zen Sun and Shiou-Chuan Sun (1966; rpt. New York: Dover, 1997). The major study of Chinese science and technology is Joseph Needham *et al.*, *Science and Civilisation in China* (Cambridge: Cambridge University Press, 1954–), which has led to a vast number of subsequent expansions, qualifications, and correctives. See particularly Francesca Bray, *Technology and Gender: Fabrics of Power in Late Imperial China* (Berkeley: University of California Press, 1997), and Bray, "Technics and Civilization in Late Imperial China: An Essay in the Cultural History of Technology," *Beyond Joseph Needham: Science, Technology, and Medicine in East and Southeast Asia*, ed. Morris F. Law, *Osiris*, 2nd series 13 (1998), 11–33. For comparative views of Chinese and European science and technology, see R. Bin Wong, *China Transformed: Historical Change and the Limits of*

European Experience (Ithaca: Cornell University Press, 1997); Toby Huff, *The Rise of Modern Science: Islam, China, and the West* (Cambridge: Cambridge University Press, 1993); and Arnold Pacey, *Technology in World Civilization: A Thousand-Year History* (Cambridge, MA: MIT Press, 1990).

27. See George Elison, *Deus Destroyed: The Image of Christianity in Early Modern Japan* (Cambridge, MA: Harvard University Press, 1973); C. R. Boxer, *The Christian Century in Japan: 1549–1650* (Berkeley: University of California Press, 1951); and Andrew C. Ross, *A Vision Betrayed: The Jesuits in Japan and China* (Maryknoll, NY: Orbis Books, 1994).

28. On Chinese population in the seventeenth century, see Mark Elvin, *The Pattern of the Chinese Past* (Stanford: Stanford University Press, 1973), 310–11, who draws on the work of Ho Ping-t'i, *Studies on the Population of China, 1368–1953* (Cambridge, MA: Harvard University Press, 1959). Ho estimates the population in 1600 at 150,000,000, Elvin almost 175,000,000. For higher estimates, see Goldstone, *Revolution and Rebellion*; and Pierre-Etienne Will and R. Bin Wong, *Nourish the People: The State Civilian Granary System in China, 1650–1850* (Ann Arbor: University of Michigan Press, 1991); on the population and prosperity of China under the Qing, see Susan Naquin and Evelyn S. Rawski, *Chinese Society in the Eighteenth Century* (New Haven: Yale University Press, 1987).

29. See, for example, Gallagher, *China in the Sixteenth Century*, 9–11.

30. On resistance to the Qing dynasty in South China, see Lynn A. Struve, *The Southern Ming 1644–1662* (New Haven: Yale University Press, 1984), and, on Cheng Ch'eng-kung, 156–93.

31. Alexander Hamilton, *A New Account of the East Indies*, 2 vols. (Edinburgh, 1727), II: 238.

32. Hamilton, *New Account of the East Indies*, II: 238.

33. On Ricci's attempts to appeal to Chinese elites by fusing elements of Christianity and Confucianism, see Mungello, *Curious Land*, 63–65; and Spence, *Memory Palace of Matteo Ricci*. For the impact of Confucianism on European philosophers, including Leibniz and Voltaire, see Yuen-Ting Lai, "Religious Scepticism and China," 11–41; and Perkins, *Leibniz and China*, 23–31.

34. On seventeenth-century descriptions of the Chinese as "white," see Lach and van Kley, *Asia in the Making of Europe*, III: 1619. The 1657 second edition of Heylyn's *Cosmographie* in the British Library, which, I believe, may be a presentation copy given by the aging author to Charles II on his restoration, includes hand-colored maps and cartouches of Asian figures. These figures are – without exception – colored in the same pink tones as Europeans, and thus distinguished from Africans and Amerindians. On the graphic depiction of the Chinese in Martini's *Atlas* and *De Bello Tartarico*, see Mungello, *Curious Land*, 117; and Timothy Billings, "Visible Cities: The Heterotropic Utopia of China in Early Modern European Writing," *Genre* 30 (1997), 105–34. On perceptions of race in the early period, see Roxanne Wheeler, *The Complexion of Race: Categories of Difference in Eighteenth-Century British Culture* (Philadelphia:

University of Pennsylvania Press, 2000); David Bindman, *Ape to Apollo: Aesthetics and the Idea of Race in the Eighteenth Century* (Ithaca: Cornell University Press, 2002); and Nussbaum, *The Limits of the Human*.

35. Michel Serres, *The Parasite*, trans. Lawrence Scher (Baltimore: Johns Hopkins University Press, 1982, 3–12). On triangular formations in eighteenth-century narrative, see Martha Koehler, "Epistolary Closure and Triangular Return in Richardson's Clarissa," *Journal of Narrative Technique* 24 (1994), 153–72.

36. Rachel Attwater, *Adam Schall: A Jesuit at the Court of China 1592–1666* (London: Geoffrey Chapman, 1963). Adapted from Joseph Duhr, S. J., *Un Jésuite en Chine, Adam Schall* (Paris, 1936).

37. Attwater, *Adam Schall*, 100; see also Dunne, *Generation of Giants*, 317–38.

38. Fo Lu-shu, comp. and trans., *A Documentary Chronicle of Sino-Western Relations, 1644–1820*, 2 vols. (Tucson: University of Arizona Press, 1966), 1: 17.

39. See chapter one below; for Purchas's comments, see *Pilgrimmes*, 1: 5.

40. On Dutch "illusions" see Wills, *Embassies and Illusions*, 3; on their proposals for trade, see 42.

41. Fo Lu-shu, *Documentary Chronicle*, 1: 19–20.

42. Fo Lu-shu, *Documentary Chronicle*, 1: 20.

43. Nieuhoff's travels were translated and printed in Awnsham and John Churchill, eds., *A Collection of Voyages and Travels, Some Now First Printed from Original Manuscripts. Others Translated out of Foreign Languages*, 4 vols. (London, 1704–05). See II: 1–156, for Nieuhoff's travels in Brazil; and II: 181–366 for his travels to India, Southeast Asia, and Taiwan, entitled *Mr. John Nieuhoff's Remarkable Voyages and Travels to the East-Indies*.

44. All quotations are from this edition. On Chinese–Russian relations, see Mancall, *Russia and China*; Sechin Jagchid and Van Jay Symons, *Peace, War, and Trade along the Great Wall* (Bloomington: Indiana University Press, 1989); and Terrence Armstrong, "Russian Penetration into Siberia up to 1800," in *The European Outthrust and Encounter* ed. Cecil H. Clough and P. E. H. Hair (Liverpool: Liverpool University Press, 1994), 119–40.

45. Adam Brand, *A Journal of an Embassy from their Majesties John and Peter Alexowits, Emperors of Muscovy into China* (London, 1698), 30.

46. See Oxnam, *Ruling from Horseback*, 3–16, on Chinese–Manchu relations in the 1660s; Jonathan D. Spence, *Emperor of China: Self-Portrait of K'ang-Hsi* (1974; rpt. New York: Vintage, 1988); Helen Dunstan, *Conflicting Counsels to Confuse the Age: A Documentary Study of Political Economy in Qing China, 1644–1840* (Ann Arbor: Center for Chinese Studies, University of Michigan, 1996); and Pamela Kyle Crossley, *A Translucent Mirror: History and Identity in Qing Imperial Ideology* (Berkeley: University of California Press, 1999).

47. See Edwin van Kley, "An Alternative Muse: The Manchu Conquest of China in the Literature of Seventeenth-Century Northern Europe," *European Studies Review* 6 (1976), 21–43. On Dryden, see Derek Hughes, *Dryden's Heroic Drama* (Lincoln: University of Nebraska Press, 1982), and Bridget Orr, *Empire on the English Stage 1660–1714* (Cambridge: Cambridge University Press, 2001).

48. For the Emperor's response to the Russian embassy, see Fo Lu-shu, *Documentary Chronicle*, I: 106–07.

49. Fo Lu-shu *Documentary Chronicle*, I: 106.

50. J[oachim] Bouvet, *The History of Cang-Hy, the Present Emperour of China* (London, 1699), 2. All quotations are from this edition.

51. See Jeannie Dalporto, "The Succession Crisis and Elkanah Settle's *The Conquest of China by the Tartars,*" *The Eighteenth Century: Theory and Interpretation* 45 (2004), 131–46.

52. Hamilton, *New Account*, II: 270. On Hamilton's voyage to Canton and the reopening of East India Company trade to China, see Hosea B. Morse, *The Chronicles of the East India Company Trading to China 1635–1834*, 5 vols. (Oxford: Clarendon, 1926), I: 83–103; and Keay, *The Honourable Company*, 205–12.

CHAPTER 4

Heroic merchants: trade, nationalism, and abjection in Dryden's Amboyna

STAGING TORTURE

In act five of Dryden's tragedy *Amboyna*, first produced in 1672 on the eve of the Third Dutch War, cruel Dutch merchants torture their virtuous English counterparts, setting their fingers on fire and wrapping their necks in oiled cloths, then forcing them to drink until they swell to grotesque proportions. The dramatist is not reticent about depicting the horrors of torture that his countrymen endured in 1623 on this Southeast Asian island; the stage direction in act five reads, "The SCENE opens, and discovers the English tortured, and the Dutch tormenting them" (v i 85).[1] But unlike the torture scenes in other contemporary plays such as Elkannah Settle's *Empress of Morocco*, the spectacle of violence is not distanced by its exotic setting. By presenting seventeenth-century Englishmen as victims of an implacable enemy, Dryden's tragedy complicates neo-Foucaultian efforts to read the history of torture as a means to inscribe on the body of the "other" the political power and juridical authority of the torturer.[2] Dryden's hero, the head of the English factory, Gabriel Towerson, may voice stirring defenses of his countrymen's nobility and generosity, but, in an important sense, English nationalism in the play emerges in and through the spectacle of its merchants being falsely accused of treason, tortured, and executed. Dryden, however, can recast England's humiliation on Amboyna as the martyrdom of national virtue, liberty, and nobility only by simplifying a complex history of international rivalry in Southeast Asia to a mercantile morality play that mystifies the sources and nature of Anglo-Dutch conflict. While the Governor General of the VOC in Batavia had broad legal, political, and military authorities, EIC merchants had fewer rights and their allegiance – despite patriotic rhetoric and displays – often was as much to the Company's directors in London as it was to an idealized concept of the nation. In transforming abject Jacobean merchants into patriotic heroes, Dryden paradoxically demonstrates the instabilities within the discourses of nationalism, free trade, and gentlemanly civility that the play overtly champions.[3]

This effort to identify and celebrate the innate qualities of English national character as they emerge in opposition to Dutch cruelty reveals the performative, ultimately imaginary basis of any sense of an essential national identity; this is one reason why the play, despite its aesthetic shortcomings, recently has received a fair amount of critical scrutiny. James Thompson, for example, suggests that, in contrast to *The Conquest of Granada*, "this play may appear laughable," although he goes on to question the aesthetic and ideological suppositions that underlie such value judgments.[4] But for Dryden and his contemporaries, English abjection in the Spice Islands was no laughing matter during the Third Dutch War. In effect, *Amboyna* displaces profound insecurities about the economic strength and political will of England – indeed the integrity of the nation – into the form of heroic tragedy and the theatrics of political martyrdom. Unlike the Jesuit descriptions of China and Japan and geographies, like Heylyn's *Cosmographie*, that almost obsessively characterized the peoples, civilizations, and landscapes of the Far East, Dryden's tragedy concentrates on inter-European rivalries and banishes the Ambonese, except for the victimized heroine, Ysabinda, to the margins of a moralistic conflict between noble Englishmen and tyrannical Dutch merchants. Rather than a foundational discourse, nationalism in the play thus emerges as a second-order ideological construct that works imperfectly to repress the anxieties described by other writers on Asia during the period: the fears that profits will overwhelm considerations of national interest, legal obligation, and individual integrity; that European rivals are conspiring with Asians to monopolize trade; that national identities will be corrupted by foreign customs and foreign contacts; and that the riches of the Far East are not, as often advertised in the seventeenth century, inexhaustible but subject to a logic of scarcity that produces – inevitably – competition, insecurity, and violence.[5] The imperfect workings of nationalism in Dryden's play, and in the historical accounts that serve as his sources, are not primitive forms of what later will become an ostensibly coherent ideology of the centralized state. *Amboyna* reveals instead the inconsistencies, gaps, and anxieties that constitute the fiction of an essential, transhistorical national identity. As Foucault argues, ideologies survive by exciting dissent, by exploiting fractures among and within groups and individuals in order to justify continuing efforts to reinscribe an always imperfect, an always imaginary, order – for example, coherent, unassailable national, racial, class, and gender identities.[6] In this sense, to understand the workings of nationalism in Dryden's play, it is necessary to look closely at the complex historical processes that the dramatist must repress in order to forge a popular, nationalistic art. In both *Amboyna* and his 1667 poem *Annus Mirabilis*, Dryden must transmute national abjection into a defense of the nation.

RIVAL STRATEGIES: COERCION AND "QUIET TRADE"

Although *Amboyna* is set in 1623, its obsession with the Dutch commercial empire in Southeast Asia reflects the political conflicts of the later seventeenth century. Anthony Reid argues that in 1600 Southeast Asian powers interacted with Europeans as equals; by 1700, inequalities, both military and economic, had begun to appear.[7] In 1672–73, European merchants still confronted sophisticated networks of states, dynasties, and political, military, and mercantile alliances throughout the region, but the VOC had turned several small islands into slave labor camps for the production of spices; the Company had colonized or partially controlled through surrogates and alliances several regional states in addition to Amboyna: Malacca on the Malay peninsula, Macassar on Celebes, Ternate, and Tidore; and it had captured Portuguese forts on Ceylon and the Malabar coast.[8] In analyzing the gradual dominance of European military and economic power that emerged in Asia by the late eighteenth century, O. H. K. Spate suggests that

> the Europeans' strongest weapon was perhaps not so much in gunnery or capital or book-keeping as in their possession of a coherent policy with the one over-riding objective of trade expansion . . . In contrast, the congeries of local states (as in the break-down of late Mogul India) had no one central aim and were riddled not only by inter-state rivalries but by intra-state dynastic feuds, the two often running in harness. In such an "international anarchy" the short-term advantage of securing European aid led to a long-term creeping take-over by the "great and powerful friend," whether the EIC in India or the VOC in the Indies.[9]

The "over-riding objective of trade expansion" may have functioned as a "coherent policy," but this coherence was enforced by the investors in the two trading companies rather than by a strong, centralized state. In England, the number of investors in the EIC never exceeded a few hundred, and the relationships among these investors, their employees, the Company's directors, and the "nation" were complex and vexed. In the distant outposts scattered across Asia, the merchants of the EIC and VOC may have been the agents for furthering national interests and reproducing discourses of national identity, but those interests and discourses were contested, as the numerous defenses of and attacks on the EIC's trade of bullion for cloth and luxury items indicate. Both *Annus Mirabilis* and *Amboyna* work to shore up the problematic identification of national interest with the EIC's need to return sizeable profits. Part of Dryden's difficulty in this undertaking lies in his being forced to acknowledge that the Dutch were better equipped financially and organizationally than the English to exploit opportunities for trade – and therefore to increase the Company's wealth and to exercise the nation's military and economic power.

In resurrecting the tragedy on Amboyna for propagandistic purposes, Dryden reanimates disputes and conflicts that date back sixty years. In one respect, he relives as traumatic memory the incidents that provoked Milton's outrage: the humiliation of English military and economic power and the threat to the ideology of trade that animated English and Dutch ventures to Southeast Asia. The VOC began in 1602 with a capital of £540,000, eight times the money invested in the EIC two years earlier; the British, consequently, could muster only one-third the number of ships in Asia as the Dutch.[10] English joint-stock companies in the sixteenth and seventeenth centuries were underfunded and their ventures (although often profitable) geared to turning a quick profit rather than establishing, as the Dutch did, a financial and administrative system capable of sustaining a diversified trade over a longer period of time. As the size of their investment suggests, the Dutch perceived the VOC as the instrument of a unified national interest, or, to take a different perspective, the Company became the agent that reinscribed, through trade, a sense of national identity that depended, in large measure, on exploiting the wealth of the Indies. Unlike the East India Company, whose stock remained in the hands of a few hundred wealthy shareholders, the VOC raised significant capital by opening investment to all citizens, including merchants, academics, clergymen, teachers, and manual workers – 6.5 million guilders in investments ranging from 50 to 850,000 guilders.[11] The Dutch were better financed and better equipped to deal with the complexities of a trade that demanded time, patience, and negotiating skills. Because pepper and other spices became expensive to purchase directly with bullion brought from Europe, the VOC sold its silver in China (where it brought higher prices than in Europe), and reinvested those profits in Chinese silks, which then were sold in Japan for copper and gold. These metals were exported to India and used to buy textiles, which finally were exchanged in the Spice Islands for cloves, mace, and nutmeg. At each juncture, the VOC turned a profit by delivering goods in demand at local and regional markets, and forcing other merchants, both European and Asian, to pay prices demanded by its factors. By the time VOC ships docked in the Moluccas, the value of their cargoes had increased significantly. The EIC, shut out of buying either Japanese silver or Moluccan spices at their sources, were at a comparative disadvantage, trading through Dutch middlemen (and paying higher prices) to purchase cloves, nutmeg, pepper, and mace.[12]

Given their financial and strategic handicaps, shareholders in the EIC characteristically shied away from promoting military adventures (except for privateering raids on foreign ships) or long-term colonial commitments, arguing that force would be unprofitable, if not self-defeating. Thomas Roe, sent by the Company on an embassy to the Moghul's court between 1615 and 1618, wrote that at Surat, as elsewhere in the East Indies,

A warr and traffique are incompatible ... [Y]ou shall no way engage your selves [in battle] but at sea, wher you are like to gayne as often as to loose. It is the beggering of the Portugall, notwithstanding his many rich residences and territoryes [in India], that hee keepes souldiers that spendes it; yet his garisons are meane. He never profited by the Indyes, since hee defended them. Observe this well. It hath beene also the error of the Dutch, who seeke Plantation heere by the Swoord. They turne a woonderfull stocke, they proule in all Places, they Possess some of the best; yet their dead Payes consume all the gayne. Let this bee received as a rue that if you will Profitt, seeke it at Sea, and in quiet trade.[13]

For Roe, as for most shareholders in the EIC, colonial garrisons and military adventures are simply too costly to maintain. Thomas Mun offers a similar analysis of the troubles of the Portuguese–Spanish forces that "infinitely exhaust their treasure" by "that canker war."[14] For Roe and Mun, the limitations of the EIC dictate both short-term mercantile strategy and a moral sense of its mission that downplays the kind of aggressive, gun-barrel strategies practiced by the Dutch. In contrast, Jan Pieterszoon Coen, later Governor General of the VOC in Asia, wrote to the Company's directors in 1614, "Your Honours should know by experience that trade in Asia must be driven and maintained under the protection and favor of Your Honours' own weapons, and that the weapons must be paid for by the profits from the trade; so that we cannot carry on trade without war nor war without trade."[15] Coen's rhetoric suggests that war, trade, Company policy, and (at least implicitly) the integrity of the nation are implicated in each other. Like some of his successors, Coen took advantage of the long delays in communications between Batavia on the northeast coast of Java and the VOC's directors, the Heren XVII, in Amsterdam to consolidate territorial and political power through military adventurism, repression, and slave labor. The expansion of Dutch power in the Spice Islands by 1620 began to assume colonialist forms that were regarded skeptically, if not hostilely, by some of the directors and many of the investors in the VOC.[16] Coen's career as a brutal administrator suggests that he, rather than his employers or investors, assumes the role of embodying a "national" interest that many Dutch men and women find abhorrent. In this respect, the nation is not a preexistent or essentialized agent that engages in trade, war, financial dealings, and a variety of other activities; rather economic trans-actions and military adventures are the "symptoms" that are always in the process of reconstituting the nation as an imaginary whole.[17] Roe and Coen, in this regard, voice different responses to ongoing crises of national identity, different means to repress the recognition that the nation itself must be constantly reinscribed by the practices of trade and by always supplementary narratives of self-identity.

The English claim to "quiet trade" in the Moluccas stemmed from Drake's visit to Ternate in 1579, and then from the handful of factories that the EIC had established in the Banda Islands, on Java, and Amboyna. Like the Dutch, the English sought to carve out a share of the traffic in cloves, nutmeg, pepper, and mace that the Portuguese had dominated since the middle of the sixteenth century. By 1606, the Dutch had driven the Portuguese out of much of the region and become the primary traders in pepper, nutmeg, and cloves. By the middle of the next decade, as I discussed in chapter one, the Dutch were on their way to monopolizing this trade. Outgunned and outfinanced, the English were forced to sign a treaty in 1619 guaranteeing the Dutch two-thirds of the trade in the region; both nations pledged to resolve disputes peacefully, and each agreed to provide ten ships to defend mutual interests in Southeast Asia or, as it turned out, to harass Portuguese and Spanish shipping. The EIC, however, lacked the resources to honor its commitment and conflicts ensued almost immediately.

Harsh debates centered on the trading relationships that each company had established with local merchants, chiefs, and growers. In a pamphlet published in Amsterdam, *The Hollanders Declaration of the Affaires of the East Indies* (1622), the Dutch author accused the English of aiding the natives of Banda in 1617 in their "warrage" against the VOC, a conflict which interrupted trade in "the fruits and spices, which the Bandaneseis were tyed [by a 1609 treaty] to deliver"; of then violating the terms of the 1619 Treaty by failing to supply ten ships "toward the common defence"; and finally of encouraging rebellions against the Dutch by the natives of Ternate and Amboyna.[18] The English responded by denying these "false and fabulous slanders," protesting the "cruell and inhumane wrongs done by the Hollanders to the English," and claiming they were only defending those villagers on Great Banda and Neira islands "with whom [the English] had free trade and trafficke, who lovingly and with free consent sold to the English their spices, &c. who put themselves under the protection of . . . the King of England."[19] The rhetoric of the English response may seem almost Lockean in its emphasis on consent, freedom, and the voluntary submission of several chiefs to English authority, but it is hardly disinterested. The English favor what they term a free trade in the region only because they cannot compete with the Dutch militarily, financially, or administratively; the Dutch insist on the letter of the treaty because they had dictated its conditions. To enforce rigorously the Treaty of 1619 would be to squeeze the English out of the spice trade. The English and Dutch pamphlets, then, offer not only competing reconstructions of events on Banda but competing ideologies of trade that reflect the two nations' differing political and economic fortunes in the East Indies. And, by 1623, the EIC was in the process of giving up its efforts in the Spice Islands and Japan to concentrate on the trade in the Moghul Empire, where its merchants would find themselves embroiled in the complex politics of the subcontinent and barely hanging on in the 1630s.[20] In this regard, as Spate argues, Amboyna was "not the occasion for [the British] withdrawal [from Southeast Asia, but] rather a bloody epilogue" to it.[21]

PAMPHLET WARS

In the aftermath of the events on Amboyna, English and Dutch pamphleteers published radically different accounts of the trial and execution of the English merchants. These pamphlets extend many of the arguments that had been made two years earlier in *The Hollanders Declaration* and the *Answere* and offer, in effect, different bases for imagining national identity. As previous editors of *Amboyna* have noted, Dryden read the two pamphlets by Sir Dudley Digges, a prominent shareholder in the EIC, *A True Relation of the Vniust, Cruell, and Barbarous Proceedings against the English at Amboyna* (London, 1624) and *The Answere unto the Dutch Pamphlet, Made in Defence of the Uniust and Barbarous Proceedings against the English at Amboyna, in the East-Indies, by the Hollanders There* (London, 1624), as well as John Darrell's *A True and Compendious Narration; Or (the Second Part of Amboyna) of Sundry Notorious or Remarkable Injuries, Insolences, and Acts of Hostility which the HOLLANDERS Have Exercised from Time to Time against THE ENGLISH NATION in the East Indies* (London, 1665).[22] These accounts emphasize Dutch ingratitude, paranoia, hypocrisy, and cruelty and maintain that the VOC's account of the alleged plot against its fort on Amboyna is implausible and its after-the-fact justification of the torture and execution of the English merchants self-serving.

According to Digges's *True Relation,* a Japanese soldier employed by the Dutch asked a sentinel about his duties in defending the fort. The Dutch treated this question as an act of espionage and either acted on their fears that the English, Japanese, Ternatans, and Bandanese were conspiring against them or simply seized this opportunity to eliminate English competition in the spice trade. Under torture, the Japanese soldier began implicating EIC merchants in a plot to capture the fort, murder the Dutch, and garrison Amboyna as a stronghold from which to prey on the VOC's trade. Throughout both pamphlets, Digges challenges the Dutch interpretation of events, seeking to demonstrate that the Hollanders' fears of an Anglo-Asian conspiracy against Amboyna are absurd. Ten unarmed Englishmen and ten unarmed Japanese, he maintains, were no match for a fort defended by two or three hundred men. There were no English let alone Japanese ships within forty leagues of Amboyna when the alleged plot was uncovered, and no evidence whatsoever that the English could have expected aid from other rivals of the Dutch in the region: "The Ternatans," Towerson's alleged co-conspirators, "were enemies as well to the English as to the Dutch," Digges asserts, and then asks pointedly, "When were they reconciled?"[23] Seizing the fort would have been pointless, he continues, because the English ships in the region were outnumbered and Towerson could not have expected aid from the EIC factory in Jakarta because the English were "under command of the Dutch Fort there, and altogether subject to the Hollanders" (16). The narrative that Digges offers, based on eyewitness accounts of other European merchants and the prisoners' professions of innocence (scribbled on the backs of bills and the flyleaves of Bibles, which escaped suppression by the Dutch when the papers were returned to the EIC after the executions), thus casts English strategic weakness as a form of moral superiority: the desire for "a fair and free commerce" (A4r). In effect, the credibility of his version of events depends on the political and military impotence of his countrymen.

Thirty years later, in the Treaty of Westminster (1654) ending the First Dutch War, the Dutch tacitly conceded many of Digges's points by agreeing to pay compensation of £85,000 for seizing English factories in Southeast Asia and £3,615 to the heirs of the men executed on Amboyna.[24] This vindication, such as it is, of Digges's interpretation becomes particularly important for understanding Dryden's troping of the events on Amboyna as tragedy. Although the playwright does not allude directly to the settlement, it offers him a moral touchstone for his heroicizing of Towerson and the other English victims and a basis for his championing a political philosophy of national aggrandizement by "quiet trade." It also suggests that Dryden, in writing the play, is not seeking justice for unpunished crimes but reliving a nightmare of national abjection; like Digges and Darrell, he is forced to argue that the English martyrdom on Amboyna is essential to legitimizing the moral and political authority – the integrity of national identity – that he celebrates. In this respect, the military achievements that characterize his heroes in tragedies such as *The Indian Queen* and *The Conquest of Granada* give way to a theatrics of martyrdom as a strategy of self-definition.

The English pamphlets, despite their tacit legitimation by the Treaty of Westminster, though, tell only half the story; *A True Declaration of the News that came out of the East-Indies ... concerning a Conspiracy discovered in the Iland of Amboyna* (Amsterdam, 1624) gives the Dutch version of the events, and, in the process, discloses the insecurities and fears that tormented and motivated the VOC authorities. The Dutch writer's insistence that the Japanese conspirators arrested on Amboyna must have been part of a larger, European-led plot to break the emerging Dutch monopoly of the clove trade is characteristic of the triangulated politics of European expansion in the region. Acting alone, without the aid of western ships bristling with canons, he asserts, "the Indians (of themselves) durst not offer to undertake any such great designe [the seizing of the Dutch fort and factory in Amboyna], without some great helpe of some of *Europe*, either of the *Spaniards, Portugalls*, or some other." To bolster this claim, he declares that native merchants and chiefs in other ports in the Moluccas "had great secret correspondence with the English Merchants."[25] The Dutch writer seems less worried about an East Indian "other" (a projection of the weaknesses of the European self, externalized and vilified) than the prospect of a Moluccan–English alliance, a "secret correspondence" that invests economic transactions – the Moluccans shopping their commodities for the best price – with a sinister political and military intent. The Dutch author does not voice a nineteenth-century fear of being contaminated or overwhelmed by an alien "other" but reveals the obsessive, even paranoid logic that informed Coen's strategies of dealing with competition: the writer assumes that the same tactics the Dutch employ – setting rival sultanates, dynastic factions, and merchants against each other – are being turned against them. The nightmare image of an Anglo-Moluccan alliance thus mirrors and projects onto the other the ruthless logic of Coen's identification of war and trade. Displacing the violence of mercantile aggrandizement onto the English, the Dutch pamphlet-writer, like his countrymen on the island a year earlier, challenges the EIC's version of events by delegitimizing the English claims to responsible nationhood – that is, to the commercial integrity that results from honoring one's contracts, abiding by treaties, and adhering to the letter of the law.

In responding to Digges's narrative, the Dutch author attempts to reclaim the moral high ground by defending tenaciously the legality of the executions on Amboyna. Unlike the EIC, the VOC had the legal authority not only to enforce laws, try and punish criminals, and enter into trading agreements, but also to declare war, seize and annex territories, and make treaties. He maintains that, according to Dutch law, the English "prisoners were all lawfully and orderly examined, and it appeared by them ioyntly, according to their own confession (every one having underwritten it with his owne hand)" (6). If they were tortured to produce this confession, the author insists, then "it [was] done according to the lawes of this Government" which distinguish between "extraordinary and cruell torture" and "ordinary torture" (16).[26] This distinction, common on the Continent but not in England, is then used to argue that any confession produced under "ordinary" torture must be considered voluntary. The signatures of the prisoners become revelations of the true state of the conscience of the conspirators, unambiguous testimony of a criminal conspiracy against the property of the United Provinces and its agents. The VOC's written record of the examination and show-trial becomes, against all logic, an unproblematic representation of events, beliefs, and intentions. The Dutch writer claims that he has "overlooked every ones confession, but I finde not one word in any one, which maketh any mention of such [extraordinary] torture." "Some of the prisoners," he contends, confessed to the plot "before any torture; others, after a little (or rather a touch) of it" (18). The Dutch defense of their actions boils down to the dubious contention that the English volunteered to incriminate themselves: "no extraordinary torture was used," the writer concludes, "in such a manner as given out there, by those that would wish us evill; nay, that those few that felt any, were only touched (not punished) with ordinary torture" (18–19). For the inquisitors, the truth rests in the legal form of the proceedings, in a decontextualizing of the circumstances under which the confession was obtained: if there is no mention of torture on the page, then no torture occurred. In effect, the Dutch author must rely on a fiction of the English as political penitents stricken by the consciousness of their sins to sign their own death warrants; they must be constituted as seemingly existential moral subjects who overcome their tendency to sin, their corrupt national identity, through the encouragement of "ordinary torture." Nationalism, in this respect, becomes the motivation for their plot, the source of their evil. Projected onto the other, the very strategies that the Dutch and English use to reinscribe the ideal of a unified nation become evidence of their enemy's inherent corruption.

If the English demonstrate their moral commitment to a "fair and free commerce" by their martyrdom, the Dutch stake their claim to an idealized nationhood not by inscribing violently their power on the bodies of their English prisoners but by enforcing a contractual conception of self-identity. As a republic that only in the last century has thrown off the yoke of Spanish tyranny, the Dutch perceive themselves as a nation through the prism of their material prosperity, their ability to extend their commercial and financial power halfway across the world by signing treaties, establishing factories, increasing their trade and profits, enforcing contracts, and outmaneuvering their European rivals. Throughout the century, Dutch writers compared the people of the United Provinces to other victims of Spanish colonialism, the natives of the Americas, and debated the morality of importing into Amsterdam the very luxuries that could corrupt the mercantile virtues of tolerance, sobriety, and the sanctity of the law on which an emerging sense of national identity depended.[27] In this context, the Dutch need to downplay their torture of the EIC merchants in order to compel the English to accept a contractual basis for national identity and international responsibility, to acknowledge the ultimate authority of the written word – the Treaty of 1619 – in place of the unwritten claims of gentlemanly privilege to a "free and fair commerce." The fiction of a voluntary confession of an Anglo-Japanese plot to seize the VOC's fort becomes a means to constitute, for the Dutch, a legal basis for their claims to an unassailable national identity. A government that can compel such confessions has the moral and legal authority to condemn the English as pirates or parasites and therefore to deny the EIC's claim to cloves, pepper, and profits in the East Indies. If, for the Dutch writer, national identity is, in part, enacted by and through an ever-expanding trade, then the English commercial failures in Southeast Asia can be explained as evidence of their lack of the national resolve, foresight, and financial acumen that would constitute them as a coherent nation. In this regard, the abstract ideals of gentlemanly morality on which Digges (and later Dryden) insist seem, to the Dutch, lame excuses for acts of economic espionage, attempts to mystify the absence of a mercantile policy that alone can legitimize the English nation as an organized and profitable corporate entity.

The retreat of the EIC from the spice trade in the Indonesian archipelago had political and economic effects on international trade throughout western Europe. While the Anglo-Dutch rivalry persisted in the third and fourth decades of the seventeenth century, a precarious, de facto division of labor left the Dutch ascendant in the Baltic trade, including lucrative shipping of manufactured and luxury goods to Russia and Scandinavia in exchange for raw materials, while the English sold Indian pepper and cloth in Spain, Portugal, and Italy. The English prospered, though, almost by default because they owed much of their success to Spanish embargoes against the Dutch and raids by Spanish and Flemish privateers on VOC and West Indian Company (WIC) vessels. In practice, the Dutch monopoly of the spice trade gave them significant financial advantages. The United Provinces benefited from "more shipping, lower freight rates, a better financial system, lower interests rates, and . . . a wider range and higher quality" of manufactured goods.[28] In the late 1640s, however, the situation changed dramatically: as England struggled through the end of the Civil War, London trade to southern Europe suffered, and the Netherlands rapidly supplanted England as the principal exporter of cloth to Spain and the chief importer of Spanish wool. By 1651 England, particularly London, was in a profound economic slump. Spurred on by merchants, shippers, and textile manufacturers, a parliamentary mission to the Hague in March 1651 tried to turn back the clock to the 1580s by demanding that the Netherlands accept the kind of political subordination to England that had been imposed on Scotland. When the Dutch countered with piecemeal proposals to ease tensions, Parliament passed the Navigation Act in August 1651, an anti-Dutch measure designed to prevent the importation into England of colonial products, fish, wines, olives, and various wools and silks on Dutch ships and outlawed any commerce between the Dutch and the English colonies in the Caribbean. It also effectively licensed English privateering: 140 Dutch merchantmen were seized by the English in the Atlantic, Caribbean, and North Sea by the end of 1651 and another thirty in January 1652. By the end of that month, the two countries were at war. Although the English fleet outnumbered and outgunned the Dutch, English victories in the Channel and Irish Sea were offset in 1653 by Dutch and Danish domination of the Baltic and Dutch victories in the Mediterranean and Indian Ocean, a severe blow to the beleaguered EIC merchants in Surat. By 1654, the war had cost thousands of men and hundreds of ships on both sides, leading to a "catastrophic slump" in Dutch trade.[29] The VOC had captured a number of key ports from the Portuguese in India and Southeast Asia in the 1640s, including Malacca, and disruptions in the spice trade as well as in the Baltic and English Channel led to severe losses for the United Provinces. The treaty concluded in 1654 saw no major territorial concessions on either side, and, given their heavy losses, the Dutch were probably only too happy to make the payment of reparations for Amboyna one of their principal concessions.

The reparations granted to the widows and orphans of the merchants executed on Amboyna, however, did nothing to ease the tensions that persisted between London and Amsterdam. Trade rivalries and political antagonisms simmered in the late 1650s and rekindled with the naval arms race that began in earnest almost as soon as Charles II was restored to the English throne. English privateers continued to prey on Dutch shipping in the Caribbean and Mediterranean, and the East India Companies of the two nations had resumed an almost open war by 1664. England had more ships and more guns to bring to the fight, and the declaration of war the following year was supported by much of the London mercantile community. The opening naval battle off Lowestoft in June 1665 resulted in a resounding English victory; seventeen of the 103 Dutch warships were captured or sunk. Yet the Dutch once again closed the Baltic to English shipping, and had the resources to outspend the English in refitting their navies. Both countries suffered heavy losses among merchant vessels, but "English maritime commerce was almost completely paralysed."[30] For Dryden, trying to rally English support for a costly war, 1666 presented a daunting challenge. The Plague in London and the Great Fire were followed by a blockade of coal supplies from the north of England in the winter after *Annus Mirabilis* was published. In June 1667 the Dutch admiral Michiel de Ruyter raided English ships in the Medway, burning five vessels, and towing away the English flagship, the *Royal Charles*. The English had little choice except to negotiate a peace. The Treaty of Breda in June 1667 confirmed English control of New York but ceded Surinam, the EIC's longstanding claim to the island of Run in the Bandas, and ports in the Caribbean and West Africa to the Dutch. Writing some months before the signing of this treaty, Dryden had to contend in his poem not only with the effects of war, plague, and fire, but also with the knowledge that the hostilities had strengthened the hold of the VOC on trade to the Far East.

In dedicating *Annus Mirabilis* to the city of London, Dryden praises "the Metropolis of Great Britain" for its "invincible Courage and unshaken Constancy" in overcoming "an expensive, though necessary War, a consuming Pestilence, and a more consuming Fire" and goes so far as to describe the city as "a great Emblem of the suffering Deity."[31] This effort to identify London, a synecdoche for England as a trading nation, with the sufferings and resurrection of Christ underscores the ways in which the languages of politics, commerce, and national identity are shot through with the rhetoric of providentialist history, even eschatology.[32] In terming his poem "*Historical*, not *Epick*," Dryden admits that he cannot confine the "broken action" of 1666 to the kind of unity demanded by epic verse; there is no conclusion to the war, no triumph to celebrate, only a commercial victory to prophesize. In his long justification of its "Heroick" character, Dryden defends his decision to employ verse forms appropriate to its themes of national and spiritual resurrection, justifying his use of quatrains as the most "noble, and of greater dignity . . . then any other Verse in use amongst us" (51). Poetic form transmutes the disasters of 1666 to harbingers of a heroic, and profitable, future for the nation.

Dryden's heroicizing of London in *Annus Mirabilis* depends on both demonizing the Dutch and rallying his readers to the belief that ultimately the English are destined to supplant their rivals in the spice trade. The villainy of the Dutch is cast in terms of their monopoly on trade to the East Indies:

> Trade, which like bloud should circularly flow,
> > Stop'd in their Channels, found its freedom lost:
> Thither the wealth of all the world did go,
> > And seem'd but shipwrack'd on so base a Coast.

> For them alone the Heav'ns had kindly heat,
> > In Eastern Quarries ripening precious Dew:
> For them the *Idumaean Balm* did sweat,
> > And in hot *Ceilon* Spicy Forests grew.

(ll. 5–12)

These early stanzas suggest something of the defensiveness that informs Dryden's celebration of England's claims to national greatness. The poet – like his contemporaries – must struggle with the realization that the Dutch for half a century have outstripped England in securing the lucrative trade to the East Indies and, more recently, have driven the Portuguese out of Ceylon and established factories on the Malabar coast that threaten English trade in Bombay. His recourse is to employ all of the allusive resources at his disposal to foretell an ultimate English victory, despite the setbacks of 1666, and to reassure his countrymen and women that "the Heav'ns'" favor toward the Dutch will not last. The Dutch ships which return "brim-full . . . to the *Bel'gan* shore" are latter-day versions of the fleets of Carthage, which "swept the riches of the world from far," while England is Rome, "less wealthy, but more strong" (ll. 16, 18–19). The bloody but inconclusive naval battle that Dryden goes on to describe in the poem – the four days' battle in June 1666 – by analogy, is characterized as "our second Punick War" (l. 20), and its violence justified by the implications of this allusion: England is foreordained to triumph. Yet the very terms of heroic action are cast, in large measure, in the language of commercial rivalry. Unable to break the Dutch stranglehold on Baltic trade, the English demonstrate their prowess by burning a Dutch merchant fleet of 150 ships in the late summer that was sheltered behind the North Holland islands. The English navy sends "whole heaps of Spices" up in flames, shattering Chinese "Porc'lain," and reducing cargoes and vessels to "Aromatick splinters" on the surface of the waters (ll. 113, 115, 116). Wanton destruction cast in heroic quatrains becomes the noble vindication of English heroism.

Throughout the poem, strained images of a saintly Charles II praying for victory and then for the deliverance of London from the fire seek to invest a vicious trade war and a civic disaster with the grandeur of classical precedent and the sanctity of providential design. The poem's morality is absolute: the "wily *Dutch*" are compared to "fall'n Angels" who "fear'd/ This new *Messiah's* coming," the arrival of Prince Rupert, Charles II's nephew, to reinforce the beleaguered fleet (ll. 453–54). In turn, national destiny and providential history are identified with visions of infinite wealth. Not only does Dryden's prophetic strain promise that the English will be able to defeat a Dutch navy "fraught/With all the riches of the rising Sun" (ll. 93–94) but the future is described in explicitly alchemical language: Charles rests secure in his knowledge that the "unripe veins" will eventually mature when "time digests the yet imperfect Ore, /... and it will be Gold another day" (ll. 573, 575–56). Seventeenth-century alchemy was both a secretive and mysterious body of knowledge, accessible only to a small number of dedicated adepts, and, for some practitioners seeking funding for their experimental regimens, a means to demonstrate principles of the capitalist generation of wealth: money breeding money.[33] Alchemy functions as well as an image of spiritual and civic resurrection, but this apotheosis itself is expressed in images of the legendary wealth of pre-conquest Mexico. Dryden's yoking of mystical rebirth and material profit is suggestive of the self-referential quality of his poetic design – turning base actions into heroic grandeur. London itself will rise "from this Chymick flame,/... a City of more precious mold:/Rich as the Town which gives the *Indies* name,/ With Silver pav'd, and all divine with Gold" (ll. 1169–72). These lines conflate morality, trade, profits, and prophecy so consistently because Dryden has no other means to describe the miraculous transformation of London's smoldering ruins into a transcendent metropolis aggrandizing an infinite and divinely sanctioned wealth. *Annus Mirabilis* can conclude only by reiterating its opening rationale for the war. The glorious future that Dryden promises for England depends on London's supplanting Amsterdam as the center of the trade of "all the world" (l. 1304), a trade defined by the riches of the Far East.

> Thus to the Eastern wealth through storms we go;
> But now, the Cape once doubled, fear no more:
> A constant Trade-wind will securely blow,
> And gently lay us on the Spicy shore.
>
> (ll. 1213–16)

Dryden's description of the voyage around the Cape to the East Indies idealizes future trading ventures as idyllic cruises to welcoming and wealthy islands. The "constant" trade winds promise a metaphoric transcendence of the uncertainty and anxieties of the "storms" of 1666. The closing stanzas offer no program to achieve supremacy over the hated VOC, only images that restage the manichean conflict with the Dutch and promise the visionary apotheosis of pepper and providence.

More than any other poem of the 1660s, *Annus Mirabilis* discloses the economic basis of the rhetoric of ideological absolutism that characterized the conflicts between England and the United Provinces in the seventeenth century.[34] The poem's circular logic suggests the extent to which the economic tensions between the two countries persisted, even after the Treaty of Breda was signed. The volume of England's international trade was growing and its character changing dramatically during Dryden's lifetime (1631–1700). Woolens accounted for 92.3 percent of the nation's exports in 1640; by 1700 that figure had dropped to 72.8 percent. Lead and tin in larger quantities were being shipped to India to buy spices and cotton clothing. Imports of pepper doubled between 1630 and 1700; imports of Indian "calicoes" (a term used to describe all cotton textiles) rose by a factor of fourteen during the same period. In those seventy years, East India goods rose from 11.3 to 16.2 percent of total imports, while American goods, notably tobacco and sugar, more than tripled, from 5.3 to 18.5 percent. These figures reflect the growing significance of the re-export trade: one-third of the sugar, two-thirds of the tobacco, and nine-tenths of the pepper, Keith Wrightson suggests, were re-exported. When Dryden was writing *Annus Mirabilis*, this trade was worth 28 percent of the value of domestic goods exported and 20 percent of the import trade; by the year of his death, these figures were 45 and 34 percent. The annual value of England's foreign trade in the 1660s averaged £8,500,000; in 1700, it stood at £12,200,000, and would rise to £20,100,000 by the middle of the eighteenth century.[35] As international trade became more important to England's economy, pressures increased on the government both to avoid costly naval wars that would disrupt trade and to use the navy to defend English interests overseas and to grab an even larger share of the lucrative trade routes in the East Indies.

REVISITING AMBOYNA

Dryden rushed *Amboyna* to the stage in 1672 to stir up popular resentment against the Dutch as England prepared to wage yet another war against the United Provinces, this time in league with the French. The threat from this Anglo-French alliance of convenience forced the Dutch Republic to face its gravest military crisis in the second half of the century. After the English navy attacked a Dutch convoy, without warning, in March 1672, Louis XIV declared war on the United Provinces and sent 130,000 men, including cavalry, against the badly outnumbered Dutch forces. The Dutch were driven back by rapid French victories, and towns began capitulating without a fight. By June, Arnhem, Kampen, Zwolle, and Utrecht had fallen, and serious negotiations were underway for an abject capitulation to French demands. As a last-gasp defensive strategy, Holland flooded fields in a vast "water line" to halt the French armies before they could reach Amsterdam, Dordrecht, Rotterdam, and The Hague. As French victories multiplied in the east, anti-government riots by artisans, militiamen, and commoners, including many women, broke out; the rioters wanted a more vigorous defense of the Republic. In general, these mobs avoided random violence and directed their energies to replacing town regents who favored negotiating a settlement with Louis XIV. In The Hague, however, the rioters made their point by murdering, mutilating, roasting, and then apparently eating parts of Johan de Witt, the Pensionary of Holland (the closest approximation the province had to a chief executive), and his brother Cornelis, the leaders blamed by the mob for failing to prepare for and prosecute the war. This Organist fervor resulted in William III (the future King of England) being proclaimed Stadholder in Holland and Zeeland; William rallied the unoccupied provinces, and the Dutch began to register important victories at sea. In the summer of 1673, the smaller Dutch fleet under De Ruyter defeated a combined Anglo-French navy in three battles off the coast of Zeeland, preventing an anticipated Anglo-French invasion by sea. Dutch privateering crippled English shipping in the Atlantic and Caribbean, and the entry of Spain and the Hapsburg Empire in the land war forced Louis to divert his forces to the south. Over several months, the French were driven from occupied territories by a rebuilt and more efficient Dutch army. With his dreams of constant trade winds wafting English merchants back to the Spice Islands shattered, Charles II was forced to sign a peace treaty in 1674 without achieving a single major objective.[36]

Throughout the war and its aftermath, English supporters of the King and the unpopular Anglo-French alliance tried to convince a suspicious merchant community that the nation's future hung in the balance. John Evelyn linked military and commercial control of the seas, declaring that "whoever commands the ocean, commands the trade of the world, and whoever commands the trade of the world, commands the riches of the world, and whoever is master of that, commands the world itself."[37] Shareholders in the EIC argued that command of the seas meant a vigorous trade to the East Indies, not an endless series of naval battles that wasted ships, money, and men. "The extraordinary Endeavours of most of the *European* Nations to compass and gain the *East-India* Trade to themselves," Robert Ferguson wrote, "together with the success of the *Dutch* therein, and the vast advantage they have reaped from thence, being a main cause of that Wealth and Grandeur which hath rendered them so redoubtable to, and envied by all their Neighbors, may give an undeniable testimony of the beneficialness of this Trade."[38] As the significance of the re-export trade became apparent, Dryden's heroic images of English merchants braving storms to the "Spicy shore" were presented as sound economic reasoning. As Josiah Child, director and sometime Governor of the EIC, maintained later in the century, the "preservation" of the Company's trade was essential to England's wealth and sociopolitical stability. Because "all other Foreign Trade in Europe doth greatly depend upon *East-India* Commodities," he asserted, a Dutch monopoly would have dire consequences for individual consumers and the nation as a whole: "the excess of price which [the VOC] would make the *European* World pay for *East-India* Commodities more than they do now, would cause a disproportionable and greater increase of their Riches. The augmentation whereof would further enable them to overballance us and all others, in Trade, as well as in Naval strength."[39] Sixty years after Mun had made a similar argument and thirty years after Milton, as Latin Secretary, had demanded on England's behalf reparations for Amboyna, comparatively little had changed: Dutch domination of the spice trade threatened the integrity of the nation; EIC shareholders and merchants were a crucial bulwark against a kind of commercial hegemony; and England's future prosperity depended on its investments in the Far East.

First staged within a month of England's declaration of war against the United Provinces, *Amboyna*, in some respects, recycles the strategies that Dryden used in *Annus Mirabilis* – unabashed propaganda is poured into the mold of heroic tragedy. The play also rehashes some of the elements of Dryden's earlier tragedies of colonization, *The Indian Queen* and *The Indian Emperor*, particularly in its gendering of conflicts between Europeans and "others." As Bridget Orr and Heidi Hutner have demonstrated, Dryden relies in these plays on a familiar *topos*, the figure of the Indian queen, to represent the politics of colonial aggression in the New World as individual tragedies of love and honor. The conquest of South America and the exploitation of its resources take place metaphorically in and through the body of the native woman – her beauty symbolizes the riches of the New World, and her love for her white conqueror becomes a moral justification for her submission to European men.[40] In the figure of the "Indian" woman in *Amboyna*, Ysabinda, who falls for the heroic merchant, Gabriel Towerson, Dryden transplants the Pocahontas myth to the Spice Islands. As the play opens, we learn that the Christianized heroine (who has no counterpart in Digges or Darrell) has remained faithful during the three years her lover has been away; he returns, they pledge their love for each other, and then, in act four, marry. Ysabinda, however, is also loved by a Dutchman, Harman Junior, the son of the Governor; when she rejects his advances, he lures her away from her wedding banquet, ties her to a tree, and rapes her. Her rape testifies to the perfidy of the Dutch (Harman Junior, before giving in to his lust, had been Towerson's friend) and, at the same time, symbolizes the political issues at stake in Dryden's recasting of the events on Amboyna: the violence directed against Ysabinda stands metonymically for the illegal, tyrannical appropriation of the East Indies by the Dutch, just as her love for Towerson justifies English trade and colonization as a "mutual" desire for harmonious, and hierarchical, relations between British merchants and dutiful East Indians.

His attempt to cast Ysabinda as another version of his Indian queens, however, falls flat because Dryden must dramatize clumsy British efforts to maintain a dwindling share of the spice trade and Towerson's failure to recognize Dutch determination to monopolize this trade as noble resistance to tyranny. By reducing the commercial rivalry between the English and Dutch to Towerson's and Harman Junior's preening for Ysabinda, Dryden represses as much as possible the material bases of international conflict and turns a rich historical narrative into a fervid tragedy. As is usually the case with Dryden's tragedies, what the dramatist omits or simplifies is often as illuminating as what he chooses to put on stage.

The historical Towerson was a survivor. He had sailed with James Lancaster on the first voyage of the EIC in 1601, and had been one of the two merchants at the English factory at Bantam to survive fire, disease, and violence. After the English warehouse burned, he was the one who conducted the grisly torture of the suspected arsonists.[41] Over the next decade, he headed other factories in the East Indies and commanded the EIC vessel *Hector* on its return voyage to England in 1613. During the voyage, the English merchant William Hawkins, who had spent three years at the Moghul Court in Agra, died, leaving a young widow. Hawkins, who spoke Turkish, had become a favorite of Jehangir's and had been given, in addition to a lavish salary, a Christian Armenian "mayden" as a bride after the death of her father, a wealthy merchant. "She being willing to go where I went and live as I lived," Hawkins wrote, his wife accompanied him on board the *Hector*.[42] Before the ship reached London, she had pawned her jewels for a passage back to India and was married to Towerson. She returned with him to the East Indies, apparently rejoining her family, while he went on to serve as the President of factories at Macassar and later Amboyna. This narrative of Towerson's wife – which can be pieced together out of Hawkins's and others' letters reprinted in Purchas – ends abruptly. A woman given in marriage by the Moghul Emperor to an Englishman, much older than she is, sails with him for England, watches him die, and then chooses to return to Asia, apparently marrying the middle-aged and corpulent Towerson in order to secure her passage and return to her family. It is impossible to say to what extent her actions were voluntary once Hawkins had died, but her story is revealing both for what it suggests about the choices facing women in the small, dispersed community of Christian merchants in the East and for what it reveals about Dryden's ideological imperatives in recasting his sources. Dryden transforms what may have been her marriage of convenience into the manichean theatrics of heroic sacrifice; his sexualized Ysabinda makes no decisions – except to remain true to Dryden's romantic hero – and plaintively helps to vilify her Dutch rapist.

Dryden's rewriting of history to suit his purposes extends beyond converting a career merchant into a tragic hero and recasting an Armenian wife as an Ambonese princess. Significantly, with the exception of some male dancers who appear in act one, there are no native men present in the play: the chaste, beautiful, and rich Ysabinda is the sole representative of the Ambonese, Ternatans, and Bandanese who figure prominently in Digges's pamphlets. East Indian sultans and traders must vanish from Dryden's play because the challenges posed by the political and commercial culture of Southeast Asia call into question the oppositional models of intra-European conflict – good Englishmen versus evil Dutchmen – that dominate the play. Ysabinda, then, is herself a symptom of the dramatist's recasting of international economic conflict into a dualistic political morality. The dramatist mystifies, in suitably heroic terms, not the conquest of non-European lands and peoples but the failures of British efforts to establish a profitable trade in the East Indies in order to promote his vision of an innate national virtue that the fortunes of trade, war, and politics – the very activities that constitute the nation – cannot diminish. This feminization of Southeast Asian culture in the figure of Ysabinda thus writes out of existence both native men – particularly powerful Islamic rulers like Jehangir who give away Christian women as gifts – and those Europeans who do not conform to a manichean politics of English virtue and Dutch vice.

One of the most intriguing historical figures in Dryden's sources does not make it into his tragedy. When he is not vilifying the Dutch, Digges scapegoats an English surgeon, Abel Price, for the horrors on Amboyna. In a drunken rage, Price had threatened to set fire to a Dutchman's house, thereby poisoning relations between the English and Dutch factories and, the author implies, prompting the Hollanders to their vengeance (*TR* 5). In Digges's *Answer unto the Dutch Pamphlet*, Price is described as a "drunken debauched sot" who had threatened Towerson and who "alone of all the English . . . had some kinde of conversation with some of the Iapons; that is, he would dice and drinke with them, as he likewise did with other Blacks, and with the Dutch also" (11). Digges's sentence structure is revealing: the description of Price's drinking and gambling with "some of the Iapons," seems to concede an indiscretion which might be misinterpreted by the Dutch; but this slur is followed by the charge that his intercultural promiscuity extends to "other Blacks" and the Dutch themselves.[43] In this respect, Price represents, for Digges, the kind of figure who flourishes in the entrepôts of seventeenth-century ports, for whom gambling and drinking cut across the always provisional identities secured by language and manners. Price is a threat to the English factory as well as the Dutch because he moves easily among different national communities, undermining the imaginary coherence of the "nation" and threatening the profits on which both Company and country depend. By disrupting the equation of economic nationalism and moral superiority, he calls into question the seemingly bedrock distinctions that Digges uses to elevate the English, socially and morally, over the Dutch. Price is absent from Dryden's tragedy, then, because he threatens to disrupt the play's binary logic of demonizing the other as a strategy of national self-definition.

The construction of a national identity in Dryden's play and elsewhere thus discloses itself as an act of idealization designed to banish the Abel Prices of the world – the mediator, the parasite, who, as Michel Serres argues, makes communication possible.[44] Any acknowledgment of the complex politics of Southeast Asia would frustrate Dryden's mapping of the "essential" differences between the English and Dutch onto gendered and class-based models of self and other – models which sustain the fiction of a heroic English virtue that exists prior to and distinct from the actions and modes of representation that (re)stage the nation. Unlike Dryden's reimagined Towerson, Price cannot be idealized: he would reveal that the "real" nation, EIC merchants haggling over the price of cloves on Amboyna, is always haunted by the ideal of a mythic national unity, while this imaginary vision of national identity haunts the postlapsarian world of Dryden and his audience, upbraiding it for its irrevocable failures to measure up to its always absent, always spectral ideal.[45]

Amboyna insistently turns complex economic and political rivalries into straightforward problems of morality: Dutch mercantile power in the Spice Islands is synonymous with greed and hypocrisy; British weakness becomes "honesty" and "honour"; the sultanates of the region vanish. These distinctions are projected onto other, seemingly essential, oppositions – gentlemanly virtue versus lower-class money-grubbing, for example – that, in turn, are depicted as effects of the essential qualities of national identity that they are supposed to explain. The English merchants in the play, particularly Towerson, are given a language of nobility and mutual obligation that reinforces the values and assumptions of heroic tragedy. Having saved Harman Junior's life in a sea-fight against pirates, Towerson brushes off his friend's expressions of gratitude:

> In your deliverance I did no more,
> Than what I had myself from you expected:
> The common ties of our religion,
> And those, yet more particular, of peace
> And strict commerce betwixt us and your nation,
> Exacted all I did, or could have done.

(1 i 20)

Towerson's speech conflates characteristics of upper-class, even chivalric duty and middle-class morality to produce a rhetoric of national honor and gentlemanly civility, cast in terms of Protestant solidarity and mutual commitments to ideals of international (or at least inter-European and inter-Protestant) cooperation. Towerson embodies heroic attributes of love and honor, but they have been grafted onto a career EIC employee who seems to have cared more for profits than ideals. The historical Towerson may have survived the hell-hole of Bantam, but ironically, as it turned out, was willing to torture men he considered his enemies in order to extract confessions. His loyalty rested as much with the Company as it did with England, and he never spent more than a few months in his native land after his first voyage to the East Indies. To counter the spectre of Dutch evil, however, Dryden endows this EIC veteran with the traditional values of aristocratic honor and self-definition. This hybrid, the heroic merchant, both constitutes and is constituted by a discourse of nationalism that has jettisoned any fellow-feeling for the Dutch and rejected the appeal of the "common ties" of Protestantism. National identity, embodied by Towerson, appropriates time-honored characteristics of gentility to safe-guard its self-reflexive ideals. The hero's stoicism both invokes and seeks to transcend the memories of the first two Dutch Wars and the brutal realities of a trading system that had descended, by 1672, from "strict commerce" to a savage plantation system.

In contrast to the English, the Dutch are portrayed as a nation of upstarts and boors, the mean-spirited inhabitants of "seven little rascally provinces, no bigger in all than a shire in England" (II i 38). As this insult suggests, Dryden castigates the Dutch by attacking their interlocking claims to an idealized, transhistorical nationhood and to the status of gentlemen. The extraordinarily complex internal politics of the United Provinces are repressed into stage caricatures of money-grubbing villains. Although the Dutch characteristically voiced their belief in republican ideals, the United Provinces, in practice, were run "by a narrow, wealthy, entrenched oligarchy," men who saw themselves as guardians guaranteeing a "liberty of conscience" and the security of property.[46] Dryden's attack in *Amboyna* on the Dutch as "boors," in this respect, is motivated less by any radical differences between the social systems of the two nations than by the animosity of a half century of economic competition, entrenched ideological hatreds, and warfare. In act two, Beaumont, another noble English merchant, trades ethnic slurs with the Dutch factor, Fiscal, turning the latter's frugality to ridicule: "our merchants live like nobleman; your gentlemen, if you have any, live like boors. You traffic for all the rarities of the world, and dare use none of them yourselves so, that, in effect, you are the mill-horses of mankind, that labour only for the wretched provender you eat" (II i 39). In Beaumont's logic, luxurious living and good manners become the stylistic accessories of inherent virtue. The Dutch merchants' financial success is turned against them by his accusation that they lack those essential qualities of taste and breeding that are the bedrock values of an ideology of patrilineal privilege and gentlemanly civility. The Dutch are not social climbers but misers; they disdain those patterns of conspicuous consumption, of living to the utmost extent of (or beyond) one's means, which characterize gentlemanly civility on the Restoration stage. As "boors," they cannot comprehend the obligations that honor demands. Because they fail to spend what they earn on the clothes, carriages, and periwigs, the accoutrements of honor, they cut themselves off from the very practices of gentility that alone can secure their status as a nation, a status founded and sustained on gentlemanly privilege rather than republican aggression. Without theatrical displays of a transcultural civility, the Dutch cannot perform the demanding roles of "gentlemen," and therefore cannot lay claim to a coherent national identity. As the exchange between Beaumont and Fiscal suggests, national identities in the play – the differences between the moral economies of the English and Dutch – become projections of overdetermined theatrical differences between social classes. English merchants embody ideals of gentlemanly existence; the Dutch serve as scapegoats for the negative aspects of international commerce.

As he does in his other tragedies such as *The Indian Queen*, *The Indian Emperor*, and *The Conquest of Granada*, Dryden recasts the complicated and divided internal politics of foreign nations as conflicts between good and evil, honor and corruption. Because the Dutch lack a civilized interiority, they can be represented only as two-dimensional stage villains. In Towerson's final condemnation of Dutch efforts to justify their torture and execution of the English, the merchant-hero derides the supposed plot against their fort and declares

> Your base new upstart commonwealth should blush,
> To doom the subjects of an English king,
> The meanest of whose merchants would disdain
> The narrow life, and the domestic baseness,
> Of one of those you call your Mighty States.

(V i 83)

Unable to defend himself, Towerson retreats to snobbery. Although the languages of national virtue and class prejudice are clearly intertwined in this speech, the hero's efforts to buttress one set of ideological values and assumptions with another is obviously inadequate: the "upstart" Dutch revel in their persecution of the English and celebrate their "domestic baseness" as a kind of republican honor. The vituperation directed against the "base new upstart commonwealth" is reminiscent of the royalist invectives hurled at the Protectorate in the 1650s. Towerson's speech reinforces the discourse of nationalism with the exclusionary rhetorics of class stratification, monarchical government, and gentlemanly civility: in *Amboyna* as in *Annus Mirabilis*, the ideology of nationalism – or, more generally, ideology itself – is defined by ongoing efforts to compensate for one failed, corrupt, or incompetent language by invoking another, then using a third to supplement the shortcomings of the second, and so on. Towerson's defiance of his fate, in this sense, testifies to Digges's and Dryden's failed efforts to find a voice powerful enough to charm the Dutch out of Amboyna.

Dryden's insistence on the moral superiority of the English thus has the effect of emphasizing precisely what he wants to explain away: the inability of the English to resist Dutch power, whether in 1623 or 1666. The near-hysteria of some parts of the play can be attributed to the playwright's sense that in May 1672 the English, in league with the French, finally may have the upper hand, and that such strident language is necessary to prod his countryman into helping Louis XIV bring an "upstart commonwealth" to its knees. In the Epilogue, Dryden turns to satire to compensate for English impotence, castigating the Dutch (in a manner familiar to Restoration audiences) as ill-mannered cits:

> To one well-born the affront is worse, and more,
> When he's abused, and baffled by a boor:
> With an ill grace the Dutch their mischiefs do,
> They've both ill-nature and ill manners too.
> Well may they boast themselves an ancient nation,
> For they were bred ere manners were in fashion;
> And their new commonwealth has set them free,
> Only from honour and civility.

Dryden's name-calling cannot disguise the fact that for sixty years the English have failed to develop the very monopolistic, and profitable, practices that the Dutch employ. In adopting the language of class antagonism familiar to Restoration audiences, Dryden makes his "baffled" Englishman appear destined to play the role of a gull or fool. He assumes the characteristics of the conventional wit-would duped by sharpers; the ideal of the truewit, one "well-born" but not "baffled by a boor," significantly, is absent from the Epilogue. In a trading world of cut-throat economic competition, there is no opting out of the values of self-aggrandizement that the Dutch practice, no way to talk one's way out of being "baffled" – or executed – by boors. "Honour and civility" are not alternatives to the mercantile aggression of the Netherlands but failed or imperfect versions of it.[47] In this respect, Dryden's satiric jibes at the Dutch suggest that his play does not stage a conflict between a residual "aristocratic" and emergent "bourgeois" ideology, identified respectively with the English and Dutch. Instead, its manichean structure dramatizes an ostensibly "universal" set of social and moral values that are under attack. Dryden asks his audience, then, to engage in the kind of cynical reasoning that Žižek describes: theatergoers must act as though they do not know that England's envisioned greatness as a commercial empire is predicated on trade, violence, and competition – the very evils Dryden projects onto the Dutch.[48]

The moral distinctions on which Dryden insists between English generosity and Dutch greed disclose as well contrasting perceptions of the islands that the two nations are vying to exploit – radically different conceptions, that is, of nature and its resources. Early in the play, Towerson suggests that English generosity and sense of fair play in international trade depend on there being enough spices on Amboyna to satisfy the needs of both nations. The island, he claims, "yields spice enough for both [English and Dutch]; and Europe, ports, and chapmen, where to vend them," and goes on to suggest that although "the world was never large enough for avarice or ambition … [,] those who can be pleased with moderate gain, may have the ends of nature, not to want: Nay, even its luxuries may be supplied from her o'erflowing bounties in these parts" (1 i 21, 22). For the English merchants, if not for the offstage natives of the Moluccas, the "o'erflowing bounties" of the East Indies mark a return to a golden age in which infinite resources make conflict and competition avoidable, if not absolutely unnecessary. National virtue must be underwritten by the assumptions that the resources of the island can be exploited indefinitely without having any negative consequences for either the environment or the indigenous peoples who grow the spices for export and also must live off the produce of the land. In contrast, the Dutch, whose only religion, the audience is told repeatedly, is "interest," regard the spices and gold they covet as scarce resources that must be exploited, husbanded, and defended. The moral implications of these views of nature are overdetermined: Dryden's unremitting insistence on Dutch greed and English generosity renders as moral certainties the fantasies of an ideology that depends on ever-increasing trade – and consequently on the ever-increasing exploitation of nature – to produce ever-increasing wealth.

The discourses of nationalism, gentlemanly civility, and honor in *Amboyna* ironically downplay the significance of the commodities – spices, sandalwood, and silks – over which the English and Dutch fight, even though the imagined integrity of the nation depends on its status as the ultimate agent that buys, tallies, owns, and resells them. These commodities were hardly the pristine gifts of an "o'erflowing nature." Even before the arrival of the Portuguese, spices were grown, sold, and consumed only because they were produced within complex networks requiring capital investment; sophisticated agricultural technologies, including speciation; seaborne transportation; accounting practices; and diplomatic and trading alliances. In an important sense, Dryden's staging of Amboyna as a tragedy of national identity both depends on and reproduces the self-divided ideology that Bruno Latour has argued, in a different context, is crucial to the construction of modernity: a division between an "essential" social identity – in this instance that of a "natural" nobility and morality – and an essential nature that remains forever distinct from human interventions in it.[49] The tragedy does not reproduce a simple base-superstructure model of the relations between commodities and values, nature and culture, but reveals and then struggles to deny the recognition that the ideals of a bountiful nature and of an essential, transhistorical, and supra-material identity are mutually constitutive fictions. Dryden's championing of "quiet trade" thus attempts to secure the nation's prosperity and its moral self-definition by embracing a crucial misrecognition of the labor-intensive cultivation of spices as the gift of nature's "o'erflowing bounties." If the East Indies are not overflowing with riches, then the merchants of the EIC would have no choice except to descend to the exploitative strategies and the Hobbesian morality of the Dutch: the world would cease to support trade as a gentlemanly endeavor and become a hostile realm dominated by the logics of scarcity, aggression, and unending competition. In this respect, Dryden must seek to deny the forms of mediation that are always in the process of breaking down the division of social essence from a "real" nature that is both a fund and a limit of human endeavor.

DOWN AND OUT ON AMBOYNA

For historians and critics of early modern colonialism, including many Marxists, it may be tempting to read Anglo-Dutch conflict as an allegory of the rise of capitalism in the late seventeenth century: an older, residual ideology of gentlemanly, if not aristocratic, virtue, forced to give way to a new, cut-throat economic order. I want to resist this reading by suggesting that the mercantile "honesty" of Towerson and Beaumont which Dryden eagerly praises is less an appropriation of noble virtue by an aspiring middle class than a repressed recognition that economic competition is – and has been all along – constitutive of the aristocratic codes of honor and privilege.[50] The logic of modernity that Latour describes suggests that the struggle to deny the effects of mediation, to enforce a fundamental split between nature and culture, inevitably produces near-herculean efforts to reinforce the oppositional tactics of exclusion and demonization of the other across a variety of symbolic registers.[51] Such efforts ultimately demonstrate the inadequacy of any system that claims to be inclusive because its integrity, as Žižek argues, depends on an "originary" act of exclusion.[52] In this sense, Dryden's reliance on a language of national pride and honor breaks down ironically on two levels: first, the discourse of national civility voiced by Towerson depends on the audience's suppressing their knowledge and experience of social differences and socioeconomic conflicts within England; in other words, "civility" celebrates the complementary nature of English commercial and gentlemanly interests that play after play on the Restoration stage insist are incompatible. Dryden's heroicizing of the merchants executed on Amboyna becomes part of an ongoing and always imperfect effort to represent "the nation" by reinventing it as an idea that transcends and subsumes competing interests, specifically the class antagonisms that are displaced onto Dutch "boors." But the common interests that Dryden identifies as nationalism paradoxically call attention to social confusion, to status anxiety, in England by insisting that his audience swell with righteous indignation at the fate of "upstart" merchants working for a company that many perceived as a haven for adventurers and a drain on England's resources. Secondly, the seemingly bedrock values of national identity and religious solidarity – English and Dutch Protestants versus Spanish Catholics – collapse when characters are confronted by opportunities for economic self-aggrandizement.

   In act three, Harman Junior hires a Spaniard, Perez, a lieutenant under Towerson disgruntled at not having been paid for his services, to murder the sleeping Englishman. Poised over his would-be victim with a dagger, Perez conveniently finds a memorandum which reads that Towerson's "first action this morning shall be, to find out my true and valiant lieutenant, Captain Perez; and as a testimony of my gratitude for his honourable service, to bestow on him five hundred English pounds, making my just excuse I had it not before within my power to reward him" (III ii 41–42). Knowing he will now be paid, Perez immediately begins upbraiding himself: "Oh, base, degenerate Spaniard! Hadst thou done it, thou hadst been worse than damned: Heaven took more care of me, than I of him, to expose this paper to my timely view. Sleep on, thou honourable Englishman I'll now sooner pierce my own breast than thine" (III ii 42). Whatever Heaven's intentions, it seems clear that Perez's moral reformation is a function of his sudden wealth; money buys a steadfast morality that necessitates Perez remain loyal to Towerson, even when the Spaniard is tortured and executed by the Dutch for his alleged role in the English plot. Although the play thus seems to yoke English and Spanish traders, who possess coherent national identities, against the upstart denizens of "seven rascally provinces," who owe even their suspect nationhood to English aid against their former colonial masters, the Spanish, the scene of Perez's reformation calls attention to the economic underpinnings of morality. Perez, not surprisingly, is Dryden's creation, a kind of antithesis to the historical Abel Price. Price threatens the discourse of national virtue; Perez confirms it.

In his efforts to blacken his coreligionists, Dryden belittles the Dutch by casting them as rebels against a rightful monarch. Towerson characterizes his captors as denizens of "an infamous nation, that ought to have been slaves, ... who had cast off the yoke of their lawful sovereign" (V i 79). Viewing the scene of torture, Towerson hurls invectives at the Dutch that resonate with the horrors of the English Civil War: "original villainy was in your blood./Your fathers all are damned for their rebellion" (V i 85). Dryden insists that national character determines profound moral differences between the English and their tormentors, but then, by identifying the Dutch with English rebels of an earlier generation, testifies to the very insecurity of his moral vision: he himself had been a civil servant under Cromwell, and, like many others, had moved, with ease, from commendations of Cromwell to celebrations of Charles II's restoration. In this context, it is hard not to see in Amboyna a recasting of the logic of *Astraea Redux* and *Annus Mirabilis*: the resurrection of a defeated or banished nobility as a call to national greatness, a transcending of internal political conflict by colonial and mercantile ventures. But this call to national unity masks the dividedness within England, the weakness of the nation – in 1623, 1660, 1666, and 1672. The standards of virtue that Towerson holds aloft symbolize only an imaginary strength and unity, a fictive national identity.

The topical nature of *Amboyna* and its generic self-proclamation as a tragedy mystify the elements of fantasy that structure the play: the disappearance of Southeast Asian and Islamic rivals; the manichean morality of virtue and villainy in trade; the scapegoating of the Dutch; the vision of the Spice Islands as lands of abundant resources that can be shared among Europeans; and the image of trade as an economy of gift exchange, friendship, and mutual obligation rather than of violence and competition. In one sense, the fantasy that Dryden promotes *is* the nation; in another, it is precisely this recognition of the nation as an imaginary construct that the dramatist must seek to escape or deny. In this respect, the stage direction in act five, "The SCENE opens, and discovers the English tortured, and the Dutch tormenting them," testifies to Dryden's efforts to enforce the bodily reality of national self-definition; the marks of torture are the signs of martyrdom, of a faith in an absent ideal. But in the theater, such stage-violence reveals ironically that the nation itself must be staged in order to demonstrate its "essential" characteristics. The play, then, imagines a national identity that coheres only in the theatricality of the torture inflicted on its representatives. Dryden must show the spectacle of Englishmen tortured because the scene, in its violence, constitutes the nation as an imaginary construct that provokes real consequences – it becomes an entity capable of suffering, remembering, and exacting vengeance. Heroism in the play's present of 1623, then, is embodied only by noble suffering; England's national greatness, its ability to define itself in terms other than political martyrdom, lies in the future that the audience supposedly inhabits, but that is deferred, as it is in *Annus Mirabilis*, to a time when the EIC will aggrandize "the eastern wealth." In 1672, however, England was about to declare yet another inconclusive war with the Dutch, and the ghosts of those executed in Amboyna could only rattle their theatrical chains. A generation later, with William III, a Dutch "boor" on the throne, and Defoe, among others, peppering the monarch with plans to establish new colonies in the Pacific, the chains were still rattling: the ghost of lost opportunities in the Far East, the spectre of infinite profits in a still fallen world.

NOTES

1. Sir Walter Scott, ed.; rev. George Saintsbury, ed., *The Works of John Dryden*, vol. V (Edinburgh: William Paterson, 1883). All quotations are from this edition.
2. See Michel Foucault, *Discipline and Punish: The Birth of the Prison*, trans. Alan Sheridan (New York: Pantheon, 1979).

3. See Richard Helgerson, *Forms of Nationhood: The Elizabethan Writing of England* (Chicago: University of Chicago Press, 1992), esp. 171–73, who discusses the significance in Elizabethan England of defining national identity against the threat posed by Spain; Linda Colley, in *Britons: Forging the Nation 1707–1837* (New Haven: Yale University Press, 1992), argues that, in the eighteenth century, the English identified themselves in opposition to the French. For a general discussion of national self-definition against the threat of the other, see Benedict Anderson, *Imagined Communities: Reflections on the Origin and Spread of Nationalism*, rev. edn (London: Verso, 1991).

4. James Thompson, "Dryden's *Conquest of Granada* and the Dutch Wars," *The Eighteenth Century: Theory and Interpretation* 31 (1990), 215. See also Raman, *Framing "India"*; Derek Hughes, *English Drama 1660–1700* (Oxford: Clarendon Press, 1996), 91–92; and Bridget Orr, *Empire on the English Stage 1660–1714* (Cambridge: Cambridge University Press, 2001), 157–59.

5. In addition to the pamphlets discussed below, see Edmund Scott, *An Exact Discourse of the Subtilties, Fashions, Religion and Ceremonies of the East Indians* (London, 1606); Sir William Foster, ed., *The Voyage of Sir Henry Middleton to the Moluccas, 1604–06* (London: Hakluyt Society, 1943); and, more generally, the compilation of voyages by Samuel Purchas, *Purchas His Pilgrimmes* (London, 1625), and the entries on Southeast Asia in Peter Heylyn, *Cosmographie.*

6. See Michel Foucault, *The History of Sexuality: An Introduction*, trans. Robert Hurley (New York: Pantheon, 1978), 92–93.

7. Reid, "Introduction: A Time and a Place," in *Southeast Asia in the Early Modern Era*, 17. The decline of Southeast Asia in the seventeenth century, as Reid notes, is a topic of intense debate among historians.

8. See M. A. P. Meilink-Roelofsz, *Asian Trade and European Influence in the Indonesian Archipelago Between 1500 and 1650* (The Hague: Martinus Nijhoff, 1962); C. R. Boxer, *Jan Compagnie in War and Peace 1602–1799: A Short History of the Dutch East-India Company* (Hong Kong: Heinemann Asia, 1979); Jacobs, *In Pursuit of Pepper and Tea*, 73–82; Leonard Y. Andaya, "Cultural State Formation in Eastern Indonesia," in Reid, *Southeast Asia in the Early Modern Era* 23–41; and, in the same volume, Barbara Watson Andaya, "Cash Cropping and Upstream–Downstream Tensions: The Case of Jambi in the Seventeenth and Eighteenth Centuries," 91–122; and Israel, *The Dutch Republic.*

9. O. H. K. Spate, *The Pacific Since Magellan*, vol. II: *Monopolists and Freebooters* (Minneapolis: University of Minnesota Press, 1983), 87, 88.

10. On the East India Company, see Chaudhuri, *The English East India Company*; Steensgaard, "The Growth and Composition of the Long-Distance Trade of England and the Dutch Republic"; Andrews, *Trade, Plunder and Settlement*; Brenner, *Merchants and Revolution*; and Keay, *The Honourable Company*, 3–18.

11. Schnurmann, "'Wherever profit leads us,'" 478.

12. See Glamman, *Dutch–Asiatic Trade 1620–1740*; Steensgaard, *The Asian Trade Revolution of the Seventeenth Century*; and Israel, *Dutch Primacy in World Trade.*

13. Quoted in Andrews, *Trade, Plunder and Settlement*, 264.

14. Thomas Mun, *England's Treasure*, 59.

15. Quoted in Spate, *Monopolists and Freebooters*, 27.

16. Schnurmann, "'Wherever profit leads us,'" 484–85.

17. See Slavoj Žižek, *The Sublime Object of Ideology* (London: Verso, 1989), esp. 20–21, 72–75.

18. Anon., *The Hollanders Declaration of the Affaires of the East Indies. Or a True Relation of That Which Passed in the Island of Banda, in the East Indies: In the Yeare of Our Lord God, 1621* (Amsterdam, 1622), 2.

19. *An Answere to the Hollanders Declaration, Concerning the Occurents of the East Indies. Written by certaine Mariners, lately returned from thence into England* (London, 1622), 1, 10, 5.

20. On the English factories in India in the 1630s, see Keay, *The Honourable Company*, 114–25.

21. Spate, *Monopolists and Freebooters*, 36. On the conflicts between the Dutch and English, see Wilson, *Profit and Power*, 24–57; Israel, *Dutch Primacy in World Trade*, 174–76, and Furber, *Rival Empires of Trade in the Orient*.

22. See Montague Summers, ed., *Dryden: The Dramatic Works* (1932; rpt. New York: Gordian Press, 1968), III: 345. Darrell, according to his Dedication, sailed with Ralegh in 1615 and had spent fifty years in the East Indies.

23. Digges, *True Relation*, 14. Subsequent citations will be noted parenthetically in the text.

24. Summers, Introduction, in *Works of Dryden*, III: 345. See also C. R. Boxer, *The Anglo-Dutch Wars of the 17th Century, 1652–1674* (London: National Maritime Museum, 1974), 16–17.

25. Anon., *A True Declaration of the News*, 3, 4. All subsequent quotations are from this edition and will be noted parenthetically in the text.

26. On this distinction see Elizabeth Hanson, "Torture and Truth in Renaissance England," *Representations* 34 (1991), 53–84; and M. Neill, *Putting History to the Question*.

27. Benjamin Schmidt, *Innocence Abroad: The Dutch Imagination and the New World, 1570–1670* (Cambridge: Cambridge University Press, 2001), 241–75. See also Schnurmann, "'Wherever profit leads us,'" 474–93.

28. Israel, *Dutch Republic*, 713.

29. Israel, *Dutch Republic*, 716. See also Wilson, *Profit and Power*, 54–77; and Israel, *Dutch Primacy*, 209–13.

30. Israel, *Dutch Republic*, 773. See also Neal, "The Dutch and East India Companies Compared," 195–223.

31. *The Works of John Dryden*, vol. I: *Poems 1649–80*, ed. Edward Niles Hooker and H. T. Swedenberg, Jr. (Berkeley and Los Angeles: University of California Press, 1956), 48. All quotations are from this edition.

32. See Michael McKeon, *Politics and Poetry in Restoration England: The Case of Dryden's* Annus Mirabilis (Cambridge, MA: Harvard University Press, 1975); Laura Brown, "Dryden and the Imperial Imagination," in *The Cambridge Companion to John Dryden*, ed. Steven N. Zwicker (Cambridge: Cambridge

University Press, 2004), esp. 63–69; David Bruce Kramer, *The Imperial Dryden: The Poetics of Appropriation in Seventeenth-Century England* (Athens: University of Georgia Press, 1994), 66–74; 92–94; Steven N. Zwicker, *Politics and Language in Dryden's Poetry: The Arts of Disguise* (Princeton: Princeton University Press, 1984), 38–39; and Suvir Kaul, *Poems of Nation, Anthems of Empire: English Verse in the Long Eighteenth Century* (Charlottesville: University of Virginia Press, 2000), 75–82.

33. On alchemy's significance in seventeenth and early eighteenth-century economic thinking, see Pamela Smith, *The Business of Alchemy: Science and Culture in the Holy Roman Empire* (Princeton: Princeton University Press, 1994); and Rajani Sudan, "Mud, Mortar, and Other Technologies of Empire," *The Eighteenth Century: Theory and Interpretation* 45 (2004), 147–69.

34. Steven C. A. Pincus, *Protestantism and Patriotism: Ideologies and the Making of English Foreign Policy, 1650–1668* (Cambridge: Cambridge University Press, 1996), 75, 92–93, 256–68.

35. Keith Wrightson, *Earthly Necessities: Economic Lives in Early Modern Britain* (New Haven: Yale University Press, 2000), 237–40.

36. Israel, *Dutch Republic*, 796–806. See also James R. Jones, "French Intervention in English and Dutch Politics, 1677–88," in *Knights Errant and True Englishmen: British Foreign Policy, 1660–1800*, ed. Jeremy Black (Edinburgh: John Donald, 1989), 1–23.

37. John Evelyn, *Navigation and Commerce, Their Original and Progress* (London, 1674), 17.

38. Robert Ferguson, *The East-India Trade a Most Profitable Trade to the Kingdom* (London, 1677), 6.

39. Sir Josiah Child, *A Treatise Wherein is Demonstrated . . . that the East-India Trade is the Most National of All Trades* (London, 1681), 26, 27.

40. Orr, *Empire on the English Stage 1660–1714*; Hutner, *Colonial Women*.

41. On fire and torture on Bantam, see M. Neill, *Putting History to the Question*, 285–310. Scott's account of Bantam, *An Exact Discourse of the Subtilties, Fashions, Religion and Ceremonies of the East Indians*, was reprinted in Purchas, *Pilgrimmes*.

42. Quoted in Keay, *The Honourable Company*, 78.

43. "Blacks" emerges as generic term for Asians as early as the sixteenth century in correspondence from Jesuit missionaries in India. See Donald Lach, with Edwin J. van Kley, *Asia in the Making of Europe*, vol. III (University of Chicago Press, 1993), 1619.

44. Serres, *The Parasite*.

45. See Jacques Derrida, *Specters of Marx: The State of the Debt, the Work of Mourning, and the New International* (New York: Routledge, 1994), 41–56.

46. See Israel, *Dutch Republic*, 807–25; quotation on 809.

47. On the Dutch as the envied model for British economic writers of the seventeenth century, see Appleby, *Economic Thought and Ideology*.

48. Žižek, *Sublime Object of Ideology*, 30–33.

49. Latour, *We Have Never Been Modern*.

50. See J. G. A. Pocock, *Virtue, Commerce, and History: Essays on Political Thought and History, Chiefly in the Eighteenth Century* (Cambridge: Cambridge University Press, 1985), 103–23.
51. See Goux, *Symbolic Economies after Marx and Freud.*
52. Žižek, *Sublime Object of Ideology,* 66–68.

CHAPTER 5

"I have now done with my island, and all manner of discourse about it": Crusoe's Farther Adventures in the Far East

THE CRUSOE TRILOGY

It would be difficult to tell from much of the critical literature that Daniel Defoe published a sequel to *Robinson Crusoe*, a mere four months after the appearance of this iconic novel in 1719.[1] In their eagerness to identify *Crusoe* and its hero as standard-bearers of an emergent modernity, most critics have taken at face value the notion that his fictional island is a template for a European colonial enterprise that dominated the eighteenth-century world. In crediting the "realism" of Defoe's fantasy of his hero's twenty-eight-year marooning in the tropics, they give short shrift to Crusoe's subsequent Asian adventures in volume two of the trilogy, particularly his hyperbolic attacks on every aspect imaginable of Chinese culture.[2] Crusoe's adventures in and reflections on the Far East play a crucial – but often neglected – role in Defoe's depiction of his hero in volumes two and three of the trilogy, *The Farther Adventures of Robinson Crusoe* (1719) and *Serious Reflections* (1720). In both works Defoe abandons the narrative strategies that he employs in his first Crusoe novel, deliberately rejecting the interlocking discourses of "psychological realism," economic self-sufficiency, and one-size-fits-all models of European colonialism that dominate his hero's stay on the island.

Rather than seeing the *Farther Adventures* as an unsuccessful sequel, I take seriously Defoe's contention that "the second part . . . is (contrary to the usage of second parts) every way as entertaining as the first, contains as strange and surprising incidents, and as great variety of them; nor is the application less serious or suitable; and doubtless will, to the sober as well as ingenious reader, be every way as profitable and diverting."[3] His contemporary readers apparently agreed with Defoe's assessment: *Farther Adventures* went through seven editions by 1747 and was republished regularly with its predecessor well into the nineteenth century. As Henry Clinton Hutchins notes "the pairing off of certain editions of Part I, with certain editions of Part II, [was] a practice which continued nearly through the century." In 1753, for example, the eighth edition of *Farther Adventures* was bound with the tenth edition of *Robinson Crusoe*. In all of the examples that Hutchins studies, the editions bound together are always two apart – the seventh and fifth, the tenth and eighth – indicating that for every new reprint or issue of part one there was a corresponding edition or reissue of part two. In his 1991 study of the publishing history of *Robinson Crusoe*, Robert W. Lovett lists 1,198 separate English editions and abridgements published between 1719 and 1979; Melissa Free, in studying 1,025 of these texts, has demonstrated that before 1920 the vast majority of these editions and abridgements (roughly 75 percent) printed volumes one and two either together as a two-part "adventure" or as part of the trilogy that included *Serious Reflections of Robinson Crusoe*.[4]

Reading through the two novels as a two-part series of adventures suggests that, in its obsession with China, *Farther Adventures* marks a significant turn in Defoe's career. Instead of elaborating on a colonialist parable of European triumphalism, this novel depicts and seeks to counter nightmare visions of an embattled English identity in a hostile world. In this regard, Defoe's explicit rejection of many of the values and assumptions associated with Crusoe's years on a fictional Caribbean island has significant implications for understanding the continuing significance of China in the history of early eighteenth-century literature.[5] Rather than considering his first novel a triumphant innovation, Defoe seems to have regarded it as an experiment that did not bear repeating.

In the most compelling analyses of Crusoian identity to date, Hans Turley has reread the three *Crusoe* novels as efforts to describe a piratical, homosocial self as an alternative to the domestic ideology of a feminized, psychologized identity.[6] According to Turley, Defoe yokes capitalist expansion and Protestant evangelism to privilege Crusoe the Christian apologist over Crusoe the poster-boy for the bourgeois self. In extending his argument, I want to emphasize that these novels are marked by a crucial fantasy – one always in danger of collapse and therefore always in need of shoring up – that centers less on elaborating a conception of psychological identity than on reasserting a dream of economic self-reliance. In analyzing the liberties that Defoe takes in *Crusoe* with the history of ceramic manufacturing, Lydia Liu has called attention to the strangeness at the heart of "an otherwise thoroughly known text and context"; his shipwrecked hero produces a usable facsimile of Chinese porcelain, a feat beyond the ability of European manufacturers in 1719.[7] If Crusoe's earthenware pot is emblematic of a fantasy of economic self-sufficiency, it also suggests how little attention has been paid to *Crusoe's* "context," especially a sequel that becomes increasingly obsessed with the problems posed by the Far East for western conceptions of colonialism, capitalism, and national identity.

In the context of the trilogy as a whole, Crusoe's island and its attendant assumptions and values – the hero's puritanical self-scrutiny; the colonialist exploitation of the natural world and non-European peoples; the willing submission of "pagans" to Christianity; and economic self-reliance – constitute only one half of a dialectic. Once Crusoe leaves his colony midway through the *Farther Adventures*, Defoe develops the narrative strategies and anatomizes the ideological concerns that shape his career as a novelist. First, economic self-sufficiency is jettisoned in favor of a discourse about the networks of communication and credit – the merchants, bankers, moneylenders, factors, and middlemen – essential to Asian trade; Crusoe's implication in these networks, even as he remains free from EIC regulations and oversight, provokes an obsessive desire to reestablish a religious and national identity that can insulate the hero from cosmopolitanism and contamination. Second, the colonialist parable of *Robinson Crusoe* is abandoned for a different kind of fantasy: the *Farther Adventures* is the first of Defoe's fictional narratives that promote visions of an infinitely profitable trade to the East Indies and the South Seas. Third, the figure of the cannibal-as-convert, the embodied tribute to the powers of European technology and religion, is replaced by the hero's – and the novelist's – obsession with far more dangerous "others," the Dutch and the Chinese. And lastly, puritanical self-scrutiny becomes far less insistent in the sequel; Crusoe's formulaic protestations of his "follies" give way to fervid, nearly hysterical assertions of European – specifically British and Protestant – superiority to Asian cultures. In *Serious Reflections*, Crusoe notes that "in all the voyages and travels which I have employed two volumes in giving a relation of, I never set foot in a Christian country; no, not in circling three parts of the globe," and then devotes the rest of the chapter, entitled "An Essay on the Present State of Religion in the World," to describing the embattled position of Protestantism in a hostile world.[8] By the end of the trilogy, the transition from psychological self to fanatic crusader is marked by the bone-chilling prescription that Crusoe offers for national prosperity in a world in which "Infidels possess such Vast Regions, and Religion in its Purity shines in a small Quarter of the Globe": convert or exterminate the brutes.[9] But as the hero's adventures in the Far East already have demonstrated, his call for a *jihad* against the Eastern world can take place, at least in 1720, only in armchair fantasies thousands of miles from the Great Wall.

The bizarre prospect of Crusoe trading diamonds in Bengal; opium, cloves, and nutmeg in the Indonesian archipelago; and silks and bullion in China, in one sense, marks a re-emergence in the *Farther Adventures* of the travel narratives of the seventeenth century – the single-minded pursuit of trade cast in terms of national glory and the spreading of the gospel that, in different ways, had animated Purchas, Heylyn, Milton, and Dryden. Written at the height of the speculation in South Sea Company stock, *Farther Adventures* seeks to jump-start British ventures in the Pacific by reinvigorating the fantasies of "infinite" wealth to be made in the region. Defoe's fictional forays into the Far East in *Farther Adventures*, *Captain Singleton* (1720), and *A New Voyage Round the World* (1724) are marked by both fascination and fear. Defoe recognizes – as his contemporaries did and as Europeans had done for two centuries – that trade with China and Japan had the potential to return enormous profits; at the same time, he reacts viscerally against the difficulties that Europeans faced as supplicants for trade during a period when China and, to a lesser extent, India and Japan, dominated world trade, bullion and financial markets, and the traffic in luxury items (from spices to porcelain) that had become staples of upper-class consumption, and of elite social identity, in Europe. By the early eighteenth century, the English had significant trading ventures in Moghul India, the Ottoman Empire, and Persia, but China continued to present both practical and ideological difficulties as a trading partner.[10] As the richest and most populous nation on earth, it could dictate the terms of trade to English merchants in Canton, levy customs, restrict trading privileges, and force merchants and missionaries to accommodate themselves to Chinese demands, protocols, and practices.[11] Almost seventy years after Jan Nieuhoff traveled to Beijing, Defoe remains obsessed by the missionary and travel sources that he cites throughout *Serious Reflections*, including those of Louis Le Comte, and Fernandez Navarette. If Defoe rejects the celebrations of Chinese civilization that characterize these accounts, he remains aware that China still represents a seemingly inexhaustible source of luxury items and potential consumer desire for English goods. As we will see in the next chapter, Defoe treats Southeast Asia and the South Seas as the other half of a familiar dialectic – the discovery of the long-sought land of ideal consumers, Terra Australis Incognita. These fantasies would persist until the voyages of James Cook a half century after the publication of Defoe's novels. Yet Defoe recognizes that the Chinese cannot be transformed into the subjects or dupes of European commercial imperialism. In his *Farther Adventures*, Crusoe confronts a nightmare that lurks everywhere in early modern accounts of the Middle

Kingdom: the irrelevance of western conceptions of identity and theology in a sinocentric world.

CRUSOE'S NAMELESS ISLAND

Crusoe's *Farther Adventures* and *Serious Reflections* have troubled critics who come to the novels with the expectation that these works should continue the novelist's project of defining an emergent selfhood. In the first half of the former novel, Defoe returns Crusoe to the island and has him deal with the problems of the colony he left behind; the second half follows the hero through an episodic series of adventures in Southeast Asia, China, and Siberia. By recasting mercantile visions of the endless generation of wealth as the very stuff of Crusoe's off-island adventures, Defoe presents a compensatory narrative for the problems of colonization – the social, theological, and administrative headaches that occupy Crusoe when he returns to "his" island. By comparison, *Serious Reflections* offers few adventures except an eighteenth-century dream vision, aptly entitled "A Vision of the Angelic World." Instead, the final installment of the trilogy draws out, expands, and footnotes the first two volumes, describing additional scenes that take place on the island and redirecting the reader's attention to religious issues. In some respects, *Serious Reflections* does for *Robinson Crusoe* what the third edition of *Clarissa* does for the first. But unlike Richardson's efforts to chastise and cajole his readers toward a "correct" interpretation of the characters and events of his novel, Defoe's *Serious Reflections* is at once both an extension and a metacommentary – it offers less a formula for interpretation than a set of strategies for reading Crusoe's adventures. To understand the workings of the trilogy is to come to grips with Crusoe's – and Defoe's – recurring fears and the rhetoric of overcompensation they provoke as the hero travels through the Far East.

Reading the *Farther Adventures*, one is struck by how little Crusoe has learned from his twenty-eight years marooned on "his" island. Repeatedly in this novel, Defoe uses the same language of folly and sin to describe his hero's obsessions, wanderlust, and rejection of middle-class comfort that he had employed in his first novel. Yet the abrupt transition midway through the novel from a colonial setting to the exotic lands of merchant-adventuring necessitates new narrative strategies to describe and defend both individual and national identity. The difference between the two halves of *Farther Adventures* is defined by two dreams that Crusoe relates at length: the first, at the beginning of the novel, describes his longing to return to the island; the second, years later, recounts his "anxieties and perplexities" (415) as a merchant in Southeast Asia. Although seven years after returning to England, the hero is living comfortably, he is obsessed with returning to the island. This "chronical distemper" troubles his dreams and dominates his day-to-day existence:

The desire of seeing my new plantation in the island, and the colony I left there, run in my head continually. I dream'd of it all night, and my imagination run upon it all day; it was uppermost in all my thoughts, and my fancy work'd so steadily and strongly upon it, that I talk'd of it in my sleep; in short, nothing could remove it out of my mind; it even broke so violently into all my discourses, that it made my conversation tiresome; for I could talk of nothing else, all my discourse run into it, even to impertinence, and I saw it my self. (251–52)

Crusoe succumbs to "such extasies of vapours" that he imagines himself back on the island and concludes that, while he cannot account for the etiology of his dreams or "what secret converse of spirits injected it, yet there was very much of it true" (252). While his dream may foreshadow the action of the first half of the *Farther Adventures*, the collapse of distinctions between dreaming and waking underscores the cautionary remarks offered in *Serious Reflections* (*SR*): "Dreams are dangerous things to talk of . . . the least encouragement to lay any weight upon them is presently carried away by a sort of people that dream waking, and that run into such wild extremes about them, that indeed we ought to be very cautious what we say of them" (*SR* 260). The nature of Crusoe's obsession, his tendency to "dream waking," is not made explicit; but if "very much" of his dreaming about the island is "true," then his "desire" takes the form of exercising an authority that the hero describes as "patriarchal." His dreams become both externalized, half-attributed to supernatural powers, and introjected so that the fantasies of commanding subjects and administering justice express his desire to repossess the island and reassert the sociopolitical and moral integrity of a self committed to colonial administration and religious instruction. Yet midway through the novel Crusoe's daydreams about the island give way to nightmares in the Far East. These violent dreams give shape to fears that are greater than those of being eaten by cannibals – fears of bodily and psychic dissolution that are emblematic of the threats to the Christian, mercantile self in a hostile world.

The first half of *Farther Adventures* set on Crusoe's island "colony" is didactic, even theologically coercive, in its insistence that the hero's administrative and juridical control depends on reclaiming sinners, notably the hell-raising Will Atkins, and reintegrating them into a social order that exemplifies the virtues of penitence and probity. Battles with natives are

interspersed with long colloquies about the necessity for religious toleration and the virtues of Christian marriage – native women must be
converted and married to their pirate and Spanish lovers to maintain social
and theological order. But if the enabling fiction of *Robinson Crusoe* is that
self-interest and colonization are compatible, that enterprising individuals
can transform the wilderness without draining England's wealth or
exhausting indigenous resources, then in the *Farther Adventures* Crusoe
confronts the dilemmas that had been finessed in the first volume: competing economic interests within the colony, contested political authority, and
religious differences among Catholics, Protestants, and "pagans."

His concern with colonial politics and Christian conversion may explain
why, in fictionalizing the account of Alexander Selkirk, Defoe changes
the location of the island in *Robinson Crusoe* on which his hero has
been marooned. Juan Fernandez, off the coast of Chile, was a resort for
buccaneers, a stopover for European expeditions to the Pacific, and a
potential naval base. Selkirk's tale was well known, as was the story of the
Moskito Indian Will, who had been marooned on the island in the 1670s
and proved more resourceful than his European counterpart.[12] Much to
Defoe's chagrin, England had no "plantations" in the Pacific, and the
EIC's intermittent voyages to the China Sea were not efforts to establish
colonies but to establish toeholds in regional trading networks.[13] By ship-
wrecking Crusoe in the Caribbean, then, Defoe locates his narrative within
a New World economy of slave trading, sugar plantations, and the prospect
of colonial improvement. This setting renders plausible the "colonization"
of the island in a region where England could point to some success, and
where Crusoe's dreams, as the hero tells the reader in *Serious Reflections*,
reconfirm his faith in his eventual rescue: "in my greatest and most hopeless
banishment I had such frequent dreams of my deliverance, that I always
entertained a firm and satisfying belief that my last days would be better
than my first; all which has effectually come to pass" (261–62). These
frequent dreams of "deliverance" – not depicted in *Robinson Crusoe* –
serve as after-the-fact confirmation of the moral and theological values
that Defoe promotes. These values are, in a sense, geographically specific to
a Caribbean world that by 1719 was well known and well prospected by the
English in their efforts to contain Spanish and French influence in the
Americas. Displaced into East Asia, Crusoe confronts the nightmares of
English irrelevance that he can ignore on his island.

The problems that Crusoe adjudicates, however, cannot mask the fact
that his island is an out-of-the-way and unprofitable backwater. He has no
dreams that foreshadow his delivering the colony to profitability. Rather

than rehash the adventures of the first Crusoe novel or continue the moralizing of the first half of its sequel, Defoe abruptly abandons the projects of colonization and conversion. Having cajoled, proselytized, and shamed the European men on the island into marrying their native wives and having brokered agreements among bickering colonists, Crusoe disclaims any long-term plans or nationalist intention: "I never so much as pretended to plant in the name of any government or nation, or to acknowledge any prince, or to call my people subjects to any one nation more than another; nay, I never so much as gave the place a name" (374). His dreams are gone, and he leaves the nameless island unceremoniously, never to return. He entrusts the administration of the colony to a nameless partner and the new governor, Will Atkins, declaring, "I have now done with my island, and all manner of discourse about it; and whoever reads the rest of my memorandums would do well to turn his thoughts entirely from it" (374). The vehemence of this admonition is startling, and Defoe is explicit: as an experiment in or as a model of colonialism, Crusoe's island is a failure. Neither ideals of toleration nor the internalized discourses of self-policing can prevent the nameless island from succumbing to the well-documented problems of such colonies – diminishing resources, political and religious conflicts, and external threats:

> the last letters I had from any of them was by my partner's means; who afterwards sent another sloop to the place, and who sent me word, tho' I had not the letter till five years after it was written, that they went on but poorly, were malecontent with their long stay there; that Will. Atkins was dead; that five of the Spaniards were come away, and that tho' they had not been much molested by the savages, yet they had had some skirmishes with them; and that they begg'd of him to write me, to think of the promise I had made to fetch them away, that they might see their own country again before they dy'd. (374–75)[14]

This outright rejection of the discourses and practices of colonialism suggests that Crusoe already has succumbed to the lure of trade and that Defoe has recognized the incompatibility of the languages of administrative control and infinite profits. In retrospect, the hero's rejection of the dictates of colonialism reveals that the "realism" of *Robinson Crusoe* has been predicated all along on the fantasy that one man is an island – economically as well as psychologically.

To introduce his subsequent adventures, Crusoe berates himself in much the same language that he had used when he left home forty years earlier: "expect to read of the follies of an old man, not warn'd by his own harms, much less those of other men, to beware of the like; not cool'd by almost forty years' misery and disappointments, not satisfy'd with prosperity beyond expectation, not made cautious by affliction and distress beyond imitation" (374). But this moralistic rhetoric hardly describes his subsequent adventures in Southeast Asia and China. When Crusoe leaves the island, he leaves behind the moral-juridical structures that he has sought to establish as well as the internalized "reflections" of a man well aware of his own "follies." Although Friday is killed in a battle at sea and Crusoe is forced off his nephew's ship after remonstrating with the crew for massacring 150 villagers on Madagascar, he realizes a fortune from his years in Asia as an independent trader. His "new variety of follies, hardships, and wild ventures; wherein the justice of Providence may be duly observed, and we may see how easily Heaven can gorge us with our own desires" is long on gorging and short on both physical and psychological consequences of this septuagenarian's "wild-goose chase" (374). Crusoe's characteristic self-doubts and upbraidings quickly give way to denunciations of the civilizations he encounters, the idolatry of the East, and ultimately, in Siberia, to acts of violence. The self, it seems, is no longer held together by moral injunctions and Foucaultian self-scrutiny but rendered coherent only as an instrument of providential fury against threats to Christianity.

"INHUMAN TORTURES AND BARBARITIES": CRUSOE'S NIGHTMARES

Crusoe's second set of dreams occurs when he and his partner discover they have bought, inadvertently, a pirate ship and fear that they will be captured and hanged by the Dutch authorities in Batavia. In recounting these nightmares, the hero mentions no Christian patience, no martyrdom, no sense of placing himself in divine hands:

both my partner and I too scarce slept a night without dreaming of halters and yard-arms, that is to say, gibbets; of fighting and being taken; of killing and being kill'd; and one night I was in such a fury in my dream, fancying the Dutch men had boarded us, and I was knocking one of their seamen down, that I struck my double fist against the side of the cabin I lay in, with such force as wounded my hand most grievously, broke my knuckles, and cut and bruised the flesh; so that it not only wak'd me out of my sleep, but I was once afraid that I should have lost two of my fingers. (414)

This dream extends beyond individual "imagination"; it is shared by Crusoe's partner and forces the hero to lash out in his sleep and break his knuckles. Crusoe does not use the rhetoric of guilt, sin, and unworthiness to describe his psychological turmoil. If this language has a precedent in his adventures, it is to be found in his fantasies of massacring the cannibals after he has discovered human remains on his island. But the "fury" of this dream, "of killing and being kill'd," threatens the hero's own person as much as it does the Dutch. The self-inflicted wound to his hand signifies a threat more troubling than his fear of cannibals in the *Strange Surprising Adventures*. The nightmares that Crusoe and his partner experience, in the Dutch-dominated waters of Southeast Asia, mark the irruption of a familiar national bogeyman into their consciousness: the trial and execution of twelve British merchants on Amboyna a century earlier by the VOC.

Nearly fifty years after the first performance of Dryden's *Amboyna*, the execution of Gabriel Towerson and other British merchants remains a crucial – indeed defining – national trauma for the British: it continues to mark England's exclusion from the lucrative spice trade; it underscores the limitations of British naval power; and it exposes the tenuousness and contingency of a British national identity that takes commercial success as a providential sign that England, and not the Netherlands, is the true defender of the Protestant faith.[15] In *Atlas Maritimus & Commercialis* (1728), Defoe denounces at length "the horrid Massacre" of English merchants by the Dutch, "a Scene so full of Barbarity, and not only unchristian but also inhuman Cruelty," that its specifics of torture, forced confession, and execution are "not to be express'd."[16] By invoking Amboyna in *Farther Adventures*, the novelist conjures up a threat to the fundamentals of a national identity founded on the interlocking value systems of enlightened self-interest, civility, and religious faith: the martyred Englishmen, he declares in 1728, "were used in the most violent and inhuman manner, without respect to their Quality or Nation, being Merchants of good repute, and Men of untainted Character."[17] Social status, nationality, professional honesty, and moral probity all are undone by the nightmare of Amboyna. Although Crusoe visits the usual stations of the cross by acknowledging that "Providence might justly inflict this punishment [of wandering through Asia as a merchant], as a retribution" (415), his own dream is not that of a penitent confronted by the consequences of his sin and enjoined to an unending self-examination, but of profit-taking, violence, and vengeance.

The hero's analysis of his nightmares describes a pattern that is repeated later in *Farther Adventures*: the threats he encounters in Asia are compared to and found more terrifying than the prospect of being eaten by "savages." His response to the cultural memory of Amboyna oscillates between "talking my self up to vigorous resolutions, that I would not be taken" by the Dutch and fears that he will be "barbarously used by a parcel of mercyless wretches in cold blood." For Crusoe, the VOC authorities are far more terrifying than New World cannibals:

it were much better to have fallen into the hands of savages, who were man-eaters ... than [into] those who would perhaps glut their rage upon me, by inhuman tortures and barbarities; ... it was much more dreadful, to me at least, to think of falling into these men's hands, than ever it was to think of being eaten by men, for the savages, give them their due, would not eat a man till he was dead, and kill'd them first, as we do a bullock; but that these men had many arts beyond the cruelty of death. (415)

Dutch "cruelty" both subsumes and goes beyond the fear of disincorporation. "Inhuman tortures" threaten the integrity of the body politic – the equation of the merchant's body with the coherence and self-reliance of the nation. If "his" island represents a failure of colonialism, Crusoe's obsession with Amboyna reveals "the anxieties and perplexities" that attend making himself into an instrument of his overriding desire for profit. Torture lays bare the greed, "barbarism," and amorality that providentialist and patriotic justifications for international trade mystify. Consequently, the hero's response to his dream is radically different from the soul-searching and moral accounting that he undertakes in *Robinson Crusoe*; he externalizes the divisiveness of sin, projecting a false "national" identity as a means to safeguard body, nation, and profits. Crusoe is the first, but not the last, of Defoe's heroes to fly a false flag at sea, to counterfeit a "national" identity in order to escape the entanglements and uncertainties of a "free commerce." In this respect, his fears of being victimized by pirates and mistaken for a pirate represent the ambiguities of the independent trader seeking cargoes and deals in the entrepôts of Southeast Asia: the "patriarch" of the island has become enmeshed in the ongoing negotiations and recalibrations of commercial identities in the East.

His nightmare of being tortured by the Dutch, however, may be the most serious threat that Crusoe faces in the second half of the novel. The colonial authorities in Batavia remain offstage; there is no heroic confront-ation with the Dutch, no grappling with internal demons, no vindication of Crusoe's honor and honesty against an evil commercial rival. In short, no consequences follow from his dreams: Crusoe sells the ship and follows a trading opportunity to China. In contrast to Anna Neill, who concludes that in *Farther Adventures* "Crusoe's reflections become increasingly less authoritative, and his identity less secure," I agree with Turley that the hero's travels in China and Siberia are crucial to shoring up Defoe's sense of national and theological identity.[18] Idolatry, Catholicism, and despair – the

principal threats against which Crusoe struggles to define his moral identity in part one – pose far fewer difficulties for the hero (and his creator) in
the sequel.[19] Although the Dutch may haunt Crusoe's nightmares, his true
antagonists in *Farther Adventures* and *Serious Reflections* are the Chinese
because they embody a fundamental contradiction that Defoe cannot
resolve – a virtuous and prosperous "heathen" civilization that threatens
Anglocentric fantasies of infinite profits, religious zeal, and a secure
national identity.

   A long-time critic of the India trade, Defoe consistently, even obsessively, advocated British expansion into the South Seas; trading posts on
the west coast of South America, he maintained, would establish a profitable trade with both New Spain and the nations of the Far East. As it
reworks material from his *Review of the State of the English Nation* (published serially from 1704 to 1713), Defoe's *New Voyage*, as I suggest in the
next chapter, reveals his and his culture's fascination with trade across the
Pacific as a means for England to realize its dreams of a coherent national
identity and international economic power. The Crusoe trilogy appeared
at a significant time in British efforts to open new markets and amid
ongoing debates about the value of the East India trade. As it had a century
earlier, England imported far more from India, China, and Southeast Asia
than it exported, and most of its exports still were in bullion. In 1718 and
1719, when Defoe was writing his Crusoe novels, a total of four East India
Company ships called at Canton, and all four carried more than 90 percent
of their cargo as silver. The four ships were the *Carnovan* (£2,796 in goods,
£28,000 in silver); the *Hartford* (£2,482 in goods, £28,000 in silver),
Sunderland (£2,688 in goods and £31,000 in silver), and the *Essex* (£2,923
in goods and £31,000 in silver). Only one Company ship before 1750
carried as much as one-third of its cargo in goods, and as late as 1754
80 percent of England's exports to Asia were in bullion.[20] Defoe's criticism
of the East India trade – sending out bullion and receiving luxury items and
cotton cloth which competed directly with British woolen mills – is
extended in *Farther Adventures* to the burgeoning tea trade.[21] While EIC
merchants "some times come home with 60 to 70 and 100 thousand
pounds at a time" from "the innumerable ports and places where they
have a free commerce" (393), the nation is threatened by its huge trade
imbalance with China and India. In the second half of the novel, these
lands become, for Defoe, *both* an imaginative space of infinite profits *and* a
nightmarish realm where personal and national identities are threatened
with disintegration. To counter the prospects of Dutch control of seaborne
trade in Southeast Asia and Chinese hegemony to the north, *Farther*

Adventures develops compensatory narratives that deny or repress the limitations of English power in the Far East.

CRUSOE IN CHINA

Crusoe has no dreams in China or Siberia, but his characterizations of both lands assume an almost hallucinogenic quality as Eurocentric fantasies of Protestant power and profit replace the moral realism of *Robinson Crusoe*. His vilification of the Chinese is without precedent in the vast European literature on the Middle Kingdom that I discussed in chapters two and three. Jonathan Spence notes in his discussion of *Farther Adventures* that "every previously described positive aspect of China [by the Jesuits and others] is negated, and every negative aspect of China is emphasized."[22] By rejecting accounts that celebrated China's wealth, socioeconomic stability, good government, and presumed monotheism, Defoe goes farther than Milton's studied disinterest in Jesuit and royalist idealizations of China and transforms the literature of diplomatic and tributary missions into mercantilist fantasies of outmaneuvering a people he depicts as backward, dishonest, and slow-witted.

For other writers in the late seventeenth and early eighteenth centuries, Qing China remained an upgraded version of the imperial powers of the ancient world: Greece, Egypt, Persia, and Rome. In England in the 1690s, Sir William Temple and William Wotton clashed bitterly over the significance that China and India played in the quarrel between the ancients and the moderns. Temple identified the Chinese as equal or superior to the hallowed philosophers of the antique Mediterranean. He asserts that the

Great and Renowned *Confutius* . . . began [with] the same Design, [as Socrates] of reclaiming men, from useless and endless Speculations of Nature, to those of Morality. But with this Difference, that the Bent of the *Grecian*, seemed to be chiefly, upon the Happiness of private Men or Families, but that of the *Chinese*, upon the good Temperament and Felicity of such Kingdoms or Governments, as that was, and is known to have continued for several Thousand of Years, and may be properly called, a Government of Learned Men, since no other, are admitted into the Charges of the State.[23]

Temple's emphasis on the lineal descent of Chinese morality and political authority reinforces a conservative tradition of learning and language. Confucius seems to out-Socrates Socrates. As we have seen in chapters two and three, this logic informs the lessons that English royalists draw in idealizing the Middle Kingdom as a model for Europe to emulate.[24] By the late seventeenth century, plays such as Elkannah Settle's *The Conquest of China by the Tartars* (1676) had transformed Martini's history of the collapse of the Ming dynasty into a tragicomedy that provided a fantasy solution to the problem of the English royal succession.[25] Jesuit commentators went farther in their efforts to counter criticism by the Dominicans, in particular, of their accommodationist strategies. In praising the reigning Qing Emperor Kangxi, as "the most potent Prince in the World, both in respect of his vast Revenues, and the great extent and Goodness of his Territories," the Jesuit Joachim Bouvet provided European readers with a biography – or (as we have seen in chapter three) something closer to a hagiography.[26] While acknowledging that "the Constitution of the *Chinese* Government is absolutely Monarchical," Bouvet maintains that the Emperor's virtue and constant vigilance render his rule, delegated to those of "approved Integrity and Probity[,] . . . Proof against all manner of Corruption."[27] Kangxi is presented as the ideal monarch, "endow'd with a Quick and piercing Wit, a vast Memory, and Great Understanding; His Constancy is never to be shaken by any sinister Event, which makes him the fittest Person in the World, not only to undertake, but also to accomplish Great Designs." Resisting the luxuries of sensual indulgence and the tyranny of absolute power, he rules with a kind of universal moral consent of both Manchus and Chinese: "his People stand in Admiration of his Person, being equally charmed with his Love and Justice, and the Tenderness he shews for his Subjects, and with his vertuous Inclinations; which as they are always guided by the Dictates of Reason." This political virtue is mirrored by what is described as his near-monotheism. He rejects the "degenerated" worship of the Chinese who "adore the Material Heavens," and instead offer "publick Prayers and Sacrifices . . . to the Supream Lord of Heaven and Earth."[28] In Bouvet's account, Kangxi becomes the true accommodationist, trying to lead the Chinese back by his example to an exemplary virtue. He is the agent for the restoration of the purity of an ancient, monotheistic religion as well as the virtuous sociopolitical order that is both the cause and effect of empire's wealth.

For critics of Jesuit accommodationism, the reasoning of Temple and Bouvet provoked anxieties that Qing China had emerged from the civil wars of the middle of the seventeenth century with its economic power intact and its reputation as an embodiment of an idealized sociopolitical order founded on absolute monarchy and absolute obedience enhanced. In England, William Wotton attacked Temple's views on China and India, ridiculed oriental medicine and religion, and claimed that if the Jesuits had printed Confucius's sayings under their own names, they "would soon have been called an incoherent Rhapsody of Moral Sayings, with which good Sense and tolerable Experience might have furnished any Man, as well as *Confucius*."[29] Wotton's view, though, was not widely shared. Bouvet's portrait of Kangxi contributed to the continuing fascination, particularly in France, with China and its rulers as alternatives to orthodox theology and royalist politics. For Pierre Bayle, and later Voltaire, China provides, as David Porter suggests, "a secure exterior vantage point from which to refute western hegemonic claims." Where Wotton sees China marked by degenerate forms of idolatry and absolutism, Temple, Bayle, and Voltaire credit the Middle Kingdom with both the order and virtue celebrated by the Jesuits and a more secular "monopoly of Deist religious truth."[30] Such laudatory views were reinforced by the persistent emphasis on China's economic prosperity and sociopolitical stability under the Qings.

Eyewitness accounts available to Defoe almost uniformly agreed with the Jesuit Louis Le Comte that "of all the Kingdoms of the Earth *China* is the most celebrated for Politeness and Civility, for grandeur and magnificence, for Arts and Inventions."[31] The translation of Confucius into European vernaculars led a number of philosophers on the Continent, notably Gottfried Wilhelm Leibniz, to begin extensive comparative studies of European and Chinese systems of thought, and Yu Liu recently has argued for the foundational significance of a redacted version of Confucianism in Leibniz's later work.[32] For a committed Protestant like Defoe, China in the early eighteenth century posed more problems than it had for Milton in the 1650s as EIC ships began plying a semi-regular trade to Canton. Although Defoe shares his contemporaries' views of the potential for trade to China and the East Indies, the prospect of a "pagan" empire resistant to his critiques of tyranny and idolatry forces him into overdetermined rhetorical assaults to counter the challenges that the Middle Kingdom poses to his vision of a godly commerce that would counter the designs of "universal" monarchs from Paris to Beijing. This commerce, however, rests not in the monopolies of the EIC and VOC but in the castaway turned merchant-adventurer.

In both *Farther Adventures* and *Serious Reflections*, Crusoe castigates the Chinese at far greater length than he does any other people or culture. In fact, his long digression on China and its civilization is the only time that he singles out a nation for explicit comment, let alone censure. "As this is the only excursion of this kind which I have made in all the account I have given of my travels," he maintains, "so I shall make no more descriptions of countrys and people; 'tis none of my business, or any part of my design" (423). In *Serious Reflections*, he dismisses the Moghul empire in two sentences and the entire Islamic world in a couple of pages but devotes twenty-three hefty paragraphs, many of them more than a page long, to castigating the Chinese for their pride, immorality, technological backwardness, corrupt government, hideous art, and political tyranny. The revenge that Crusoe can only dream about earlier in the novel – fighting back against the Dutch – is enacted rhetorically as a compensatory fantasy that dominates the latter part of the novel of European moral righteousness and supposed technoscientific superiority. In identifying the Chinese as the "other" against whom he defines his political, religious, and economic sense of identity, Crusoe finds the structure of fantasy more certain than the uncertainty of his dreams.[33]

Defoe launched his first broadside against the Chinese more than a decade before the Crusoe novels. In his satiric fantasy, *The Consolidator* (1705), he targets China as the antithesis of the political and religious values that he champions. His satire takes the form of a mock-encomium that travesties Chinese learning, technological accomplishments, absolutist politics, and claims to a pre-Mosaic antiquity. Satirizing John Webb's theory that China was founded by Noah, Defoe has his credulous narrator promise his readers "A Description of a Fleet of Ships of 100000 Sail, built at the Expense of the Emperor *Tangro* the 15th; who having Notice of the General Deluge, prepar'd these Vessels," escaped the Flood, and consequently preserved the antediluvian "Perfections" of their culture and a "most exact History of 2000 Emperors."[34] For Defoe, China's widespread renown for its antiquity, virtue, and social stability is merely a cover for the noxious political and religious doctrines – notably the monarchical absolutism and passive obedience that he savaged throughout his career as a journalist and pamphlet-writer. His narrator avows that there is no "Tyranny of Princes, or Rebellion of Subjects" in any of China's histories, and concludes that these annals offer proof "that Kings and Emperors came down from Heaven with Crowns on their Heads, and all their Subjects were born with Saddles on their Backs" (12, 13–14). If such absolutism has been decreed by heaven, then Chinese history can be invoked by apologists for tyranny to "explain, as well as defend, all Coercion in Cases invasive of Natural Right" (14). In *The Consolidator*, China, not France, symbolizes the political repression and false religion that Defoe spent a lifetime attacking.

Fifteen years later, Crusoe's obsession with the Chinese occasions his vehement attacks on Jesuit accommodationism. Although Defoe accepts the Jesuits' wishful characterization of "Confucius's maxims" as an analogue of European "theology," he echoes Wotton in denouncing these texts (widely translated into European vernaculars by 1720) as "a rhapsody of words, without consistency, and, indeed, with very little reasoning." He then declares that there are "much more regular doings among some of the Indians that are pagans in America, than there are in China; and if I may believe the account given of the government of Montezuma in Mexico, and of the Uncas of Cusco in Peru, their worship and religion, such as it was, was carried on with more regularity than these in China" (*SR* 123). As he does in vilifying the Dutch, Crusoe compares the Chinese unfavorably to the "pagans" of the Americas. But in China "idolatry" goes beyond ignorance or devil-worship to violate the principles that anchor western conceptions of reality and representation. In a garden near Nanking, Crusoe finds a horrifying Chinese "idol":

It had a thing instead of a head, but no head; it had a mouth distorted out of all manner of shape, and not to be described for a mouth, being only an unshapen chasm, neither representing the mouth of a man, beast, fowl, or fish; the thing was neither any of the four, but an incongruous monster; it had feet, hands, fingers, claws, legs, arms, wings, ears, horns, everything mixed one among another, neither in the shape or place that Nature appointed, but blended together and fixed to a bulk, not a body, formed of no just parts, but a shapeless trunk or log, whether of wood or stone, I know not[.] (*SR* 126)

This "celestial hedgehog" is too grotesque "to have represented even the devil"; yet, if the reader wishes to form a picture in her mind's-eye of Chinese deities, Crusoe asserts, "let imagination supply anything that can make a misshapen image horrid, frightful, and surprising" and the Chinese will worship "such a mangled, promiscuous-gendered creature" (*SR* 126). Crusoe overreacts: Chinese art by 1720 was well known in the West: porcelain was a prized import, and silks, furniture, screens, and fans made Chinese artistic conventions familiar and popular.

   Much later in the eighteenth century, Sir William Chambers explicated and defended the aesthetic and ecological values that informed Chinese landscape architecture, and his appreciation casts into relief the near-hysteria of Defoe's rhetoric. Rather than imposing pre-determined designs or patterns on the landscape, "the Chinese Gardeners take nature for their pattern; and their aim is to imitate all her beautiful irregularities." Consequently, "they shape their garden to the terrain, whether it be flat or sloping; hilly or mountainous; small or of considerable extent; abounding with springs and rivers, or labouring under a scarcity of water; whether woody or bare, rough or even, barren or rich; and whether the transitions be sudden, and the character grand, wild or tremendous; or whether they be gradual, and the general bent placid, gloomy or cheerful."[35] Unlike Defoe, who decontextualizes the Chinese "idol," Chambers (and perhaps those members of the upper classes who followed his advice) recognizes that an appreciation of oriental gardening must take into account not only ecological considerations and aesthetic principles but also the complex psychological effects of landscape design. His descriptive vocabulary is intent on rendering the "disposition" of the garden as an embodied experience of walking through a landscape, noticing the "irregularities" of what we would now call its geology, biota, and hydrology. Contrast this appreciation of an idealized Chinese view of nature to Crusoe's perception of "his" island as a storehouse of use-value awaiting exploitation.

For Defoe, the "hedgehog's" confusion of physiology, gender, and religion challenges a western ethics and ideology of representation and therefore an entire worldview. He rejects the intercultural commerce that, in different ways, intrigues Leibniz, Voltaire, and Chambers. It is not simply that this "incongruous monster" represents the idolatrous other against which an English Protestant self must be defined, but that Chinese moral philosophy and representational practices threaten to rewrite the very principles of theology, gender, and self-identity. Cannibals, like Friday, can be converted; they are amenable to reason and candidates for revelation. Catholics, like the helpful French priest on Crusoe's island, can become allies against idolatry. Even the Dutch, with their "inhuman tortures and barbarities," are Protestants who can be understood as antagonists within the representational and political contexts of national interest and international rivalry for trade. But it is the Chinese *lack* of interest in European manufactured goods and overtures for trade that poses a greater threat than disincorporation by cannibalism or psychic disintegration at the hands of torturers. China threatens to incorporate Europeans within its standards of civilization, its conceptions of morality, trade, and civic order. Even as he tolerates "subtle *Jesuites*" in his country, the Kangxi Emperor and his subjects remain largely unmoved by their designs, forcing the missionaries, according to Le Comte's anonymous English translator, to adapt "their Model [of religion] to the philosophy of *Confucius*, seldom or never Teaching the Crucifixion and Godhead of Christ, and frequently allowing the worship of *Pagods*."[36] Going native in early Qing China does not mean reverting to "savagery" but conforming to the assumptions, values, and practices of a powerful and, particularly for Defoe, alien civilization.

Yet even Defoe's insults reveal his familiarity with the vast literature on China available in the early eighteenth century. Crusoe's route across Siberia from Beijing to Archangel follows, in large measure, the itinerary described by the Czar's emissary to Kangxi, Evret Ysbrants Ides, in *Three Years Travels from Moscow Over-Land to China*, discussed in chapter three.[37] Defoe reads Ides selectively. After lavishly praising China's wealth, civility, architecture, magnificence, and women, as we have seen in chapter three, Ides spends the final two pages of his narrative criticizing the "rude and barbarous" judiciary system of the Chinese and the "perfect Pagan idolatry" of their religion; he concludes that "the great share of Wisdom, Arts and Sciences, for which they are so highly extolled by many Writers, comes far short of the *Europeans*" (108–09). Such belated denunciations and perfunctory criticisms were trotted out by Jesuit writers to reassure European readers that the threat China posed to western notions of religious, political, and cultural supremacy could be mitigated or contained. However eager merchants and missionaries may have been to flatter the Emperor and the Mandarin officials in order to secure trading privileges or build churches, they were quite conscious of explorers and their patrons who invested huge sums of money in both trading ventures and religious missions. Employed by Peter the Great but seeking to establish himself in the caravan trade between Beijing and Moscow, Ides was eager to placate a monarch who entertained his own imperial ambitions; and he needed to put the best possible spin on the message that he brought back from Beijing: while a limited caravan trade was permitted, the Czar's letters to the Kangxi Emperor were rejected by the Board of Rites because they violated the proper protocols for a barbarian tributary mission. Similarly, Le Comte flatters Louis XIV, bogged down in a costly war in Europe, by reflecting "on the facility with which *Lewis* the Great would subdue those Provinces [bordering the Great Wall], if Nature had made us a little nearer Neighbours to *China*; he whom the stoutest Places in *Europe* can at best withstand but during a few days."[38] Given the praise that he elsewhere lavishes on Chinese civilization, this sop to French ambitions is less a sober military assessment than a means of flattering the King into continuing to patronize Jesuit missions in the Far East. As such, it misrepresents the situation of which Jesuits in China were well aware. Faced with the extraordinarily difficult problems of policing thousands of miles of their northern and western borders against incursions by nomads, the Qing dynasty extended the Ming policy of avoiding, whenever possible, prolonged and inconsequential military campaigns. Although intermittent hostilities were par for the course, the Manchu government favored commerce over conquest as a strategy of pacification: the nomadic tribes gained access to Chinese luxury goods and widened their opportunities for trade across the border; the Chinese and Manchus south of the Great Wall imported horses, meat, milk products, hides, and wool from the nomads.[39]

Defoe amplifies Ides's perfunctory criticism and Le Comte's formulaic flattery of Louis XIV into an all-out assault on Chinese civilization. He is shrewd enough to know that he cannot mimic the density of detail that characterizes firsthand accounts of China, so generic diatribes substitute for the descriptive strategies of literary-cartographic realism. China's vaunted prowess, Crusoe asserts, is the effect of the low expectations that Europeans hold for "a barbarous nation of pagans": "the greatness of their wealth, their trade, the power of their government, and the strength of their armies, is surprising to us," he maintains, "because . . . we did not expect such things among them; and this indeed is the advantage with which all their greatness and power is represented to us; otherwise in it self it is nothing at all" (421). It is difficult to convey how jarring an assertion this is in the early eighteenth century: the idealized Empire of Jesuit-inspired literature is replaced by a country caricatured as, at once, backward, tyrannical, and decadent. In confronting the threat that China poses to his vision of national identity and economic prosperity, Defoe describes a land he has never seen only in debased relation to European conceptions of religious truth, military power, and technological sophistication. Crusoe elaborates authoritative-sounding comparisons that structure his (and his creator's) fantasy of European superiority. "A million of their foot [soldiers]," he claims, "could not stand before one embattled body of our infantry . . . 30,000 German or English foot, and 10,000 French horse, would fairly beat all the forces of China" (422). This vision of well-trained and well-equipped European forces united against the Chinese army, "a contemptible herd or crowd of ignorant sordid slaves" (422), becomes an imaginary compensation for the wealth and "greatness" of the Chinese empire, not to mention the 900,000 soldiers garrisoned along its northern frontier. This battle of East and West takes place only in a virtual realm where fictional pronouncements about military capabilities take precedence over material reality: European garrisons in Asia well into the eighteenth century could muster, at most, only a few hundred men, and no British, French, or German soldiers were stationed within two thousand miles of Beijing. In *A New Account of the East Indies,* Hamilton calculated the taxes paid in salt and rice in the province of

Canton and suggests that its "military Expence ... may amount to 1000000 of *Tayels* yearly," the equivalent of approximately £300,000, and Adam Brand describes a China "by both Art and Nature made impregnable."[40] Crusoe's claim is not a serious challenge or a reflection of the relative strengths of the two nations but a compensatory rhetorical gesture in the face of superior economic power.

Crusoe's tirades cannot disguise the fact that Chinese luxuries remain objects of intense desire, such as the £3,500 of raw silk, cloth, and tea which the hero brings back to sell in Europe. Much of his stay in China is devoted to negotiating with shady, often dishonest traders who are presented as characteristic of their nation. These scenes, too, present fantasies of wealth and empowerment in the guise of narrative realism. All the eyewitness accounts that Defoe could have read testify to the wealth, business acumen, and ingenuity of the Chinese. Englishmen such as Hamilton, who in 1703 in Canton had to sell his ship's cargo at half its market value, were aware that they were dealing with shrewd merchants who drove hard bargains.[41] Some sense of how shrill, even hysterical, Defoe's attack on China must have seemed to his contemporaries can be gleaned from two important eyewitness accounts published at the same time as *The Consolidator*, Fernandez Navarette's *An Account of the Empire of China, Historical, Political, Moral, and Religious* and Giovanni Francisco Gemelli Careri's *A Voyage Round the World*, which devotes its longest section to China.[42] To a greater extent than Ides or Nieuhoff, these writers find grounds for mutual respect in their day-to-day negotiations with the Chinese for the products and services of a wealthy and civilized society.

Careri, an Italian jurist, traveled through Asia to China in 1695–96 without governmental or religious sponsorship. His memoirs echo (and often paraphrase) the comments of earlier missionary accounts, even as he supplements them with his own observations. Noting the "extraordinary industry" of the "very sharp Witted" Chinese, he admits that they "exceed the *Europeans* in Ingenuity."[43] This view is shared by Navarette, a Dominican friar who drew on his two decades in China to produce a detailed account of social and economic life during the early Qing period. The "Nature, Method, and disposition of the *Chinese* Government is admirable," Navarette asserts, "and may be a Pattern or Model to many in the World."[44] This sociopolitical stability is reflected in the economic life of the Empire. Canton is a city of superb workmen, who produce both exotic items and knockoffs of European imports "counterfeited ... so exactly, that they sell them in the Inland for Goods brought from *Europe*." Even as they undercut the market for western imports, the Chinese more than hold their own against the Europeans as manufacturers of luxury merchandise:

The Curiosities they make and sell in the Shops amaze all *Europeans*. If four large Galeons were sent to the City *Nan King*, to that of *Cu Cheu*, to *Hang Cheu*, or any other like them, they might be loaden with a thousand varieties of Curiosities and Toys, such as all the World would admire, and a great Profit be made of them, tho sold at reasonable Rates. All things necessary to furnish a Princely House, may be had ready made in several parts of any of the aforesaid Citys, without any further trouble than the buying, and all at poor Rates in comparison of what is sold among us.[45]

Navarette is explicit: the Chinese are better businessmen than the Europeans, equaling or bettering the quality of European goods at much cheaper prices. Throughout his narrative, he quotes the prices he has paid for various staples, marveling at how inexpensively he can purchase food, paper, clothes, and servants. His view of commercial life in China, in short, differs starkly from the fictional descriptions that Defoe offers. Navarette describes Chinese "Traders and Merchants" as "all very obliging and civil; if they can get any thing [in the way of profit], tho never so little, they don't slip the opportunity."[46] This willingness to negotiate prices marks the Chinese as members of a civilized, transnational class of merchants whose business practices indicate that they share the same moral, social, and financial values as the Europeans. In turn, these values become the external manifestations of a fundamental similarity of worldviews. Careri finds that in dealing with merchants "their Oath is Inviolable, and they will hazard their Head to keep their Word."[47] This "civil and obliging" behavior guarantees that the Chinese share a psychology characterized by the universal desires for profit, civility, and ultimately, Navarette implies, Christian enlightenment. In this regard, like Careri, Navarette accepts his status as a foreign guest in an empire that – except for religion – out-civilizes as well as out-produces the nations of western Europe.

Le Comte, in many respects, confirms Navarette's account of the Chinese, but his comments on their business practices suggest a darker perception of the psychological costs of commercial acumen. The desire for profit turns inward upon China's merchants so that they become the victims as well as the perpetrators of mercantile obsession:

There is no Nation under the Sun, that is more fit for Commerce and Traffick, and understand them better: One can hardly believe how far their Tricks and Craftiness proceed when they are to insinuate into Mens affections, manage a fair Opportunity, or improve the Overtures that are offered: The desire of getting torments them continually, and makes them discover a thousand ways of gaining ... Every thing serves their turn, every thing is precious to the *Chinese*, because there is nothing but they know how to improve ... The infinite Trade and Commerce that is carried on every where, is the Soul of the People, and the *primum mobile* of all their Actions.[48]

This passage almost reads like a gloss on the advice that Defoe doles out in *The Complete English Tradesman.* In his chapter on diligence, he states that "trade is a daily employment, and must be followed as such, with the full attention of the mind, and full attendance of the person; nothing but what are to be called the necessary duties of life are to intervene, and even these are to be limited so as not to be prejudicial to business."[49] If Crusoe's dreams of his island at the beginning of *Farther Adventures* are any indication, Defoe's tradesman may spend nights as well as days with the "full attention of [his] mind" on business. Chinese merchants embody the very strategies that Defoe's heroes and heroines adopt over the course of their careers. Like Moll and Roxana, these profit-seekers thrive on their ability to outmaneuver European men, yet remain obsessed with perfecting their "thousand ways of gaining." As Le Comte warns his European readers, "a Stranger will always be cheated, if he be alone." Most threateningly, for Defoe, China's "infinite Trade" marks the sinicization of capitalist self-interest, a preemptive appropriation of the strategies of bourgeois self-definition, including the psychological "torments" of Crusoian obsession. If a European, says Le Comte, employs a "trusty *Chinese*, who is acquainted with the Country, who knows all the Tricks ... you will be very happy, if he that buys [for you] and he that sells [to you], do not collogue together to your Cost, and go snips in the profit."[50] In contrast to the fictions of economic self-sufficiency, labor, and the devotion of a virtuous servant, China presents Crusoe with confusing networks of "infinite Trade and Commerce," double-dealing and dependency, and self-interested and untrustworthy locals. In China, Defoe's hero threatens to fall from "patriarch" to dupe because the prosperity and acumen of the Chinese undermine the links between sin and scarcity, virtue and abundance, that underlie Protestant visions of self-identity and national greatness.

The novelist's response to the threat posed by the Chinese is to remove Crusoe from the complications of international trade that Hamilton encountered, to downplay the difficulty of transcultural negotiations, and to idealize the merchant as a free agent in a hostile world. Consequently, Defoe must gloss over how an empire "imperfect and impotent" in "navigation, commerce, and husbandry" (428) can dominate European markets for luxury goods and for re-export to the Americas. Crusoe's invectives can prompt no action; his assertion that the English

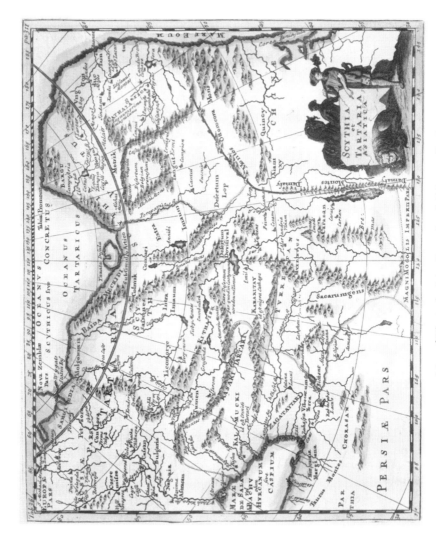

FIGURE 4. Map of Siberia, by John Senex (1721). Private collection.

could "batter . . . down in ten days" "this mighty nothing call'd a wall" (431) can have no consequences, provoke no vindication such as his victory, decades earlier, over the cannibals. His taunts can be acted on only after he has left the Qing Empire and the crises of self-representation that it provokes, only when the opportunity arises for Crusoe to assert the superiority of Christian culture against a far weaker antagonist on the steppes of Siberia.

CRUSOE THE AVENGER

To get his hero back from Beijing to Europe, Defoe creates a fictional Russian caravan.[51] The nine caravans that followed Ides's route between 1696 and 1719 were the monopoly of the Czar (figure 4), an effort to control the trading of furs to China in exchange for gold, damask, and silk. Although Ides had returned a 48 percent profit on the state's investment, by 1710 Chinese imports had saturated the tiny Russian market for luxury items and had to be resold in the Baltic for considerably less than they had previously commanded.[52] These caravans across Siberia offered nothing like the fantastic profits that Crusoe reaps in the *Farther Adventures*. Yet however fanciful his hero's "wild ventures" may seem, Defoe was fascinated by the narrative possibilities that such an epic trek offered. Having sent Crusoe five thousands miles across Asia, the novelist has Singleton lead a shipwrecked band of pirates across Africa on foot, and, in *A New Voyage*, fifty sailors walk from Peru, across South America, to Brazil. In the latter two novels, these improbable treks allow the sailors to accumulate vast amounts of gold in regions which are free from competition: the natives in Africa are relatively few; the Amazon basin is a bucolic and unpopulated countryside of verdant hills, abundant game, and rivers of gold. While all three novels fantasize about trading opportunities with "savages," usually willing to part with mounds of gold for brass pots and rusty hatchets, *Farther Adventures* makes Crusoe an improbable agent in rendering Siberia a comparatively safe byway for Christian merchants. In brief, the anxieties provoked by China are displaced onto the nomadic "Tartars"; railing that has no consequences in China becomes a righteous – and violent – vindication of Christian belief on the borders of the Czar's dominions where the few "profess'd Christians" are out-numbered by thousands of "meer pagans" (440). In this regard, the fear and desire provoked by China can be unleashed as holy indignation against nomadic tribesmen and backward villagers who can be pigeonholed, albeit with some difficulty, as the colonized subjects of a Christian empire.

Crusoe seizes the opportunity to reaffirm his faith when he encounters a village where the "pagans" worship an idol. After seventy years of hardship, isolation, and danger, Crusoe declares, "I was more mov'd at their stupidity and brutish worship of a hobgoblin, than ever I was at any thing in my life; to see God's most glorious and best creature . . . sunk and degenerate to a degree so more than stupid, as to prostrate it self to a frightful nothing" (441). His response to this "brutish worship" both recalls and exceeds those moments in *Robinson Crusoe* when he fantasizes about killing scores of cannibals. On Madagascar, earlier in *Farther Adventures*, Crusoe had tried to stop his sailors from slaughtering villagers as grim retribution for the death of a shipmate, and his ceaseless upbraiding had led them to put him ashore in India. Now, confronted by the spectre of idolatry, he describes to one of his Scots companions, how his shipmates "burnt and sack'd the village there, and kill'd man, woman, and child, . . . and when I had done, I added that I thought we ought to do so to this village" (443). The excesses of "so bloody and cruel an enterprise" on Madagascar leave Crusoe, at the time, "pensive and sad" (386); now idolatry provokes in him thoughts of genocide. Trade in Asia has not civilized the aged hero but made him more intransigent, less introspective, and more convinced than ever that any action – including mass murder – can be justified by Protestant self-righteousness. Fortunately, his Scots comrade, Captain Richardson, "famous for his zeal [against] devilish things," points out that because the idol is carried from village to village in this region, it is more cost-effective to destroy it rather than wage war against every pagan settlement that the caravan encounters. The episode thus becomes a revenge fantasy for the imagined insults of Dutch torturers and shrewd Chinese merchants.

Although Crusoe declares that his vengeance is intended "to vindicate the honour of God, which is insulted by this devil worship" (442), his language of nearly chivalric honor is compromised by his actual escapade. He, Richardson, and another Scots merchant raid the village at night, tie up several pagan priests, and force them to watch as the British consign their idol to flames. Having struck this blow for their faith, Crusoe and his fellows hurry off with their caravan, never acknowledging to the Russian governor of the region or their Russian fellow-travelers that they are responsible for an incident that provokes a major confrontation between the Czar's officials in Nerchinsk and the "Tartars" who are "thirty thousand" strong (446). The nomads then pursue the caravan across the steppes, and what follows is an extended chase scene across a "vast nameless desert" (447), a strategic standoff in a wood, and yet another narrow escape for the British merchants. The flight across Siberia, in one respect, is a flight

from the consequences of cultural and theological conflict and the difficulties of colonial administration: torch the idol, play dumb, and leave the
Czar's governor to deal with thousands of angry Mongol horsemen. As acts
of Christian faith, burning the idol and then fleeing seem uncomfortably
similar to the logic behind flying false colors at sea: vindicating the honor of
God looks suspiciously like vandalism. Ironically, Crusoe has adopted the
strategy of the Jesuit missionaries who, according to the translator of Le
Comte's *Memoirs and Observations*, assume "the Characters of Physicians,
Painters, Merchants, Astrologers, Mechanicians, *&c.* and are receiv'd as
such in the Courts of *Asia*, which are too fine to suffer openly the
propagation of a strange Religion."[53] Like the Jesuits, Crusoe preaches, it
seems, only to the credulous and unarmed. He does not converse with the
Siberian nomads; they do not assume Friday's posture of submission before
western technology and theology; he rescues no one; and he asserts no
theological or political authority in a reshaped *polis*. Instead *Farther
Adventures* offers the prototypical logic of the action-adventure genre: the
reconfirmation, through juvenile acts of "heroism," of moralistic denunciations of alien cultures, the imposition of western standards of morality as
universal truths, and violence as a means to an end.[54] At seventy-one,
Crusoe reestablishes the hyper-masculinity of the merchant-adventurer
by burning a phallic log and claiming a victory over idolatry. Such
declarations ultimately pose no threat to the safety of the caravan or the
hero's profits because we recognize that, once outside the borders of China,
providence smiles on Christian merchants who use deception as a basic
strategy of survival, profitability, and self-definition, who adopt, in effect,
the characteristics and strategies of their Chinese counterparts.

If *Farther Adventures* disorients readers who may expect another tale
of "man's" triumph over "nature," it also reorients the values and assumptions which traditionally have defined *Robinson Crusoe* and the realist "rise"
of the novel.[55] It is significant, in this regard, that the *Crusoe* trilogy
concludes with a set piece that harks back to the medieval dream vision,
the hero's imaginative ascent to the "angelic world." Crusoe's vision is
the generic form to which realism tends: if zealotry is the form that fantasy
takes to obscure the relative weakness of Protestant England in an Asian-
dominated world, the hero's transcendence of the material world ironically
reveals the surreal quality of his "serious reflections" on his adventures.
All along, this dream vision suggests, readers have been assured by the
generic certainty of a faith-based memoir, Crusoe's after-the-fact *apologia*
for the engaging literary strategies that shape his years on the island and
his travels in Asia. In one sense, *Serious Reflections* reads like the moralizing

passages left out of the second half of *Farther Adventures*, belated efforts to bridge the gaps and resolve the inconsistencies within the Eurocentric ideologies of selfhood, economic individualism, and colonialist appropriation.

If Defoe's moral and aesthetic imperatives remain the same in the first two volumes of the trilogy, as the novelist claims, *Farther Adventures* represents a broader range of narrative possibilities which Defoe exploits throughout his career: the protean self whose integrity can be guaranteed only by protestations of faith; the balance sheet that shows only profits, and not the costs or consequences of money-making; the business enterprise that can be left at a moment's notice without affecting profits; and a nationalism that picks its rhetorical fights very carefully. Both the "profit-ability" and "diversion" of this sequel, then, depend on a dialogic interac-tion among competing genres: the moral apology, the administrative treatise, the travel narrative, the trade embassy, and what we might call the Protestant revenge fantasy. After 1724, Defoe ceased writing novels, and in his last years produced an astonishing array of polemical texts ranging from *The Complete English Tradesman* to *Conjugal Lewdness*; these works are anticipated more by the literary experimentation of *Farther Adventures* than they are by the "realism" of its predecessor. In this sequel, Defoe sketches the beginnings of an alternative – and as yet unwritten – history of the eighteenth-century novel, one that depends on adventure, profit, and Protestant fanaticism to turn readers' thoughts from the fate of Crusoe's nameless island. Defoe in 1719 had already done with his island; and his desire to chart the conditions for an infinitely profitable trade demands that the second installment of his trilogy assuage the "anxieties and per-plexities" that such fantasies produce. At the end of his career as a novelist, in *A New Voyage Around the World*, his fantasies are more insistent and the anxieties only strategic in a vast region of infinite promise – the South Seas.

NOTES

1. See, for representative readings, Ian Watt, *The Rise of the Novel* (Berkeley: University of California Press, 1957); J. Paul Hunter, *The Reluctant Pilgrim: Defoe's Emblematic Method and the Quest for Form in Robinson Crusoe* (Baltimore: Johns Hopkins University Press, 1966), and *Before Novels: The Cultural Contexts of Eighteenth-Century English Fiction* (New York: Norton, 1990); John Richetti, *Defoe's Narratives: Situations and Structures* (Oxford: Clarendon, 1975); Paula Backscheider, *Daniel Defoe: Ambition and Innovation* (Lexington: University of Kentucky Press, 1986), and *Daniel Defoe: His Life* (Baltimore: The Johns Hopkins University Press, 1989); Michael McKeon, *The Origins of the English*

Novel 1600–1740 (Baltimore: Johns Hopkins University Press, 1987); Nancy Armstrong and Leonard Tennenhouse, *The Imaginary Puritan: Literature, Intellectual Labor, and the Origins of Personal Life* (Berkeley and Los Angeles: University of California Press, 1992); Thompson, *Models of Value*; William Beatty Warner, *Licensing Entertainment: The Elevation of Novel Reading in Britain, 1684–1750* (Berkeley and Los Angeles: University of California Press, 1998); Sandra Sherman, *Finance and Fictionality in the Early Eighteenth Century: Accounting for Defoe* (Cambridge: Cambridge University Press, 1996); and Wolfram Schmidgen, "*Robinson Crusoe*, Enumeration, and the Mercantile Fetish," *Eighteenth-Century Studies* 35 (2001), 19–39.

2. Recent critics who have dealt with the second and third installments of the *Crusoe* trilogy include Anna Neill, "Crusoe's *Farther Adventures*: Discovery, Trade, and the Law of Nations," *The Eighteenth Century: Theory and Interpretation* 38 (1997), 213–30; Jeffrey Hopes, "Real and Imaginary Stories: *Robinson Crusoe* and the *Serious Reflections*," *Eighteenth-Century Fiction* 8 (1996), 313–28; and Minaz Jooma, "Robinson Crusoe Inc(corporates): Domestic Economy, Incest and the Trope of Cannibalism," *Lit* 8 (1997), 61–81.

3. *The Farther Adventures of Robinson Crusoe* (New York: Peebles Classics, 1927), 250. All citations are from this edition.

4. Henry Clinton Hutchins, *Robinson Crusoe and Its Printing 1719–1731: A Bibliographical Study* (New York: Columbia University Press, 1925), 113; Robert W. Lovett, assisted by Charles C. Lovett, *Robinson Crusoe: A Bibliographical Checklist of English Language Editions, 1719–1979* (New York: Greenwood, 1991); and Melissa Free, "Un-Erasing Crusoe: *Farther Adventures* in the Nineteenth Century," *Book History*, forthcoming.

5. On the implications of the Caribbean setting of Crusoe's island, see Peter Hulme, *Colonial Encounters: Europe and the Native Caribbean 1492–1797* (1986; rpt. New York: Routledge, 1992), 184–222; Aparna Dharwadker, "Nation, Race, and the Ideology of Commerce in Defoe," *The Eighteenth Century: Theory and Interpretation* 39 (1998), 63–84; Markman Ellis, "Crusoe, Cannibalism, and Empire," in *Robinson Crusoe: Myths and Metamorphoses*, ed. Lieve Spaas and Brian Stimpson (New York: St. Martin's Press, 1996), 45–61; and Roxanne Wheeler, "'My Savage,' 'My Man': Racial Multiplicity in *Robinson Crusoe*," *ELH* 62 (1995), 821–61.

6. Hans Turley, "Protestant Evangelism, British Imperialism, and Crusoian Identity," in Kathleen Wilson, ed., *A New Imperial History: Culture, Identity and Modernity in Britain and the Empire, 1660–1840* (Cambridge: Cambridge University Press, 2004); "The Sublimation of Desire to Apocalyptic Passion in Defoe's Crusoe Trilogy," in Philip Holden and Richard J. Ruppel, eds., *Imperial Desire: Dissident Sexualities and Colonial Literature* (Minneapolis: University of Minnesota Press, 2003), 3–20; and *Rum, Sodomy, and the Lash: Piracy, Sexuality, and Masculine Identity* (New York: New York University Press, 1999).

7. Lydia H. Liu, "Robinson Crusoe's Earthenware Pot," *Critical Inquiry* 25 (1999), 757.

8. *Serious Reflections during the Life and Surprising Adventures of Robinson Crusoe*, introduced by G. H. Maynadier (Boston: Beacon Classics, 1903), 116. All quotations are from this edition.

9. Daniel Defoe, *Vindication of the Press* (London, 1718), 4.

10. Alexander Hamilton, *A New Account of the East Indies*, 2 vols. (Edinburgh, 1727), II: 230–39.

11. On the economic dominance of China before 1800, see the sources cited in the notes to chapters two and three.

12. For the stories of Will and Selkirk, see Glyndwr Williams, *The Great South Sea: English Voyages and Encounters 1570–1750* (New Haven: Yale University Press, 1997), 93–96, 176–77; and Philip Edwards, *The Story of the Voyage: Sea-Narratives in Eighteenth-Century England* (Cambridge: Cambridge University Press, 1994), 41–42. Will's resourcefulness is described by William Dampier, *A Collection of Voyages*, 4 vols. (London, 1729), 80–86.

13. See Spate, *Monopolists and Freebooters*, 155–65; 205–12; Glyndwr Williams, "'The Inexhaustible Fountain of Gold': English Projects and Ventures in the South Seas, 1670–1750," in *Perspectives of Empire: Essays Presented to Gerald S. Graham*, ed. John E. Flint and Glyndwr Williams (London: Longman, 1973), 27–53; Williams, *Great South Sea, passim*; and Jonathan Lamb, *Preserving the Self in the South Seas, 1680–1840* (Chicago: University of Chicago Press, 2001), 174–76.

14. These "last letters" may reflect Defoe's own problems with colonial trade; twice in the 1690s he was sued for failing to deliver on ventures in Massachusetts and Maryland, which precipitated his first bankruptcy for £17,000. See James Sutherland, "Some Early Troubles of Daniel Defoe," *Review of English Studies* 9 (1933), 275–90.

15. On the English–Dutch rivalry in Southeast Asia, see Furber, *Rival Empires of Trade*, as well as the notes to chapter four.

16. [Defoe], *Atlas Maritimus*, 202, 226. On Defoe's authorship of this work, see Maximillian Novak, *Daniel Defoe: Master of Fictions* (Oxford and New York: Oxford University Press, 2001), 687–90.

17. Defoe, *Atlas Maritimus*, 226.

18. A. Neill, "Crusoe's *Farther Adventures*: Discovery, Trade, and the Law of Nations," 226; Turley, "The Sublimation of Desire to Apocalyptic Passion in Defoe's Crusoe Trilogy," 3–20.

19. On constructions of "Englishness" in the eighteenth century, see Colley, *Britons: Forging the Nation 1707–1837*; and Colin Kidd, *British Identities before Nationalism: Ethnicity and Nationhood in the Atlantic World, 1600–1800* (Cambridge: Cambridge University Press, 1999).

20. Hosea B. Morse, *The Chronicles of the East India Company Trading to China 1635–1834*, 5 vols. (Oxford: Clarendon, 1926, 1929), I: 308; I: 122–23. See also Barrett, "World Bullion Flows, 1450–1800," in *Rise of Merchant Empires*, 224–53.

21. Between 1710 and 1720, England imported £1,316,534 of goods from Asia and ran a trade deficit of over £300,000. By 1719, 417,000 kilograms of tea from

Canton were imported into Britain; within twenty years this figure more than doubled. See Steensgaard, "The Growth and Composition of the Long-Distance Trade of England and the Dutch Republic," 104–10.

22. Spence, *The Chan's Great Continent*, 67.

23. Sir William Temple, "An Essay Upon Ancient and Modern Learning," in *Miscellanea. The Second Part. In Four Essays* (London, 1690), 21–22.

24. See David Porter, *Ideographia: The Chinese Cipher in Early Modern Europe* (Stanford: Stanford University Press, 2001). On the royalist use of China as a model for England, see Ramsey, "China and the Ideal of Order," 483–503.

25. See Dalporto, "The Succession Crisis," 131–46.

26. Bouvet, *History of Cang-Hy*, 29–30.

27. Bouvet, *History of Cang-Hy*, 23–24.

28. Bouvet, *History of Cang-Hy*, 2, 28.

29. William Wotton, *Reflections upon Ancient and Modern Learning*, 2nd edn (London, 1697), 156. On the Temple–Wotton controversy, see Eun Min, "China between the Ancients and the Moderns," *The Eighteenth Century: Theory and Interpretation* 45 (2004), 115–29.

30. Porter, *Ideographia*, 128.

31. Louis Le Comte, *Memoirs and Observations Topographical, Physical, Mathematical, Natural, Civil, and Ecclesiastical, Made in a Late Journey through the Empire of China* (London, 1697), A3r (translator's preface). This is a translation of the first volume of Le Comte's *Nouveaux mémoires sur l'état présent de la Chine*, 3 vols. (Paris, 1696–98).

32. Yu Liu, "The Jesuits and the Anti-Jesuits." The literature on Leibniz's interest in China is extensive. See particularly David Mungello, *Leibniz and Confucianism: The Search for an Accord* (Honolulu: University of Hawaii Press, 1977); Daniel J. Cook and Henry Rosemont, Jr., "The Pre-established Harmony between Leibniz and Chinese Thought," *Journal of the History of Ideas* 42 (1981), 253–67; and Perkins, *Leibniz and China*.

33. On fantasy see particularly Slavoj Žižek, *Tarrying with the Negative: Kant, Hegel, and the Critique of Ideology* (Durham: Duke University Press, 1993), 45–82.

34. Daniel Defoe, *The Consolidator* (London, 1705), 60–61, 13. All quotations are from this edition.

35. Sir William Chambers, *A Dissertation on Oriental Gardening* (London, 1772), 12–13.

36. Le Comte, *Memoirs and Observations* (translator's preface), A1r.

37. Ides, *Three Years Travels from Moscow Over-Land to China* (London, 1706).

38. Le Comte, *Memoirs and Observations*, 75.

39. Thomas J. Barfield, "The Shadow Empires: Imperial State Formation along the Chinese–Nomad Frontier," in Susan E. Alcock, Terrence N. D'Altroy, Kathleen D. Morrison, and Carla M. Sinopoli, eds., *Empires: Perspectives from Archaeology and History* (Cambridge: Cambridge University Press, 2001), 10–41, and C. Pat Giersch, "'A Motley Throng': Social Change on

Southwest China's Early Modern Frontier, 1700–1880," *Journal of Asian Studies* 60 (2001), 67–94.

40. See Hamilton, *A New Account of the East Indies*, II: 239; Brand, *A Journal of an Embassy*, 102. On the "marginality of European military" power in Asia during this period, see Jeremy Black, *European Warfare, 1660–1815* (New Haven: Yale University Press, 1994), 19–23.

41. See Hamilton, *A New Account of the East Indies*, II: 220–35, and Morse, *Chronicles of the East India Company*, 102–03.

42. Both works appeared in English translation in Awnsham and John Churchill's collection of previously unpublished manuscripts or untranslated foreign accounts, *A Collection of Voyages and Travels*, 4 vols. (London 1744–48). In their preface to Navarette's account, the Churchills assert, "those that have read him in the Original [i.e. Spanish] give a high Commendation of his Learning, Judgment, and Sincerity … he delivers nothing but upon the best grounds, as an Eye-witness, where he could be so, or else upon the Authority of *Chinese* Histories, which he search'd and very well understood, or upon the Information of credible Persons; ever mentioning on which of these the Reader is to rely for the Truth of what he relates" (11). On the significance of this collection, see P. J. Marshall and Glyndwr Williams, *The Great Map of Mankind: British Perceptions of the World in the Age of Enlightenment* (London: Dent, 1982), 49–51.

43. Careri, in *Collection of Voyages and Travels*, IV: 363.

44. Navarette, in *Collection of Voyages and Travels*, I: 52.

45. Navarette, in *Collection of Voyages and Travels*, I: 58.

46. Navarette, in *Collection of Voyages and Travels*, I: 60. On the markets of late Ming and early Qing China see particularly Adshead, *Material Culture in Europe and China*, and Xu Tan, "The Formation of an Urban and Rural Market Network in the Ming-Qing Period and Its Significance," *Social Studies in China* 22, 3 (2001), 132–39. On consumerism in Europe see Lisa Jardine, *Worldly Goods: A New History of the Renaissance* (London: Macmillan, 1996).

47. Careri, in *Collection of Voyages and Travels*, IV: 372.

48. Le Comte, *Memoirs and Observations*, 237.

49. Daniel Defoe, *The Complete English Tradesman* (New York: Alan Sutton, 1987), 39.

50. Le Comte, *Memoirs and Observations*, 237.

51. See Mancall, *Russia and China*. On the significance of trade in the areas that Crusoe traverses, Jagchid and Symons, *Peace, War, and Trade*; Thomas J. Barfield, *The Perilous Frontier: Nomadic Empires and China, 221 BC to AD 1757* (Oxford: Blackwell, 1989); Terrence Armstrong, "Russian Penetration into Siberia up to 1800," in Cecil H. Clough and P. E. H. Hair, eds., *The European Outthrust and Encounter* (Liverpool: Liverpool University Press, 1994), 119–40; James A. Millward, *Beyond the Pass: Economy, Ethnicity, and Empire in Qing Central Asia, 1759–1864* (Stanford, CA: Stanford University Press, 1998); Giersch, "'A Motley Throng,'" 67–94; and Vermeer, "Population and Ecology," 235–81.

52. Mancall, *Russia and China*, 201. Ironically, at the time Defoe was writing *Farther Adventures*, a Scotsman, John Bell, was traveling through Siberia to China. His memoirs were not published until 1763. See Spence, *The Chan's Great Continent*, 45–51.

53. Le Comte, *Memoirs and Observations*, A3r–A3v.

54. On the action-adventure genre, see Martin Green, *Dreams of Adventure, Deeds of Empire* (New York: Basic Books, 1979).

55. See Srinivas Aravamudan, "In the Wake of the Novel: The Oriental Tale as National Allegory," *Novel* 33 (1999), 5–31.

CHAPTER 6

"So inexhaustible a treasure of gold": Defoe, credit, and the romance of the South Seas

DEFOE'S NEW VOYAGES

If comparatively few critics of Defoe have paid much attention to *Farther Adventures*, even fewer have examined his writings on the South Seas, despite the fact that he spends a good deal of time and energy in his journalism and fiction urging his readers to take advantage of opportunities for trade in the Pacific. His view of these opportunities remained remarkably consistent from the early 1690s, when he first broached the idea of English trade to South America to the King, until 1724 when he published his final and little-read novel, *A New Voyage Round the World*.[1] This consistency is striking because, unlike many of his contemporaries, Defoe was not scared off by the collapse of stock prices in the South Sea Bubble of 1720; if anything, his fascination with the unexplored regions of the South Pacific and South America intensified in the 1720s.[2] In this chapter, I concentrate on Defoe's views of exploration and trade in the South Seas before and after the Bubble, particularly the twelve numbers of the *Review of the State of the British Nation* in 1711 that he devoted to the founding of the South Sea Company, and his fictional treatment of the Pacific in *A New Voyage*. The complex relations among early modern economics, ecology, and national identity appear in a markedly different and, in some respects, more ideologically revealing form in this novel than they do in the first two volumes of *Robinson Crusoe*. While Crusoe in *Farther Adventures* and Bob Singleton venture into the Indian Ocean and the far western Pacific in search of profits and prey, their adventures are opportunistic, and their decisions to traipse, respectively, across Siberia and Africa are motivated by expediency and short-term gain rather than any nationalistic intention. In translating his arguments for colonizing the South Seas from political journalism to fiction in *A New Voyage*, however, Defoe reveals the ways in which mercantilist fantasies of infinite profits inform the narrative logic of a novel predicated on a profoundly anti-ecological economics.

Underlying Defoe's vision of the South Seas before and after the Bubble are the constitutive assumptions of European writings on the Pacific from the sixteenth to the nineteenth centuries – that its lands and peoples can produce wealth in excess of the capital expenditures required to exploit them. The importance of *A New Voyage*, in particular, lies in its creating a basis in fiction for the "financial euphoria" that characterizes the instabilities of capitalist speculation.[3] Although Defoe's novel extends many of the idealizations of infinite productivity that characterize seventeenth-century European writings on China and Southeast Asia, it redirects his readers' attention from the Middle Kingdom and its environs to the vast, comparatively unexplored regions of the South Seas. In this regard, rather than sorting through the difficulties of colonization and trade or the moral quandaries of piracy, Defoe adapts the genre of the travel and trade narrative to describe the imaginary conditions under which humankind, or at least British, upper-class, male humankind, can prosper indefinitely.

In several respects, then, *A New Voyage*, like *Farther Adventures*, challenges some fundamental assumptions about the "rise" of the novel and its relationship to the rise of the middle class.[4] It, too, intervenes in, and recasts, the interlocking discourses of trade, golden-age dreaming, and the infinite extension of use-value in its efforts to secure an imaginary future of prosperity and natural greatness. In this context, I examine four interrelated ways in which the novel registers the gaps and disruptions within what Jean-Joseph Goux terms the "symbolic economies" of early modern culture – in the structures of knowledge and belief that shape moral, political, and monetary value.[5]

First, the novel takes as its foundational assumption the idea that nature's resources – and therefore humankind's ability to exploit them – are inexhaustible, at least in the South Seas. Defoe's fascination with blank spaces on the map – Africa in *Captain Singleton* and the Pacific and South America in *A New Voyage* – follows from his desire to imagine a natural world that transcends the logic of scarcity and its implications. In his final novel, the imaginary conditions of infinite profitability render "nature" as a symbolic extension of a golden-age world in which, to borrow Locke's phrase, "All the world was America."[6] Defoe becomes both poet and theorist of the Lockean assumption that use-value – cabined, cribbed, and confined in Britain – can be extended indefinitely in colonies yet to be planted in the South Seas. If nature in the distant reaches of the Pacific is infinitely productive, then postlapsarian conditions of scarcity and competition can be overcome, and the Hobbesian war of all against all – or of England against the Dutch and French – can be displaced or tempered by economic aggrandizement. The merchants and crew in *A New Voyage*, for example, resort to violence against the natives they encounter only when efforts at profitable trade fail. For Defoe as for Dryden, the fault-lines of power follow the paths of trade.

Second, the novel displaces labor into two related (and by 1720 well-rehearsed) fictions: capital itself is sufficient to generate wealth and the nature it exploits is inexhaustible, its resources infinite. Significantly, Defoe does not mystify the ways to make money in the South Seas – privateering, illegal trading in Spanish and Dutch ports, and bartering trinkets for gold all figure prominently in the novel. Instead, he uses the notion of wealth in excess of labor to assuage the anxieties which underlie and inform postlapsarian political economy: resources are always scarce; competition therefore is inevitable; power derives from controlling these scarce resources; and one's power – one's property – is always actually or potentially under attack.[7] In this regard, the abundance of nature frees "man," or at least the novel's narrator, from the curse of labor, from the ideology of scarcity.

Third, in an imaginary world of abundance, wealth does not depend on the strictures of the Protestant ethic to justify the exploitation of a fallen world. Although it shares the episodic narrative structure of the second half of *Farther Adventures* and *Singleton*, *A New Voyage* gives little indication of Defoe's theological beliefs: there are no penitent sinners, no self-upbraidings, no tag lines to suggest that getting rich needs to be mitigated or balanced by religious scruples. The erasure of moral consciousness, the studied lack of interiority characteristic of the novel's unnamed narrator, suggests that Defoe is intent on dramatizing the kind of character, a version of his complete tradesman, able to compartmentalize his scruples, capable of triumphing over the grim calculus of scarcity. Moral self-consciousness gives way to managerial expertise. The narrator's strategies may be complicated, even opaque, but they are always guided by the imperatives of maximizing profits and minimizing risks. This nameless merchant stakes Defoe's claim to be the great poet of middle management.

Because *A New Voyage* sails fictional seas of abundance, it presents no sustained accounts of the risks and frustrations of trade that trouble Crusoe during his travels through Asia. In this regard, it makes the accounts of the trade embassies to China by Jan Nieuhoff and Evret Ysbrants Ides that I discussed in chapter three seem almost dystopian. Lastly, then, in its assumptions about the natural and political world, Defoe's novel models a "rise" of venture capitalism that is less a break with than a displacement of an aristocratic ethos. In imagining what political economy might look like if it could be constructed within and by an ideology of abundance, Defoe offers his readers a vision of trade and exploration as an idealized extension of upper-class existence: many labor, few profit.[8] At the heart of Defoe's novel lies a dream of the South Seas that fascinated explorers, buccaneers, merchants, and investors – a dream that does not die with the Bubble: getting something for nothing.

SOUTH SEA VENTURES

Defoe's writings on the Pacific, like those of his contemporaries, are entangled in the histories of exploration, trade, piracy, and the financial manipulation exemplified by the Bubble. Any attempt to understand his or his contemporaries' attitudes toward the South Seas must take into account the economic and political constraints on British ventures to the Pacific and the complicated history of the South Sea Company between 1711 and 1721. Perhaps because discussing the South Sea Bubble transports us through the looking-glass and into a realm in which voyages, profits, and credit prove illusory, it is worth examining how and why the difficulties of English trade to the South Seas in the early eighteenth century take a back seat to the financial fantasies of the Bubble.

By the early eighteenth century, the British still were shut out of a significant share of trade in the Far East. The Dutch remained the dominant European commercial power in Southeast Asia and Japan, and Spain, despite raids by British and French privateers, still monopolized trade between the Philippines and South America.[9] After the disaster at Amboyna, the English made intermittent attempts for the next century and a half to gain a share of the lucrative trade to the Far East and New Spain, employing two often overlapping strategies: efforts to discover new trading partners – and exploit new markets – outside of the Spanish and Dutch spheres of influence and attacks on Spanish shipping off the west coast of South America. Crucial to both exploration and privateering was the need to generate huge profits in order to offset the costs of sending ships across the Atlantic, around the Cape, and into the Pacific. Expeditions required substantial capital investments for salaries and provisions, goods to trade (if possible) in Chile and Peru, bullion for ventures in China, and additional sums for marine insurance with rates as high as 20 percent. Financial risks were spread among multiple investors who bought shares in ships and cargoes.[10]

Even by seventeenth or eighteenth-century standards, however, British expectations of profits in the Pacific were wildly optimistic, conditioned more by the privateering successes of Drake in the sixteenth century than by cold-eyed assessments of the risks and difficulties involved. As early as 1604, the English translation of Jose de Acosta's *The Naturall and Morall Historie of the East and West Indies* suggested that the Spanish "have found out the Ilands which they call Salomon, and which are many and greate" eight hundred leagues west of Peru and that other ships may have discovered "some firm lande neere unto" them.[11] The next year Pedro de Quiros and Luis Vaez de Torres sailed in search of the southern continent they believed lay to the west of the Marquesas. Landing in Vanuatu, de Quiros proclaimed the island the tip of this continent, though his plan to found a settlement failed and he was forced to retreat to Mexico. Glyndwr Williams describes the numerous memorials that de Quiros subsequently wrote before his death in 1615 as prospectuses for exploration "inflated . . . to epic and mystical proportions."[12] In these pleas for financing, he claims that the great southern continent "in probabillitie [is] twice greater in Kingdoms and Seignories, then all that which at this day doth acknowledge subiection and obedience" to Spain. The islands he visited abound in "Siluer and Pearl" and "another Captaine in his Relation, doth report that he hath seen Gold."[13] This fanciful account was read out loud to sailors on board the Dutch expedition of Jacob Le Maire and Isaac Schouten in 1615 "which aimed to evade the monopoly rights of the VOC by sailing into the Pacific from the east."[14] The Dutch had no more success than the Spanish expeditions, although Abel Tasman's voyages in the 1640s marked the first extensive charting of New Zealand and Australia by European explorers.[15] The eagerness with which English readers devoured such accounts persisted well into the eighteenth century. The dream of enormous profits, "the vision or mirage of a great colony, an easy, godly, and profitable protectorate based on harnessing Indian resistance to the Spaniards [in South America], and tapping all the wealth of the Indies," O. H. K. Spate maintains, "begins with Hakluyt in the flush of enthusiasm kindled by Drake's South Sea exploit, takes a more concrete if aborted form with Raleigh in Guiana, revives with [John] Narborough and the buccaneers, and remains a constant in British projecting throughout the eighteenth century."[16] In the context of this history, the fantastic profits reaped by Defoe's heroes in *Singleton* and *New Voyage* testify to the author's and his readers' fascination with the prospects for trade and plunder in the South Seas.

English adventures in the Pacific never discovered the imaginary treasures envisioned by de Quiros and Defoe. In writing *A New Voyage*, Defoe had to resort to fiction to describe a heroically profitable voyage to the South

Seas because his sources – the extremely popular narratives of John Narborough, William Dampier, George Shelvocke, and Woodes Rogers – testify to the difficulties of command and discipline on board ship as well as the extraordinary problems confronting eighteenth-century voyages to the Pacific: maintaining the health of the crew against the omnipresent threat of scurvy, controlling often unruly seamen, securing provisions, especially fresh water, and navigating in the absence of reliable charts and maps.[17] These accounts fall into two loosely defined and overlapping genres: voyage narratives by captains of vessels financed by the Crown and tell-all memoirs of buccaneers who raided along the coasts of Central and South America in the 1670s and 1680s. The latter made better reading.

Narborough's account of his clumsy efforts at commercial espionage in Chile and Peru in 1670–71 is ridiculed by Defoe in the opening pages of *New Voyage*. On the coast of Patagonia, Narborough sought to induce the natives to reveal the location of the gold mines that he assumed were close by. Without a translator who could communicate with the indigenous people, he had to resort to what Williams calls an "amicable but futile dumbshow." Narborough explains how he "laid Gold and bright Copper into the Ground, and made as if I found it there, and looked to and fro on the Earth as if I looked for such things; they looked one on another and spake to each other some words, but I could not perceive that they understood me, or what I meant."[18] This pantomime of prospecting reveals not only the problems of translation that hampered English efforts in the South Seas but also the limitations of the ostensibly universal languages of gold-hunting and mutually beneficial trade. Narborough's dumbshow could work only if the values and assumptions of mercantile self-interest *already* had been interiorized by the natives of Patagonia. His efforts were no more successful with the Spanish settlements in Peru. Arriving at Valdivia on the coast of Chile in 1670, Narborough attempted to establish relations with tribes hostile to the Spanish; his actions infuriated colonial authorities and some of his men were captured and imprisoned. Despite the failure of his mission to the South Seas, Narborough nonetheless claimed that "the most advantageous Trade in the World might be established in those Parts" by pouring more ships and money into yearly expeditions – a theme which Defoe would sound repeatedly.[19]

There were less complicated and expensive ways to make one's fortune in the region, and in the 1670s and 1680s, the British government encouraged or turned a blind eye toward raids off the west coast of New Spain. In 1680–81, a ragtag crew of buccaneers marched across the isthmus of Panama, sacked the port of Panama, and, in captured Spanish ships, raided along the west coast of South America, before heading west across the Pacific. Although the ship commanded by Bartholomew Sharp captured twenty-five vessels and an estimated four million pesos, their most valuable prize was "a Spanish manuscript of prodigious value," as the buccaneer Basil Ringrose described it, a collection of charts and sailing directions that covered the western coast of the Americas from Acapulco to Tierra del Fuego.[20] Convinced that they had captured the key to unlocking the riches of the South Seas, William Dampier and many of the other buccaneers returned to the west coast of South America by 1684 and continued to raid Spanish shipping. They found, however, the defenses of Panama strengthened and the authorities in New Spain more vigilant. Nonetheless, by 1686 English buccaneers had taken seventy-two coastal traders, two-thirds of the Spanish merchant fleet in the South Seas. Their exploits became the basis for two histories of these raiding ventures by A. O. Exquemelin and Ringrose.[21]

The most significant of these accounts, though, was authored by Dampier, a buccaneer turned naturalist and ethnographer. Dampier's reputation as naturalist has led some historians to downplay his efforts to open the South Seas for British mercantile exploitation. During his adventures in the 1680s in particular, he took copious notes and preserved them throughout his years of intermittent raiding in the Caribbean and Central America, carrying them at one point in a sealed, water-tight bamboo pole through the jungles of Panama.[22] Dampier published an account of the first of what would be his three circumnavigations of the globe in 1697 as *A New Voyage Round the World*, and it was an instant success; three editions were published that year, a fourth in 1699, as well as a hustled together collection of leftover material, *Voyages and Descriptions* (1699). Although much of Dampier's popularity can be traced to the excitement of his first-hand account of buccaneering, Williams demonstrates that significant differences exist in all of the buccaneer accounts between the sailors' manuscripts and the published versions. The narratives of John Cox, William Dick, Ringrose, Sharp, Lionel Wafer, and, most significantly, Dampier's *New Voyage* indicate the presence of a ghostwriter (or ghostwriters) engaged in "a process of enlargement and literary polishing."[23] From the 1680s through the voyages of Captain Cook nearly a century later, descriptions of the South Seas rested on such literary efforts to turn mariners' logs and episodic notes into a hybrid genre of sanguinary adventures, naturalist observations, and commercial reconnaissance. The title given to Dampier's first account – *A New Voyage Round the World* – was appropriated frequently, almost slavishly, by later writers and publishers besides Defoe: Rogers, Shelvocke, William Betagh, and Dampier's disgruntled mate on his third circumnavigation, William Funnell.[24] This often-used title reveals clearly both the efforts of writers, ghostwriters, and their publishers to cash in on a popular genre and the assumptions that informed the thinking of the British government and individual investors: voyages around Cape Horn into the Pacific could raid Spanish shipping on the west coast of South America and then continue to the East Indies or Canton. There the ships could trade their booty (or part of it) for tea, silks, spices, and porcelain before returning to England by sailing west around the Cape of Good Hope.

The literary success of his *New Voyage* resulted in Dampier being given command of a voyage with orders to chart the coast of Terra Australis Incognita – the vast southern continent that supposedly lay in the temperate zones south and southeast of Indonesia – and to assess the potential for trade in the far western Pacific. On his earlier voyage in 1688, Dampier had landed on Australia and returned an unpromising description of the land and an unflattering portrait of its inhabitants. But his landfall was enough to convince him and his backers in London that Australia and its environs might provide a way to circumvent the Dutch stranglehold on trade in the Spice Islands and the East Indies. His account of this contentious and unprofitable mission, *A Voyage to New Holland* (1704), reiterates themes that were as popular in the eighteenth century as they had been in the seventeenth and that figure prominently in Defoe's *New Voyage* – specifically, the idea that the islands of New Guinea and eastern Indonesia can be exploited for both the natural resources they harbor and the markets for English exports they offer. Although Dampier never explored the interior of New Britain, for example, he remains confident that "this Island may afford as many rich Commodities as any in the World; and the Natives may be easily brought to Commerce, though I could not pretend to it under my present Circumstances."[25] In this episode and throughout *A Voyage to New Holland*, Dampier's profits from "Commodities" and "Commerce" remain only imaginary. The nature of the lands he sails past must be extrapolated from what he knows of those islands that lie to the west, namely the Spice Islands, still at the end of the seventeenth century the strongest link in the Dutch commercial network in Southeast Asia. In the first chapter of his 1709 *Continuation of a Voyage to New Holland* he tells his readers, "I could not but hope to meet with some fruitful Lands, Continent, or Islands, or both, productive of any of the rich Fruits, Drugs, or Spices (perhaps Minerals also, &c.) that are in other Parts of the Torrid Zone, under equal Parallels of Latitude."[26] The commercial potential of

these islands must await further exploration, trade negotiations with presumably friendly natives, and colonization; the fact that these "fruitful
lands" remain undiscovered only whets the imagination of Dampier's
readers. His attempt to find a profitable trade free from French, Spanish,
and particularly Dutch competition depends ultimately on a faith in the
alchemical powers of commerce rather than on British experience in the
region, the series of false starts, disasters, and failures that date back to
Amboyna. In an important sense, this faith – his belief in undiscovered
opportunities for profit – is both a plea for and a justification of the credit,
the investment, needed to finance further expeditions to these "fruitful
lands." Yet despite his avowed faith in commerce, like other British adventurers before and after him, Dampier turned a profit by raiding Spanish
ships rather than discovering new sources of "Fruits, Drugs, or Spices."

The British launched no successful commercial ventures in the Pacific
(with the exception of clandestine trading by EIC merchants) from
the middle of the seventeenth until the nineteenth century; "British private
enterprise" in the South Seas, Spate declares, "meant privateering."[27] The
French, however, were more successful, and used trade with New Spain to
finance Louis XIV's armies during the War of Spanish Succession: between
1698 and 1725, they dispatched 168 ships to the South Seas (although not all
of them made it to the Pacific) and returned profits from this trade that
Rogers estimated at £25,000,000.[28] Only three accounts of this lucrative
trade found their way into print, and only one appeared in English: a 1717
translation of A. F. Frézier's *A Voyage to the South-Sea*.[29] In contrast, the
only way the British found to tap the "inexhaustible … treasure" of the
Pacific was state-sanctioned piracy, as the enthusiasm which greeted
the successful raiding voyages of Woodes Rogers and later, in the 1740s,
George Anson suggests. Just before the South Sea Company assumed the
national debt in 1711, Rogers captured a smaller ship accompanying the
Manila Galleon, the annual Spanish vessel that sailed from Acapulco to
the Philippines; he returned from his "cruising" voyage across the Pacific
with gross profits of £148,000, a 100 percent return for the owners,
although legal wrangling over the shares owed to the crew went on for
years.[30] The most successful of the early eighteenth-century raiding voyages
directed against Spanish shipping, Rogers's mission stirred patriotic hopes
that England could outpace the French and outmaneuver the Spanish
in the South Seas. Even more than Dampier's promise of "rich
Commodities," his success fueled the economic speculation that led to
the Bubble. For investors weary of two decades of war on the Continent,
the dream of huge profits proved hard to resist.

THE SOUTH SEA COMPANY AND THE FICTIONS OF CREDIT

The South Sea Company (SSC), the brainchild of Robert Harley, Defoe's patron, was born of the Tory ministry's desire to consolidate the national debt of nine million pounds. Holders of unfunded government securities that constituted the debt were issued stock in a company empowered to carry on

the sole trade and traffick, from 1 August 1711, into[,] unto and from the Kingdoms, Lands, etc. of America, on the east side from the river Aranoca, to the southernmost part of the Tierra del Fuego, on the west side thereof, from the said southernmost part through the South Seas to the northernmost part of America, and into[,] unto and from all countries in the same limits, reputed to belong to the Crown of Spain, or which shall hereafter be discovered.[31]

In addition to the monopoly on trade, the SSC was guaranteed payments of 6 percent of the debt (£568,279 annually), plus management charges. In practice, the company would have to undertake this trade entirely on credit because the 6 percent granted to it by Parliament had to be used to pay the interest on the debt to its shareholders. It had no capital to outfit trading – or raiding – expeditions to the vast territories granted to it in its Charter; and the nature of its legitimate trade was narrowly circumscribed. In negotiations with France in 1711 to end the War of Spanish Succession, the British delegation, led by Matthew Prior, asked for four ports in New Spain, two on the Atlantic and two on the Pacific. This concession, had it been made, would have allowed England to make huge inroads – legal and illegal – into the lucrative Caribbean and Pacific trade. What England got instead was a thirty-year lease on the French *asiento* to supply New Spain with slaves, a money-losing proposition that the French had few qualms about surrendering. This traffic was restricted from Panama to Peru, vessels had to be locally hired, voyages to Europe were prohibited, and the King of Spain got 29 percent of the profits. This trade, the only legitimate business of the South Sea Company, was intended as little more than "a shoehorn for a vast illicit commerce."[32] John Carswell argues that the Company's directors, led by John Blunt, "meant to use [its] privileges as a facade behind which they could continue the business of financial manipulation"; "as a business proposition," he continues, the Company "was from the first a sham."[33] Some financial historians, in contrast, have tried to untangle the logic behind the expansion of paper credit and unsecured loans during the Mississippi and South Sea Bubbles. Larry Neal emphasizes the "orderly" development of financial markets in the eighteenth century; his study draws extensively on quantitative data on stock prices and exchange rates

in Paris, Amsterdam, and London to argue for the integration of international capital markets and to recast the Mississippi and South Sea
Bubbles as provoked by and provoking liquidity crises.[34] But in the context
of enthusiasm for the South Seas, the Bubble is an important moment in
the history of economics not because it points towards the development of
rational economic mechanisms but because it reveals the irrationality that
lies at the heart of capitalism's repression of the ecological constraints on
"infinite" production.

In practice, as Spate notes, the activities of the Company "appear
disjointed and even at times almost incoherent" and "the accounts [for
the *asiento*] were never settled to anyone's satisfaction, least of all the King
of Spain's."[35] There were plans drawn up by the Company in 1712–13 for a
vast armada of ships to sail around the Cape to the Pacific; but the very
aggressiveness of the plan violated the treaty provisions of 1711, and the
government provided no economic support. In addition, the South Sea
Company was restricted to ventures only three hundred leagues from the
coast of the Americas; other islands and trading opportunities were claimed
by the influential East India Company that was determined to increase its
trade to Canton and other ports in Siam and Southeast Asia. But as the
penchant for recycling the title of Dampier's *New Voyage Round the World*
suggests, the only rationale for the SSC that made any sense depended on
potential profits that could be realized by sailing across the Pacific and
using looted Spanish gold and merchandise as capital for trading ventures
in Canton, Batavia, and Bombay. Such contradictions and sleights of hand
were displaced into the virtual spaces of speculation: although the SSC
never sent a ship into the Pacific, at its peak in the summer of 1720 its stock
was selling for ten times its face value.

Despite the contradictions in the logic of its charter, the Company was
anything but a fly-by-night outfit. Its directors included many of the
richest merchants in England, and numerous peers and members of their
extended families invested heavily in SSC stock, motivated, in part, by the
brokers and the Company's directors, who argued that their stock provided
a Tory alternative to the Whig-dominated Bank of England. In the years
before the Bubble, members of both houses of Parliament and influential
civil servants were intimately involved with the speculators and stock
jobbers of Exchange Alley: the lure of huge profits often overrode the sort
of social snobbery exploited by satirists in the period to castigate stock-
jobbers and charlatans alike. George I was made Governor of the Company
and apparently invested heavily in it. Huge bribes were paid in the form of
stock issued to the members of Parliament: they did not pay for their

shares, but they could, and often did, sell them and pocket enormous profits.[36]

The involvement of the aristocracy and members of Parliament in the South Sea Bubble is significant because it suggests that "sham" may be a necessary but not sufficient term to describe the mindset behind the Company's "illicit commerce" and "financial manipulation." The financial and naval piracies that constituted the business of the SSC share the assumption that it is possible to generate wealth in excess of expenditures of capital or labor; both project onto the vast spaces of the Pacific fantasies of what Defoe calls "so inexhaustible a treasure of gold."[37] The Company's activities – its penchant for financial manipulation and its studied avoidance, after the Treaty of Utrecht, of actually sending any expeditions to the Pacific – suggest both a willful belief in the potential of Dampier's "fruitful lands" and a cynicism that allowed directors and investors to go on profit-taking, even as they acknowledged they were engaged in speculating on the market rather than investing in plausible opportunities for trade. After 1713, the Company seems to have lost interest in proposals to establish bases in South America, although its directors were sent proposals by Thomas Bowrey, among others, that envisioned naval bases on both the Atlantic and Pacific coasts of the continent and an overland route between them.[38] In an important sense, the Company played to the assumptions and values of its well-to-do investors. Its financial schemes – however dubious they seem in retrospect – did not mark a radical break with the thinking of the landed classes but reproduced, in large measure, the biases of men who viewed investment in trade as an extension of a logic of upper-class privilege: one should not have to work to make money.[39]

In this regard, what animated much of the speculation in South Sea stock was neither outright fraud nor rational analysis of the possibilities of trade or colonization in New Spain but a faith in the ability of stock certificates to represent accurately the infinite productivity of the natural world, a fiction that captivated agricultural improvers, merchants, investors, and political economists throughout the seventeenth century.[40] In 1690, Nicholas Barbon, the most prominent builder (or as we would now call him, real-estate developer and slumlord) in London after the Great Fire of 1666, extended familiar arguments about the open-ended nature of agricultural productivity to assert what he considered more general economic laws. He maintains that "the Stock of a Nation [is] infinite, and can never be consumed; For what is Infinite, can neither receive Addition by Parsimony, nor suffer Diminution by Prodigality."[41] The metaphoric translation from "Stock" to "stock" is significant: Barbon, a successful and unscrupulous entrepreneur who made a fortune in putting up substandard housing in London, takes a term from the vocabulary of estate management and applies it generally to encompass all forms of production. As early as the sixteenth century, "stock" became not merely an inventory of existing commodities but a representation of potential wealth, of returns yet to be realized.[42] What becomes "infinite," for Barbon, is not the daily or annual production of specific estates or ship-yards but the potential for that production to continue indefinitely if it is imaginatively freed from ecological, social, and political constraints. The imaginary conditions of infinite production in both finance and trade, in this sense, project idealized images of the bounty of nature, of organic generation and growth, onto the instruments that seemingly embody rather than passively reflect or conserve imagined riches.

The logic of speculation, in this regard, is a logic of abstraction, of attributing to stock the ability to grow without coming up against eco-logical constraints. In 1720, 1929, and the 1990s, financial markets responded to a faith in the seemingly self-sustaining increase in the value of stock, in the "financial euphoria" that results from a boom market in signs signifying a confidence in the alchemy of investment itself. When that faith is shaken, stock prices collapse. As an anonymous author, one of the few critics of the rampant speculation that gripped financial markets early in 1720, wrote on the eve of the Bubble:

The additional rise of [South Sea Company] stock above the true capital [its par value of 100 pounds per share] will be only imaginary; one added to one, by any rules of vulgar arithmetic, will never make three and a half; consequently, all the fictitious value must be a loss to some persons or other, first or last. The only way to prevent it to oneself must be to sell out betimes, and so let the Devil take the hindmost.[43]

As the writer recognizes, the generation of paper wealth can be only "fictitious," and the faith in credit, the "imaginary" ability of wealth to generate wealth, extends Barbon's view of the infinite productivity of nature. One added to one makes three and a half only if one shares a faith in the infinite productivity of a "Stock" that can be generated without ecological consequences and then reproduced in a form that represents reflexively a faith in nature's unending exploitability. If the South Sea Company is the extension of this logic, then Defoe might be its greatest poet: in his journalism as well as his fiction he casts the exploitation of the infinite resources of the South Seas within the form of a romance – a paratactic tale of unending profit. Denying the logic of scarcity, and the conflicts and constraints that doom Crusoe's island colony to failure in *Farther Adventures*, *A New Voyage* rewrites the dream of financial euphoria as a narrative of exploration and profit: the desire for more wealth produces, at least in fiction, more wealth.

CREDIT AND VALUE

In July and August of 1711, Defoe devoted twelve numbers of the *Review* to promoting the South Sea Company as a means to drive the French from South America and to advance English trade and colonization in the vast areas of the continent unoccupied by the Spanish. In contrast to those who saw the Company's charter as an invitation to unrestricted trade with New Spain, Defoe emphasizes the difficulties of dealing with the Spanish. "During the War [of Spanish Succession]," he argues, "New Spain will prevent [British trade; and], After a Peace, Old Spain will never consent to it."[44] Mocking those supporters of the SSC who "will propose immediately Shipping [to South America], the prodigious Glut of your Manufacture, &c. which now fills your Mouths with Bluster, and talk of nothing but bringing Home Freights of Gold and Silver" (VIII: 50, July 19, 1711), Defoe attacks "imaginary" views of the Company's project and demands realistic assessments of its prospects for trade. Yet his debunking of fantasies of unfettered trade to New Spain is itself based on an imaginary vision of South American riches that are sufficient to satisfy both the English and Spanish. For Defoe, the uncolonized regions of the continent offer abundant resources and the prospect of establishing "an easy, godly, and profitable protectorate."[45]

As I have suggested, the crucial term for Defoe in describing the South Seas and its contiguous lands is "infinite." It appears repeatedly in the *Review* when he seeks to promote the South Sea Company: the "mighty Circulation of Commerce . . . is infinitely Gainful as well to Old-Spain, as to all the rest of Europe"; the trade between New Spain and Old is "infinitely Profitable" (VIII: 42, June 30, 1711); the King of France finds his trade to New Spain during the war "infinitely Advantageous" (VIII: 45, July 7, 1711); should England seize some ports in New Spain under the authority of the Grand Alliance, they will prove "Fruitful of infinite Advantages" (VIII: 47, July 12, 1711); and Defoe characterizes the Bill to charter the South Sea Company as "a Proposal to Supplant the French in the South-Seas, and make that Profit [Britain's] own[.] . . . that such a Trade may be settled to infinite Advantage, is no more a Question to me, than it is, Whether there is Silver at Potosi, or Gold at Chili" (VIII: 49,

July 17, 1711). The "infinite Advantages" of colonies yet to be planted and trade yet to be undertaken allow Defoe to envision a way to secure English interests without provoking another war with New and Old Spain: "there is Room enough on the Western Coast of America, call'd the South Seas," he asserts, "for us to Fix, Plant, Settle, and Establish a Flourishing Trade, without Injuring, Encroaching on, or perhaps in the least Invading the Property or Commerce of the Spaniards" (VIII: 49, July 17, 1711). In contrast to Louis XIV, who described the War of Spanish Succession as a contest to control the "commerce of the Indies and the riches they produce," Defoe offers a vision of peace and prosperity by imposing on the uncharted regions of the Pacific an updated version of de Quiros's and Dampier's assertions: he recycles the myth of infinite productivity of the islands and coasts of the South Seas.[46] In this respect, he attempts to soothe his readers worried about the possibility of another war over "the commerce of the Indies" by invoking what he takes to be a shared faith both in the fecundity of nature and in the consequent ability of investments in trade and colonization to generate returns "infinitely" greater than the expenditures required to outfit ships, provision and pay sailors, and capture Spanish vessels. This faith informs other works by Defoe as well as the maps and atlases produced by the geographer Herman Moll in the first quarter of the eighteenth century.[47]

Defoe's faith in the infinite extension of trade and profit, however, is marked by anxieties that have their source not in doubts about whether there is gold and silver in South America but in the contradictory views of nature prevalent in the seventeenth and early eighteenth centuries. On the one hand, for natural philosophers such as Isaac Newton, Robert Boyle, and John Ray, the beauty and order of nature offer evidence of God's perfect wisdom; on the other, however, the natural world is fallen and corrupt, the demonized realm of Protestant theology.[48] This contradiction is carried over into economic discourse throughout the seventeenth century. The fecundity of nature reproduces the logic of the biblical grant to man of "dominion" over the natural world; abundance, like Newton's rainbow, marks a covenant between a benevolent deity and humankind. Scarcity, in contrast, is the primary consequence of the Fall, and labor the mark of a nature irrevocably corrupt, as it is for Milton in the concluding books of *Paradise Lost*.[49] These unstable, almost manichean constructions of nature – at once theological, ecological, and economic – both inform and are informed by a logic of value that works constantly to reproduce the oppositional structures which Goux identifies as crucial to western thought.

Extending Marx's account of the money form of value, Goux suggests that the Father in the symbolic economy of subjectivity, the phallus in that of desire, and language in that of representation function, like gold, as "general equivalents," the "excluded, idealized element[s]" that underwrite all forms of exchange as universal measures of value but that remain aloof from the consequences of individual transactions.[50] This binary logic, this structure of value, is always unstable, whether in the seventeenth century or the twenty-first: it seeks to divide the world into the "sexualized oppositions" that have defined western metaphysics since Plato – male/female, idea/matter, form/substance, mind/body, and so on. But these absolute oppositions are always abstractions mediated by the processes of "interposition," the "'inter' of a third term" that undoes and reinscribes the separation of ideal and material realms.[51] Interposition, then, is what we might call "literature" or "political economy": the always incomplete effort to imagine conditions under which we can resolve or escape from the antithetical constructions – abundance and scarcity, for example – that structure our actions, beliefs, and self-conceptions. Defoe's contribution to both literature and political economy is to recognize intuitively the logic of value that underlies economic systems that require an idealized vision of the endless generation of wealth. The system, always in crisis, must sustain itself by resorting to the imaginary realm in which the contradictions between pristine and fallen nature, faith and despair, euphoria and nightmare give way to the fantasies of "infinite Advantage."

Goux's description of the logic of value provides one way to understand the structural similarities between Defoe's faith in the ability of nature to generate "inexhaustible Treasure[s] of gold" and his faith in the systems of credit, of signification, that constitute the potential of the South Sea Company to generate such profits. Credit, for Defoe, like nature, is always internally divided, marked by the distinction between corrupt, culturally feminized forms of exchange (stock jobbing, for example) and what Goux calls the "paterial reproduction" of the idea of credit, the faith that must underwrite investment. J. G. A. Pocock, Sandra Sherman, James Thompson, Laura Mandell, and Catherine Ingrassia have called attention to Defoe's and his contemporaries' feminizing and denigrating of credit; but, it is significant that Defoe also defends the idea of public credit, particularly during the period when he is promoting schemes for securing trade in the South Seas.[52] Defoe links credit to the ancient, honorable, and masculinist institutions that comprise his vision of the "Constitution" of the nation: "Publick Credit is no more or less, than the Satisfaction the People have in the Faith and Honour of the Government: By the

Government, is here to be understood not the Ministry, not this or that Party, no, not the Queen personally – But the Constitution, the Queen or King for the Time being, and Parliament . . . I lay it down as an undoubted Truth, That the Foundation of our Credit is the Constitution, as is above noted, and nothing else" (VIII: 59, August 9, 1711). By making credit an article of faith, Defoe constitutes it not only as an instrument of exchange, a form of currency, but also as a general equivalent, a measure of a supposedly absolute confidence in the infinite productivity of both nature and trade. Credit, then, assumes two dialectically related and often gendered forms, and each of these terms is itself divided: credit is feminized either as a marker for the luxury and complacence that enervate the nation or as the spectre of promises unfulfilled and expectations shattered. Yet, like gold, credit is masculinized either as the immutable measure of all transactions, the guarantor of the integrity of the symbolic order – theological, political, and economic – represented by "the Constitution" or as the marker of diligence, exchange, and mercantile energy. Because it fulfills or can be made to fulfill contradictory functions, credit transcends the divisiveness of partisan politics and temporal institutions – it becomes the guarantee of both political stability and a future of unending prosperity, even if that future can be secured only in the hubbub of Exchange Alley.

To the extent that credit displaces and supplements gold as the guarantee of all economic transactions, it takes on a phantasmagoric quality, as we shall see in *A New Voyage*. Gold is not only the unmoved mover that underwrites all negotiations of value but a symbolic promise of the inexhaustibility of material and financial resources. In other words, if credit is the promise to pay in gold, gold becomes the promise of an unending extension of credit, of a systemic faith in a future of "infinite Advantages," however distant that future sometimes appears. Gold and credit, then, exist in a symbiotic relationship in which each assumes the ability to generate value and each must be reinforced by a faith in the commodifed status of the other. Gold must guarantee credit and credit must guarantee the value of gold. The danger, of course, in seeing credit as the necessary supplement of gold is that the money form of value stands revealed as contingent, subject to endless negotiation, rather than as absolute. If gold becomes a commodity subject to the negotiations of the marketplace, then credit must emerge as the means to imagine stable systems of value – it must function as a general equivalent and, as Defoe seems to recognize, it can do so only by reproducing itself endlessly, by deferring the promise of payment into an indefinite, almost millenarian future. But the infinite production of credit, like the vision of an infinite "Stock," presupposes conditions – an inexhaustible nature, the idealized consensus represented by the Constitution – which are themselves imaginary. Credit is everywhere and nowhere: this is the paradox of its insinuation into the money form of value. In travel narratives and stock transactions, credit takes the form of imaginary riches that must remain always out of sight, the "Commodities" that Dampier knows are in the interior of New Britain but has not seen, the wealth represented by slips of paper. Only in fiction, it seems, can we visualize – and credit – realms of gold.

REALMS OF GOLD

A New Voyage is a fictional rendering of the argument Defoe had made in 1711. That summer he asked rhetorically, "Are not the Countries in [the tropical] Latitudes, infinitely beyond the Plantations of New England, Virginia, &c. in the Fruitfulness of the Soil, Kind of Production, and other Advantages?" (VIII: 58, August 7, 1711); thirteen years later his final novel makes the case for exploiting the unknown lands of the Pacific and the interior of South America by dramatizing what might lie "infinitely beyond" the disappointments of North American colonization and stock jobbing. Defoe's narrator begins the novel by disparaging his historical predecessors, whose tales of their circumnavigations of the globe, demonstrate that "a very good sailor may make but a very indifferent author" (1). These "long journals [and] tedious accounts . . . have little or nothing of story in them for the use of such readers who never intend to go to sea" (3). In contrast, the narrator announces, he will "give an account of my voyage, differing from all that I had ever seen before, in the nature of its observations, as well as in the manner of relating them; and as this is perfectly new in its form, so I cannot doubt but it will be agreeable in the particulars, seeing either no voyage ever made before had such variety of incidents, happening in it, so useful and so diverting, or no person that sailed on those voyages has thought fit to publish them after this manner" (3–4). What distinguishes this narrative from those of Narborough and (though he is not mentioned by name) Dampier, however, is not its "form" or its "variety of incidents" but its redefinition of the usefulness of voyage literature. Previous narratives of circumnavigation, the narrator asserts, "are generally filled up with directions for sailors coming that way, the bearings of the land, the depth of the channels, entrances, and bars at the several ports, anchorage in the bays and creeks, and the like things, useful indeed for seaman going thither again – and how few are they? – but not at all to the purpose when we come expecting to find the history of the voyage" (2–3). English voyages to the South Seas during the seventeenth and eighteenth century, as we have seen, were marked by mutinies, disasters, privation for the common sailors, disease, and death.[53] The narratives of these voyages are filled with tales of scurvy, dissension, mutiny, and violence; these "variety of incidents" must be suppressed in order for Defoe to develop a new kind of voyage literature. The elimination of sailing instructions, scientific cataloguing, and the hardships described by Dampier and others is essential for the novelist's idealization of a new sort of managerial ethos. "History," for the narrator and for Defoe, requires a plot, a "form"; but this "form" depends less on artistic design or the psychological and moral depiction of a character such as Crusoe than on a coherent and "useful" purpose. If *Roxana*, published in the same year as *A New Voyage*, can be read as a cautionary tale about the seductions of luxury and sin, then Defoe's final novel offers an inverted image: a demonstration of how to subordinate one's "character" for the betterment of ship, investors, self, and nation.

In this context, recall Northrop Frye's description of romance as a paratactic series of tales that goes on as long as the narrator has stories to tell.[54] But the romance is a purposeful, if open, form; it describes the conditions – the ongoing collapse of Arcadia into history – that bring it into existence. In *A New Voyage*, the romance is not a tale of exile but of ongoing, anti-ecological exploitation. The novel projects into the future the imaginary conditions – the inexhaustible resources of nature – of a golden-age past that has been reimagined by, among others, John Locke.[55] Listening to his Spanish host in Chile assert that "'there is more gold every year washed down out of the Andes . . . into the sea and lost there, than all the riches that go from New Spain to Europe in twenty years," Defoe's narrator tells us succinctly, "This discourse fired my imagination" (217). His host's tales of "the infinite wealth" of New Spain inscribe reflexively within the novel a unity of purpose that motivates the narrator and his creator: firing the imagination of his English readers to explore and exploit the lands that the novel describes.

A New Voyage might be subtitled "Easy Money." In contrast to the spirit of the Protestant ethic which looms over the first installment of *Crusoe*, this novel is dominated by the aura of an unerringly successful con game. Defoe rewrites the voyage literature of his predecessors, transmuting the dangers and uncertainties of exploration and trade into a narrative of profit and the exercise of a power that is, at once, nearly invisible and relentlessly efficient. *A New Voyage* depicts the narrator and his crew sailing almost unnervingly from success to success. Although they have some luck at privateering, hoisting French colors to prey on Spanish shipping, they make most of their profits in one of three ways: by clandestine trading in the ports of Manila and Santiago, where Spanish colonists pay outrageous prices for English and Asian goods; by trading "toys" (glass beads, needles, cheap cloth, and rusty hatchets) to Pacific islanders for lumps of gold; and picking up gold from the ground in the Andes where, the narrator insists, it is so abundant that it is not worth the effort of the natives to stoop to collect it. The sailors dive for pearls, haul fresh water aboard ship, and kill bountiful game almost everywhere they touch land, but this labor is presented as secondary to the gathering of valuable goods and gold. Defoe's narrator and his subordinates expend no more energy than Locke's primal property-owner who gathers acorns and apples for his own use and thereby lays claim to the land on which he finds them.[56]

By devaluing labor, *A New Voyage* functions as a handbook for eighteenth-century investors hoping to make their fortunes effortlessly. In contrast to its straightforward propaganda for a new voyage to the South Seas, it offers a sophisticated model for new forms of command, new strategies of power. What is needed to exploit the material riches of Chile, the novel implies, is a form of authority suited to the tasks of resource hunting, trade, and the management of men. This authority must be vested in an individual capable of molding his crew, and his readers, into desiring subjects who willingly define their identities in and through the disseminated power of credit and profit. The hero of *A New Voyage* earns his right to command by persuading his men to consent to his plans, not by terrifying or browbeating them into obedience. At times, he seems a textbook illustration of Foucault's account of the operations of power.[57] Initially, he conceals his authority, pretending to be a merchant while allowing the French Captain to present himself as the commander of the voyage. Later, the narrator reveals himself but continues to act on behalf of the nameless owner in England, who, we learn in the last sentence of the novel, has died during the course of the voyage, leaving much of his newly made fortune to the narrator. Strategies seem more important than strategists. Historically, conflicts on board ship between merchants and captains were often bitter and divisive, but, in Defoe's novel, political authority, moral responsibility, and psychological realism are displaced into and by the romance of trade. In 1713, Defoe had written, "It is a great Mistake to say that every Trading Man is only separately interested in, or concern'd for the Trade he himself carries on: There is a Relation in Trade to itself in every Part, every Branch of Trade has a concern in the Whole, and the Whole in every Part."[58]

Defoe's vocabulary in this passage verges on the metaphysical: trade is self-referential, a coherent yet complex system that displays essential similarities between the whole and its parts. The "Trading Man" becomes less a psychological figure than a Leibnizian monad, whose existence reflexively guarantees and is guaranteed by its replication of the system's integrity.[59] Identity in *A New Voyage* becomes a function of the quest for infinite profits, rendered coherent by its dedication to a purpose that is at once individual and collective. The narrator serves as a metonymic guarantee that the romance of infinite profits and self-perpetuating trade will continue.

Defoe's narrators, of course, have been the focus of scholarly attention for decades, and, to a great extent, the crucial questions in the criticism of his novels have been framed in terms of reliability and psychology: can we trust what Moll says? Is Roxana a consistent character? Is Defoe aware that by internalizing moral issues within Robinson Crusoe's imagination he is creating (the first) modern, novelistic consciousness?[60] If these questions seem beside the point in *A New Voyage*, it is because the novelist has transformed the conditions under which psychological notions of identity take shape. To a greater extent than *Farther Adventures*, Defoe's last novel jettisons moral and theological commentary to harness the effects of power that, as Foucault suggests, are "both intentional and nonsubjective."[61] In his adventures in the South Seas, the narrator raises to a fine art the trading and subterfuge that are counseled by Quaker William in *Singleton*. The rationalizations of Defoe's earlier heroes – Crusoe's self-criticism of his profit-seeking in Asia as "the follies of an old man," for example – give way to the narrator's willingness to present himself as a retrospective effect of the power he exercises. The integrity of the self can be secured only as a back formation, judged paradoxically from an imaginary future of individual prosperity. Unlike Dryden's Towerson in *Amboyna*, a merchant endowed with traditional heroic values, the narrator of *A New Voyage* can validate his actions and the ideology of trade only from this strange and self-reflexive narrative future. The self has done what it had to do in order to become a coherent narrative voice that can account for its stratagems as the necessary precursors to its own existence. While David Hume suggests that memory becomes the means by which the individual's discrete sensory observations, "variable or interrupted," are granted "a perfect identity . . . as invariable and uninterrupted," this fiction of selfhood is inverted by Defoe.[62] The hero's managerial consciousness enables him to manipulate effectively and unobtrusively his crew and the various peoples of the Pacific, and, in the process, to fashion an identity that shapes and renders this behavior as the demonstration of "a perfect identity" that has banished psychological interiority.

Early in the novel, the narrator is forced to put down a mutiny by sailors who resist the idea of sailing east across the Indian Ocean to reach the Pacific. The narrator, who until this time has concealed his command of the voyage, halts the mutiny by guile and generosity: "I have ever thought, and have found it by experience to be the best way, that men were always secured in their duty by a generous kindness, better than by absolute dominion and severity" (47). "Generous kindness," however, is not a mark of sentiment or good nature but a strategy of control, a way to enhance and mask the effects and nature of power. The narrator pardons all but two of the mutineers, then sends one of them, the second mate and ringleader of the attempted mutiny, to spy on a crew of pirates on Madagascar. His adventures in this section of the novel might be read as a revision of the Madagascar episodes in *Captain Singleton*; piracy in *A New Voyage* has become less profitable than trade, and the exercise of delegated authority becomes, for the second mate, the means of his moral reclamation. After landing, he quickly learns that the pirates "were in no condition to undertake anything, for that they were a crew of unresolved divided rogues; that they were never two days of a mind; that they had nobody to command, and therefore nobody to obey; . . . that, in short, they thought of nothing but of shifting every one for themselves as well as they could" (64–65). The narrator uses this knowledge to have his mate encourage a gunner and other pirates discouraged or repulsed by their immoral, and not very profitable, ways to commandeer one of their stolen ships and to join the expedition for the remainder of the voyage. The second mate is named captain of this vessel, having demonstrated his worthiness to command by his mastering the techniques of power that the narrator embodies: guile, strategic lying, foresight, a knowledge of human nature that sees morality and duty as functions of money, and a self-effacing quality that makes the "securing" of duty a product of the consent of the governed. The novel dramatizes, then, the exercise and dissemination of power by nameless owners and captains through the consent of those under them. Defoe intuits what Locke only grudgingly admits: consent itself can be the effect rather than the originary cause of unequal distributions of socioeconomic power.

Unlike Defoe's other heroes and heroines, the narrator of *A New Voyage* does not suffer from pangs of conscience or indict himself for his sins. He has nothing to repent and no guilt to expiate or explain away. His lack of self-reflection suggests the extent to which the novel gives voice to a materialist view of the world and of human nature. Trekking through the Andes, the narrator warns his Chilean host that the riches of his country make it a target for potential enemies:

You live in a golden country, seignior, said I; my men are stark mad to see so much gold and nobody to pick it up. Should the world know what treasure you have here, I would not answer for it that they should not flock hither in armies and drive you all away. They need not do that, seignior, says he, for here is enough for them and for us too. (279)

In this passage, morality becomes a function of political economy as surely as it does in Behn's "The Golden Age": scarcity produces sin, greed, and war; abundance seemingly ensures peace and prosperity.[63] If *Moll Flanders* and *Bob Singleton* reform after they have become rich, the narrator of *A New Voyage* has no need to leave a life of rampant acquisitiveness because he already exists in a privileged state, the retrospective validation of his actions and identity. As a "Trading Man," a "Branch . . . of the Whole," he participates in and is uplifted by an ideology of abundance: the belief that, in the blank spaces on the maps of the South Seas, gold "enough for them and for us too" must exist becomes an article of narrative faith, of the moral certainty which underwrites the familiar logic of mercantile aggrandizement. In a world of infinite resources, "men are stark mad" if they remain trapped by the assumptions and values of Hobbesian competition. But the problem with defining moral and psychological identity by the strategic exercise of power and the accumulation of riches is that the integrity of the individual becomes no less imaginary than the vision of nature that underwrites his or her profitable existence. The fiction of abundance, of limitless profits, in short, enables the fiction of a coherent if temporally dislocated self: the "Trading Man" is always about to become rich. Without the prospect of "Infinite Advantage," the narrator would have no way to justify his retrospective celebrations of his triumphs over both scarcity and the internal divisiveness of sin, and presumably he would relapse into the ambiguities that surround the penitent declamations of Singleton and Moll. Cut off from the "Whole," he would fall victim to a moral psychology, the inevitable consequence of a corrupt world of labor, scarcity, sin, and retribution. As *A New Voyage* stands, however, the hero seems Defoe's attempt to paper over the contradictions – moral, economic, and ecological – that inhere in systems of self and social definition predicated on the imaginary prospect of "Infinite Advantage."

Slavoj Žižek, following Lacan, argues persuasively that all systems are inconsistent because they are constituted by an excluded element that resists symbolization: the Real. The totality of any system, he suggests, is imaginary because the rupture of exclusion is necessary to constitute it as a symbolic whole. When one confronts the Real, the Symbolic collapses into new forms of projection – the Imaginary – but the Imaginary now constituted as already and irrevocably in crisis.[64] *A New Voyage round the World*, in this context, seems the essential constituent of the very system – capitalism, "Trade" – that it claims to represent and therefore from which it, as a mere fiction, must be excluded. If the Real is forever on the edge of our dreams, then perhaps Defoe's final novel gives form to a dream that economists never can quite remember: their privileging of imaginary constructs in the place of those elements that resist representation and analysis. The novel's most fantastic passages, significantly, occur precisely when the narrator seems most intent on presenting factual information about England's economic situation.

Having made a fortune in the imaginary islands southeast of Indonesia, the narrator disparages the India trade, a common complaint among economic writers of the time who decried buying luxury items with bullion and denounced the competition for English products from South Asian imports.[65] The "necessary or useful things" brought back to England by this trade – "pepper, salt-petre, dyeing-woods and dyeing-earths, drugs, … shellac, … diamonds, … some pearl, and raw silk" – are of far less consequence than such "trifling and unnecessary" imports as "china ware, coffee, tea, japan works, pictures, fans, screens, &c." and "returns that are injurious to [Britain's] manufactures": "printed calicoes, chintz, wrought silks, stuffs of herbs and barks, block tin, cotton, arrack, copper, indigo." "For all these," he declares, "we carry nothing or very little but money, the innumerable nations of the Indies, China, &c., despising our manufactures and filling us with their own" (155–56). A century after Thomas Mun's defense of the EIC's trade, Defoe decries the arrogance of those "innumerable nations" that outproduce England. His solution to this trade imbalance is to have his narrator assert that England's commercial future lies in the undiscovered lands of the Pacific:

the people in the southern unknown countries, being first of all very numerous, and living in a temperate climate which requires clothing, and having no manufactures or materials for manufactures of their own, would consequently take off a very great quantity of English woolen manufactures, especially when civilized by our dwelling among them and taught the manner of clothing themselves for their ease and convenience; and in return for these manufactures, it is evident we should have gold in specie, and perhaps spices, the best merchandise and return in the world . . . Nor can it be objected here that this nook of the country [where the narrator and his crew have reaped huge profits] may not easily be found by any one but us that have been there before . . .; for not to enter into our journal for their direction, I lay it down as a foundation, that whosoever, sailing over the South Seas, keeps a stated distance from the tropic to the latitude of fifty-six to sixty degrees, and steers eastward towards the Straits of Magellan, shall never fail to discover new worlds, new nations, and new inexhaustible funds of wealth and commerce, such as never were yet known to the merchants of Europe. (156)

This description of unknown lands (lying roughly south southeast of a yet to be explored New Zealand) is less a fiction than an expression of faith, less evidence of a "sham" than of the ongoing breakdown of oppositions between fiction and fact, speculation and investment. These uncharted regions are the imaginary – and essential – landscape of the ideology of capitalist expansion, the dream of "inexhaustible funds of wealth and commerce." Their promise renders schemes of trade and exploration, even the SSC's incoherent plans and abortive projects, seemingly rational enterprises, even as these "new worlds" remain outside the regimes of truth, fact, and exploitation. These "new nations" must remain imaginary because to discover them would bring them into the logic, and the economy, of scarcity, self-interest, and commercial competition. If that were to happen, as the history of economic theorizing suggests, the crucial function they perform – constituting the system of trade by offering a vision of "infinite Advantage" – would need to be relocated elsewhere. For Defoe, elsewhere is the uncharted Amazon Basin.

In the last section of *A New Voyage*, Defoe imagines the interior of South America as an unpeopled, bucolic landscape that stretches from the eastern slopes of the Andes to the Atlantic coast. Filled with gold and game, it stands as the imaginary vision of a land of infinite resources and riches – a fictional embodiment of the plan Defoe presented to William thirty years earlier to colonize the South Seas without encroaching on Spanish interests in Chile and Peru. Trooping across the Andes,

we that were Englishmen could not refrain smiling at one another to think how we passed through a country where the gold lay in every ditch, as we might call it, and never troubled ourselves so much as to stoop to take it up; so certain is it that it is easy to be placed in a station of life where that very gold, the heaping up of which is here made the main business of man's living in the world, would be of no value, and not worth taking off from the ground; nay, not of signification enough to make a present of; for that was the case here. Two of three yards of Colchester baize, a coarse rug-like manufacture, worth in London about fifteen pence half-penny per yard, was here a present for a man of quality; when for a handful of gold dust the same person would scarcely thank you[.] (266–67)

Recall Locke's phrase to describe the golden age: "All the world was America." The spectre of the Hobbesian war of all against all gives way to an economy of idealized gift-exchange which promotes both the ideal of mutual satisfaction and, for those returning to London, seemingly limitless profits.[66] Underlying this version of the Imaginary is the Lockean logic of an infinitely elastic use-value: one can use the land and its resources but one cannot use them up. The use and the structure of value itself become culturally contingent, and their contingency – the lack of "signification" for gold in Chile, the "surplus" value of cheap English cloth in the Andes – underscores Defoe's belief that the profitable exchange of commodities is a logistical problem rather than an inaccessible ideal. In the unpeopled interior of South America both English and Spanish can profit.

A New Voyage is unlikely to find many readers in the future, and unlikelier still to force scholars to reconsider their ideas about the development of the English novel or the history of exploration in the South Seas. But it remains a historically significant text because it lays bare the implications of Lockean, consensualist myths of the origins of property and government. At the heart of the middle-class myth of managerial expertise lie fantasies of abundance, of the infinite elasticity of use-value, of recasting the aristocratic assumption that the value of labor is less than the wealth it generates. Financial euphoria, though, can be sustained only if resources are infinite; when they become scarce, dreams of "infinite Advantage" give way to nightmares of trade wars, colonialism, and people gone "stark mad." In one sense, Defoe's final novel might stand as the "positive unconscious" of capitalist speculation, a means both to acknowledge and repress the anxieties that trade and profits in a postlapsarian world are always limited.[67] As the violent and tragic history of European expansion into the South Pacific in the late eighteenth and nineteenth centuries attests, indigenous peoples catch onto the rusty hatchet scam very quickly.[68] However comic we may find Defoe's geography in imagining a pastoral countryside in the Amazon Basin, we should recognize that the ecological devastation of the rain forest in our own century is, in part, the consequence of our "infinite" expansion of use-value, the credit we still give to the economic postulates of Defoe's romance: profits without end.

NOTES

1. See Defoe's *Review of the State of the English Nation*, vol. VIII, number 50, July 19, 1711.
2. On Defoe's interest in trade and travel literature, see particularly John McVeagh, "Defoe and the Romance of Trade," *Durham University Journal* 70 (1978), 141–47; "Defoe and Far Travel," in *English Literature and the Wider World*, vol. I: *1660–1780: All the World Before Them*, ed. McVeagh (London: Ashfield, 1990), 115–26; Joel Reed, "Nationalism and Geoculture in Defoe's History of Writing," *Modern Language Quarterly* 56 (1995), 31–53; and Aparna Dharwadker, "Nation, Race, and the Ideology of Commerce in Defoe," *The Eighteenth Century: Theory and Interpretation* 39 (1998), 63–84.
3. See John Kenneth Galbraith, *A Short History of Financial Euphoria* (New York: Whittle, 1990), esp. 34–41, who links the South Sea Bubble to the crash of 1929 and the junk bond craze of the 1980s.
4. See particularly Ian Watt, *The Rise of the Novel* (Berkeley and Los Angeles: University of California Press, 1957); McKeon, *The Origins of the English Novel*; and Thompson, *Models of Value*. On the literary production of the middle class, see Nancy Armstrong, *Desire and Domestic Fiction: A Political History of the Novel* (New York: Oxford University Press, 1987), and Armstrong and Tennenhouse, *The Imaginary Puritan*.
5. Goux, *Symbolic Economies after Marx and Freud*.
6. John Locke, *Two Treatises of Government*, ed. Peter Laslett (Cambridge: Cambridge University Press, 1960), II: par. 49.
7. See Robert Markley, "'Credit Exhausted': Satire and Scarcity in the 1690s," in *Cutting Edges: Contemporary Essays on Eighteenth-Century Satire*, ed. James Gill, Tennessee Studies in Literature (Knoxville: University of Tennessee Press, 1995), 110–26.
8. On aristocratic ideology see McKeon, *Origins of the Novel*, 206–11. In an episode of BBC's *Blackadder III* an exiled French aristocrat in 1790s London is asked if he wants to earn fifty pounds; he replies: "No. I do not want to earn money. I want someone else to work for the money and give it to me."
9. On international commerce see Boxer, *The Dutch Seaborne Empire*, and Boxer, *Jan Compagnie*; Glamann, *Dutch–Asiatic Trade*; Furber, *Rival Empires of Trade in the Orient*; Israel, *Dutch Primacy in World Trade*; and Israel, *The Dutch Republic*.
10. On the East India trade, see Ralph Davis, *The Rise of the English Shipping Industry in the Seventeenth and Eighteenth Centuries* (London: Macmillan, 1962), 257–66; and Peter Klein, "The China Seas and the World Economy between the Sixteenth and Nineteenth Centuries: The Changing Structures of World Trade," in *Interactions in the World Economy: Perspectives from International Economic History*, ed. Carl-Ludwig Holtfrerich (Hemel Hempstead: Harvester, 1989), 61–89.
11. Jose de Acosta, *The Naturall and Morall Historie of the East and West Indies*, trans. Edward Grimstone (London, 1684), 83.
12. Williams, *South Sea*, 57.

13. Pedro Fernando de Quiros, *Terra Australis Incognita, or a New Southerne Discoverie, Containing a Fifth Part of the World* (London, 1617), 18.
14. Williams, *South Sea*, 59. See also J. C. Beaglehole, *The Exploration of the Pacific*, 3rd edn (Stanford: Stanford University Press, 1966), 58–80.
15. See William Eisler, *The Furthest Shore: Images of Terra Australis from the Middle Ages to Captain Cook* (Cambridge: Cambridge University Press, 1995).
16. Spate, *Monopolists and Freebooters*, 158.
17. In addition to Williams, *South Sea*, see Lamb, *Preserving the Self in the South Seas*, and Edwards, *The Story of the Voyage*, 17–43.
18. Williams, *South Sea*, 78. Narborough's journals were published in William Hacke, ed., *A Collection of Original Voyages* (London, 1699); the quotation is on 63.
19. Anon., *An Account of Several Late Voyages & Discoveries to the South and North* (London, 1694), 110.
20. Derek Howse and Norman Thrower, eds., *A Buccaneer's Atlas: Basil Ringrose's South Sea* (Berkeley and Los Angeles: University of California Press, 1992), 22. This "waggoner," so-called after the Dutch cartographer L. J. Wagenhenaer, who published the first compendium of such charts in 1584, was copied numerous times in subsequent years; see Williams, *South Sea*, 87–88. On the ships the buccaneers raided see Peter T. Bradley, *The Lure of Peru: Maritime Intrusions into the South Sea* (New York: St. Martin's Press, 1989); and, for the significance of piracy in English literary culture between 1650 and 1800, Turley, *Rum, Sodomy, and the Lash*. For the exploits of the buccaneers, see A. O. Exquemelin, *Bucaniers of America ... Inlarged with two Additional Relations, viz. The One of Captain Cook, and the Other of Captain Sharp* (London, 1684), and Basil Ringrose, *Bucaniers of America. The Second Volume Containing the Dangerous Voyage and Bold Attempts of Captain Bartholomew Sharp and Others; Performed upon the Coasts of the South Sea* (London, 1685).
21. Spate, *Monopolists and Freebooters*, 135, 152.
22. See Diana and Michael Preston, *A Pirate of Exquisite Mind: The Life of William Dampier: Explorer, Naturalist and Buccaneer* (Sydney: Doubleday, 2004).
23. Williams, *South Sea*, 113.
24. See William Funnell, *A Voyage Round the World* (London, 1707); Woodes Rogers, *A Cruising Voyage Round the World* (London, 1712); George Shelvocke, *A Voyage Round the World by Way of the Great South Sea* (London, 1726); and William Betagh, *A Voyage Round the World* (London, 1728).
25. Dampier, *A Voyage to New Holland: The English Voyage of Discovery to the South Seas in 1699*, ed. James Spencer (London: Alan Sutton, 1981), 224.
26. Dampier, *Voyage to New Holland*, 147.
27. Spate, *Monopolists and Freebooters*, 202.
28. Williams, *South Sea*, 135–36.
29. Frézier, *A Voyage to the South-Sea*. On French interests in the Pacific, see James Pritchard, *In Search of Empire: The French in the Americas, 1670–1730* (Cambridge: Cambridge University Press, 2004), 320–32; and Catherine Manning, *Fortunes à Faire: The French in the Asian Trade, 1719–48* (Aldershot: Variorum, 1996).

30. On Woodes Rogers, see Spate, *Monopolists and Freebooters*, 198–99; Jonathan Lamb, "Eye-Witnessing in the South Seas," *The Eighteenth Century: Theory and Interpretation* 38 (1997), 201–12; and Williams, *South Sea*, 143–59. Anson turned a disastrous voyage into a success when he captured the Manila galleon in 1743. He returned to London a hero, and with a profit of £500,000, despite the fact that he lost three ships and 1,300 men – four in action, the rest by disease and starvation. See Glyn Williams, *The Prize of All the Oceans: The Dramatic True Story of Commodore Anson's Voyage Round the World and How He Seized the Spanish Treasure Galleon* (New York: Viking, 1999).

31. Parliamentary Statutes: 9 Anne, cap. XXI. Quoted in John Carswell, *The South Sea Bubble* (Stanford: Stanford University Press, 1960). On the South Sea Bubble, see also John G. Sperling, *The South Sea Company: An Historical Essay and Bibliographical Finding List* (Boston: Baker Library, Harvard University, 1962); Neal, *The Rise of Financial Capitalism*, 62–117; Edward Chancellor, *Devil Take the Hindmost: A History of Financial Speculation* (New York: Farrar, Strauss, Giroux, 1999), chapters one and two; and, on the Mississippi Bubble in France, Antoin E. Murphy, *John Law: Economic Theorist and Policy-maker* (New York: Oxford University Press, 1997); and Janet Gleeson, *Millionaire: The Philanderer, Gambler, and Duelist Who Invented Modern Finance* (New York: Simon and Schuster, 1999).

32. Walter Louis Dorn, *Competition for Empire 1740–63* (1940; rpt New York, 1963), 123.

33. Carswell, *South Sea Bubble*, 54–55, 56.

34. Neal, *Rise of Financial Capitalism*, 62–117. On the complex relationships between debt and party politics, see David Stasavage, *Public Debt and the Birth of the Democratic State: France and Great Britain, 1688–1789* (Cambridge: Cambridge University Press, 2003), 99–129.

35. Spate, *Monopolists and Freebooters*, 205.

36. Carswell, *South Sea Bubble*, 121–24.

37. Defoe, *A New Voyage round the World*, ed. George Aitkin (London, 1902), 73. Variants of this phrase appear throughout Defoe's non-fictional work as well as in other eighteenth-century writings on the Pacific. See, for example, Williams, "'The Inexhaustible Fountain of Gold,'" 27–53.

38. On Bowrey, see Williams, *South Sea*, 164–65.

39. See Appleby, *Economic Thought and Ideology in Seventeenth-Century England*, 135: there is "little evidence of a deep division between [seventeenth-century] capitalists associated with trade and manufacturing and those with landed wealth. Rather than challenge the sensibilities of their age, the economic writers tended to resituate their commercial virtues into the older social outlook."

40. On agricultural improvement literature in the seventeenth century, see McRae, *God Speed the Plough*.

41. Nicholas Barbon, *A Discourse of Trade* (London, 1690), 6.

42. See Scott, *The Constitution and Finance of English, Scottish and Irish Joint-Stock Companies*, I: 4–17.

43. Anon., *Letter of Thanks from the Author of the Comparison to the Author of the Argument* (London, 1720), cited in Carswell, *South Sea Bubble*, 120.

44. Defoe, *Review of the State of the English Nation* VIII: 47 (July 12, 1711). Subsequent references are noted by number and date in the text.

45. See Williams, *South Sea*, 167–69.

46. Quoted in Spate, *Monopolists and Freebooters*, 184.

47. Defoe, *Essay on the South Sea Trade* (London, 1711), and Herman Moll, *A View of the Coasts, Countrys, & Islands within the Limits of the South-Sea Company* (London, 1711). On Moll, see Dennis Reinhartz, "Shared Vision: Herman Moll and his Intellectual Circle and the Great South Sea," *Terrae Incognitae* 19 (1988), 1–10.

48. See Markley, *Fallen Languages*, 116–30, 144–53.

49. See, for example, Goodman, *The Fall of Man*.

50. Goux, *Symbolic Economies after Marx and Freud*, 4.

51. Goux, *Symbolic Economies after Marx and Freud*, 239.

52. Pocock, *Virtue, Commerce, and History*, 99–100; Sherman, *Finance and Fictionality*; Thompson, *Models of Value*; Laura Mandell, *Misogynous Economies: The Business of Literature in Eighteenth-Century Britain* (Lexington: University of Kentucky Press, 1999), and Catherine Ingrassia, *Authorship, Commerce, and Gender in Early Eighteenth-Century England: A Culture of Paper Credit* (Cambridge: Cambridge University Press, 1998). On the widespread use of credit as a commercial instrument, see Patrick Brantlinger, *Fictions of State: Culture and Credit in Britain, 1694–1994* (Ithaca: Cornell University Press, 1996); Margot C. Finn, *The Character of Credit: Personal Debt in Eighteenth-Century Culture* (Cambridge: Cambridge University Press, 2003); William J. Ashworth, *Customs and Excise: Trade, Credit, and Consumption in England 1640–1845* (Oxford: Oxford University Press, 2003), 87–93; and Brewer, *The Sinews of Power*, 186–88.

53. For the conditions on board ship in the eighteenth century, see Spate, *Monopolists and Freebooters*, 256–68, James Davis, *Rise of the English Shipping Industry*, and Jonathan Lamb, "Minute Particulars and the Representation of South Pacific Discovery," *Eighteenth-Century Studies* 28 (1995), 281–94. Many, if not most British voyages to the Pacific, produced mutinies, desertions, and, when the contending parties returned to England, rival accounts of what had happened at sea. John Welbe, for example, deserted Dampier's expedition to New Holland along with William Funnell, wrote an account attacking Dampier for incompetence, became the target of the latter's *Vindication of a Voyage to the South Seas*, and then responded with *An Answer to Captain Dampier's Vindication* (London, 1707). In 1713 Welbe advanced a plan to colonize the South Seas; in 1720, its shares were selling at thirty-two times their par value. See Spate, *Monopolists and Freebooters*, 209, and Carswell, *South Sea Bubble*, 60. Welbe's plan is reprinted in *Some Proposals for Establishing Colonies in the South Seas*, ed. G. Mackaness (Dubbo, New South Wales: Australian Historical Monographs, 1981), 8–11.

54. Northrop Frye, *An Anatomy of Criticism* (Princeton: Princeton University Press, 1957), 186–87.

55. See Robert Markley, "'Land Enough in the World': Locke's Golden Age and the Infinite Extensions of 'Use,'" *South Atlantic Quarterly* 98 (1999), 817–37.

56. Locke, *Two Treatises of Government*, II, pars. 49, 301.

57. See Foucault, *The History of Sexuality*, 92–93.

58. Daniel Defoe, *A Brief Account of the Present State of the African Trade* (London, 1713), 53.

59. On Leibniz, see Michel Serres, *Le Système de Leibniz et ses modèles mathematiques* (Paris: Presses Universitaires de France, 1968), 2 vols.

60. In addition to the critics cited above, see Backscheider, *Daniel Defoe: Ambition and Innovation* and *Daniel Defoe: His Life*; Michael Boardman, *Defoe and the Uses of Narrative* (New Brunswick: Rutgers University Press, 1983); Richetti, *Defoe's Narratives*; David Trotter, *Circulation: Defoe, Dickens, and the Economies of the Novel* (New York: St. Martin's Press, 1988); and Robert Mayer, *History and the Early English Novel: Matters of Faction from Bacon to Defoe* (Cambridge: Cambridge University Press, 1997). For brief comments on *A New Voyage* see Paul K. Alkon, *Defoe and Fictional Time* (Athens: University of Georgia Press, 1979), 133; John Richetti, *Daniel Defoe* (Boston: Twayne, 1987), 62; John Robert Moore, *Daniel Defoe: Citizen of the Modern World* (Chicago: University of Chicago Press, 1958), 297; Peter Earle, *The World of Defoe* (New York: Athenaeum, 1977), 54–57; and Maximillian E. Novak, *Economics and the Fiction of Daniel Defoe* (Berkeley and Los Angeles: University of California Press, 1962), 142–43.

61. Foucault, *History of Sexuality*, 93.

62. David Hume, *A Treatise of Human Nature*, ed. David Fate Norton and Mary Norton (Oxford: Oxford University Press, 2000), 114.

63. See Robert Markley and Molly Rothenberg, "The Contestations of Nature: Aphra Behn's 'The Golden Age' and the Sexualizing of Politics," in *Rereading Aphra Behn: History, Theory, and Criticism*, ed. Heidi Hutner (Charlottesville: University of Virginia Press, 1993), 301–21.

64. Žižek, *The Sublime Object of Ideology*.

65. See Michel Morineau, "The Indian Challenge: Seventeenth to Eighteenth Centuries," trans. Cyprian P. Blamire, in *Merchants, Companies, and Trade: Europe and Asia in the Early Modern Era*, ed. Sushil Chaudhury and Michel Morineau (Cambridge: Cambridge University Press, 1999), 243–75.

66. On gift theory, see Cynthia Klekar, "'Her Gift was Compelled': Gender and the Failure of the Gift in *Cecilia*," *Eighteenth-Century Fiction* 18 (2005), 107–26.

67. Michel Foucault, *The Order of Things* (New York: Vintage, 1971), xi.

68. On the colonization of Australasia in this period, see Nicholas Thomas, *Possessions: Indigenous Art/Colonial Culture* (London: Thames & Hudson, 1999), and Alex Calder, Jonathan Lamb, and Bridget Orr, eds., *Voyages and Beaches: Pacific Encounters, 1769–1840* (Honolulu: University of Hawai'i Press, 2000). On the literary fascination with the South Seas, see Neil Rennie, *Far-Fetched Facts: The Literature of Travel and the Idea of the South Seas* (Oxford: Clarendon Press, 1995).

CHAPTER 7

Gulliver, the Japanese, and the fantasy of European abjection

It is very usual for Civiliz'd and Polite Nations to look upon all others as barbarous . . . *Europe* now being the Seat of Learning, and Science, wherein learned Academies are set up for the Discovery of Hidden Secrets in Nature, we take all the Rest of Mankind for meer Barbarians: But Those who have Travel'd into *China* and *Japan*, must confess those People far surpass us in the endowments, both of body and mind.

Jean Crasset, 1705[1]

SWIFT AND JAPAN

To a greater extent than Defoe's *Farther Adventures of Robinson Crusoe*, books two and four of *Gullivers Travels* have become important texts for critics concerned with European attitudes toward exploration, and exploitation, in the South Seas.[2] Book three, in contrast, has received comparatively little attention – both because the hero's episodic adventures do not fit the pattern of European encounters with "barbaric" peoples (the Irish, Native Americans, and Pacific Islanders) and because Swift's satire is directed exclusively at European institutions (the Royal Society) and vices (luxury, political corruption, and absurd philosophies).[3] Gulliver's wanderings among the imaginary islands of the western Pacific, however, are bookended by his only encounters with natives of "real" realms: his capture by a Japanese pirate captain and Dutch pirate at the beginning of book three, and, at its conclusion, his audience with the Emperor of Japan and subsequent voyage back to Europe with the suspicious crew of a Dutch vessel. In 1722, after Swift had begun drafting *Gullivers Travels*, he noted that he was reading "many diverting Books of History and Travels,"[4] and while scholars have speculated about possible sources for his depiction of Japan, only Anne Barbeau Gardiner has noted the significance of these Japanese encounters in the context of Swift's vitriolic attacks on the Dutch.[5] In this chapter, I examine Gulliver's voyage to Japan in the context of three important bodies of literature widely available in the early eighteenth century: accounts of the short-lived English trading post in Hirado (1613–23); histories of the expulsion of the Jesuits and the extirpation of Catholicism in Japan in the 1630s; and narratives of the Dutch willingness after 1638 to perform the ritual of *yefumi* – literally trampling on the crucifix – in order to maintain their trading privileges in Japan. Gulliver's encounters with the Japanese suggest both that Swift knew this literature and that he was well aware of the deeply unsettling implications that Japan posed for Eurocentric visions of trade, history, and theology. If Defoe sees the Pacific as a region ripe for English expansion, Swift takes a more sardonic view of the possibilities that await projectors, mariners, and merchants in their encounters with a powerful and alien civilization. His unfinished satire, *An Account of the Court and Empire of Japan*, uses the far-eastern nation as a satiric standard to lambaste the corruption of the courts of George I and George II, and in *Gullivers Travels*, Japan serves as a means to underscore Swift's critique of England's imperial ambitions.[6] In their combination of fantasy and political satire, Gulliver's encounters with the Japanese register profound anxieties about the limitations of English economic power, national identity, and morality in a world that, as we have seen, until 1800 was dominated economically by the empires of South Asia and the Far East.[7]

Japan, like China, has been given short shrift in much postcolonial criticism of the early modern era. While many scholars recognize that the history of Japanese–European relations cannot be conflated with straightforward narratives of colonialism or imperialism, there has been surprisingly little work done on the role that Japan played in challenging or disrupting Europeans' self-perceptions in the seventeenth and eighteenth centuries. In a sense, the Shogunate's policy of *sakoku* (literally "closed country") that was enforced from 1638 to 1853 paradoxically allows most critics and historians to underestimate Japan's significance and to ignore western fantasies of reopening the country to commerce. While China remained the goal of most European traders and the subject of much of the vast literature on the Far East, Japan presented different but no less substantial challenges to Eurocentric views of the Christian world's technological, military, and economic power. In this respect, the revisionist projects of Andre Gunder Frank, Frank Perlin, and Kenneth Pomeranz, among other historians I have discussed in previous chapters, have profound implications for the historiography of European relations with Japan in the seventeenth century, calling into question the ways in which that nation has been marginalized or ignored in the narratives of an emerging

European hegemony in the early modern world.[8] Swift's depiction of Gulliver's encounters with the Japanese disrupts such Eurocentric narratives and calls attention to the ways in which a commitment to monolithic views of western imperialism constrains our ability to read the complexities of English abjection in the far western reaches of the Pacific. Even the vilified Dutch remain "bird[s] in a gilded Japanese cage," and Swift revels in satirizing their willingness to sing in order to please their masters.[9]

Like many of his contemporaries, if not his twentieth-century critics, Swift recognized the limitations of British economic and naval power in the Far East. Unlike Defoe, however, who devotes much of *Farther Adventures* and *A New Voyage round the World* to fantasizing about trading opportunities in China and the South Pacific, Swift sets book three of *Gullivers Travels* in the context of England's failures to dent the Dutch monopoly of trade in Japan and Southeast Asia. Like China, Japan presented fundamental challenges to the rhetoric and practices of eighteenth-century European imperialism: it was a "heathen" empire that, after its civil wars in the sixteenth century, had rejected Christianity, cut off almost all contact with Europeans, and yet continued to prosper. In dedicating his translation of Engelbert Kaempfer's *History of Japan* (1727) to George II, John Gaspar Scheuchzer, a Fellow of the Royal Society, characterized his subject as "a valiant and invincible Nation, a polite, industrious and virtuous People, enrich'd by a mutual Commerce among themselves, and possess'd of a Country, on which Nature hath lavish'd her most valuable Treasures."[10] Scheuchzer's language reflects a consensus among European commentators that the Japanese rivaled or surpassed the English, French, and Dutch in their standards of living, technological sophistication, civility, business acumen, and military prowess. Perhaps the most urbanized society in the early modern world, with a population that dwarfed that of any country in Europe, Japan boasted "cities that were infinitely cleaner and safer than anywhere else in the world"; water quality, sewage systems, and trash removal were more advanced and efficient than in London or Paris. Commoners "enjoyed a high degree of literacy," a "varied and nutritious" diet, "cheap entertainment," religious freedom (except for Christianity), and "relatively good and cheap medical care."[11] Will Adams, as we have seen in chapter one, praised the Japanese as "curteous above measure, and valiant in warre" and declared that there was "no Land better governed in the world by civill Policie."[12] For Adams as for Scheuchzer more than a century later, the Japanese embody idealized, transcultural characteristics (good nature, courtesy) that the English both see as fundamental to their own sense of national identity and identify as universal qualities of civility. Unlike the nations of Europe, wracked by warfare throughout the seventeenth and eighteenth centuries, however, Japan by 1720 had enjoyed peace and comparative prosperity for a century.

Before and after the nation was closed to most European trade, Japan was considered an extraordinarily important economic power. The goal of European merchants since the sixteenth century, it remained after 1638 an object of speculative desire, a mirror image of China's capacity for production and consumption. In one of the most popular atlases of his day, Swift could have read that Japan

abounds in all manner of Necessaries . . . with Mines of Silver and other Metals, and a great many fine Towns and Fortresses. The Emperor surpasses all the Monarchs of *Europe* in Splendor. The Kings, Princes, and Noblemen, who are his Vassals, have vast Riches in their Territories, which they spend in Luxury.[13]

Descriptions such as this motivated the EIC to imagine schemes to circumvent the Dutch and reopen trade with the Tokugawa regime. Although plans for a joint Dutch–Japanese invasion of the Philippines in 1637 were shelved, the VOC was allowed, with myriad restrictions, to trade cotton, spices, and silk for Japanese silver, a crucial privilege at a time when silver mining had declined in South America. The Dutch monopoly on European trade to Japan rankled with the English who, as always, were still seeking a market for their cloth. Josiah Child, the sometime Governor of the EIC, complained that the VOC "industriously avoid[s] introducing our English Cloth [to Japan]. Which Country being exceeding large, rich and populous, and lying in such a Northern Latitude, might vent as much of our English Manufactures, as *Spain* or *Portugal*, if we could gain a footing into that Trade."[14] The expensive effort to sell English woolens to a country far enough north to need heavy clothing could be justified only if this trade could be justified as essential to the nation's prosperity as well as to the Company's profits. Seventeenth-century voyages to Hudson's Bay searching for the Northwest Passage carried letters from James I to the Emperor of Japan promising friendship and enumerating the advantages to both countries of a regular commercial route through the imagined waterway.

Fifty years after the English had shut down their factory at Hirado, the East India Company mounted a costly voyage to Nagasaki to try to re-establish this trade. Writing in the 1677, Robert Ferguson described the Company's failed mission in terms that emphasized both its costs and the benefits that could accrue to shareholders and to the nation at large if trade could be revived in Canton and Hirado:

though [merchants of the EIC] have met with very great difficulties and disappointments in the attempts that they have made, one undertaking about three years since for the gaining of that Trade, though designed with all the care and circumspection possible, proved ineffectual, to the Companies loss of at least 50 thousand pounds; which, though a very great sum, was not ruinous to any, because of the great number of persons that bear it.[15]

The English ships were rebuffed without being allowed to land. The motivation for this venture was England's longstanding dream of finding a substantial Asian market for its broadcloth that would stanch the flow of bullion from London and allow the English to buy their way back into the spice trade. The Company's instructions to its merchants declared that "our chiefest end of vndertaking the Iapon trade is the vent of Cloth, and other English Manufacture, and for the procuring of Gold, Silver & Copper for the supply of our other Factories in East India yt wee may not send Gold & Silver" from England.[16] The English (particularly the "great number of persons" who invested in the failed mission) were, in brief, trying to mimic the strategies that the Dutch successfully employed: trading Indian cottons for Japanese silver, then using that silver both to trade with China for porcelain and silk and to finance their expenses throughout the Far East. For Swift's readers fifty years after this failed venture, Tokugawa Japan was both a promised land from which the English were banished and a reminder of the limits of England's commercial power.

Swift's decision to send Gulliver to Japan represents a crucial (if necessarily brief) disruption of Eurocentric discourses of imperialism and barbarism. Unlike contemporaries such as Leibniz or Voltaire who idealized Chinese civilization as a model for a corrupt Europe to emulate, Swift has little interest in trying to explain (or explain away) the paradoxical tag "heathen civilization" that was applied to both China and Japan.[17] Instead, Gulliver's audience with the Emperor in Edo (Tokyo) marks the historical and conceptual limits of a European-dominated commerce, English imperial designs, and western morality. For Swift, the Tokugawa policy of *sakoku* isolates Japan from the corruptions of modern Europe that are satirized throughout *Gullivers Travels*. The Emperor, however, is not the King of Brobdingnag or the Master Houyhnhnm, neither a satiric scourge nor an impossible ideal. He is a means to an end: Gulliver's audience offers a fantasy – conniving with the Japanese against the Dutch – that discloses *as* fantasy Eurocentric discourses of economic imperialism, moral probity, and technocultural superiority. Gulliver's Japanese encounters mortify English pride by revealing the *irrelevance* of the assumptions, values, and logic on which the self-congratulatory rhetoric of Eurocentrism depends. Where Defoe responds to a similar threat by castigating the Chinese, Swift uses Japan's isolation to counter both English adventurism and Eurocentric denunciations of non-western cultures.

JAPAN AND THE CRISIS IN EUROPEAN HISTORIOGRAPHY

In writing about Japan, European authors after 1640 had to confront the defeat of western hopes that Japan could be easily converted to Christianity and the country opened to profitable trade. In the late sixteenth century, Jesuit missionaries had converted 220,000 Japanese (approximately 3 percent of the population), and Portuguese merchants from Macao engaged in a lucrative commerce that provided the silver bullion essential for their trafficking throughout Asia. During the century of civil wars in Japan, the Jesuits and Portuguese frequently contributed material and spiritual support as a means to induce feudal warlords and their retainers to convert to Christianity. After the victory and consolidation of power by the Tokugawa Shogunate, some missionaries confidently predicted the imminent conversion of the entire population. Beginning in 1587, however, Hideyoshi and his successors, Ieyasu and Hidetaka, issued a series of edicts to clamp down on Christians who were suspected of political subversion.[18] Intensifying repression followed, and by 1615 foreign missionaries had been deported, martyred, or chased underground; Japanese Christians were forced to recant or die. In 1637 and 1638, confronted by famine and crushing taxes, peasants rebelled in the former Christian stronghold of Shimabara, resurrecting the rhetoric of apocalyptic Christianity as a rallying cry. The rebels threatened to "slay all village magistrates and heathen bonzes [priests] without sparing even one; for judgment day is at hand," but they themselves were besieged and eventually massacred by the Shogun's forces with the help of a Dutch warship.[19] The once-flourishing trade with the Portuguese ended, and Dutch merchants were confined to the tiny trading post on Deshima. The German naturalist Engelbert Kaempfer (1651–1716), the physician for the VOC merchants in 1691–92, described conditions on this tiny artificial island as "an almost perpetual imprisonment"; cut off from Nagasaki by armed sentries on the bridges to their outpost, the Dutch "patiently and submissively [had] to bear the abusive and injurious behaviour of these proud Infidels" (325). The dominant European sea-power in Asia was confined to a mercantile ghetto.

Japan, in short, provoked a crisis in seventeenth and eighteenth-century historiography because the defeat of Christianity and the ongoing abjection of the Dutch on Deshima mocked the values and assumptions of Eurocentric ideology. Peter Heylyn's treatment of Japan reveals dramatically the problems that the island nation posed for Europeans. In the first edition of his *Microcosmos* (1621), Heylyn is characteristically terse in his treatment of the Jesuit missionaries. "This Island . . . is much frequented by the *Iesuites*, of whom 200 are said to liue here; *Xavier* one of *Ignatius* first companions leading the way."[20] In the eighth edition (1639), Heylyn repeats this sentence (and the paragraph from which it is taken) verbatim. The type has been reset and the punctuation altered but the wording is unchanged; there is no mention of the increasing repression or the failed uprising of 1637–38. More tellingly, in his *Cosmographie*, first published in 1652, Heylyn adds a good bit of detail about the Jesuit mission in the sixteenth century, but he does *not* allude to any events later than the repression of 1587, reported in the *Epistolae Japanicae* from which he and other seventeenth-century historians derived much of their information:

Of late times by the care and dilligence of the *Jesuits*, *Christianity* hath begun to take footing here; whether with such a large increase as their letters, called *Epistolae Japanicae*, have been pleased to tell us, I am somewhat doubtfull. They tell us there of some Kings of these Islands, whom they have converted and baptized; that within 50 miles of *Meaco*, they had 50 Churches, 200 at the least in all; and that in the year 1587 the number of their Converts was two hundred thousand. Of this, if the one half be but true, we have great cause to praise God for it, and to give them the commendatiou[n] of their pains and industry: not letting pass the memory of the first *Adventurer*, who was Father *Xavier*, one of the first foundation of this *Society*, (employed in this business by *Ignatius*, the first founder of it) who first landed here about the year 1556.[21]

Heylyn's account is sixty years out of date and stubbornly ignores anything in his sources related to the repression of Christianity. In a geography cited by Heylyn, first published in 1592, Giovanni Botero had noted the resistance of many Japanese to "the preaching of the Iesuits," and reported accurately both the determination of Hideyoshi "to banish them all, and to weed vp that good vine [of Christianity] which began to take deepe roote in those prouinces," and the resulting agitation among many Japanese converts. His source for this information is the "aduisoes of the last yeere," that is, the same Jesuit letters, the *Epistolae Japanicae*, that Heylyn, sixty years later, cites in describing the progress of Christianity.[22] Other works in this genre published before *Microcosmos* note the disturbing developments in early seventeenth-century Japan. After reporting on the number of conversions between 1569 and 1590, Pierre d'Avity, writing in 1614, describes the recent persecutions in the context of battles that had occurred between 1609 and 1611: "Since, there hauue beene great wars, and great persecutions against the Christians, euen vnder *Taicosama*, who raignes at this present: yet the faith doth still flourish and extends it selfe in many places."[23] While d'Avity tends to downplay the dire conditions for Christian converts and locates his account within the larger metanarrative of Christian triumphalism, he makes the effort to keep his readers up to date. His final clause seeks to recoup a situation that Heylyn simply ignores. Because Heylyn's account of Japan is drawn, in part, from Botero, we can assume that he was aware of the persecutions, then thirty years old, in 1621; by 1652 most educated people in Europe knew about the extirpation of Christianity in Japan. Although, in his preface, Heylyn laments the loss of his books during the Interregnum, it is evident throughout *Cosmographie* that he consulted new sources after the publication of the eighth edition of *Microcosmos* because many of his entries on European nations refer to events of the 1640s. He refuses to explain or even acknowledge what, for many Europeans, defied explanation: the overthrow of the grand narrative of Judeo-Christian history.

Heylyn's outdated description of Japan testifies to the difficulties faced by European writers in dealing – or not dealing – with the defeat of Christianity. When ideological expectations confront brutal experience, the recent events are suppressed but the dream of an infinitely profitable commerce to a civilized island nation remains. In *Cosmographie*, Heylyn reiterates the well-known but dated history from the sixteenth century celebrating the inroads of Christianity, but concentrates on describing those qualities of the country and its people that seem most conducive to future opportunities for trade. Like other writers for the next two centuries, he describes a country that is characterized by its civilized morality, good government, and rigorous adherence to the rule of law, and yet that cannot be located unproblematically on a hierarchical scale of civilized – that is, commercial – nations because it rejects the very grounds of that civility: a desire for and commitment to trade.

Because Japan is too enticing a potential trading partner to be condemned outright, Heylyn must find a rhetorical strategy to describe a people who confound the principles that underlie English readers' perceptions of their own national identity. The Japanese, he tells his readers, are

of good understanding, apt to learn, and of able memories; cunning and subtile in their dealings. Of body vigorous and strong, accustomed to bear Arms untill 60 years old. Their complexion of an Olive-Colour, their beards thin, and the half of the hair of their heads shaved off. Patient they are of Pain, ambitious of glory, uncapable of suffering wrong, but can withall dissemble their resentments of it till opportunity of revenge. They reproach no man for his poverty, so it come not by his own untruthfulness, for which cause they detest all kinds of gaming, as the wayes of ill-husbandry and generally abhor Slandering, Theft, and Swearing ... The very Antipodes of our world in customs, though not in site: and the true type or Figure of the old English Puritan, opposite the Papists in things fit and decent, though made ridiculous many times by that opposition. (915)

Heylyn's description employs two strategies of triangulation: the Japanese are opposed to "Papists" and identified with "the old English Puritan" – not the regicide of the 1640s but a "ridiculous" figure closer to the stage-caricatures of the Jacobean theater, such as Ben Jonson's Zeal-of-the-Land Busy. These images allow the non-Puritan reader, such as Heylyn's fellow royalists, to judge "objectively" the strengths and weaknesses of the Japanese – identifying with them against Catholics and holding them at arm's length when they are associated with the pride, rigidity, moralistic self-denial, and economic aggrandizement of the Puritans. But these two triangular comparisons fail to resolve the problem of a people who offer a radical alternative to western ideas of a mutually profitable and civilizing commerce. If the Japanese are "cunning and subtile in their dealings," they are also "ambitious of glory" in a manner that resonates with Heylyn's praise of the "heroic Acts" of the English in his preface. In both respects, they are motivated by a self-interest that mirrors and opposes the self-image of the nation. Like the Christian woman worshiping Venus and Cupid aboard Saris's ship in Nagasaki in 1613 (described in chapter one), Heylyn's Japanese translate into their own terms European desires for a "mutual" trade. Rather than conforming to western desires, "their dealings" serve their own ends in "cunning and subtile" ways. If they are "the very Antipodes of [Europe] in customs," their rejection of gambling, swearing, and prodigality (the venal sins of a profligate European aristocracy) marks them as worthy antagonists, policing conceptual boundaries that European merchants, missionaries, and readers cannot easily cross. Heylyn's analogies, then, ultimately confront the limitations of a worldview that cannot force into signification a wealthy and virtuous nation that has rejected the commercial and religious bases of European, specifically English, self-definition.

Although in England, Heylyn and later geographers could rely on anti-Catholic prejudices to mitigate the horror of Christian converts recanting their faith, Europeans had no ready-to-hand analytical vocabulary to explain either the suppression of Christianity or the abject behavior of the Dutch. Besides Jesuit letters from a past that had been violently eradicated, the Dutch literature on Japan was both sparse and tightly censored by the directors of the VOC who were intent on maintaining their monopoly on a still-profitable trade. The Dutch outpost on Deshima was denied intercourse with all but a handful of Japanese, and communicated only through a hereditary guild of interpreters whose success was judged by the amount of money they could wring out of the red-haired barbarians. Before the publication of Kaempfer's *History of Japan* in 1727, the only eyewitness accounts published in England after the early seventeenth century were the short history by François Caron, a VOC merchant, and the compilation of Dutch reports collected and edited by Arnoldus Montanus and translated by John Ogilby as *Atlas Japannensis*.[24] Defoe characterizes Caron's history as "a tedious but very imperfect Account of the Country," and Montanus's work was never reprinted, although it frequently was cannibalized in geographies and atlases for a half century after its publication, including Defoe's *Atlas Maritimus & Commercialis* (1728).[25] With the Japanese forced to swear an oath, in Kaempfer's words, "not to discourse with [the Dutch] nor to discover any thing . . . of the Condition of their Country," up-to-date information about Japan was a scarce and valuable commodity (ii).

Nonetheless, Swift and his contemporaries could read several accounts of Japan that reinforced views of the Empire as alien, alluring, and powerful. Purchas's *Pilgrimmes* included Will Adams's letters and the narratives of John Saris, the captain of the first trading venture to Japan in 1613 (see chapter one), and Richard Cocks, the head of the English factory at Hirado from 1616 to 1623. Even more troublesome than the failure of English attempts to establish a profitable trade were the implications of reports that reached Europe during the Japanese persecutions of Christians in the 1630s. In 1633, the Vice-Provincial for Japan, a Portuguese missionary for thirty-seven years, who had been in the country for more than two decades, Christovão Ferreira, turned apostate under agonizing torture, and later served the Shogun as a translator, anti-Christian propagandist, and inquisitor.[26] Ferreira was excommunicated in 1636, but two groups of Jesuits from Macao encountered him when they were captured trying to enter Japan, despite the edicts issued by the Shogun. The second of these groups was taken into custody in 1643, and the priests tortured. In *Atlas Japannensis*, Montanus provides a harrowing description, taken from the reports of a Dutch trading mission, of Ferreira, now called Sawano Chuan, or, as the VOC merchants knew him, "*Syovan* the Apostate Priest," interrogating the four Jesuits who had come to rescue him. This remarkable account includes long ventriloquized passages of the apostate Christian taunting the members of his former order:

O despairing *Jesuits*! What confidence can you repose in your God, who hath so shamefully forsaken you? Is he the Creator and Governor of all Things? Why doth he not release you from your Troubles, by which your Bodies rather seem to be Anatomies than Living Creatures? Cannot the *Japan* Emperor do with you whatever he pleases, without asking leave of the *Christian* God?[27]

It is difficult to imagine the response of a seventeenth-century reader to this passage: the familiar language of biblical faith is inverted and used to humiliate four men already tortured to such an extent that they resemble corpses on a dissecting table. The Jesuits answer, as their contemporaries in Europe would expect, by claiming that God has not forsaken them, that they are suffering for the true faith, and that while their bodies are corruptible and susceptible to the Emperor's power, their souls are not. This response is emblematic of a Christian mission that persisted in asserting its faith in a hopeless cause: the Jesuits sent to Japan after 1615 had been taught to embrace their coming martyrdom and to prepare Japanese converts and members of their own order to withstand torture.

In 1643, the four priests were under no illusions about their fate. But their persistence in reasserting their principles and faith was met by their interlocutor with scorn, derision, and a litany of charges that the apostate Jesuit had borrowed from previous Japanese attacks on Christianity.

[H]e look'd very fiercely upon them, notwithstanding he had formerly been one of their Order, and in a scoffing manner said, "No fie upon you *Jesuits*, that make this World in an Uproar. How you vapor of your God and Salvation? Are none sav'd but *Jesuits*, or those that embrace your Opinion? In what consists your Interest in Heaven? Is it because you privately dissemble with, and defraud all Princes; and gathering, hoard up the Worlds Treasure? Had you remain'd still in your usual Pleasures, the *Japan* Prisons had not harbor'd such a crue of Antichrists; nay, *Japan* had never shed so much Blood: for thousands, by your Delusions, were taken from their Worship of the ancient Gods *Amida*, *Xaca*, and *Canon*, and embrac'd the *Christian* Religion, for which they sufferd'd the cruellest Deaths. Was it under a pretence to win Souls? And why did you plot to bring *Japan* under the Subjection of the *Spanish* Tyrant, and so to order all things according to your pleasure? But now, what is the Power of the *Christian* God? Look upon your miserable Bodies; can he not help you? Where then is he omnipotent? Will he not help you? Where is his Mercy? O foolish thought of Salvation! You are distracted, to continue thus in your stubborn humor, imagining to receive great Rewards from God, and great Esteem of your Successors, in suffering willfully your Bodies to be thus tormented. I ask once again, Why doth not your God help you? Certainly your Life is not in his Hands, but in the Emperours of *Japan*, who when he pleaseth can punish and torture you more than ever he hath done yet."

This the *Hollanders* understood very well . . . But whilst *Syovan* rail'd thus at the *Jesuits*, he seem'd exceedingly to please two of the *Japan* Council.[28]

Some of the insults attributed to Ferreira by the Dutch follow closely the charges that were made frequently in anti-Catholic polemics in England and the Netherlands during the seventeenth century.[29] For die-hard Protestants, the Jesuits appear as a kind of fifth column within Japan, agents of the Spanish monarch, and part of a corrupt order as dedicated to material gain and political subversion as it is to promoting the true faith. But the apostate priest also mocks Christianity itself: martyrdom is a delusional attempt to gain the favor of a remote or nonexistent God; it is a newfangled innovation that threatens to disrupt the social order and religious practices of a prosperous and politically stable country that wants to be left to its own devices. Christianity is stripped of its metaphysical rewards and punishments and brought down to the level of a brute materialism: the experience of bodily torture for the lost cause of the Jesuit mission in Japan. While it is tempting to conclude that Montanus includes this account – and John Ogilby translates it for English readers – as a mortification of Jesuit pride, it seems that the voice of the apostate Ferreira echoes in subsequent efforts to explain, or explain away, the failure of Christianity to take root in Japan and China. For the next sixty years, most accounts of Japan drew on Montanus, and registered the contradictory impulses that underlay European perceptions of a civilized nation that refused to trade and refused to sanction even the limited presence of Christian missionaries.

In the atlases of the cartographer Herman Moll, English readers could find (in translation) short descriptions of Japan culled from Montanus and the Jesuits, such as a 1701 Latin entry by Johann Luyts, a professor at Utrecht: "The Japanese are reckon'd ingenious in Handicraft, just in Dealing, temperate, valiant and trusty, but at the same time addicted to Dissimulation and Cruelty, and are apt to lay violent Hands upon themselves; they are gross Idolaters, worshipping especially the Sun."[30] In this caricature, the Japanese embody contradictory qualities: "civilized" virtues (technological sophistication, temperance, and military prowess) and "barbarous" attributes usually displaced onto "heathens" (suicidal tendencies, cruelty, and idolatry). They are both "trusty" – trusting and presumably trustworthy – and given to dissimulation. Luyts does not try to resolve these contradictory impressions, in part because the sources he cites offer no means to explain how the Japanese can dictate the terms of their contact with Europeans. Only "the Dutch," he continues, "by despising the Pictures and Images of the Virgin *Mary*, and other Fopperies of the Portuguese; and . . . delivering up their very Bibles to the Flames, [have] persuaded the Inhabitants, they were not Christians; and prevail'd upon them to permit Traffick there."[31] Luyts's strategy of packaging apostasy as Protestant iconoclasm failed to impress either English or Jesuit writers, who accused the Dutch of willingly sacrificing their beliefs to their lust for Japanese gold and silver.[32]

The most important of these Jesuit commentators was Jean Crasset, whose two-volume history of the Jesuit mission was translated into English in 1705 as *The History of the Church of Japan*, and ransacked by the anonymous author of the section on Japan in Moll's *A System of Geography* (1721). Writing a half century after the Jesuits had been expelled from Japan, Crasset devotes almost 1,400 pages to describing, with gruesome specificity, the tortures endured by Christian martyrs and trying to explain away Ferreira's apostasy. Paradoxically, he is more positive than Luyts in characterizing the Japanese. After praising this "most extreamly Courteous and Civil" people for their hatred of avarice, "their wonderful Courage in Adversity," the excellence of their education, and "their great Moderation," he declares that they "far surpass [Europeans] in the endowments, both of body and mind."[33] Crasset turns the Japanese into a heroic race who replace western models of elegance and virtue; they embody the qualities of mind and body that Sir William Temple, as I have suggested in chapter two, attributes to the Chinese. In praising the Japanese, Crasset describes their language as "grave, elegant, and copious, and surpassing without dispute both the Greek and Latine in the number of words, and variety of expressions" (I: 6). Crasset displaces the Greeks and Romans – the progenitors of western civilization – as a source of cultural, linguistic, and secular authority.[34] Japan wants only the revealed word of the Judeo-Christian God, and the path to salvation is precisely what Catholic missionaries offer. Crasset ultimately conjures into being an imagined future, once "the Persecution blows over," of the resurrection of Christianity in Japan (II: 547). This future spreading of the gospel represents the *only* contribution that Europeans can make to an otherwise superior people. The Jesuits, according to Crasset, see themselves reliving the early history of the Church when the faithful suffered martyrdom to bring true religion to the great empires of the ancient world. The heroism of Japanese converts in the face of bone-chilling tortures, in this regard, testifies to a national and racial identity founded on courage, loyalty, and stoic endurance; the Japanese have become the spiritual heirs of an apostolic Christianity. Their martyrdom offers a powerful example to their European brethren who have fallen prey to heresy (Protestants), rivalry (Dominicans), and political and military conflict.

As armchair editors, Luyts and Crasset sift through firsthand accounts of Japan, rewrite their material, and make grand pronouncements about the country and its inhabitants. Like other seventeenth-century commentators, they lift passages from various sources, usually unacknowledged, and then transform the disparate experiences of priests, merchants, and officials into seemingly authoritative discourses. In contrast, Kaempfer's account of his experiences in Japan emphasizes the psychological costs of being subject to the slights and abuses of "proud Infidels" (325). Using his interpreter as an intermediary, Kaempfer bribed officials so that he could have access to dozens of Japanese sources for his history, and consequently provides a wealth of information that surpasses the syncretic accounts in Montanus. He strives to give European readers a sense of what it is like to suffer the "shocking" indignities of subaltern status (325).[35]

Kaempfer's description of the VOC merchants on Deshima defines their relationship to the Japanese in terms of *abjection*.[36] The Dutch do not simply comply with edicts from the Shogunate and regional authorities; they repeatedly demonstrate their "submissive readiness" to grovel before Japanese demands, including, in 1638, the order to aid in the "final destruction . . . of a people [the Christian rebels on Shimabarra], with whom [the Dutch] otherwise agree in the most essential parts of their faith" (324–25). The reward for bombarding fellow Christians and then surrendering the ship's canon to the Japanese is circumscribed trading privileges and confinement on an island the size of a baseball field. Although the Dutch claim that they have proved themselves "sincerely faithful to a foreign Monarch" by trampling on the crucifix, burning their Bibles, and neglecting Christian worship, they never allay Japanese suspicions of their intentions (325). Their submission is neither a single act nor a carefully staged performance during their annual tribute mission to Edo but an ongoing test of their willingness, at any and every moment, to sacrifice religion, national and personal honor, and weaponry to placate Japanese authorities. Kaempfer, an employee of the VOC, not a fellow national, is both complicit in Dutch rituals of abjection and critical of such compliance.

Although Kaempfer's history was published a year after *Gullivers Travels*, the manuscript had been purchased by Sir Hans Sloane in 1723, and Scheuchzer had taken over its translation by 1725.[37] Subscriptions were being solicited by the end of that year, and it is tempting to speculate, as J. Leeds Barroll has done, that Swift added the Japanese episodes when he was in London in 1726 to a work otherwise substantially complete. Swift may have known of the manuscript as early as 1724 through his friendship with John, Lord Carteret, who subscribed to the first edition; but Scheuchzer's translation had not been completed when Carteret was in Ireland that year. Swift's only opportunity to have seen Kaempfer's work would have been two years later when he was in London and making final revisions to *Gulliver*.[38] Whether or not Swift had seen Kaempfer's work, he had read enough about the Japanese to be able to contrast their "heathen" virtues to Dutch corruption, and to realize that this contrast could be used to satirize England's long-time commercial rival in the Far East. By emphasizing Dutch malevolence and hypocrisy, Swift focuses the reader's attention on the moral failings of England's erstwhile Protestant allies rather than on the customs, language, or religion of the Japanese. He ignores much of what had been written about Japan: the warfare and political strife of the sixteenth century, the failure of the English factory, and the violent end to Japan's Christian century. The reader learns far more about Lilliput, Brobdingnag, the Island of the Houyhnhnms, Laputa, and Luggnagg than she does about Scheuchzer's "valiant and invincible Nation." Swift's depiction of Japan depends on the triangular dynamics of rivalry and exclusion: the Japanese are represented, in one respect, only in terms of their difference from the Dutch. Japan resists representation precisely because it controls the cultural and economic terms of its encounters with red-haired barbarians. To participate in the discursive regime of the Japanese is to risk assimilation (Adams), martyrdom (the Jesuits), apostasy (Ferreira), or submission (the Dutch). Consequently, Gulliver cannot engage in extended conversations with the Japanese Emperor as he does with the Brobdingnagian King or his Houyhnhnm Master; he can only lie, connive, and evade the abject, sacrilegious behavior that has become, Swift implies, an "essential" part of the Dutch national character.

AUDIENCES WITH THE SHOGUN: REAL AND IMAGINARY

Gulliver's adventures in book three begin when he tries to enter the lucrative inter-Asian country trade as a merchant. He sails from Tonquin in command of a sloop, bound for "neighbouring islands." Like his other endeavors, Gulliver's stint as a trader comes to an abrupt and unsuccessful end when his ship is captured by Japanese pirates, a fictional rendering of the raiders who preyed on coastal shipping in the China Seas. The villain of this encounter, however, is not Japanese but Dutch:

I observed among them a *Dutchman*, who seemed to be of some Authority, although he were not Commander of either ship. He knew us by our Countenances to be *Englishmen*, and jabbering to us in his own Language, swore we should be tyed Back to Back, and thrown into the Sea. I spoke *Dutch* tolerably well; I told him who we were, and begged him in Consideration of our being Christians and Protestants, of neighbouring Countries, in strict Alliance, that he would move the Captains to take some Pity on us. This inflamed his Rage, he repeated his Threatnings, and turning to his Companions, spoke with great Vehemence, in the *Japanese* Language, as I suppose, often using the Word *Christianos.*[39]

After the expulsion of the Jesuits, the practice of Christianity was a capital offense in Tokugawa Japan, and the label "*Christianos*" is potentially a death sentence. The Dutchman jabbers, threatens, and curses; his language lies beyond the pale of both civility and Protestant solidarity. During the years covered by book three (1707–09), England and the Netherlands were allies in the increasingly unpopular war against France. In his pamphlets of 1711 and 1712 Swift attacks the prosecution of the war by the Whig ministry, its staggering expense, and the duplicitous, self-serving behavior of the Dutch. The "Folly, the Temerity, the Corruption, [and] the Ambition" of the Whigs, he declared, was matched by the "Insolence, Injustice, and Ingratitude" of the Dutch, who, he maintains, gained territory and trading concessions at England's expense, while British armies did most of the fighting.[40] Swift was not alone in his opinion of the United Provinces and the conduct of the war. His November 1711 pamphlet, *The Conduct of the Allies*, sold 11,000 copies in two months and became the basis for Tory arguments in Parliament for ending the war; Swift claimed credit for securing the votes that pushed the Ministry toward a negotiated settlement.[41] The bloodthirsty Dutchman in *Gullivers Travels*, in short, embodies the pride, maliciousness, and avarice that Swift attributes to a nation that engages in "insolent Hostilities" against the English throughout "the *East-Indies*."[42] Whatever political differences he may have had with Defoe over the war, international trade, and England's imperial ambitions, Swift shares his view of Dutch perfidy.

In contrast to the Dutchman, the Japanese captain of one of the "Pyrate ships" is civilized and even merciful. He speaks "a little *Dutch*, but very imperfectly," and, having questioned Gulliver, refuses to allow the Dutchman to have him executed.

I made the Captain a very low Bow, and then turning to the *Dutchman*, said, I was sorry to find more Mercy in a Heathen, than in a Brother Christian. But I had some reason to Repent those foolish Words; for that malicious Reprobate, having often endeavoured in vain to persuade both Captains that I might be thrown into the Sea (which they would not yield to after the Promise made me, that I should not die), however prevailed so far as to have a Punishment inflicted on me, worse in all human Appearance than Death it self . . . I should be set a-drift in a small Canoe, with Paddles and a Sail, and four Days Provisions; which last the *Japanese* Captain was so kind to double out of his own Stores, and would permit no Man to search me. I got down into the Canoe, while the *Dutchman*, standing upon the Deck, loaded me with all the Curses and injurious Terms his Language could afford. (139)

The difference between the behavior of the Dutchman and the Japanese captain hardly could be more marked. The Japanese captain is a man of his word, even "kind," doubling Gulliver's provisions "out of his own Stores." He is the antithesis of the apostate Christian, a "Heathen" seemingly as virtuous as those figures called up from the dead later in book three as foils for a debased modern philosophy of self-interest and exploitation. The Dutchman seems the evil genius of the pirate ships, cursing an innocent victim and demanding the severest punishment.

When Gulliver later lands in Luggnagg, he must lie to a "Customs-House Officer, by whom [he is] examined very strictly." Seeking to gain passage back to England, he admits that "I thought it necessary to disguise my Country, and call my self a *Hollander*, because my intentions were for *Japan*, and I knew the Dutch were the only *Europeans* permitted to enter into that Kingdom" (187). As Barroll suggests, aspects of the hero's stay in Luggnagg may be derived from Swift's sources on Japan: the custom-house interrogation was familiar to European merchants in Nagasaki as well as Canton, and Gulliver's description of his audience with the King of Luggnagg, whom he approaches "crawl[ing] upon [his] Belly, and lick[ing] the Floor as [he] advanced" and then "striking [his] forehead seven times upon the Ground" (189), satirically exaggerates the rituals of the Shogun's Court.[43] By posing as a Dutchman, Gulliver is able to avoid the protocols of abjection – *yefumi*, trampling on the cross – that define Dutch subservience to the Japanese. Ironically, he must assume the guise of his enemies in order to distinguish himself from them.

Gulliver's audience with the Japanese Emperor resurrects nostalgically images of Englishmen at the Shogun's Court a century earlier, particularly the reception ultimately afforded Adams, the English pilot of a Dutch vessel who landed in Japan after a harrowing voyage through the Straits of Magellan and across the Pacific. Brought before Ieyasu, Adams was accused by Jesuits at court of being a spy. Yet the Englishman found the Shogun "wonderfull favourable" and eventually convinced him, after repeated interrogations, that he was neither an Iberian spy nor a pirate, and that the English (or Dutch) would provide an effective counter-balance to the Portuguese Jesuits (II: 127). Ieyasu's questions to Adams indicate that he quickly grasped the value of playing the English and Dutch against the Portuguese, even if the Japanese remained puzzled by the nature of the theological disputes between Protestants against Catholics.

Adams spent the rest of his life in Japan as a translator and advisor to Ieyasu, and proved essential to the English efforts to establish a factory at Hirado.[44] Official sanction for the mission had to be obtained from the Shogunate, and in 1613, Saris traveled to Edo for the first official encounter between a representative of James I and the Japanese ruler. The audience he described paradoxically was both a nerve-wracking and anti-climactic affair. No diplomatic breakthroughs were achieved, and the Englishmen were outmaneuvered by the better-financed and more persistent Dutch.

Although Saris was guided by Adams through the protocols for a foreign ambassador, he still managed to bungle matters. Before Saris entered the audience chamber, he delivered "Presents sent from our kinge to the Emperour as alsoe those, (which according to the custome of the countrie) I gave into the Emperour as from my self." These "Presents" (luxury items from England and South and Southeast Asia) signify differently for the English ambassador and the Japanese ruler: for Saris, they encode a reciprocal semiotics of civility that depends on idealized conceptions of exchange among equals; for the Japanese they are symbolic markers of the tributary status of another nation of European barbarians who nonetheless can be used to counter-balance Portuguese merchants and Jesuit missionaries and their converts.[45] After the Shogun takes his seat, Saris offers this brief description of his audience:

Comminge to the Emperour, according to our English complements, I delivered our kinges letter vnto his Maiestie, who tooke it in his hande, and putt it vpp towardes his forehead, and commaunded his Interpretour whoe sate a good distaunce from him behinde, to will Mr Adams to tell me, that I was wellcome from a wearisome Iourney, that I should take my rest for a daie or two, and then his aunswer should be readie for our kinge. Soe takinge my leave of the Emperour, . . . with my Attendaunts [I] returned to my lodgings.[46]

A bizarre figure with limited diplomatic skills, Saris apparently tried to hand-deliver James I's letter to Ieyasu, assuming that his "English complements" would satisfy Japanese protocol.[47] The Japanese Court, however, imposed a severe regimen of ritual addresses and protocols to elevate the

FIGURE 5. Kaempfer performs for the Shogun, from Engelbert Kaempfer, *The History of Japan* (1727). Reproduced by permission of the British Library.

Shogun far above a mere ship's captain. Even Adams had to communicate through an official interpreter, and although he, like the Jesuits, describes himself as an invaluable advisor and confidant to the Shogun, his status, like theirs, seems akin to that of a favorite pet.[48] Englishmen in the Shogun's palace have roughly the same standing as Gulliver at the Court of Brobdingnag. They wishfully misinterpret their situation, transforming their tributary missions into evidence of Japanese interest in their factory and the prospect of an expanding commerce.

Kaempfer's account of his audience in 1692 as a member of the annual tribute mission reveals how rigid the protocols of seventeenth-century European embassies to Edo were. Saris's sanitized fiction of diplomatic reciprocity for his superiors in the EIC lacks the experiential and psychological specificity that is a hallmark of Kaempfer's narrative. Kaempfer describes at length the passage of the Dutch through the palace before they enter the audience chamber in which the Shogun, court officials, and women sit behind lattice-work screens (see figure 5). The chief of the Dutch trade mission is granted the temporary rank of minor *daimyo* (feudal warlord) to elevate his status just enough to allow him to perform the ceremonies required of such vassals. He sits to the viewer's right, while the two merchants kneel, and Kaempfer performs for the Court. Arriving in the audience chamber, the four VOC representatives "first [make their] obeyances after the Japanese manner, creeping and bowing our heads to the ground," and deliver their "most humble thanks … for having [been] graciously granted … liberty of commerce" (535). After this ritual is completed, however, "the succeeding part of this solemnity [becomes] a perfect farce." Although the ambassador is spared having "ridiculous and comical commands" laid upon him by the Shogun, the other three tribute-bearers are "ask'd a thousand ridiculous and impertinent questions" and then forced to perform for the amused nobility. Kaempfer and the merchants are ordered to remove their

Garment[s] of Ceremony, then to stand upright, that [the Shogun] might have a full view of us; again to walk, to stand still, to compliment each other, to dance, to jump, to play the drunkard, to speak broken Japanese, to read Dutch, to paint, to sing, to put our cloaks on and off. Mean while we obey'd the Emperor's commands in the best manner we could, I join'd to my dance, a love-song in High German. In this manner, and with innumerable such other apish tricks, we must suffer ourselves to contribute to the Emperor's and the Court's diversion. (535)

Kaempfer's description answers the question of whether the European subaltern can speak at the Japanese Court – he can, but only according to a script that others write and direct for him. The commands to which the author and the merchants are subjected turn them into farcical entertainers, and the accomplishments that might otherwise mark them as gentlemen and exemplary citizens of a civilized nation – painting, dancing, and singing – are rendered ridiculous by being reduced to pantomime and farce. Kaempfer can articulate his resentment at such treatment only after the fact.

Yet his resentment is undermined by the accompanying plate. An elaborate key (letters and numbers are explained on a separate page) introduces European readers to the complex semiotics of the Shogun's court. Before the courtiers and officials, kneeling in the foreground and to the viewer's left of the Dutch ambassador, Kaempfer performs his "love-song in High German of [his] own composition" (535) and dances. An interpreter kneels on a raised platform facing him, and the Shogun and the ladies of the court are concealed behind the latticework screen to the right, an unseen audience. As Annette Keogh demonstrates in her discussion of this song, Kaempfer's verse seek to remasculinize the Dutch through the conventions of European love lyrics.[49] The performer of "apish tricks" casts himself in the archetypal role of the wandering but faithful lover, disdaining the riches

of far-off lands for his mistress. The song concludes with lines addressed to
and ultimately dismissive of the wealth of the Shogun:

> Great Ruler, Son of Heaven,
> Lord of these distant lands,
> Rich in gold and great of power,
> By your throne I swear:
> All the radiance
> Of your wealth and splendor
> Of your women with painted faces
> I prize less than my angel.
> Away with you, court of empty pleasures!
> Away with you, land of immense treasures!
> Nothing can give me earthly pleasure
> But the chaste loveliness,
> Of my precious Florimene.
> Deeply longing for each other,
> She for me, and I for her.[50]

Despite their sentiments of undiminished love, the lyrics of Kaempfer's
love-song reinforce a visual semiotics that turns the physician-poet into a
performer. It is not surprising, in this regard, that the love-song was not
printed in Scheuchzer's 1727 translation or subsequent eighteenth-century
editions in other European languages because the illustration of the author
undermines the values of love and fidelity by emphasizing the theatricality
of his command performance. The Shogun's "hall of audiences" resembles
a proscenium stage with the audience in the foreground and to the viewer's
left; the reader sees the scene as though she were seated in an imaginary
balcony. The vast interior dwarfs the Europeans, and the military hardware
that borders the plate suggests a power that encloses and contains the scene,
emblematic of the Shogun's absolute authority. The contrasts that structure
the poem – "precious Florimene" set against the wealth and splendor of the
court – call attention to the idealized semiotics of a romantic love that can
exist only as a distant memory; after his extensive travels in the Middle East,
including a bout of illness in Ormuz, Kaempfer had not been in Europe in
more than six years. In this respect, his banishing of the splendors of Court
for a long-distance love appropriates a familiar lyric *topos* and makes his
expressions of fidelity to Florimene emblematic of both the impotence of
the Dutch mission in Edo and its members' mercantile loyalties to the
VOC's directors and shareholders in the Netherlands. An attachment to a
far-off ideal becomes a talisman to ward off the indignities of performing
for the amusement of the Shogun, his concubines, and his courtiers.

If the situation that Kaempfer describes were reversed – if a European monarch were ordering representatives from a small, far-off country to "speak broken" English or Dutch, dance, sing a love-song in a language no one at Court understands, and endure the indignity of performing "apish tricks" – postcolonial critics would have little trouble analyzing (and deploring) this spectacle. Such a scene might stand synecdochally for a history of European imperialism and its sophisticated appropriations of the culture and cultural identity of non-western peoples. But Kaempfer's description of his audience points to the limits of narratives of Eurocentric "colonialism" or "imperialism" in the Far East. The Japanese treatment of Kaempfer and his cohorts not only inverts the expectations of postcolonial readings of European–Asian relations, it demonstrates some of the ways in which the lived experience and psychology of European abjection in the Far East reflect aspects of the larger historical realities described, in different ways, by Frank, Pomeranz, Gunn, and Perlin. In this context, Gulliver's audience with the Emperor of Japan becomes an important text in deploying and ironically undercutting one of the persistent cultural fantasies that Europeans develop to translate such "obeyances" into the languages of friendship and mutually beneficial exchange – the "liberty of commerce" that defines Dutch self-justification.

A PASSAGE ON THE *AMBOYNA*

At the end of his adventures in book three, Gulliver takes a ship from imaginary Luggnagg to Xamoschi on "the South-East Part of Japan" (the region near Tokyo, marked on Moll's maps, that Swift takes for a "small Port-Town" [199]). The Japan that Swift imagines, however, is as much a fantasy as Luggnagg, though stripped of satiric description. Gulliver's letter of introduction from the King of Luggnagg to the Emperor ensures that he is treated by the Japanese "as a publick Minister" and "provided . . . with Carriages and Servants" as well as expenses for his trip to Edo. There is no description of this journey, no account of the land or its people. In a single sentence, Gulliver moves from his landing at Xamoschi to his audience with the Emperor. Swift reduces the lengthy descriptions of the palace and the elaborate protocols of the Japanese Court recorded by Saris and Kaempfer to a single phrase: Gulliver's letter is "opened with great Ceremony." Rather than licking the floor in ritual humiliation or experiencing endless delays, Gulliver is told simply "that [he] should signify [his] Request; and whatever it were, it should be granted for the sake of his Royal Brother of Luggnagg" (200). Swift's device of an alliance between a real empire and an imaginary island allows him to circumvent the problem of *sakoku*. Rather than being portrayed as a xenophobic nation, ferociously resistant to international trade or friendship, Japan is engaged in "perpetual Commerce" with Luggnagg, a relationship cemented by royal friendship (200). Swift's radical departure from his sources has two effects: it brings Japan (or at least its Emperor) within the idealized semiotics described by Crasset – Gulliver is again treated with civility and generosity, as he had been by the pirate captain – and it evokes distant memories of Adams's account of his reception and acculturation a century earlier.

Although Gulliver is posing as a Dutchman, the sympathetic connection he forges with the Emperor is founded on victimizing the Dutch. Having secured safe passage on a Dutch ship bound for Europe, he asks that the Emperor,

excuse my performing the Ceremony imposed on my Countrymen of *trampling upon the Crucifix*, because I had been thrown into his Kingdom by my Misfortunes, without any Intention of trading. When this latter Petition was interpreted to the Emperor, he seemed a little surprised; and said he believed I was the first of my Countrymen who ever made any Scruple in this Point; and that he began to doubt whether I was a real *Hollander* or no; but rather suspected I must be a CHRISTIAN. However, for the Reasons I had offered, but chiefly to gratify the King of Luggnagg, by an uncommon Mark of his Favour, he would comply with the singularity of my Humour; but the Affair must be managed with Dexterity, and his Officers should be commanded to let me pass as it were by Forgetfulness. For he assured me, that if the Secret should be discovered by my Countrymen, the Dutch, they would cut my Throat in the Voyage. (200–01)

With the connivance of the Emperor, Gulliver avoids apostasy, the test of *yefumi* that all Japanese nationals and foreigners had to perform to demonstrate their rejection of Christianity and hence their loyalty to the Tokugawa Shogunate. Anti-Christian behavior and immorality are displaced onto the "*Hollander*[s]," continuing a tradition in the pamphlet literature of the 1670s (and afterwards) anathematizing the Dutch for their "submissive readiness" to stomp on Catholic icons. Significantly, as the Emperor's warning suggests, the "real *Hollander*[s]" are not temporizing when they perform this ritual: having internalized their abjection as a measure of self-identity, the Dutch elevate apostasy to a perverse article of faith.

Before the ship departs, Gulliver is "often asked by some of the Crew, whether I had performed the Ceremony," and escapes detection, without lying, only by "evad[ing] the Question by general Answers, that I had satisfied the Emperor and Court in all Particulars" (201). The Dutch sailors' and merchants' obsession with *yefumi* suggests an inward corruption unmitigated by resentment directed at either the Japanese or at their own complicity in their ongoing abjection. The Dutch no longer perceive themselves as Christians but as the submissive subjects of a heathen prince. Although Gulliver's audience is mediated through the Emperor's relationship with the fictitious king of an imaginary country, the ultimate fantasy – one that Swift lets pass without overt satiric commentary – lies in imagining that the Emperor is willing to circumvent the law in order to allow Gulliver to escape apostasy. This benevolence, even if it is intended primarily as a gesture to the King of Luggnagg, allows an (imaginary) Englishman to outwit the Dutch in one of the key outposts of their lucrative Eastern trade.

Gulliver's Japanese encounters, then, allow Swift to paper over internal political divisions within England by scapegoating a common adversary, the jabbering Dutchmen. But where Dryden in *Amboyna* uses a similar strategy to shore up the fiction of a coherent national identity, Swift contrasts the corruption of contemporary England to the imagined ideality that refuses commercial and imperial adventurism. Gulliver returns from Japan on a Dutch ship named *Amboyna*, and the allusion, for his contemporaries, was unambiguous and chilling. For Swift, as for Milton, Dryden, and Defoe, to write about the Far East is to confront the spectre of Dutch commercial and naval supremacy; throughout the seventeenth and eighteenth century, the spectre of Amboyna haunted the coherence of a British national identity that depended, in part, on commercial success as a sign of providential favor. The tendency to invoke Amboyna as both a rallying cry and a nightmare image of English abjection in the South Seas cut across political and religious divisions within England. By having Gulliver and the Emperor outwit the Dutch, Swift offers his readers a satiric revenge fantasy for a century of indignities.

Framing the hero's episodic adventures in book three are the satires in Brobdingnag and Houyhnhnmland of European immorality, deceit, tyranny, violence, and hypocrisy. As the Brobdingnagian King tells Gulliver after the hero has described the supposed virtues of England, "the Bulk of your Natives" must be "the most pernicious Race of little odious Vermin that Nature ever suffered to crawl upon the Surface of the Earth" (116). Gulliver's brief encounters with the Japanese raise questions about the extent to which such satiric judgments project into an imaginative or conceptual space what Europeans imagine – or fear – must be going through the minds of the Japanese (and Chinese). To some extent, the attitudes toward red-haired barbarians ascribed by generations of western writers to the Courts of Edo, Beijing, and Agra are refracted versions of

European descriptions of the "savages" that merchants and missionaries encountered in the Americas, the Pacific, and Africa. A country "exceeding large, rich, and populous," Japan forces European writers to imagine an antipodal inversion of the rhetoric, values, and assumptions that define the colonization of the Americas.

For Swift, Japan offers an ideal satiric foil for his anti-Dutch agitprop: a rich and populous land, both real and nearly inaccessible, that is inflexible in making the Dutch complicit in their own humiliation. Japan thus anchors and defamiliarizes Swift's satiric strategies by inverting the self-congratulatory rhetoric of European-driven trade: at the end of book three of *Gullivers Travels* lies the possibility that, in Edo and Beijing, the "pernicious Race" of red-haired "vermin" have encountered an alterity more threatening to their self-conception than giants or talking horses.

NOTES

1. Jean Crasset, *The History of the Church of Japan*, trans. N. N., 2 vols. (London, 1705), 5.

2. See Clement Hawes, "Three Times Round the Globe: Gulliver and Colonial Discourse," *Cultural Critique* 18 (1991), 187–214; Brown, *Ends of Empire*, 170–200; Claude Rawson, *God, Gulliver, and Genocide: Barbarism and the European Imagination, 1492–1945* (New York: Oxford University Press, 2001); Bruce McLeod, *The Geography of Empire in English Literature, 1580–1745* (Cambridge: Cambridge University Press, 1999), 181–86; and Anna Neill, *British Discovery Literature and the Rise of Global Commerce* (London: Palgrave, 2002), 110–19.

3. Douglas Lane Patey, "Swift's Satire on 'Science' and the Structure of *Gullivers Travels*," *English Literary History* 58 (1991), 809–39; Robert Fitzgerald, "Science and Politics in Swift's Voyage to Laputa," *Journal of English and Germanic Philology* 87 (1988), 213–29; and William Freedman, "Swift's Struldbruggs, Progress, and the Analogy of History," *Studies in English Literature* 35 (1995), 457–72.

4. Harold Williams, ed., *The Correspondence of Jonathan Swift* (Oxford: Clarendon Press, 1963), 2: 430.

5. Anne Barbeau Gardiner, "Swift on the Dutch East India Merchants: The Context of the 1672–73 War Literature," *Huntington Library Quarterly* 54 (1991), 234–52. See also Rennie, *Far-Fetched Facts*, 76–82; John A. Dussinger, "Gulliver in Japan: Another Possible Source," *Notes and Queries* 39, n.s. (1992), 464–67; and Herman Real and Heinz Vienken, "Swift's 'Trampling upon the Crucifix' Once More," *Notes and Queries* 30, n.s.(1983), 513–14.

6. See Maurice Johnson, Kitagawa Muncharu, and Philip Williams, *Gulliver's Travels and Japan* (Doshisha, Japan: Doshisha University, Amherst House, 1977); Williams, *South Sea*, 208–12; and Gunn, *First Globalization*, 55–56.

7. See Frank, *ReOrient*; Pomeranz, *Europe, China, and the Making of the Modern World Economy*; Chaudhuri, *Asia before Europe*; Goldstone, *Revolution and Rebellion*; and Perlin, *"The Invisible City."*

8. Wallerstein, *Mercantilism and the Consolidation of the European World Economy*; Braudel, *Civilization and Capitalism*. On the Eurocentrism of the languages of economic history, see particularly, Perlin, "The Other 'Species' World," 145–73.

9. Schnurmann, "'Wherever profit leads us,'" 489.

10. Engelbert Kaempfer, *The History of Japan*, trans. J. G. Scheucher (London, 1727), N.p.

11. Louis G. Perez, *Daily Life in Early Modern Japan* (London: Greenwood, 2002), 13, 15. Japan's population grew from 17,000,000 in 1600 to 30,000,000 by 1700. For economic and demographic analyses of Japan, see Hanley, "Tokugawa Society," 660–705; Hanley and Yamamura, *Economic and Demographic Change*; Katsuhisa Moriya, "Urban Networks and Information Networks," trans. Ronald P. Toby, in *Tokugawa Japan: The Social and Economic Antecedents of Modern Japan*, ed. Chie Nakane and Shinzaburo Oishi (Tokyo: University of Tokyo Press, 1990), 97–123; Conrad Totman, *Early Modern Japan* (Berkeley and Los Angeles: University of California Press, 1993); and Gary Leupp, *Servants, Shophands, and Laborers in the Cities of Tokugawa Japan* (Princeton: Princeton University Press, 1991).

12. Samuel Purchas, *Purchas His Pilgrimmes*, II: 128.

13. [Herman Moll], *Atlas Geographus*, 5 vols. (London, 1712–17), III: 818. Moll reissued different versions of his atlases under different titles and often with new descriptions of countries. See note 30 below.

14. Child, *A Treatise Wherein is Demonstrated*, 9.

15. Ferguson, *The East-India Trade*, 22.

16. Quoted in Massarella, *A World Elsewhere*, 356; see also 355–69; and Keay, *The Honourable Company*, 198–99.

17. For a different view, see Frank Boyle, *Swift as Nemesis: Modernity and its Satirist* (Stanford: Stanford University Press, 2000), 61–77. Boyle argues that Swift echoes Sir William Temple's account of the Chinese but satirizes its Confucian idealizations in the figure of the Houyhnhnms. On Voltaire and Leibniz, see Porter, *Ideographia*.

18. See Mary Elizabeth Berry, *Hideyoshi* (Cambridge, MA: Harvard University Press, 1982), 92–94. The standard account of the limitations and fall of Christianity in Japan is George Elison's *Deus Destroyed: The Image of Christianity in Early Modern Japan* (Cambridge, MA: Harvard University Press, 1973); Elison offers a skeptical account of the claims of some of the champions of the Christian mission. See Boxer, *The Christian Century in Japan*; Ross, *A Vision Betrayed*; Kazuyoshi Enozawa, "Missionaries' Dreams and the Realities in the Land of Warriors – Some Problems in the Early Jesuit Missions to Japan, 1549–1579," *The Hiyoshi Review of English Studies* 23 (1994), 54–73; and Ohashi Yukihiro, "New Perspectives on the Early Tokugawa Persecution," trans. Bill Garrad, in *Japan and Christianity: Impacts and*

Responses, ed. John Breen and Mark Williams (New York: St. Martin's Press, 1996), 46–62.

19. From a circular of 1638, translated in Elison, *Deus Destroyed*, 220.
20. Heylyn, *Microcosmos*, 2nd edn (Oxford, 1625), 695.
21. Heylyn, *Cosmographie*, 916.
22. Botero, *The Travellers Breviat*, 159.
23. D'Avity, *The Estates, Empires, & Principalities of the World*, 750.
24. François Caron and Joost Schorten, *A Description of the Mighty Kingdoms of Japan and Siam*, trans. Roger Manley (London, 1671); Arnoldus Montanus, *Atlas Japannensis: Being Remarkable Addresses by Way of Embassy from the East-India Company of the United Provinces to the Emperor of Japan*, trans. John Ogilby (London, 1670).
25. [Defoe], *Atlas Maritimus*, 200.
26. On Ferreira, see Hubert Cieslik, "The Case of Christovão Ferreira," *Monumenta Nipponica* 29 (1974), 1–54; Elison, *Deus Destroyed*, 185–88; and Jacques Proust, *Europe through the Prism of Japan: Sixteenth to Eighteenth Centuries*, trans. Elizabeth Bell (Notre Dame: University of Notre Dame Press, 2002), 44–56.
27. Montanus, *Atlas Japannensis*, 357.
28. Montanus, *Atlas Japannensis*, 357–58.
29. Raymond D. Tumbleson, *Catholicism in the English Protestant Imagination: Nationalism, Religion, and Literature, 1660–1745* (Cambridge: Cambridge University Press, 1998).
30. Herman Moll, *A System of Geography: or a New and Accurate Description of the Earth*, 4th edn (London, 1723), II: 51. This work originally was published in 1721.
31. Ibid.
32. Gardiner, "Swift on the Dutch East India Merchants," 243–47.
33. Crasset, *History of the Church of Japan*, I: 5; I: 13. All quotations are from this edition.
34. On European conceptions of the purity of the Japanese language see, Annette Keogh, "Oriental Translations: Linguistic Explorations into the Closed Nation of Japan," *The Eighteenth Century: Theory and Interpretation* 45 (2004), 171–91.
35. See Paul van der Velde, "The Interpreter Interpreted: Kaempfer's Japanese Collaborator Imamura Genemon Eisei," in Bodart-Bailey and Massarella, eds., *The Furthest Goal: Engelbert Kaempfer's Encounter with Tokugawa Japan* (Folkestone, Kent: Japan Library, 1995), 44–70, and, in the same volume, Beatrice M. Bodart-Bailey, "Writing *The History of Japan*," 17–43, on Kaempfer's use of VOC sources. On Kaempfer's stay in Japan, see Detlef Haberland, *Engelbert Kaempfer, 1651–1716: A Biography*, trans. Peter Hogg (London: British Library, 1996), 65–82.
36. On the complexities of this term, see Julia Kristeva, *Powers of Horror: An Essay on Abjection*, trans. Leon S. Roudiez (New York: Columbia University Press, 1982).
37. See Derek Massarella, "The History of *The History*: The Purchase and Publication of Engelbert Kaempfer's *The History of Japan*," in Bodart-Bailey

and Massarella, eds., *The Furthest Goal*, 96–131. See J. Leeds Barroll, "Gulliver in Luggnagg: A Possible Source," *Philological Quarterly* 36 (1957), 504–08, and, on Swift's friendship with Carteret, Irvin Ehrenpreis, *Swift: The Man, His Works, and the Age*, 3 vols. (London: Methuen, 1962–83), III: 437.

38. See Johnson, Muncharu, and Williams, *Gullivers Travels and Japan*.

39. Herbert Davis, ed., *Gullivers Travels*, in *Prose Works of Jonathan Swift* 14 vols. (Oxford: Shakespeare's Head Press, 1941), XI: 138. All quotations are from this edition.

40. Swift, *Conduct of the Allies* (1711) in *Political Tracts 1711–1713*, vol. VI of *Prose Works of Jonathan Swift*, ed. Herbert Davis (Oxford: Basil Blackwell, 1939–68), 15.

41. Jeremy Black, *Parliament and Foreign Policy in the Eighteenth Century* (Cambridge: Cambridge University Press, 2004), 34: see Davis, *Prose Works of Swift*, XVI: 480–82.

42. *Some Remarks on the Barrier Treaty* (1712), in Davis, *Prose Works of Swift*, VI: 97. On Swift's anti-Dutch attitudes, see Ian Higgins, *Swift's Politics: A Study in Disaffection* (Cambridge: Cambridge University Press, 1994), 183–90.

43. Barroll, "Gulliver in Luggnagg," 504–08.

44. See Massarella, *A World Elsewhere: Europe's Encounter with Japan*, 71–130, and Giles Milton, *Samurai William*, 106–14; 291–97. Invariably, the English refer to the Shogun they meet (whether Ieyasu, Hidetaka, or Iemitsu) as "the Emperor."

45. On the politics of diplomatic gift-giving, see Cynthia Klekar, "'Prisoners in Silken Bonds': Obligation and Diplomacy in English Voyages to Japan and China," *Journal for Early Modern Cultural Studies* 6 (2006).

46. John Saris, *The First Voyage of the English to Japan*, ed. Takanobu Otsuka (Tokyo: Toyo Bunko [The Oriental Library], 1941), 184. On the different manuscripts of Saris's account, see Otsuka's introduction, vii–xix. European audiences with the Shogun are reprinted in Michael Cooper, ed., *They Came to Japan: An Anthology of European Reports on Japan, 1543–1640* (Berkeley: University of California Press, 1965), 109–27.

47. See Giles Milton, *Samurai William*, 194–97.

48. On pethood, see Srinivas Aravamudan's discussion of Aphra Behn's Oroonoko in *Tropicopolitans*, 33–49.

49. Keogh, "Oriental Translations: Linguistic Explorations into the Closed Nation of Japan 171–91."

50. Although Kaempfer's love-song was not included in the original 1727 edition, it is published in the modern translation of his *History* by Beatrice Bodart-Bailey, *Kaempfer's Japan: Tokugawa Culture Observed* (Honolulu: University of Hawaii Press, 1999). See also Bodart-Bailey, "Kaempfer Restor'd," *Monumenta Nipponica* 43 (1988), 1–33.

Epilogue: The ideology of trade

In 1745, a consortium of eight booksellers published a revised and enlarged edition of John Harris's 1704 collection, *Navigantium atque Itinerantium Biblioteca*. In his dedication to "The Merchants of Great Britain," the editor, John Campbell, reiterates a view of international trade that dates back in England almost two centuries: "To Commerce we owe our Wealth; for though Labor may improve, though Arms may extend, yet Commerce only can enrich a Country."[1] Well into the eighteenth century, atlases, geographies, collections, and compilations devoted far more space to Asia than they did to the Americas, and Campbell's updated edition of *Navigantium atque Itinerantium Biblioteca* reveals the extent to which the lure of trade to the Far East continued to dominate conceptions of international commerce. Tellingly, the longest volume in the collection (615 pages) is devoted to "the Discovery, Settlement, and Commerce of the East-Indies," and Campbell introduces it by telling his readers that "there are few Subjects more instructive, or more entertaining, than that of the History of the *Indies*, or which have exercised the Pens of more able Men" (I: 369). These "able Men" seem to have been much less interested in the West Indies: only 187 pages deal with English, French, and Dutch discoveries, settlements, and commerce in North America. In addition, one of the five sections devoted to European travel actually concerns the fruitless quest for the Northwest Passage through Hudson Bay and into the Pacific (79 pages). "If ever a Passage could be this Way found into the South Seas," Campbell claims, "we might, very probably, reach, in six Weeks, Countries that we cannot now visit in twelve or fifteen Months" (II: 399).[2] Even this quixotic, if often tragic quest, had as its goal those countries that fired the imaginations of Milton, Dryden, and Defoe. In addition to providing a shortcut to Japan, the Northwest Passage "would give us a much more facile Passage . . . to those Parts of the *East Indies*, with which we have no Correspondence, and consequently would, in that respect, be absolutely a new Branch of Commerce, probably of much greater Benefit to this Nation, than the whole of our *East India* Trade, as it is now carried on." Only a decade before the Battle of Plessy, the East Indies remain a far more appealing goal than India, and the possibility of opening trade to new lands and new markets continues to provoke booksellers into investing "very great Expence and Labour" in efforts to capitalize on a dream two centuries old.

In editing hundreds of texts into "a natural and easy Order" and "regular Progression," Campbell transforms miscellaneous accounts of commercial voyages into a narrative of the history of trade and commerce since biblical times. He adapts the genre of universal history to a commercial ideology – an ideology at once both providentialist and progressivist. Unlike earlier compendia of travels, Campbell includes only accounts written by merchants or early explorers; although Ides's mission is featured prominently, all of the Jesuit accounts of the Middle Kingdom are omitted. Even as trade is accommodated to traditional systems of inheritance and the transmission of property, it becomes a kind of absolute measure of the progress of nations and peoples toward an idealized state of prosperity, liberty, and "the equal and just Distribution of Property." Campbell reasserts truisms that had been current since Elizabeth wrote to the Sultan of Aceh: "the greatest Differences between Nations, arise chiefly from the Degrees, and Nature of their Commerce, and according as it is, either little or large, extended or confined; the People are Civilized or Rude, Rich or Poor, Powerful or Weak, Brave or Base, and finally, Free or Slaves." The diffusion of wealth means that "the Evils created by Trade, are corrected by Trade," a phrasing that suggests – with the objectivity of an economic law – that the principles of international commerce are true transhistorically and transculturally. The wealth pouring in from the importation and re-exportation of the luxuries of the Far East underwrites Campbell's efforts to finesse, if not reconcile, the tensions between progressivist views of history and fears that the world either cycles through epochs of prosperity and corruption or is locked into a process of irreversible decline. In this context, international trade offers a means to transcend the theological identification of sin and scarcity and to displace anxieties about diminishing returns, higher prices, and environmental degradation. Since trade continues to be promoted as the be-all and end-all for judging the morality and progress of nations, those countries that refuse to trade must be either ignored or explained away: there are no accounts of Japan in the collection. It is as though the previous history of failed Christian conversion in that empire no longer can be factored into the calculus of international trade.

The second half of the eighteenth century frequently is described as a watershed in terms of both European disillusionment with Chinese civilization and the fascination with *chinoiserie*, the luxury items that figured prominently in patterns of elite consumption in western Europe.[3] This book ends with Defoe and Swift, before the outpouring of literature from the 1740s on. The names that figure prominently in the history of European perceptions of China and the Far East in the eighteenth and nineteenth centuries are, for many scholars, much more familiar than Peter Heylyn's or Alexander Hamilton's: George Anson, Voltaire, Arthur Murphy, Oliver Goldsmith, William Chambers, Abbé Raynal, William Robertson, and George Macartney. But Campbell's decision to reproduce voyage literature from the seventeenth and early eighteenth centuries should give pause to any scholars content to simplify the complex relations between western Europe and the Far East into a linear and progressivist narrative beginning in 1640, 1700, or even 1740. China still signifies for Raynal as it had for du Halde; Adam Smith perceives China's role in the world economy very differently from Karl Marx in the middle of the nineteenth century; and the more scholars explore the histories of China and even India in the eighteenth century, the more complex the narratives seem to become.[4] At the very least, in an age that has tried to lay claim to having invented or discovered globalization, it seems that a revisionist reading of writers from Anson and his ghostwriters to Marx and his followers is needed to shed light on the rise, progress, and discontents of the vexed ideologies of orientalism. But the subject of the East and the European imagination from 1740 to 1850 is too important to be tucked into an epilogue, and the heirs of Heylyn, Martini, and Defoe require a study of their own.

NOTES

1. John Harris, *Navigantium atque Itinerantium Biblioteca. Or a Complete Collection of Voyages and Travels Consisting of Above Six Hundred of the Most Authentic Writers ... Whether Published in English, Latin, French, Italian, Spanish, Portuguese, High and Low Dutch, or in any other European Language*, rev. edn [ed. John Campbell] (London, 1744–48). All quotations are from this edition.
2. On the continuing fascination with the Northwest Passage in the eighteenth century, see Glyn Williams, *Voyages of Delusion: The Quest for the Northwest Passage* (New Haven: Yale University Press, 2002).
3. See Maxine Berg and Helen Clifford, eds., *Consumers and Luxury: Consumer Culture in Europe 1650–1850* (Manchester: Manchester University Press, 1999); and Maxine Berg and Elizabeth Eger, eds., *Luxury in the Eighteenth Century: Debates, Desires and Delectable Goods* (New York: Palgrave, 2003); and Beth

Kowaleski-Wallace, "Tea, Gender, and Domesticity in Eighteenth-Century England," *Studies in Eighteenth-Century Culture* 23 (1994), 131–45.

4. See, for example, Hevia, *Cherishing Men from Afar*; and Jeng-Guo S. Chen, "The British View of Chinese Civilization and the Emergence of Class Consciousness," *The Eighteenth Century: Theory and Interpretation* 45 (2004), 193–205.

Bibliography

PRIMARY SOURCES

Acosta, Jose de. *The Naturall and Morall Historie of the East and West Indies.* Trans. Edward Grimstone. London, 1604.

Anon. *An Answere to the Hollanders Declaration, concerning the Occurents of the East Indies.* London, 1622.

Anon. *The Hollanders Declaration of the Affaires of the East Indies. Or a True Relation of That Which Passed in the Island of Banda, in the East Indies: In the Yeare of Our Lord God, 1621 and Before. Faithfully Translated According to the Dutch Copie.* Amsterdam, 1622.

Anon. *A True Declaration of the News that came out of the East-Indies . . . concerning a Conspiracy discovered in the Island of Amboyna, and the punishment following thereupon, according to the course of iustice, in March 1624, comprehended in a letter-missive; and sent from a friend in the Low-Countries, to a friend of note in England, for information of him in the truth of those passages.* N.p., 1624.

Anon. *An Account of Several Late Voyages & Discoveries to the South and North.* London, 1694.

Atlas Geographus: or, a Compleat System of Geography. Ancient and Modern. Containing What is of most Use in Bleau [sic], Varenius, Cellarius, Culverius, Brietius, Sanson, &c. With the Discoveries and Improvments of the Best Modern Authors to this Time. Illustrated with about 100 New MAPS, done from the latest Observations, by Herman Moll, Geographer; and many other CUTS by the best Artists. 5 vols. London, 1712[-17].

Barbon, Nicholas. *A Discourse of Trade.* London, 1690.

Barnard, John. *Theologico-Historicus, or the True Life of the Most Reverend Divine, and Excellent Historian Peter Heylyn.* London, 1683.

Betagh, William. *A Voyage Round the World.* London, 1728.

Blaeu, Joan. *Atlas Maior.* 11 vols. Amsterdam, 1662.

Botero, Giovanni. *The Travellers Breviat, or An Historicall Description of the Most Famous Kingdomes in the World.* Trans. Robert Johnson. London, 1601.

Bouvet, J[oachim]. *The History of Cang-Hy, the Present Emperour of China.* London, 1699.

Boyer, Abel. *The History of the Life and Reign of Queen Anne.* London, 1722.

Brand, Adam. *A Journal of an Embassy from their Majesties John and Peter Alexowits, Emperors of Muscovy into China.* London, 1698.

Careri, Francis Gemelli, *A Voyage Round the World.* In Awnsham and John Churchill, comp. *A Collection of Voyages and Travels, Some Now First Printed from Original Manuscripts. Others Translated out of Foreign Languages.* 4 vols. London, 1704–05, IV: 1–605.

Caron, François and Joost Schorten, *A Description of the Mighty Kingdoms of Japan and Siam.* Trans. Roger Manley. London, 1671.

Chambers, Sir William. *A Dissertation on Oriental Gardening.* London, 1772.

Child, Sir Josiah. *A Treatise Wherein is Demonstrated . . . that the East-India Trade is the Most National of All Trades.* London, 1681.

Churchill, Awnsham and John, eds. *A Collection of Voyages and Travels, Some Now First Printed from Original Manuscripts. Others Translated out of Foreign Languages.* 4 vols. London, 1704–05.

Crasset, Jean. *The History of the Church of Japan.* Trans. N. N. 2 vols. London, 1705 [vol. I], 1707 [vol. II].

Dampier, William. *A New Voyage Round the World.* London, 1697.

　　A Voyage to New Holland: The English Voyage of Discovery to the South Seas in 1699. Ed. James Spencer. London: Alan Sutton, 1981.

　　A Collection of Voyages. 4 vols. London, 1729.

[Dapper, Olfert]. *Atlas Chinensis: Being a Second Part of a Relation of Remarkable Passages in Two Embassies from the East-India Company of the United Provinces, to the Vice-Roy Singlamong and General Taising Lipovi, and to Konchi, Emperor of China and East-Tartary.* Trans. John Ogilby. London, 1671.

Darrell, John. *A True and Compendious Narration; Or (the Second Part of Amboyna) of Sundry Notorious or Remarkable Injuries, Insolences, and Acts of Hostility which the HOLLANDERS Have Exercised from Time to Time against THE ENGLISH NATION in the East Indies.* London, 1665.

d'Avity, Pierre. *The Estates, Empires, & Principalities of the World.* Trans. Edward Grimstone. London, 1615.

Defoe, Daniel. *Review of the State of the English Nation*, 9 vols. London, 1704–13.

　　The Consolidator. London, 1705.

　　Essay on the South Sea Trade. London, 1711.

　　A Brief Account of the Present State of the African Trade. London, 1713.

　　Vindication of the Press. London, 1718.

　　Captain Singleton. London, 1720.

　　The Farther Adventures of Robinson Crusoe. 1720. New York: Peebles Classics, 1927.

　　Serious Reflections during the Life and Surprising Adventures of Robinson Crusoe. Intro. G. H. Maynadier. 1721. Boston: Beacon Classics, 1903.

　　A New Voyage round the World by a Course Never Sailed Before. 1724. Ed. George A. Aitkin. London: Dent, 1902.

　　Atlas Maritimus & Commercialis; or a General View of the World . . . London, 1728.

　　The Complete English Tradesman. New York: Alan Sutton, 1987.

Digges, Dudley. *The Answer unto the Dutch Pamphlet, Made in Defence of the Uniust and Barbarous Proceedings against the English at Amboyna in the East-Indies, by the Hollanders there.* London, 1624.

   A True Relation of the Vniust, Cruell, and Barbarous Proceedings against the English at Amboyna. London, 1624.

Dryden, John. *Dryden: The Dramatic Works.* Ed. Montague Summers. 1932. 3 vols. Rpt. New York: Gordian Press, 1968.

   The Works of John Dryden, vol. 1: *Poems, 1649–80.* Ed. Edward Niles Hooker and H. T. Swedenberg, Jr. Berkeley and Los Angeles: University of California Press, 1956.

du Halde, Jean Baptiste. *The General History of China.* 4 vols. London, 1736.

Eden, Richard. Newly Set in Order, Augmented, and Finished by Richarde Willes. *The History of Trauayle.* London, 1577.

Evelyn, John. *Navigation and Commerce, Their Original and Progress.* London, 1674.

Exquemelin, A. O. *Bucaniers of America . . . Inlarged with two Additional Relations, viz. The One of Captain Cook, and the Other of Captain Sharp.* London, 1684.

Ferguson, Robert. *The East-India Trade a Most Profitable Trade to the Kingdom. And Best Secured and Improved in a Company and a Joint-Stock.* London, 1677.

Forster, John Reinhold. *Observations Made during a Voyage Round the World on Physical Geography, Natural History, and Ethic Philosophy.* London, 1778.

Frézier, A. F. *A Voyage to the South-Sea, and Along the Coasts of Chili and Peru.* London, 1717.

Funnell, William. *A Voyage round the World.* London, 1707.

Gallagher, Louis, S. J., ed. *China in the Sixteenth Century: The Journals of Matthew Ricci 1583–1610.* New York: Random House, 1953.

Goodman, Godfrey. *The Fall of Man: Or the Corruption of Nature.* London, 1616.

Hacke, William, ed. *A Collection of Original Voyages.* London, 1699.

Hakluyt, Richard. *The Principall Navigations, Voiages & Discoveries of the English Nation.* London, 1598–1600.

Hale, Matthew. *The Primitive Origination of Mankind, Considered and Examined According to the Light of Nature.* London, 1677.

Hamilton, Alexander. *A New Account of the East Indies.* 2 vols. Edinburgh, 1727.

Harris, John. *Navigantium atque Itinerantium Biblioteca. Or a Complete Collection of Voyages and Travels Consisting of Above Six Hundred of the Most Authentic Writers . . . Whether Published in English, Latin, French, Italian, Spanish, Portuguese, High and Low Dutch, or in any other European Language.* Rev. edn [by John Campbell]. London, 1744–48.

Heylyn, Peter. *Microcosmos: Or, A Little Description of the Great World.* 1621. 2nd edn. Oxford, 1625.

   Cosmographie. 2nd edn. London, 1657.

Horn, Georg. *Arcae Noae sive historia imperiorum et regnorum a condito orbe ad nostra temporum.* Leiden, 1666.

Howse, Derek and Northan Thrower, eds. *A Buccaneer's Atlas: Basil Ringrose's South Sea.* Berkeley and Los Angeles: University of California Press, 1992.

Hume, David. *A Treatise of Human Nature*. Ed. David Fate Norton and Mary Norton. New York: Oxford University Press, 2000.

Ides, Evret Ysbrants. *Three Years Travels from Moscow Over-Land to China*. London, 1706.

Isaacson, Henry. *Saturni Ephemerides*. London, 1633.

Kaempfer, Engelbert. *The History of Japan*. Trans. J. G. Scheuchzer, FRS. London, 1727.

Kircher, Athanasius. *China Illustrata*. Amsterdam, 1667.

La Peyrere, Isaac. *A Theological Systeme upon that Presupposition That Men were before Adam*. London, 1655.

 Men Before Adam. London, 1656.

LeClerc, Jean. *Compendium Historiae Universalis: A Compendium of Universal History from the Beginning of the World to the Reign of Charles the Great*. London, 1699.

Le Comte, Louis. *Nouveaux mémoires sur l'état présent de la Chine*. 3 vols. Paris, 1696–98.

 Memoirs and Observations Topographical, Physical, Mathematical, Natural, Civil, and Ecclesiastical, Made in a Late Journey through the Empire of China. London, 1697.

Linschoten, Jan van. *Iohn Huighen van Linschoten his Discours of Voyages into ye Easte and West Indies*. London, 1598.

Lockyer, Charles. *An Account of the Trade in India*. London, 1711.

Magaillans [Magalhães], Gabriel. *A New History of China*. London, 1688.

Malynes, Gerald. *Consuetudo vel Lex Mercatoria, or the Ancient Law-Merchant*. London, 1629.

Martin, François. *Description du Premier Voyage Facit aux Indes Orientales par les François en l'an 1603*. Paris, 1604.

Martini, Martinus. *Sinicae Historiae Decas Prima, Res a Gentis Origine ad Christum Natum in Extrema Asia, sive Magno Sinarum Imperio Gestas Complexa*. Amsterdam, 1659.

 De Bello Tartarico Historia. Amsterdam, 1655.

 Novus Atlas Siensis. Amsterdam, 1655. Published as vol. XI of Joan Blaeu's *Atlas Maior*.

Mendoza, Gonzalez de. *The Historie of the Great and Mightie Kingdome of China, and the Situation Thereof: Togither with the Great Riches, Huge Cities, Politike Gouernement, and Rare Inuentions in the Same*. Trans. R[obert] Parke. London, 1588.

Mendoza, Juan de Palafox y. *The History of the Conquest of China by the Tartars*. London, 1671.

Milton, John. *Works of John Milton*. Ed. Frank Allen Patterson *et al*. 18 vols. New York: Columbia University Press, 1931–38.

 The Complete Poetical Works of John Milton. Ed. Harris Francis Fletcher. New York: Houghton Mifflin, 1941.

 Complete Prose Works of John Milton. Ed. Don M. Wolfe. 8 vols. New Haven: Yale University Press, 1953–82.

Paradise Lost. Ed. Merritt Y. Hughes. New York: Odyssey Press, 1962.

Miscellanea Curiosa. Containing a Collection of Curious Travels, Voyages, and Natural Histories of Countries, as They Have Been Delivered to the Royal Society. Vol. III. 2nd edn. Ed. W. Derham, F.R.S. London, 1727.

Moll, Herman. *A View of the Coasts, Countrys, & Islands within the Limits of the South-Sea Company.* London, 1711.

[Moll, Herman]. *Atlas Geographus.* 5 vols. London, 1712–17.

A System of Geography: or a New and Accurate Description of the Earth, in all its Empires, Kingdoms and States. Illustrated with History and Topography and Maps of Every Country, Fairly Engraven on Copper, according to the latest Discoveries and Corrections. 4th edn. London, 1723.

The Compleat Geographer: or, the Chorography and Topography of all the Known Parts of the Earth. 4th edn. London, 1723.

Montanus, Arnoldus. *Atlas Japannensis: Being Remarkable Addresses by Way of Embassy from the East-India Company of the United Provinces to the Emperor of Japan.* Trans. John Ogilby. London, 1670.

Mun, Thomas. *A Discovrse of Trade, from England vnto the East-Indies: Answering to diuerse Obiections which are usually made against the same.* London, 1621.

England's Treasure by Forraign Trade. London, 1660.

Navarette, Domingo Fernandez. *An Account of the Empire of China, Historical, Political, Moral, and Religious.* In Awnsham and John Churchill, comp. *A Collection of Voyages and Travels, Some Now First Printed from Original Manuscripts.* 4 vols. London, 1704, I: 1–424. Translation of the first edition [Madrid, 1676].

Nieuhoff, Jan. *An Embassy from the East-India Company of the United Provinces, to the Grand Tartar Cham Emperour of China; Delivered by their Excellencies Peter de Goyer, and Jacobs de Keyzer, At his Imperial City of Peking.* Trans. John Ogilby. London, 1669.

Ogilby, John. *Asia, The First Part being An Accurate Description of Persia, and the Several Provinces thereof. The Vast Empire of the Great Mogol, and other Parts of India: and Their Several Kingdoms and Regions.* London, 1673.

Pinto, Fernão Mendes. *The Travels of Mendes Pinto.* Ed. Rebecca D. Catz. Chicago: University of Chicago Press, 1989.

Purchas, Samuel. *Purchas His Pilgrimmes.* 5 vols. London, 1625.

Quiros, Pedro Fernando de. *Terra Australis Incognita, or a New Southerne Discoverie, Containing a Fifth Part of the World.* London, 1617.

Ralegh, Sir Walter. *The History of the World.* London, 1614.

Ricci, Matteo. *China in the Sixteenth Century: The Journals of Matthew Ricci 1583–1610.* Ed. Louis J. Gallagher, S. J. New York: Random House, 1953.

Ringrose, Basil. *Bucaniers of America. The Second Volume Containing the Dangerous Voyage and Bold Attempts of Captain Bartholomew Sharp and Others; Performed upon the Coasts of the South Sea.* London, 1685.

Rogers, Woodes. *A Cruising Voyage Round the World.* London, 1712.

Saris, John. *The First Voyage of the English to Japan.* Ed. Takanobu Otsuka. Tokyo: Toyo Bunko [The Oriental Library], 1941.

Scott, Edmund. *An Exact Discourse of the Subtilties, Fashions, Religion and Ceremonies of the East Indians.* London, 1606.

Scott, Sir Walter, ed. *The Works of John Dryden.* Rev. edn. Ed. George Saintsbury. ed. Vol. v. Edinburgh: William Paterson, 1883.

Semedo, Alvarez. *The History of that Great and Renowned Monarchy of China.* London, 1655.

Senex, John. *A New General Atlas of the World.* London, 1721.

Settle, Elkannah. *The Conquest of China by the Tartars.* London, 1676.

Shelvocke, George. *A Voyage Round the World by Way of the Great South Sea.* London, 1726.

Sung Ying-Hsing. *Chinese Technology in the Seventeenth Century: T'ien-Kung K'ai-Wu.* Trans. E-Tu Zen Sun and Shiou-Chuan Sun. 1966; rpt. New York: Dover, 1997.

Swift, Jonathan. *Prose Works of Jonathan Swift.* 14 vols. Ed. Herbert Davis. Oxford: Basil Blackwell, 1938–51.
  The Correspondence of Jonathan Swift. Ed. Harold Williams. Oxford: Clarendon Press, 1963.

Tallents, Francis. *A View of Universal History.* London, 1695.

Temple, Sir William. "An Essay Upon Ancient and Modern Learning." *Miscellanea. The Second Part. In Four Essays.* London, 1690.
  Miscellanea. The Third Part. London, 1701.

Thomas, Pascoe. *A True and Impartial Journal of a Voyage to the South Seas.* London, 1745.

Toland, John. *Propositions for Uniting the Two East-India Companies.* London, 1701.
  The Destiny of Rome, or the Probability of the Speedy and Final Destruction of the Pope. London, 1718.
  A Collection of Several Pieces of Mr. John Toland. 2 vols. London, 1726.

Vernon, George. *The Life of the Learned and Reverend Dr. Peter Heylyn.* London, 1682.

Vossius, Gerard. *De Theologia Gentili et Physiologia Christiana.* 1641. Rpt. New York: Garland, 1976.

Vossius, Isaac. *Dissertatio de vera aetate mundi, qua ostenditur Natale mundi tempus annis minimum 1400 vulgarem aeram anticipare.* The Hague, 1659.

[Walter, Richard and Benjamin Robins]. *A Voyage Round the World, in the Years MDCCXL, I, II, III, IV.* By George Anson, Esq. London, 1748.

Webb, John. *An Historical Essay Endeavoring a Probability That the Language of the Empire of China is the Primitive Language.* London, 1669.

Welbe, John. *An Answer to Captain Dampier's Vindication.* London, 1707.

Wotton, William. *Reflections upon Ancient and Modern Learning.* 2nd edn. London, 1697.
  A Defense of the Reflections upon Ancient and Modern Learning. London, 1705.

SECONDARY SOURCES

Abu-Lughod, Janet. *Before European Hegemony: The World System A.D. 1250–1350.* New York: Oxford University Press, 1989.

Achinstein, Sharon. *Literature and Dissent in Milton's England*. Cambridge: Cambridge University Press, 2003.

Adams, Percy. *Travel Literature and the Evolution of the Novel*. Lexington: University of Kentucky Press, 1983.

Adas, Michael. *Machines as the Measure of Men: Science, Technology, and Ideologies of Western Dominance*. Ithaca: Cornell University Press, 1989.

Adshead, S. A. M. *Material Culture in Europe and China, 1400–1800: The Rise of Consumerism*. London: Palgrave, 1997.

Alkon, Paul. *Defoe and Fictional Time*. Athens: University of Georgia Press, 1979.

Amorose, Thomas. "Milton the Apocalyptic Historian: Competing Genres in *Paradise Lost*, Books XI–XII." In *Milton Studies 17*, ed. Richard S. Ide and Joseph Wittreich. Pittsburgh: University of Pittsburgh Press, 1983, 141–62.

Andaya, Barbara Watson. "Cash Cropping and Upstream–Downstream Tensions: The Case of Jambi in the Seventeenth and Eighteenth Centuries." In *Southeast Asia in the Early Modern Era: Trade, Power, and Belief*. Ithaca: Cornell University Press, 1993, 91–122.

Andaya, Leonard Y. "Interactions with the Outside World and Adaptation in Southeast Asian Society, 1500–1800." In *The Cambridge History of Southeast Asia*. Vol. 1 *From Early Times to c. 1800*. Ed. Nicholas Tarling. Cambridge: Cambridge University Press, 1992, 345–401.

"Cultural State Formation in Eastern Indonesia." In Anthony Reid, ed., *Southeast Asia in the Early Modern Era: Trade, Power, and Belief*. Ithaca: Cornell University Press, 1993, 23–41.

Anderson, Benedict. *Imagined Communities: Reflections on the Origin and Spread of Nationalism*, rev. edn. London: Verso, 1991.

Andrea, Bernadette. "Columbus in Istanbul: Ottoman Mapping of the 'New World.'" *Genre* 30 (1997), 135–65.

Andrews, Kenneth R. *Trade, Plunder and Settlement: Maritime Enterprise and the Genesis of the British Empire, 1480–1630*. Cambridge: Cambridge University Press, 1984.

Appleby, Joyce Oldham. *Economic Thought and Ideology in Seventeenth-Century England*. Princeton: Princeton University Press, 1978.

Arasaratnam, Sinnappah. *Maritime Trade, Society and the European Influence in Southern Asia, 1600–1800*. Aldershot: Variorum, 1995.

Aravamudan, Srinivas. "In the Wake of the Novel: The Oriental Tale as National Allegory." *Novel* 33 (1999), 5–31.

Tropicopolitans: Colonialism and Agency, 1688–1804. Durham: Duke University Press, 1999.

Archer, John Michael. *Old Worlds: Egypt, Southwest Asia, India, and Russia in Early Modern English Writing*. Stanford: Stanford University Press, 2001.

Arditi, Jorge. *A Genealogy of Manners: Transformations of Social Relations in France and England from the Fourteenth to the Eighteenth Century*. Chicago: University of Chicago Press, 1998.

Armitage, David. *The Ideological Origins of the British Empire*. Cambridge: Cambridge University Press, 2000.

Armstrong, Nancy. *Desire and Domestic Fiction: A Political History of the Novel.* New York: Oxford University Press, 1987.

Armstrong, Nancy and Leonard Tennenhouse. *The Imaginary Puritan: Literature, Intellectual Labor, and the Origins of Personal Life.* Berkeley and Los Angeles: University of California Press, 1992.

Armstrong, Terrence. "Russian Penetration into Siberia up to 1800." In Cecil H. Clough and P. E. H. Hair, eds., *The European Outthrust and Encounter.* Liverpool: Liverpool University Press, 1994, 119–40.

Ashworth, William J. *Customs and Excise: Trade, Production, and Consumption in England 1640–1845.* Oxford: Oxford University Press, 2003.

Attwater, Rachel. *Adam Schall: A Jesuit at the Court of China 1592–1666.* London: Geoffrey Chapman, 1963.

Azim, Firdous. *The Colonial Rise of the Novel.* New York: Routledge, 1993.

Backscheider, Paula. *Daniel Defoe: Ambition and Innovation.* Lexington: University of Kentucky Press, 1986.

   Daniel Defoe: His Life. Baltimore: Johns Hopkins University Press, 1989.

Bairoch, Paul. *Economics and World History: Myths and Paradoxes.* Hemel Hempstead: Harvester/Wheatsheaf, 1993.

Banerjee, Pompa. "Milton's India and *Paradise Lost.*" *Milton Studies* 37 (1999), 142–65.

Barfield, Thomas J. *The Perilous Frontier: Nomadic Empires and China, 221 BC to AD 1757.* Oxford: Blackwell, 1989.

   "The Shadow Empires: Imperial State Formation along the Chinese–Nomad Frontier." In Susan E. Alcock, Terrence N. D'Altroy, Kathleen D. Morrison, and Carla M. Sinopoli, eds., *Empires: Perspectives from Archaeology and History.* Cambridge: Cambridge University Press, 2001, 10–41.

Barroll, J. Leeds. "Gulliver in Luggnagg: A Possible Source." *Philological Quarterly* 36 (1957), 504–08.

Bartlett, Beatrice S. *Monarchs and Ministers: The Grand Council in Mid Ch'ing China, 1723–1820.* Berkeley: University of California Press, 1991.

Beaglehole, J. C. *The Exploration of the Pacific.* 3rd edn. Stanford: Stanford University Press, 1966.

Berg, Maxine and Helen Clifford, eds. *Consumers and Luxury: Consumer Culture in Europe 1650–1850.* Manchester: Manchester University Press, 1999.

Berg, Maxine and Elizabeth Eger, eds. *Luxury in the Eighteenth Century: Debates, Desires and Delectable Goods.* New York: Palgrave, 2003.

Berry, Mary Elizabeth. *Hideyoshi.* Cambridge, MA: Harvard University Press, 1982.

Bhattacharya, Nandini. *Reading the Splendid Body: Gender and Consumerism in Eighteenth-Century British Writing on India.* Newark: University of Delaware Press, 1998.

   "James Cobbs, Colonial Cacophony, and the Enlightenment." *Studies in English Literature 1500–1900* 41 (2001), 583–603.

Billings, Timothy. "Visible Cities: The Heterotropic Utopia of China in Early Modern European Writing." *Genre* 30 (1997), 105–34.

Bin Wong, R. *China Transformed: Historical Change and the Limits of European Experience.* Ithaca: Cornell University Press, 1997.

Bindman, David. *Ape to Apollo: Aesthetics and the Idea of Race in the Eighteenth Century.* Ithaca: Cornell University Press, 2002.

Black, Jeremy. *European Warfare 1660–1815.* New Haven: Yale University Press, 1994.
    Parliament and Foreign Policy in the Eighteenth Century. Cambridge: Cambridge University Press, 2004.

Blackmore, Josiah. *Shipwreck Narrative and the Disruption of Empire.* Minneapolis: University of Minnesota Press, 2002.

Blaut, J. M. *The Colonizer's Model of the World: Geographical Diffusionism and Eurocentric History.* New York: Guilford Press, 1993.

Boardman, Michael. *Defoe and the Uses of Narrative.* New Brunswick: Rutgers University Press, 1983.

Bodart-Bailey, Beatrice M. "Kaempfer Restored." *Monumenta Nipponica* 43 (1988), 1–33.

Bodart-Bailey, Beatrice M., ed. *Kaempfer's Japan: Tokugawa Culture Observed.* Honolulu: University of Hawai'i Press, 1999.

Bodart-Bailey, Beatrice M. and Derek Massarella, eds. *The Furthest Goal: Engelbert Kaempfer's Encounter with Tokugawa Japan.* Folkestone, Kent: Japan Library, 1995.

Boxer, C. R. *The Christian Century in Japan: 1549–1650.* Berkeley and Los Angeles: University of California Press, 1951.
    "A Note on Portuguese Reactions to the Revival of the Red Sea Spice Trade and the Rise of Acheh, 1540–1600." *Journal of Southeast Asian History* 10 (1969), 416–19.
    The Anglo-Dutch Wars of the 17th Century, 1652–1674. London: National Maritime Museum, 1974.
    The Dutch Seaborne Empire 1600–1800. 1965; rpt. London: Hutchinson, 1977.
    Jan Compagnie in War and Peace 1602–1799: A Short History of the Dutch East-India Company. Hong Kong: Heinemann Asia, 1979.

Boyle, Frank. *Swift as Nemesis: Modernity and its Satirist.* Stanford: Stanford University Press, 2000.

Bradley, Peter T. *The Lure of Peru: Maritime Intrusions into the South Sea.* New York: St. Martin's Press, 1989.

Brantlinger, Patrick. *Fictions of State: Culture and Credit in Britain, 1694–1994.* Ithaca: Cornell University Press, 1996.

Braudel, Fernand. *Civilization and Capitalism: 15th–18th Century.* Vol. II. *The Wheels of Commerce.* Trans. Sian Reynolds. Berkeley and Los Angeles: University of California Press, 1982.
    Civilization and Capitalism 15th–18th Century. Vol. III. *The Perspective of the World.* Berkeley and Los Angeles: University of California Press, 1992.

Bray, Francesca. *Technology and Gender: Fabrics of Power in Late Imperial China.* Berkeley: University of California Press, 1997.
    "Technics and Civilization in Late Imperial China: An Essay in the Cultural History of Technology." In *Beyond Joseph Needham: Science, Technology, and*

Medicine in East and Southeast Asia. Ed. Morris F. Law, *Osiris,* second series 13 (1998), 11–33.

Brenner, Robert. *Merchants and Revolution: Commercial Change, Political Conflicts, and London's Overseas Traders, 1550–1633.* Cambridge: Cambridge University Press, 1993.

Brewer, John. *The Sinews of Power: War, Money and the English State, 1688–1783.* Cambridge, MA: Harvard University Press, 1990.

Brook, Timothy. *The Confusions of Pleasure: A History of Ming China (1368–1644).* Berkeley and Los Angeles: University of California Press, 1998.

Brotton, Jerry. *Trading Territories: Mapping the Early Modern World.* Ithaca: Cornell University Press, 1998.

Brown, Laura. *Ends of Empire: Women and Ideology in Early Eighteenth-Century English Literature.* Ithaca: Cornell University Press, 1993.

"Dryden and the Imperial Imagination." In *The Cambridge Companion to John Dryden.* Ed. Steven N. Zwicker. Cambridge: Cambridge University Press, 2004.

Bryson, Anna. *From Courtesy to Civility: Changing Codes of Conduct in Early Modern England.* Oxford: Clarendon Press, 1998.

Buck-Morss, Susan. "Envisioning Capital: Political Economy on Display." *Critical Inquiry* 21 (1995), 434–67.

Burton, Jonathan. "English Anxiety and the Muslim Power of Conversion: Five Perspectives on 'Turning Turk' in Early Modern Texts." *Journal for Early Modern Cultural Studies* 2 (2002), 35–67.

Traffic and Turning: Commerce, Conversion, and Islam in English Drama. Newark: Delaware University Press, 2005.

Calder, Alex, Jonathan Lamb, and Bridget Orr, eds. *Voyages and Beaches: Pacific Encounters, 1769–1840.* Honolulu: University of Hawai'i Press, 2000.

Carswell, John. *The South Sea Bubble.* Stanford: Stanford University Press, 1960.

Catz, Rebecca. "The Portuguese in the Far East." In Cecil H. Clough and P. E. H. Hair, eds., *The European Outthrust and Encounter.* Liverpool: Liverpool University Press, 1994, 97–117.

Cavanaugh, Michael. "A Meeting of Epic and History: Books XI and XII of *Paradise Lost.*" *English Literary History* 38 (1971), 206–22.

Cawley, Robert Ralston. *Milton and the Literature of Travel.* Princeton: Princeton University Press, 1951.

Chancellor, Edward. *Devil Take the Hindmost: A History of Financial Speculation.* New York: Farrar, Strauss, Giroux, 1999.

Chaudhuri, K. N. *The English East India Company: A Study of an Early Joint Stock Company, 1600–1640.* New York: Kelley, 1965.

Asia before Europe: Economy and Civilisation of the Indian Ocean from the Rise of Islam to 1750. Cambridge: Cambridge University Press, 1990.

"The English East India Company in the 17th and Early 18th Centuries: A Pre-Modern Multinational Organization." In *The Organization of Interoceanic Trade in European Expansion, 1450–1800.* Ed. Pieter Emmer and Femme Gaastra. Aldershot, Hampshire: Variorum, 1996, 187–204.

Chen, Jeng-Guo S. "The British View of Chinese Civilization and the Emergence of Class Consciousness." *The Eighteenth Century: Theory and Interpretation* 45 (2004), 193–205.

Chen Yuan. "A Study of the Israelite Religion in Kaifeng." In *Jews in Old China: Studies by Chinese Scholars*. Rev. edn, ed. and trans. Sidney Shapiro. New York: Hippocrene Books, 2001, 15–45.

Ching, Julia and Willard Oxtoby, eds. *Discovering China: European Interpretations in the Enlightenment*. Rochester, NY: Rochester University Press, 1992.

Cieslik, Hubert. "The Case of Christovão Ferreira." *Monumenta Nipponica* 29 (1974), 1–54.

Clark, Gregory, Michael Huberman, and Peter H. Lindert. "A British Food Puzzle, 1770–1850." *Economic History Review* 48 (1995), 215–37.

Clay, C. G. A. *Economic Expansion and Social Change: England 1500–1700*. 2 vols. Cambridge: Cambridge University Press, 1984.

Coffey, John. "Pacifist, Quietist, or Patient Militant? John Milton and the Restoration." *Milton Studies* 42 (2002), 149–74.

Cohn, Bernard S. *Colonialism and Its Forms of Knowledge: The British in India*. Princeton: Princeton University Press, 1996.

Colley, Linda. *Britons: Forging the Nation 1707–1837*. New Haven: Yale University Press, 1992.

Cook, Daniel J. and Henry Rosemont, Jr. "The Pre-established Harmony between Leibniz and Chinese Thought." *Journal of the History of Ideas* 42 (1981), 253–67.

Cooper, Michael, ed. *They Came to Japan: An Anthology of European Reports*. London: Thames and Hudson, 1965.

This Island of Japan. New York and Tokyo: Kodansha, 1973.

Crosby, Alfred W. *Ecological Imperialism: The Biological Expansion of Europe, 900–1900*. New York: Cambridge University Press, 1986.

The Measure of Reality: Quantification and Western Society. Cambridge: Cambridge University Press, 1997.

Crossley, Pamela Kyle. "Thinking about Ethnicity in Early Modern China." *Late Imperial China* 11 (1990), 1–34.

A Translucent Mirror: History and Identity in Qing Imperial Ideology. Berkeley: University of California Press, 1999.

Crouzet, François. *A History of the European Economy, 1000–2000*. Charlottesville: University Press of Virginia, 2001.

Crumley, Carole. "Historical Ecology: A Multidimensional Ecological Orientation." In *Historical Ecology: Cultural Knowledge and Changing Landscapes*, ed. Carole Crumley. Santa Fe: School of American Research Press, 1994, 1–11.

Curtin, Philip D. *Cross-Cultural Trade in World History*. Cambridge: Cambridge University Press, 1984.

Dalporto, Jeannie. "The Succession Crisis and Elkanah Settle's *The Conquest of China by the Tartars*." *The Eighteenth Century: Theory and Interpretation* 45 (2004), 131–46.

Das, Harihar. *The Norris Embassy to Aurangzib (1699–1702)*. Calcutta: K. L. Mukhopadhyay, 1959.

Dash, Mike. *Batavia's Graveyard*. New York: Crown, 2002.

Daunton, Martin and Rick Halpern, eds. *Empire and Others: British Encounters with Indigenous Peoples, 1600–1850*. Philadelphia: University of Pennsylvania Press, 1999.

Davis, James. *The Rise of the English Shipping Industry in the Seventeenth and Eighteenth Centuries*. London: Macmillan, 1962.

Davis, Mike. *Late Victorian Holocausts: El Niño Famines and the Making of the Third World*. London: Verso, 2001.

de Bary, William Theodore and Richard Lufrano, comps. *Sources of Chinese Tradition*. Second edn. Vol. II. New York: Columbia University Press, 2000.

Dening, Greg. *Performances*. Chicago: University of Chicago Press, 1996.

Derrida, Jacques. *Specters of Marx: The State of the Debt, the Work of Mourning, and the New International*. Trans. Peggy Kamuf. New York: Routledge, 1994.

Des Forges, Roger V. *Cultural Centrality and Political Change in Chinese History: Northeast Henan in the Fall of the Ming*. Stanford: Stanford University Press, 2003.

Dharwadker, Aparna. "Nation, Race, and the Ideology of Commerce in Defoe." *The Eighteenth Century: Theory and Interpretation* 39 (1998), 63–84.

Dobbs, Betty Jo Teeter. *The Janus Faces of Genius: The Role of Alchemy in Newton's Thought*. Cambridge: Cambridge University Press, 1992.

Dorn, Walter Louis. *Competition for Empire 1740–63*. 1940. Rpt. New York, 1963.

Duchesne, Ricardo. "Between Sinocentrism and Eurocentrism: Debating Andre Gunder Frank's *Reorient: Global Economy in the Asian Age*." *Science and Society* 65 (2001–02), 428–63.

Dunne, Gregory, S. J. *Generation of Giants: The Story of the Jesuits in China in the Last Decades of the Ming Dynasty*. Notre Dame: Notre Dame University Press, 1962.

Dunstan, Helen. *Conflicting Counsels to Confuse the Age: A Documentary Study of Political Economy in Qing China, 1644–1840*. Ann Arbor: Center for Chinese Studies, University of Michigan, 1996.

"Official Thinking on Environmental Issues and the State's Environmental Roles in Eighteenth-Century China." *Sediments of Time: Environment and Society in Chinese History*. Ed. Mark Elvin and Liu Ts'ui-jung. Cambridge: Cambridge University Press, 1998, 585–615.

Dussinger, John A. "Gulliver in Japan: Another Possible Source." *Notes and Queries* 39, n.s. (1992), 464–67.

Earle, Peter. *The World of Defoe*. New York: Athenaeum, 1977.

Edney, Matthew. "Cartography without Progress: Reinterpreting the Nature and Historical Development of Mapmaking." *Geographia* 30, 3 (1993), 54–68.

Edwards, Philip. *The Story of the Voyage: Sea-Narratives in Eighteenth-Century England*. Cambridge: Cambridge University Press, 1994.

Ehrenpreis, Irvin. *Swift: The Man, His Works, and the Age*. 3 vols. London: Methuen, 1962–83.

Eisler, William. *The Furthest Shore: Images of Terra Australis from the Middle Ages to Captain Cook*. Cambridge: Cambridge University Press, 1995.

Elison, George. *Deus Destroyed: The Image of Christianity in Early Modern Japan.* Cambridge, MA: Harvard University Press, 1973.

Ellis, Markman. "Crusoe, Cannibalism, and Empire." In *Robinson Crusoe: Myths and Metamorphoses.* Ed. Lieve Spaas and Brian Stimpson. New York: St. Martin's Press, 1996, 45–61.

Elvin, Mark. *The Pattern of the Chinese Past.* Stanford: Stanford University Press, 1973.

Enozawa, Kazuyoshi. "Missionaries' Dreams and Realities in the Land of Warriors – Some Problems in the Early Jesuit Missions to Japan, 1549–1579." *Hideyoshi Review of English Studies* 23 (1994), 54–73.

Farrington, Anthony. *The English Factory in Japan, 1613–23.* 2 vols. London: British Library, 1991.

  Trading Places: The East India Company and Asia 1600–1834. London: British Library, 2002.

Fausett, David. *Writing the New World: Imaginary Voyages and Utopias of the Great Southern Land.* Syracuse: Syracuse University Press, 1993.

Ferguson, Arthur B. *Utter Antiquity: Perceptions of Prehistory in Renaissance England.* Durham: Duke University Press, 1993.

Ferguson, Moira. *Subject to Others: British Women Writers and Colonial Slavery, 1670–1834.* New York: Routledge, 1992.

Fernández-Armesto, Felipe. *Civilizations: Culture, Ambition, and the Transformation of Nature.* New York: Free Press, 2001.

Finn, Margot C. *The Character of Credit: Personal Debt in Eighteenth-Century Culture.* Cambridge: Cambridge University Press, 2003.

Fischer, David Hackett. *The Great Wave: Price Revolutions and the Rhythm of History.* New York: Oxford University Press, 1996.

Fitzgerald, Robert. "Science and Politics in Swift's Voyage to Laputa." *Journal of English and Germanic Philology* 87 (1988), 213–29.

Fo Lu-shu, comp. and trans. *A Documentary Chronicle of Sino-Western Relations, 1644–1820.* 2 vols. Tucson: University of Arizona Press, 1966.

Foss, Theodore N. "A Western Interpretation of China: Jesuit Cartography." In *East Meets West: The Jesuits in China, 1582–1773.* Ed. Charles E. Ronan, S. J. and Bonnie B. C. Oh. Chicago: Loyola University Press, 1988, 209–51.

Foster, Sir William, ed. *The Voyage of Sir Henry Middleton to the Moluccas, 1604–06.* London: Hakluyt Society, 1943.

Foucault, Michel. *The Order of Things.* New York: Vintage, 1971.

  The History of Sexuality: An Introduction. Trans. Robert Hurley. New York: Pantheon, 1978.

  Discipline and Punish: The Birth of the Prison. Trans. Alan Sheridan. New York: Vintage, 1979.

Frank, Andre Gunder. *ReOrient: Global Economy in the Asian Age.* Berkeley and Los Angeles: University of California Press, 1997.

Free, Melissa. "Un-Erasing Crusoe: *Farther Adventures* in the Nineteenth Century," *Book History,* forthcoming.

Freedman, William. "Swift's Struldbruggs, Progress, and the Analogy of History." *Studies in English Literature 1500–1900* (1995), 457–72.

Frye, Northrup. *An Anatomy of Criticism*. Princeton: Princeton University Press, 1957.

Furber, Holden. *Rival Empires of Trade in the Orient, 1600–1800*. Minneapolis: University of Minnesota Press, 1976.

Galbraith, John Kenneth. *A Short History of Financial Euphoria*. New York: Whittle, 1990.

Gao Xiang. "On the Trends of Modernization in the Early Qing Period." *Social Sciences in China* 22, 4 (2001), 108–27.

Gardiner, Anne Barbeau. "Swift on the Dutch East India Merchants: The Context of the 1672–73 War Literature." *Huntington Library Quarterly* 54 (1991), 234–52.

Gernet, Jacques. *China and the Christian Impact: A Conflict of Cultures*. Trans. Janet Lloyd. Cambridge: Cambridge University Press, 1985.

Giersch, C. Pat. "'A Motley Throng': Social Change on the Southwest China's Early Modern Frontier, 1700–1880." *Journal of Asian Studies* 60 (2001), 67–94.

Glamman, Kristof. *Dutch–Asiatic Trade 1620–1740*. 1958, Rpt. 's-Gravenhage: Martinus Nijhoff, 1981.

Gleason, John B. "The Nature of Milton's *Moscovia*." *Studies in Philology* 61 (1964), 640–49.

Gleeson, Janet. *Millionaire: The Philanderer, Gambler, and Duelist Who Invented Modern Finance*. New York: Simon and Schuster, 1999.

Goldstone, Jack A. *Revolution and Rebellion in the Early Modern World*. Berkeley and Los Angeles: University of California Press, 1991.

Goux, Jean-Joseph. *Symbolic Economies after Marx and Freud*. Trans. Jennifer Curtiss Gage. Ithaca: Cornell University Press, 1990.

Green, Martin. *Dreams of Adventure, Deeds of Empire*. New York: Basic Books, 1979.

Grossman, Marshall. *"Authors to Themselves": Milton and the Revelation of History*. Cambridge: Cambridge University Press, 1987.

Guibbory, Achsah. *The Map of Time: Seventeenth-Century English Literature and Ideas of Pattern in History*. Urbana: University of Illinois Press, 1986.

Gunn, Geoffrey. *First Globalization: The Eurasian Exchange, 1500–1800*. Lanham, MD: Rowman & Littlefield, 2003.

Haberland, Detlef. *Engelbert Kaempfer, 1651–1716: A Biography*. Trans. Peter Hogg. London: British Library, 1996.

Hadden, Richard W. *On the Shoulders of Merchants: Exchange and the Mathematical Conception of Nature in Early Modern Europe*. Albany: SUNY Press, 1994.

Hamilton, Gary D. "The *History of Britain* and its Restoration Audience." In *Politics, Poetics, and Hermeneutics in Milton's Prose*. Ed. David Loewenstein and James Grantham Turner. Cambridge: Cambridge University Press, 1990, 241–55.

Hanley, Susan B. *Everyday Things in Premodern Japan: The Hidden Legacy of Material Culture.* Berkeley: University of California Press, 1997.

"Tokugawa Society: Material Culture, Standard of Living, and Life-Styles." In John W. Hall and James L. McCain, eds., *Early Modern Japan*, vol. IV in the *The Cambridge History of Japan.* Cambridge: Cambridge University Press, 1997, 660–705.

Hanley, Susan B. and Kozo Yamamura. *Economic and Demographic Change in Preindustrial Japan, 1600–1868.* Princeton: Princeton University Press, 1977.

Han Qi. "Sino-British Scientific Relations through Jesuits in the Seventeenth and Eighteenth Centuries." In *La Chine entre Amour et Haine: Actes du VIIIe Colloque de Sinologie de Chantilly*, ed. Michel Cartier. Paris: Desclée de Brouwer, 1998.

Hanson, Elizabeth. "Torture and Truth in Renaissance England." *Representations* 34 (1991), 53–84.

Harris, Marvin. *Cannibals and Kings: The Origins of Cultures.* New York: Random House, 1977.

Hawes, Clement. "Three Times Round the Globe: Gulliver and Colonial Discourse." *Cultural Critique* 18 (1991), 187–214.

Hay, Jonathan. "Ming Palace and Tomb in Early Qing Jiangning: Dynastic Memory and the Openness of History." *Late Imperial China* 20 (1999), 1–48.

Helgerson, Richard. *Forms of Nationhood: The Elizabethan Writing of England.* Chicago: University of Chicago Press, 1992.

Heuschert, Dorothea. "Legal Pluralism in the Qing Empire: Manchu Legislation for the Mongols." *International History Review* 20 (1998), 310–24.

Hevia, James. *Cherishing Men from Afar: Qing Guest Ritual and the McCartney Embassy of 1793.* Durham: Duke University Press, 1995.

Higgins, Ian. *Swift's Politics: A Study in Disaffection.* Cambridge: Cambridge University Press, 1994.

Holmes, Geoffrey. *The Making of a Great Power: Late Stuart and Early Georgian Britain 1660–1772.* London: Longman, 1993.

Ho Ping-t'i. *Studies on the Population of China, 1368–1953.* Cambridge, MA: Harvard University Press, 1959.

Hopes, Jeffrey. "Real and Imaginary Stories: *Robinson Crusoe* and the *Serious Reflections.*" *Eighteenth-Century Fiction* 8 (1996), 313–28.

Hoskins, Janet. "Spirit Worship and Conversion in Western Sumba." *Indonesian Religions in Transition.* Ed. Rita Kipp and Susan Rodgers. Tucson: University of Arizona Press, 1987, 144–58.

Hostetler, Laura. "Qing Connections in the Early Modern World: Ethnography and Cartography in Eighteenth-Century China." *Modern Asian Studies* 34 (2000), 623–62.

Qing Colonial Enterprise: Ethnography and Cartography in Early Modern China. Chicago: University of Chicago Press, 2001.

Huang, Ray. *1587, A Year of No Significance: The Ming Dynasty in Decline.* New Haven: Yale University Press, 1981.

Huff, Toby. *The Rise of Modern Science: Islam, China, and the West.* Cambridge: Cambridge University Press, 1993.

Hughes, Derek. *Dryden's Heroic Drama.* Lincoln: University of Nebraska Press, 1982.

English Drama 1660–1700. Oxford: Clarendon Press, 1996.

Hulme, Peter. *Colonial Encounters: Europe and the Native Caribbean 1492–1797.* New York: Routledge, 1986.

Hummel, Arthur W., ed. *Eminent Chinese of the Ch'ing Period (1644–1912).* 2 vols. Washington, D.C.: Government Printing Office, 1943.

Hung-Kay Luk, Bernard. "A Serious Matter of Life and Death: Learned Conversations at Foochow in 1627." In *East Meets West: The Jesuits in China, 1582–1773.* Ed. Charles E. Ronan, S. J. and Bonnie B. C. Oh. Chicago: Loyola University Press, 1988, 173–206.

Hunter, J. Paul. *The Reluctant Pilgrim: Defoe's Emblematic Method and the Quest for Form in Robinson Crusoe.* Baltimore: Johns Hopkins University Press, 1966.

Before Novels: The Cultural Contexts of Eighteenth-Century English Fiction. New York: Norton, 1990.

Hutchins, Henry Clinton. *Robinson Crusoe and its Printing 1719–1731: A Bibliographical Study.* New York: Columbia University Press, 1925.

Hutner, Heidi. *Colonial Women: Race and Culture in Stuart Drama.* New York: Oxford University Press, 2001.

Ingrassia, Catherine. *Authorship, Commerce, and Gender in Early Eighteenth-Century England: A Culture of Paper Credit.* Cambridge: Cambridge University Press, 1998.

Israel, Jonathan. *Dutch Primacy in World Trade, 1585–1740.* Oxford: Clarendon Press, 1989.

The Dutch Republic: Its Rise, Greatness, and Fall 1477–1806. Oxford: Oxford University Press, 1995.

Jacob, Els M. *In Pursuit of Pepper and Tea: The Story of the Dutch East India Company.* 3rd edn. Amsterdam: Netherlands Maritime Museum, 1991.

Jagchid, Sechin and Van Jay Symons. *Peace, War, and Trade along the Great Wall.* Bloomington: Indiana University Press, 1989.

Jardine, Lisa. *Worldly Goods: A New History of the Renaissance.* London: Macmillan, 1996.

Jensen, Lionel. *Manufacturing Confucianism: Chinese Traditions and Universal Civilization.* Durham: Duke University Press, 1997.

Johnson, Chalmers. *The Sorrows of Empire: Militarism, Secrecy, and the End of the Republic.* New York: Metropolitan Books, Henry Holt, 2004.

Johnson, Maurice, Kitagawa Muncharu, and Philip Williams. *Gulliver's Travels and Japan.* Doshisha, Japan: Doshisha University, Amherst House, 1977.

Jones, James R. "French Intervention in English and Dutch Politics, 1677–88." In *Knights Errant and True Englishmen: British Foreign Policy, 1660–1800.* Ed. Jeremy Black. Edinburgh: John Donald, 1989, 1–23.

Jooma, Minaz. "Robinson Crusoe Inc(corporates): Domestic Economy, Incest and the Trope of Cannibalism," *Lit* 8 (1997), 61–81.

Joseph, Betty. *Reading the East India Company, 1720–1840: Colonial Currencies of Gender*. Chicago: University of Chicago Press, 2004.

Kamps, Ivo. "Colonizing the Colonizer: A Dutchman in *Asia Portuguesa*." In *Travel Knowledge: European "Discoveries" in the Early Modern Period*. Ed. Ivo Kamps and Jyostna G. Singh. London: Palgrave, 2001, 16–84.

Kathirithamby-Wells, Jeyamalar. "Restraints on the Development of Merchant Capitalism in Southeast Asia before *c*. 1800." In *Southeast Asia in the Early Modern Era: Trade, Power, and Belief*. Ed. Anthony Reid. New York: Cornell University Press, 1993, 123–48.

Katz, David S. "Isaac Vossius and the English Biblical Critics 1670–1689." *Scepticism and Irreligion in the Seventeenth and Eighteenth Centuries*. Ed. Richard H. Popkin and Arjo Vanderjagt. Leiden: Brill, 1993, 142–84.

Kaul, Suvir. *Poems of Nation, Anthems of Empire: English Verse in the Long Eighteenth Century*. Charlottesville: University of Virginia Press, 2000.

Keay, John. *The Honourable Company: A History of the English East India Company*. New York: Macmillan, 1991.

India: A History. New York: Atlantic Monthly Press, 2000.

Keogh, Annette. "Oriental Translations: Linguistic Explorations into the Closed Nation of Japan." *The Eighteenth Century: Theory and Interpretation* 45 (2004), 171–91.

Kessler, Lawrence D. *K'ang-Hsi and the Consolidation of Ch'ing Rule 1661–1684*. Chicago: University of Chicago Press, 1976.

Kidd, Colin. *British Identities before Nationalism: Ethnicity and Nationhood in the Atlantic World, 1600–1800*. Cambridge: Cambridge University Press, 1999.

Klein, Peter. "The China Seas and the World Economy between the Sixteenth and Nineteenth Centuries: The Changing Structures of World Trade." *Interactions in the World Economy: Perspectives from International Economic History*. Ed. Carl-Ludwig Holtfrerich (Hemel Hempstead: Harvester, 1989), 61–89.

Klekar, Cynthia. "'Her Gift was Compelled': Gender and the Failure of the Gift in *Cecilia*." *Eighteenth-Century Fiction* 18 (2005), 107–26.

"'Prisoners in Silken Bonds': Obligation and Diplomacy in English Voyages to Japan and China." *Journal for Early Modern Cultural Studies*, 6 (2006).

Knoespel, Kenneth B. "Milton and the Hermeneutics of Time: Seventeenth-Century Histories and the Science of History." *Studies in the Literary Imagination* 22 (1989), 17–35.

"Newton in the School of Time: The *Chronology of Ancient Kingdoms Amended* and the Crisis of Seventeenth-Century Historiography." *The Eighteenth Century: Theory and Interpretation* 30 (1989), 19–41.

Knoppers, Laura Lunger. *Historicizing Milton: Spectacle, Power, and Poetry in Restoration England*. Athens: University of Georgia Press, 1994.

Koehler, Martha. "Epistolary Closure and Triangular Return in Richardson's *Clarissa*," *Journal of Narrative Technique* 24 (1994), 153–72.

Koeman, Cornelius. *Joan Blaeu and His Grand Atlas*. Amsterdam: Theatarum Orbis Terrarum. 1970.

Kowaleski-Wallace, Beth. "Tea, Gender, and Domesticity in Eighteenth-Century England." *Studies in Eighteenth-Century Culture* 23 (1994), 131–45.

Kramer, David Bruce. *The Imperial Dryden: The Poetics of Appropriation in Seventeenth-Century England*. Athens: University of Georgia Press, 1994.

Kristeva, Julia. *Powers of Horror: An Essay on Abjection*. Trans. Leon Roudiez. New York: Columbia University Press, 1982.

Kutcher, Norman. *Mourning in Late Imperial China: Filial Piety and the State*. Cambridge: Cambridge University Press, 1999.

Lach, Donald, with Edwin J. van Kley. *Asia in the Making of Europe*. 3 vols. Chicago: University of Chicago Press, 1965–93.

Lamb, Jonathan. "Minute Particulars and the Representation of South Pacific Discovery." *Eighteenth-Century Studies* 28 (1995), 281–94.

"Eye-Witnessing in the South Seas." *The Eighteenth Century: Theory and Interpretation* 38 (1997), 201–12.

Preserving the Self in the South Seas, 1680–1840. Chicago: University of Chicago Press, 2001.

Latour, Bruno. *We Have Never Been Modern*. Trans. Catherine Porter. Cambridge, MA: Harvard University Press, 1993.

Leslie, D. D. "The Chinese–Hebrew Memorial Book of the Jewish Community of K'aifeng," part three. *Ab-Nahrain* 6 (1965–66), 1–52.

Leupp, Gary P. *Servants, Shophands, and Laborers in the Cities of Tokugawa Japan*. Princeton: Princeton University Press, 1991.

Lewalski, Barbara. *The Life of John Milton: A Critical Biography*. Oxford: Blackwell, 2000.

Li Bozhong, "Changes in Climate, Land, and Human Efforts: The Production of Wet-Field Rice in Jiangnan during the Ming and Qing Dynasties." In *Sediments of Time: Environment and Society in Chinese History*. Ed. Mark Elvin and Liu Ts'ui-jung. Cambridge: Cambridge University Press, 1998, 447–85.

Lieb, Michael. *Milton and the Culture of Violence*. Ithaca: Cornell University Press, 1994.

Lin Jinshui. "Chinese Literati and the Rites Controversy." Trans. Hua Xu and ed. D. E. Mungello. In *The Chinese Rites Controversy: Its History and Meaning*, ed. D. E. Mungello. Nettetal: Steyler Verlag, 1994, 65–82.

Liu, Lydia H. "Robinson Crusoe's Earthenware Pot." *Critical Inquiry* 25 (1999), 728–57.

Locke, John. *Two Treatises of Government*, ed. Peter Laslett. Cambridge: Cambridge University Press, 1960.

Loewenstein, David. *Milton and the Drama of History: Historical Vision, Iconoclasm, and the Literary Imagination*. Cambridge: Cambridge University Press, 1990.

Representing Revolution in Milton and His Contemporaries: Religion, Politics, and Polemics in Radical Puritanism. Cambridge: Cambridge University Press, 2001.

Loomba, Ania. "'Break her will, and bruise no bone sir': Colonial and Sexual Mastery in Fletcher's *The Island Princess*." *Journal for Early Modern Cultural Studies* 2 (2002), 68–108.

Lovett, Robert W., assisted by Charles C. Lovett. *Robinson Crusoe: A Bibliographical Checklist of English Language Editions, 1719–1979*. New York: Greenwood, 1991.

Lynch, Deidre Shauna. *The Economy of Character: Novels, Market Culture, and the Business of Inner Meaning*. Chicago: University of Chicago Press, 1998.

Macauley, Melissa. *Social Power and Legal Culture: Litigation Masters in Late Imperial China*. Stanford: Stanford University Press, 1998.

McCloskey, Donald N. "The Economics of Choice: Neoclassical Supply and Demand." In *Economics and the Historian*, ed. Thomas G. Rawski, Susan B. Carter, Jon S. Cohen, Stephen Cullenberg, Peter H. Lindert, Donald N. McCloskey, Hugh Rockoff, and Richard Sutch. Berkeley and Los Angeles: University of California Press, 1996, 122–58.

MacKaness, G., ed. *Some Proposals for Establishing Colonies in the South Seas*. Dubbo, New South Wales: Australian Historical Monographs, 1981.

McKeon, Michael. *Politics and Poetry in Restoration England: The Case of Dryden's Annus Mirabilis*. Cambridge, MA: Harvard University Press, 1975.
　The Origins of the English Novel 1600–1740. Baltimore: Johns Hopkins University Press, 1987.

MacLean, Gerald. *The Rise of Oriental Travel: English Visitors to the Ottoman Empire, 1580–1720*. London: Palgrave, 2004.

McLeod, Bruce. *The Geography of Empire in English Literature, 1580–1745*. Cambridge: Cambridge University Press, 1999.

McRae, Andrew. *God Speed the Plough: The Representation of Agrarian England, 1500–1660*. Cambridge: Cambridge University Press, 1996.

McVeagh, John. "Defoe and the Romance of Trade." *Durham University Journal* 70 (1978), 141–47.
　"Defoe and Far Travel." In *English Literature and the Wider World*. Vol. 1: *1660–1780: All the World Before Them*, ed. McVeagh. London: Ashfield, 1990.

Mancall, Mark. *Russia and China: Their Diplomatic Relations to 1728*. Cambridge, MA: Harvard University Press, 1971.

Mandell, Laura. *Misogynous Economies: The Business of Literature in Eighteenth-Century Britain*. Lexington: University of Kentucky Press, 1999.

Manning, Catherine. *Fortunes à Faire: The French in the Asian Trade, 1719–48*. Aldershot: Variorum, 1996.

Markley, Robert. "The Rise of Nothing: Revisionist Historiography and the Narrative Structure of Eighteenth-Century Studies." *Genre* 23 (1990), 77–101.
　Fallen Languages: Crises of Representation in Newtonian England, 1660–1740. Ithaca: Cornell University Press, 1993.
　"'Credit Exhausted': Satire and Scarcity in the 1690s." In *Cutting Edges: Contemporary Essays on Eighteenth-Century Satire*. Ed. James Gill. Knoxville, TN: University of Tennessee Press, 1995, 110–26.
　"'Gulfes, deserts, precipices, stone': Marvell's 'Upon Appleton House' and the Contradictions of 'Nature.'" In *The Cultural Life of the Country and City: Identities and Spaces in Britain, 1550–1860*, ed. Donna Landry, Gerald Maclean, and Joseph Ward. Cambridge: Cambridge University Press, 1999, 89–105.

"'Land Enough in the World': Locke's Golden Age and the Infinite Extensions of 'Use'." *South Atlantic Quarterly* 98 (1999), 817–37.

"Newton, Corruption, and the Tradition of Universal History." In *Newton and Religion*, ed. James E. Force and Richard Popkin. Dordrecht: Kluwer Academic Press, 1999, 121–43.

Markley, Robert and Molly Rothenberg. "The Contestations of Nature: Aphra Behn's 'The Golden Age' and the Sexualizing of Politics." In *Rereading Aphra Behn*, ed. Heidi Hutner. Charlottesville: University of Virginia Press, 1993, 301–21.

Marks, Robert B. *Tigers, Rice, Silk, and Silt: Environment and Economy in Late Imperial South China*. Cambridge: Cambridge University Press, 1997.

"'It Never Used to Snow': Climatic Variability and Harvest Yields in Late-Imperial South China, 1650–1850." In *Sediments of Time: Environment and Society in Chinese History*, ed. Mark Elvin and Liu Ts'ui-jung. Cambridge: Cambridge University Press, 1998, 411–46.

Marshall, P. J. and Glyndwr Williams. *The Great Map of Mankind: British Perceptions of the World in the Age of Enlightenment*. London: Dent, 1982.

Massarella, Derek. *A World Elsewhere: Europe's Encounter with Japan in the Sixteenth and Seventeenth Centuries*. New Haven: Yale University Press, 1990.

"The History of *The History*: The Purchase and Publication of Engelbert Kaempfer's *The History of Japan*." In *The Furthest Goal: Engelbert Kaempfer's Encounter with Tokugawa Japan*, ed. Beatrice Bodart-Bailey and Derek Massarella. Folkestone, Kent: Japan Library, 1995, 96–131.

Matar, Nabil I. *Islam in Britain, 1558–1685*. Cambridge: Cambridge University Press, 1998.

Turks, Moors, and Englishmen in the Age of Discovery. New York: Columbia University Press, 1999.

"The Maliki Imperialism of Ahmad al-Mansur: The Moroccan Invasion of Sudan, 1591." In *Imperialisms: Historical and Literary Investigations, 1500–1900*, ed. Balachandra Rajan and Elizabeth Sauer. London: Palgrave, 2004, 147–62.

Mayer, Robert. *History and the Early English Novel: Matters of Fact from Bacon to Defoe*. Cambridge: Cambridge University Press, 1997.

Meilink-Roelofsz, M. A. P. *Asian Trade and European Influence in the Indonesian Archipelago between 1500 and 1650*. The Hague: Martinus Nijhoff, 1962.

Mignolo, Walter. *The Darker Side of the Renaissance: Literacy, Territoriality, and Colonization*. Ann Arbor: University of Michigan Press, 1995.

Millward, James A. *Beyond the Pass: Economy, Ethnicity, and Empire in Qing Central Asia, 1759–1864*. Stanford: Stanford University Press, 1998.

Milton, Giles. *Nathaniel's Nutmeg: Or, the True and Incredible Adventures of the Spice Trader Who Changed the Course of History*. New York: Penguin, 2000.

Samurai William: The Adventurer Who Unlocked Japan. London: Hodder and Stoughton, 2002.

Milward, Peter, ed. *Portuguese Voyages to Asia and Japan in the Renaissance Period*. Tokyo: Renaissance Institute, Sophia University, 1994.

Min, Eun. "China between the Ancients and the Moderns." *The Eighteenth Century: Theory and Interpretation* 45 (2004), 115–29.

Minamiki, George, S. J. *The Chinese Rites Controversy from Its Beginning to Modern Times.* Chicago: Loyola University Press, 1985.

Mintz, Sidney. *Sweetness and Power: The Place of Sugar in Modern History.* New York: Penguin, 1985.

Mirowski, Philip. *More Heat than Light: Economics as Social Physics, Physics as Nature's Economics.* Cambridge: Cambridge University Press, 1989.

Mokyr, Joel. *The Lever of Riches: Technological Creativity and Economic Progress.* New York: Oxford University Press, 1990.

Momigliano, Arnaldo. *On Pagans, Jews, and Christians.* Middletown, CT: Wesleyan University Press, 1987.

Moore, John Robert. *Daniel Defoe: Citizen of the Modern World.* Chicago: University of Chicago Press, 1958.

Moreland, Carl and David Bannister. *Antique Maps.* 3rd edn. London: Phaidon, 1989.

Morineau, Michel. "The Indian Challenge: Seventeenth to Eighteenth Centuries." Trans. Cyprian P. Blamire. In *Merchants, Companies, and Trade: Europe and Asia in the Early Modern Era.* Ed. Sushil Chaudhury and Michel Morineau. Cambridge: Cambridge University Press, 1999, 243–75.

Moriya, Katsuhisa. "Urban Networks and Information Networks," trans. Ronald P. Toby. In Chie Nakane and Shinzaburo Oishi, eds., *Tokugawa Japan: The Social and Economic Antecedents of Modern Japan.* Tokyo: University of Tokyo Press, 1990, 97–123.

Morse, Hosea B. *The Chronicles of the East India Company Trading to China 1635–1834.* 5 vols. Oxford: Clarendon, 1926, 1929.

Mullan, John. *Sentiment and Sociability: The Language of Feeling in the Eighteenth Century.* Oxford: Clarendon, 1988.

Mungello, David E. *Leibniz and Confucianism: The Search for an Accord.* Honolulu: University of Hawai'i Press, 1977.

   Curious Land: Jesuit Accommodation and the Origins of Sinology. Studia Leibnitiana, Supplementa XXV. Stuttgart: Steyler Verlag, 1985.

Murphy, Antoin E. *John Law: Economic Theorist and Policy-maker.* New York: Oxford University Press, 1997.

Nagtegaal, Luc. *Riding the Dutch Tiger: The Dutch East Indies Company and the Northeast Coast of Java, 1680–1743.* Trans. Beverley Jackson. Leiden: Koninklijk Institut voor Taal-, Land- en Volkenkunde, 1996.

Naquin, Susan and Evelyn S. Rawski. *Chinese Society in the Eighteenth Century.* New Haven: Yale University Press, 1987.

Neal, Larry. "The Dutch and English East India Companies Compared: Evidence from the Stock and Foreign Exchange Markets." In *The Rise of Merchant Empires, Long-Distance Trade in the Early Modern World,* ed. James D. Tracy. Cambridge: Cambridge University Press, 1990, 195–223.

   The Rise of Financial Capitalism: International Capital Markets in the Age of Reason. Cambridge: Cambridge University Press, 1990.

Needham, Joseph *et al.*, *Science and Civilisation in China*. Cambridge: Cambridge University Press, 1954–.

Neill, Anna. "Crusoe's Farther Adventures: Discovery, Trade, and the Law of Nations." *The Eighteenth Century: Theory and Interpretation* 38 (1997), 213–30.

    "Buccaneer Ethnography: Nature, Culture, and Nation in the Journals of William Dampier." *Eighteenth-Century Studies* 33 (2000), 165–180.

    British Discovery Literature and the Rise of Global Commerce. London: Palgrave, 2002.

Neill, Michael. *Putting History to the Question: Power, Politics, and Society in English Renaissance Drama*. New York: Columbia University Press, 2000.

Norbrook, David. *Writing the English Republic: Poetry, Rhetoric, and Politics, 1627–1660*. Cambridge: Cambridge University Press, 1999.

Novak, Maximillian E. *Economics and the Fiction of Daniel Defoe*. Berkeley and Los Angeles: University of California Press, 1962.

    "Friday: Or, The Power of Naming." In Albert J. Rivero, ed., *Augustan Subjects: Essays in Honor of Martin Battestin*. Newark: University of Delaware Press, 1997, 110–22.

    Daniel Defoe: Master of Fictions. Oxford and New York: Oxford University Press, 2001.

Nussbaum, Felicity A. *Torrid Zones: Maternity, Sexuality, and Empire in Eighteenth-Century English Narratives*. Baltimore: Johns Hopkins University Press, 1995.

    The Limits of the Human: Fictions of Anomaly, Race, and Gender in the Long Eighteenth Century. Cambridge: Cambridge University Press, 2003.

    "Introduction." In *The Global Eighteenth Century*, ed. Felicity A. Nussbaum. Baltimore: Johns Hopkins University Press, 2003, 1–18.

Orr, Bridget. *Empire on the English Stage 1660–1714*. Cambridge: Cambridge University Press, 2001.

Osborne, Anne. "Highlands and Lowlands: Economic and Ecological Interactions in the Lower Yangzi Region under the Qing." In *Sediments of Time: Environment and Society in Chinese History*, ed. Mark Elvin and Liu Ts'ui-jung. Cambridge: Cambridge University Press, 1998, 203–34.

Oxnam, Robert B. *Ruling from Horseback: Manchu Politics in the Oboi Regency 1661–1669*. Chicago: University of Chicago Press, 1975.

Pacey, Arnold. *Technology in World Civilization: A Thousand-Year History*. Cambridge, MA: MIT Press, 1990.

Pagden, Anthony. *Lords of All the World: Ideologies of Empire in Spain, Britain and France c. 1500–1800*. New Haven: Yale University Press, 1995.

Parker, Kenneth, ed. *Early Modern Tales of Orient: A Critical Anthology*. New York: Routledge, 1999.

Parker, William Riley. *Milton: A Biography*. 2 vols. Oxford: Clarendon, 1968.

Patey, Douglas Lane. "Swift's Satire on 'Science' and the Structure of *Gullivers Travels*." *English Literary History* 58 (1991), 809–39.

Pearson, M. N. "The People and Politics of Portuguese India during the Sixteenth and Early Seventeenth Centuries." In Pieter Emmer and Femme

Gaastra, eds., *The Organization of Interoceanic Trade in European Expansion, 1450–1800*. Aldershot, Hampshire: Variorum, 1996, 25–49.

Pei-kai Cheng and Michael Lestz, with Jonathan D. Spence, eds. *The Search for Modern China: A Documentary Collection*. New York: Norton, 1999.

Perdue, Peter. *Exhausting the Earth: State and Peasant in Hunan, 1500–1850*. Cambridge, MA: Harvard University Press, 1987.

"Comparing Empires: Manchu Colonialism." *International History Review* 20 (1998), 255–61.

Perez, Louis G. *Daily Life in Early Modern Japan*. London: Greenwood, 2002.

Perkins, Franklin. *Leibniz and China: A Commerce of Light*. Cambridge: Cambridge University Press, 2004.

Perlin, Frank. *"The Invisible City": Monetary, Administrative and Popular Infrastructure in Asia and Europe 1500–1900*. Aldershot: Variorum, 1993.

Unbroken Landscape. Commodity, Category, Sign, and Identity: Their Production as Myth and Knowledge from 1500. Aldershot: Variorum, 1994.

"The Other 'Species' World: Speciation of Commodities and Moneys, and the Knowledge-Base of Commerce, 1500–1900." In *Merchants, Companies, and Trade: Europe and Asia in the Early Modern Era*. Ed. Sushil Chaudhury and Michel Morineau. Cambridge: Cambridge University Press, 1999, 145–73.

Peterson, Willard. "Learning from Heaven: The Introduction of Christianity and Other Western Ideas into Late Ming China." In *Cambridge History of China*, vol. VIII, part 2: *The Ming Dynasty, 1368–1644*, ed. Denis Twitchett and Frederick W. Mote (Cambridge: Cambridge University Press, 1988), pp. 810–14.

Philip, Kavita. *Civilizing Natures: Race, Resources, and Modernity in Colonial South India*. New Brunswick, NJ: Rutgers University Press, 2004.

Pincus, Steven C. A. *Protestantism and Patriotism: Ideologies and the Making of English Foreign Policy, 1650–1668*. Cambridge: Cambridge University Press, 1996.

Pluvier, Jan M. *Historical Atlas of South-east Asia*. Leiden: Brill, 1995.

Pocock, J. G. A. *Virtue, Commerce, and History: Essays on Political Thought and History, Chiefly in the Eighteenth Century*. Cambridge: Cambridge University Press, 1985.

Pollak, Michael. *Mandarins, Jews, and Missionaries: The Jewish Experience in the Chinese Empire*. 1980. Rpt. New York and Tokyo: Weatherhill, 1998.

Pomeranz, Kenneth. *The Great Divergence: China, Europe, and the Making of the Modern World Economy*. Princeton: Princeton University Press, 2000.

Porter, David. *Ideographia: The Chinese Cipher in Early Modern Europe*. Stanford: Stanford University Press, 2001.

Porter, Theodore. *Trust in Numbers: The Pursuit of Objectivity in Science and Public Life*. Princeton: Princeton University Press, 1995.

Prakash, Om. "Asian Trade and European Impact: A Study of Trade from Bengal, 1630–1720." In *The Age of Partnership: Europeans in Asia before Dominion*, ed. Blair Kling and M. N. Pearson. Honolulu: University Press of Hawai'i, 1979, 43–70.

"The Portuguese and the Dutch in Asian Maritime Trade: A Comparative Analysis." *Merchants, Companies, and Trade: Europe and Asia in the Early Modern Era*, ed. Sushil Chaudhury and Michel Morineau. Cambridge: Cambridge University Press, 1999, 175–88.

Preston, Diana and Michael. *A Pirate of Exquisite Mind: The Life of William Dampier, Explorer, Naturalist, and Buccaneer.* Sydney: Doubleday, 2004.

Pritchard, James. *In Search of Empire: The French in the Americas, 1670–1730.* Cambridge: Cambridge University Press, 2004.

Proudfoot, D. S. and D. Deslandres. "Samuel Purchas and the Date of Milton's *Moscovia.*" *Philological Quarterly* 64 (1985), 260–65.

Proust, Jacques. *Europe through the Prism of Japan: Sixteenth to Eighteenth Centuries.* Trans. Elizabeth Bell. Notre Dame: University of Notre Dame Press, 2002.

Radzinowicz, Mary Ann. "'Man as a Probationer of Immortality': *Paradise Lost* XI–XII." *Approaches to Paradise Lost: The York Tercentenary Lectures*, ed. C. A. Patrides. London: Edward Arnold, 1968, 31–51.

Rajan, Balachandra. *Under Western Eyes: India from Milton to Macaulay.* Durham: Duke University Press, 1999.

Rajan, Balachandra and Elizabeth Sauer. "Imperialisms: Early Modern to Premodernist." In *Imperialisms: Historical and Literary Investigations, 1500–1900*, ed. Balachandra Rajan and Elizabeth Sauer. London: Palgrave, 2004, 1–12.

Raman, Shankar. *Framing "India": The Colonial Imaginary in Early Modern Culture.* Stanford: Stanford University Press, 2001.

Ramsey, Rachel. "China and the Ideal of Order in John Webb's *An Historical Essay.*" *Journal of the History of Ideas* 62: 3 (2001): 483–503.

Rawski, Evelyn S. "Reenvisioning the Qing: The Significance of the Qing Period in Chinese History." *Journal of Asian Studies* 55 (1996), 829–50.

The Last Emperors: A Social History of Qing Imperial Institutions. Berkeley: University of California Press, 1998.

Rawson, Claude. *God, Gulliver, and Genocide: Barbarism and the European Imagination, 1492–1945.* New York: Oxford University Press, 2001.

Real, Herman and Heinz Vienken. "Swift's 'Trampling upon the Crucifix' Once More." *Notes and Queries* 30, n. s. (1983), 513–14.

Reed, Joel. "Nationalism and Geoculture in Defoe's History of Writing." *Modern Language Quarterly* 56 (1995), 31–53.

Reid, Anthony. *Southeast Asia in the Age of Commerce.* 2 vols. New Haven: Yale University Press, 1988–93.

"Economic and Social Change, c. 1400–1800." *The Cambridge History of Southeast Asia.* Vol. I: *From Early Times to c. 1800*, ed. Nicholas Tarling. Cambridge: Cambridge University Press, 1992, 460–507.

Reid, Anthony, ed. *Southeast Asia in the Early Modern Era: Trade, Power, and Belief.* New York: Cornell University Press, 1993.

Reinhartz, Dennis. "Shared Vision: Herman Moll and his Intellectual Circle and the Great South Sea." *Terrae Incognitae* 19 (1988), 1–10.

Rennie, Neil. *Far-Fetched Facts: The Literature of Travel and the Idea of the South Seas.* Oxford: Clarendon Press, 1995.

Richetti, John. *Defoe's Narratives: Situations and Structures.* Oxford: Clarendon, 1975.
   Daniel Defoe. Boston: Twayne, 1987.
Ricklefs, M. C. *War, Culture, and Economy in Java 1677–1726: Asian and European
   Imperialism in the Early Kartasura Period.* Sydney: Allen and Unwin, 1993.
Roach, Joseph. *Cities of the Dead: Circum-Atlantic Performance.* New York:
   Columbia University Press, 1996.
Roll, Eric. *A History of Economic Thought.* 5th edn. London: Faber and Faber, 1992.
Rosenthal, Laura J. "Owning Oroonoko: Behn, Southerne, and the Contingencies
   of Property," *Renaissance Drama* 23 (1992), 25–38.
Ross, Andrew C. *A Vision Betrayed: The Jesuits in Japan and China.* Maryknoll,
   NY: Orbis Books, 1994.
Rossi, Paolo. *The Dark Abyss of Time: The History of the Earth and the History of
   Nations from Hooke to Vico.* Trans. Lydia G. Cochrane. Chicago: University
   of Chicago Press, 1984, 141–67.
Rotman, Brian. *Ad Infinitum: The Ghost in Turing's Machine. Taking God Out of
   Mathematics and Putting the Body Back In.* Stanford: Stanford University
   Press, 1993.
Rouse, Joseph. "Philosophy of Science and the Persistent Narratives of
   Modernity." *Studies in the History and Philosophy of Science* 22 (1991), 141–62.
Rowbotham, Arnold H. *Missionary and Mandarin: The Jesuits at the Court of
   China.* Berkeley and Los Angeles: University of California Press, 1942.
Rubiés, Joan-Pau, *Travel and Ethnology in the Renaissance: South India through
   European Eyes 1250–1625.* Cambridge: Cambridge University Press, 2000.
Said, Edward. *Orientalism.* London: Routledge, 1978.
Sandiford, Keith. *The Cultural Politics of Sugar: Caribbean Slavery and Narratives
   of Colonialism.* Cambridge: Cambridge University Press, 2000.
   "Vertices and Horizons within Sugar: A Tropology of Colonial Power." *The
   Eighteenth Century: Theory and Interpretation* 42 (2001), 142–60.
Saussy, Haun. *Great Walls of Discourse and Other Adventures in Cultural China.*
   Cambridge, MA: Harvard University Press, 2001.
Scammell, G. V. *The World Encompassed: The First Maritime Empires, c. 800–1650.*
   Berkeley and Los Angeles: University of California Press, 1981.
   The First Imperial Age: European Overseas Expansion, c. 1400–1715. London:
   Unwin Hyman, 1989.
Schmidgen, Wolfram. "*Robinson Crusoe*, Enumeration, and the Mercantile
   Fetish." *Eighteenth-Century Studies* 35 (2001), 19–39.
Schmidt, Benjamin. *Innocence Abroad: The Dutch Imagination and the New
   World, 1570–1670.* Cambridge: Cambridge University Press, 2001.
Schnurmann, Claudia. "'Wherever profit leads us, to every sea and shore . . .': The
   VOC, the WIC, and Dutch Methods of Globalization in the Seventeenth
   Century." *Renaissance Studies* 17 (2003), 474–93.
Scott, W. R. *The Constitution and Finance of English, Scottish and Irish Joint-Stock
   Companies to 1720.* 3 vols. Cambridge: Cambridge University Press, 1910.
Sen, Sudipta. *Empire of Free Trade: The East India Company and the Making of the
   Colonial Marketplace.* Philadelphia: University of Pennsylvania Press, 1998.

Serres, Michel. *Le Système de Leibniz et ses modèles mathématiques*. 2 vols. Paris: Presses Universitaires de France, 1968.

  The Parasite. Trans. Lawrence Scher. Baltimore: Johns Hopkins University Press, 1982.

Shaffer, Lynda Norene. *Maritime Southeast Asia to 1500*. London: Sharpe, 1996.

Shapin, Steven. *A Social History of Truth: Civility and Science in Seventeenth-Century England*. Chicago: University of Chicago Press, 1994.

Sherman, Sandra. *Finance and Fictionality in the Early Eighteenth Century: Accounting for Defoe*. Cambridge: Cambridge University Press, 1996.

Shoulson, Jeffrey S. *Milton and the Rabbis: Hebraism, Hellenism, and Christianity*. New York: Columbia University Press, 2001.

Singh, Jyotsna G. *Colonial Narratives/Cultural Dialogues: "Discoveries" of India in the Language of Colonialism*. London: Routledge, 1996.

  "History or Colonial Ethnography: The Ideological Formation of Edward Terry's *A Voyage to East India* (1655 & 1665) and *The Merchants and Mariners Preservation and Thanksgiving* (1649)." In *Travel Knowledge: European "Discoveries" in the Early Modern Period*, ed. Ivo Kamps and Jyotsna G. Singh. London: Palgrave, 2001, 197–210.

Smith, Pamela. *The Business of Alchemy: Science and Culture in the Holy Roman Empire*. Princeton: Princeton University Press, 1994.

Spate, O. H. K. *The Pacific Since Magellan*. Vol. II: *Monopolists and Freebooters*. Minneapolis: University of Minnesota Press, 1983.

Spence, Jonathan D. *Emperor of China: Self-Portrait of K'ang-Hsi*. 1974. Rpt. New York: Vintage, 1988.

  The Memory Palace of Matteo Ricci. New York: Penguin, 1984.

  The Chan's Great Continent: China in Western Minds. New York: Norton, 1998.

  Treason by the Book. New York: Viking, 2001.

Sperling, John G. *The South Sea Company: An Historical Essay and Bibliographical Finding List*. Boston: Baker Library, Harvard University, 1962.

Stasavage, David. *Public Debt and the Birth of the Democratic State: France and Great Britain, 1688–1789*. Cambridge: Cambridge University Press, 2003.

Steensgaard, Neils. *The Asian Trade Revolution of the Seventeenth Century: The East India Companies and the Decline of the Caravan Trade*. Chicago: University of Chicago Press, 1974.

  "The Growth and Composition of the Long-Distance Trade of England and the Dutch Republic before 1750." In *The Rise of Merchant Empires*, ed. James D. Tracy. Cambridge: Cambridge University Press, 1990, 102–52.

Struve, Lynn A. *The Southern Ming 1644–1662*. New Haven: Yale University Press, 1984.

Struve, Lynn A., ed. *Voices from the Ming-Qing Cataclysm: China in Tigers' Jaws*. New Haven: Yale University Press, 1993.

Stulting, Claude N., Jr. "'New Heav'ns, new Earth': Apocalypse and the Loss of Sacramentality in the Postlapsarian Books of *Paradise Lost*." In *Milton and the Ends of Time*, ed. Juliet Cummins. Cambridge: Cambridge University Press, 2003, 184–201.

Suárez, Thomas. *Early Mapping of Southeast Asia.* Hong Kong: Periplus Editions, 1999.

Subrahmanyam, Sanjay. "Written on Water: Designs and Dynamics in the Portuguese *Estado da India.*" In Susan E. Alcock, Terrence N. D'Altroy, Kathleen D. Morrison, and Carla M. Sinopoli, eds., *Empires: Perspectives from Archaeology and History.* Cambridge: Cambridge University Press, 2001, 42–69.

Sudan, Rajani. *Fair Exotics: Xenophobic Subjects in English Literature, 1720–1850.* Philadelphia: University of Pennsylvania Press, 2002.

"Mud, Mortar, and Other Technologies of Empire," *The Eighteenth Century: Theory and Interpretation* 45 (2004), 147–69.

Sussman, Charlotte. *Consuming Anxieties: Consumer Protest, Gender, and British Slavery, 1713–1833.* Stanford: Stanford University Press, 2000.

Sutherland, James. "Some Early Troubles of Daniel Defoe." *Review of English Studies* 9 (1933), 275–90.

Thomas, Nicholas. *Possessions: Indigenous Art/Colonial Culture.* London: Thames & Hudson, 1999.

Thompson, James. "Dryden's *Conquest of Granada* and the Dutch Wars." *The Eighteenth Century: Theory and Interpretation* 31 (1990), 211–26.

Models of Value: Eighteenth-Century Political Economy and the Novel. Durham: Duke University Press, 1996.

Todd, Janet. *Sensibility: An Introduction.* London: Methuen, 1987.

Totman, Conrad. *Early Modern Japan.* Berkeley and Los Angeles: University of California Press, 1993.

Trotter, David. *Circulation: Defoe, Dickens, and the Economies of the Novel.* New York: St. Martin's Press, 1988.

Tumbleson, Raymond. *Catholicism in the English Protestant Imagination: Nationalism, Religion, and Literature, 1600–1745.* Cambridge: Cambridge University Press, 1998.

Turley, Hans. *Rum, Sodomy, and the Lash: Piracy, Sexuality, and Masculine Identity.* New York: NYU Press, 1999.

"The Sublimation of Desire to Apocalyptic Passion in Defoe's Crusoe Trilogy." In *Imperial Desire: Dissident Sexualities and Colonial Literature*, ed. Philip Holden and Richard J. Ruppel. Minneapolis: University of Minnesota Press, 2003, 3–20.

"Protestant Evangelism, British Imperialism, and Crusoian Identity." In Kathleen Wilson, ed., *A New Imperial History: Culture, Identity and Modernity in Britain and the Empire, 1660–1840.* Cambridge: Cambridge University Press, 2004.

Turnbull, George Henry. *Hartlib, Drury, and Comenius: Gleanings from Hartlib's Papers.* Liverpool: University Press of Liverpool, 1947.

Twitchett, Denis and Frederick W. Mote, eds., *The Ming Dynasty, 1368–1644, Part 2* in *The Cambridge History of China*, gen. eds. Denis Twitchett and John K. Fairbank. Cambridge: Cambridge University Press, 1998.

van der Velde, Paul. "The Interpreter Interpreted: Kaempfer's Japanese Collaborator Imamura Genemon Eisei." In *The Furthest Goal: Engelbert Kaempfer's Encounter with Tokugawa Japan*. Ed. Beatrice M. Bodart-Bailey and Derek Massarella Folkestone, Kent: Japan Library, 1995, 44–70.

van Kley, Edwin. "Europe's 'Discovery' of China and the Writing of World History." *American Historical Review* 76 (1971), 358–85.

"News from China: Seventeenth-Century Notices of the Manchu Conquest," *Journal of Modern History* 45 (1973), 361–82.

"An Alternative Muse: The Manchu Conquest of China in the Literature of Seventeenth-Century Northern Europe." *European Studies Review* 6 (1976), 21–43.

van Opstall, M. E. "Dutchmen and Japanese in the Eighteenth Century." *Trading Companies in Asia 1600–1830*. Ed. J. van Goor. Utrecht: HES Utigevers, 1986, 107–26.

van Sant, Anne Jessie. *Eighteenth-Century Sensibility and the Novel: The Senses in Social Context*. Cambridge: Cambridge University Press, 1993.

Vermeer, Eduard B. "Population and Ecology along the Frontier in Qing China." In *Sediments of Time: Environment and Society in Chinese History*, ed. Mark Elvin and Liu Ts'ui-jung. Cambridge: Cambridge University Press, 1998, 235–81.

Villiers, John. "'A Truthful pen and an impartial spirit': Batolomé Leonardo de Argensola and the *Conquista de las Islas Malucas*." *Renaissance Studies* 17 (2003), 449–73.

Vitkus, Daniel. "Introduction: Toward a New Globalism in Early Modern Studies." *Journal for Early Modern Cultural Studies* 2 (2002), v–viii.

Turning Turk: English Theater and the Multicultural Mediterranean, 1570–1630. London: Palgrave, 2003.

von Glahn, Richard. *Fountain of Fortune: Money and Monetary Policy in China, 1000–1700*. Berkeley: University of California Press, 1996.

von Maltzahn, Nicholas. *Milton's* History of Britain: *Republican Historiography in the English Revolution*. Oxford: Clarendon Press, 1991.

Wakeman, Frederic, Jr. *The Great Enterprise: The Manchu Reconstruction of Order in Seventeenth-Century China*. 2 vols. Berkeley and Los Angeles: University of California Press, 1985.

Waley-Cohen, Joanna. *The Sextants of Beijing: Global Currents in Chinese History*. New York: Norton, 1999.

Walker, William. "Typology and *Paradise Lost*, Books XI and XII." *Milton Studies* 25, ed. James D. Simmonds. Pittsburgh: University of Pittsburgh Press, 1989, 245–64.

Wallerstein, Immanuel. *The Modern World-System*, vol. I: *Capitalist Agriculture and the Origins of the European World-Economy in the Sixteenth Century*. New York: Academic Press, 1974.

The Modern World-System, vol. II: *Mercantilism and the Consolidation of the European World-Economy, 1600–1750*. New York: Academic Press, 1980.

The Modern World-System, vol. III: *The Second Era of Great Expansion of the Capitalist World-Economy, 1730–1840s*. San Diego: Academic Press, 1989.

Warner, William Beatty. *Licensing Entertainment: The Elevation of Novel Reading in Britain, 1684–1750.* Berkeley and Los Angeles: University of California Press, 1998.

Watt, Ian. *The Rise of the Novel.* Berkeley: University of California Press, 1957.

Wheeler, Roxanne. "'My Savage,' 'My Man': Racial Multiplicity in *Robinson Crusoe.*" *English Literary History* 62 (1995), 821–61.

   The Complexion of Race: Categories of Difference in Eighteenth-Century British Culture. Philadelphia: University of Pennsylvania Press, 2000.

Wilcox, Donald. *The Measure of Times Past: Pre-Newtonian Chronologies and the Rhetoric of Relative Time.* Chicago: University of Chicago Press, 1987.

Wilding, Michael. *Dragon's Teeth: Literature in the English Revolution.* Oxford: Clarendon, 1987.

Will, Pierre-Etienne. *Bureaucracy and Famine in Eighteenth-Century China.* Stanford: Stanford University Press, 1990.

Will, Pierre-Etienne and R. Bin Wong. *Nourish the People: The State Civilian Granary System in China, 1650–1850.* Ann Arbor: University of Michigan Press, 1991.

Williams, Glyn [Glyndwr]. *The Prize of All the Oceans: The Dramatic True Story of Commodore Anson's Voyage Round the World and How He Seized the Spanish Treasure Galleon.* New York: Viking, 1999.

   Voyages of Delusion: The Quest for the Northwest Passage. New Haven: Yale University Press, 2002.

Williams, Glyndwr. "'The Inexhaustible Fountain of Gold': English Projects and Ventures in the South Seas, 1670–1750." In *Perspectives of Empire: Essays Presented to Gerald S. Graham,* ed. John E. Flint and Glyndwr Williams. London: Longman, 1973, 27–53.

   "Anson at Canton, 1743: 'A Little Secret History.'" In Cecil H. Clough and P. E. H. Hair, eds., *The European Outthrust and Encounter.* Liverpool: Liverpool University Press, 1994, 270–90.

   The Great South Sea: English Voyages and Encounters 1570–1750. New Haven: Yale University Press, 1997.

Wills, John E., Jr. *Pepper, Guns, and Parleys: The Dutch East India Company and China, 1662–1681.* Cambridge, MA: Harvard University Press, 1974.

   Embassies and Illusions: Dutch and Portuguese Envoys to K'ang-hsi, 1667–1687. Cambridge, MA: Council on East Asian Studies, Harvard University, 1984.

   1688: A Global History. New York: Norton, 2001.

Wilson, Charles, *Profit and Power: A Study of England and the Dutch Wars.* London: Longmans, 1957.

Worden, Blair. "Politics and Providence in Cromwellian England." *Past and Present* 109 (1985), 55–99.

Wrightson, Keith. *Earthly Necessities: Economic Lives in Early Modern Britain.* New Haven: Yale University Press, 2000.

Wu, Silas Hsiu-liang. *Communication and Imperial Control in China: Evolution of the Palace Memorial System, 1693–1735.* Cambridge, MA: Harvard University Press, 1970.

Passage to Power: K'ang-hsi and His Heir Apparent, 1661–1722. Cambridge, MA: Harvard University Press, 1979.

Xu Tan. "The Formation of an Urban and Rural Market Network in the Ming-Qing Period and Its Significance." *Social Studies in China* 22, 3 (2001), 132–39.

Yin Gang, "The Jews of Kaifeng: Their Origins, Routes, and Assimilation." In *Jews in Old China: Studies by Chinese Scholars*. Rev. edn, ed. and trans. Sidney Shapiro. New York: Hippocrene Books, 2001, 217–38.

Yu Liu, "The Jesuits and the Anti-Jesuits: The Two Different Connections of Leibniz with China." *The Eighteenth Century: Theory and Interpretation* 43 (2002), 161–74.

Yuen-Ting Lai. "Religious Scepticism and China." In *The Sceptical Mode in Modern Philosophy: Essays in Honor of Richard H. Popkin*. Ed. Richard A. Watson and James E. Force. Dordrecht: Martinus Nijhoff, 1988, 11–41.

Yukihiro, Ohashi. "New Perspectives on the Early Tokugawa Persecution." Trans. Bill Garrad. In *Japan and Christianity: Impacts and Responses*, ed. John Breen and Mark Williams. New York: St. Martin's Press, 1996, 46–62.

Zelin, Madeleine. *The Magistrate's Tael: Rationalizing Fiscal Reform in Eighteenth-Century China*. Berkeley: University of California Press, 1984.

Žižek, Slavoj. *The Sublime Object of Ideology*. London: Verso, 1989.

Tarrying with the Negative: Kant, Hegel, and the Critique of Ideology. Durham: Duke University Press, 1993.

Zürcher, Erik. "Jesuit Accommodation and the Chinese Cultural Imperative." In *The Chinese Rites Controversy: Its History and Meaning*, ed. D. E. Mungello. Nettetal: Steyler Verlag, 1994, 31–64.

Zwicker, Steven N. *Politics and Language in Dryden's Poetry: The Arts of Disguise*. Princeton: Princeton University Press, 1984.

Index